NOT
BRAVE
ENOUGH

NOT
BRAVE
ENOUGH

MY LEAP INTO THE STRATOSPHERE

RICK BUTCHER

authorHOUSE®

AuthorHouse™ LLC
1663 Liberty Drive
Bloomington, IN 47403
www.authorhouse.com
Phone: 1-800-839-8640

Published by AuthorHouse   10/07/2013

ISBN: 978-1-4918-2181-7 (sc)
ISBN: 978-1-4918-2179-4 (hc)
ISBN: 978-1-4918-2180-0 (e)

Library of Congress Control Number: 2013917737

CONTENTS

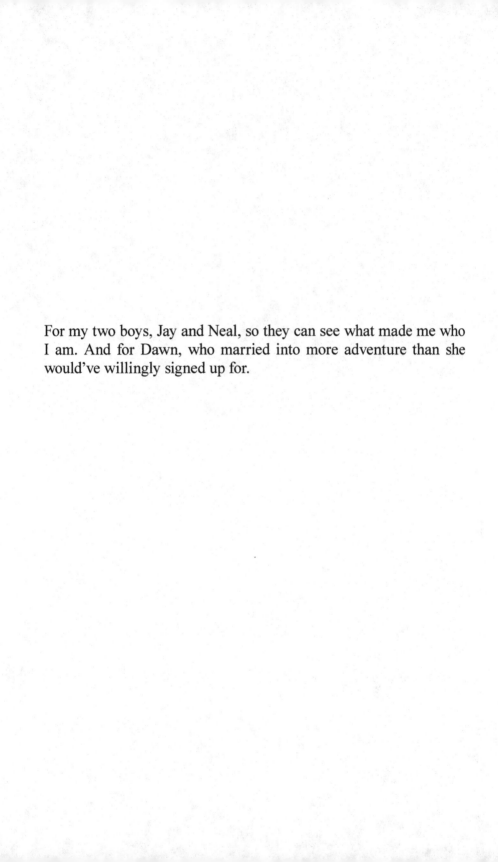

For my two boys, Jay and Neal, so they can see what made me who I am. And for Dawn, who married into more adventure than she would've willingly signed up for.

Flying Rules

Always have an out.

There are old pilots and bold pilots, but there are no old bold pilots.

Always fly (and drive) like your life depends on it, because it does.

Speed is like money in your pocket. Altitude is like money in the bank.

You can't use runway that's behind you, altitude that's above you, or fuel that's still in the truck.

Always look both ways before crossing a runway, and always write down your taxi clearance.

Hurrying can kill you, and if you really want to get there, it's safer to let someone else fly you there, because without a vested interest, they're likely to make safer decisions.

People are not good at multitasking; never trust anything to your short-term memory, and see the next rule.

Prioritize: Aviate, Navigate, Communicate.

Stay ahead of your airplane.

A thorough pre-departure briefing is an important mental rehearsal for the most dangerous moment of the flight.

Always know where the airplane needs to go and then point it there.

Always know exactly where in space your destination is, especially if you're flying on raw-data or on radar vectors.

Don't let the automation do your thinking for you.

Keep a sterile cockpit during critical phases of flights.

An unplanned contact with the ground is certain to hurt.

Always fly as if there was a fed (Federal Aviation Administration Inspector) in your jumpseat. Drive like a traffic cop is always watching.

Fly the same way, the right way, every time.

Know and respect your airplane's limitations, and understand that you have limitations too.

You can hope for the best as long as you've planned for the worst.

Optimism is overrated; it's too often followed by disappointment.

There's never shame in double-checking; there is shame in a violation or worse.

Sliding off the end of the runway is more shameful than a go-around.

To assume makes an "ass" out of "u" and "me."

You don't know what you don't know.

Never create an emergency where none exists.

You can never be too prepared for an emergency.

Learn something new at every opportunity.

If it flew in, it can probably fly out. If it came from the maintenance hangar, you never know.

It's better to be on the ground wishing you were in the air than to be in the air wishing you were on the ground.

It's okay to hate the company you fly for. Loyalty to their balance sheet can lead to bad decisions, because safety isn't cheap.

The two most important things a Captain must be able to say are *"No"* and *"Fuck no."*

Your co-pilot is worthless if he can't say any more than *"Nice landing," "Must've been a gust,"* or *"I'll take the ugly one."*

Be good to your co-pilot; he or she might be your Captain at your next airline.

If there's a disturbance in the cabin, don't open the cockpit door.

Every pilot makes mistakes on every flight. A good pilot makes sure that those mistakes won't hurt anyone.

A good pilot uses his superior aeronautical knowledge to avoid needing to use his superior aeronautical skills.

A thousand "attaboys" don't make up for one "dumbshit."

If you whore yourself out to fly airplanes, expect to be treated like a whore.

Never cross a picket line.

Don't wear your uniform to the bar, and pay your bar bill with cash, even if you've behaved.

Don't live from paycheck to paycheck.

If mama's not happy, you're not happy.

Only one pilot at your airline has seniority; everyone else has juniority.

The most coveted airline benefit, flying standby, is great when you don't need to go somewhere. If you really need to go, buy a ticket.

There are no shortcuts to experience; it can only be earned.

If you're only flying for the money and glamour, you're going to have a miserable career.

If the grass looks greener, it's probably because of all the manure that's fertilizing it.

The key to happiness is low expectations.

An Impossibly Dark Summer Night

The utter smoothness of the air and the opaque blackness of the sky were so absolute that it severed us from the world to which we belonged, a world that was now probably asleep, unaware of our anonymous passage several miles above. We were peacefully suspended somewhere between the sparse lights of Upstate New York far beneath us and the faint stars incomprehensibly far above, attached to neither. Our secluded realm was bathed in the calming soft light from a hundred instruments and panels. Too loud, but somehow not painfully so, the steady whoosh of transonic wind and faint whine of the jet engines was comforting in its familiar ceaselessness. I was back in my element, savoring every moment, at peace, on the dark side of the planet.

I had survived my first airline furlough, and I was back in the cockpit with a renewed appreciation for the good thing I had. I was having too much fun to be bitter that the coolest job in the world had been briefly taken away from me. I was enjoying the flying, certainly just as much as I ever had. The DC-9 is no Learjet, but it's a fine machine. It's comfortable, stable, built like a bridge, and even with its old-fashioned rigging of cables and control tabs, it obligingly responds to what my hands and feet ask of it. I was enjoying the camaraderie of exploring the country again with my colleagues, whom I respected and admired.

I hadn't yet lost the promise of youth, the naively optimistic feeling that everything would turn out okay. I was enjoying a new degree of contentment with my career, the feeling that I had arrived. This was the job I would retire from. Airline pilots often sarcastically quip "living the dream," in the same breath with which they are voicing their grievances. I really was living the dream, in a way that I couldn't truly have understood without having had it temporarily taken away.

We were repositioning a nearly empty airplane back to Milwaukee after a mechanical problem had left the airplane stranded in Boston all day. Two mechanics were reclined in the dark cabin, soundly sleeping, obviously confident in the fine work they had performed to get the old bird back in the air.

In the cockpit jumpseat was an unlikely occupant, a company employee who had been setting up new computer equipment in the Boston station that day. It suddenly seemed like everyone in the company claimed to be jumpseat qualified, although they really didn't know what that meant, nor would they actually be able to ever sit in the cockpit on revenue flights.

Our jumpseater and all the others who now claimed access to our private space were scabs in training. In preparation for a flight attendant strike that never came, the company had rushed every live body through an accelerated replacement course to learn, but certainly not master, emergency procedures.

No one can truly understand a flight attendant's job until they've seen them shouting orders and efficiently pushing people to safety during an evacuation, something I get to see annually in recurrent training. How would these replacements handle a real emergency evacuation? Would they be able to quickly help all of the passengers out of a burning aluminum tube, or would they just panic as the passengers trampled each other to death while futilely pushing on the plug doors, unable to escape? Fortunately, we never found out.

I didn't hold her replacement training against her. She, and all the other potential scabs, had only done what they had been told to do, seduced by a false illusion of glamour, oblivious to the bonds of solidarity that the flight crews knew. Her presence in the cockpit that night was actually welcome. The cockpit is a secluded place that is never really seen by outsiders. This was a rare occasion for someone to observe something unfamiliar to them and then to ask us questions from a perspective that we hadn't thought about in years, if ever, actually giving us a fresh look at our mundane realm. Plus, she was positively thrilled to be sitting in the least comfortable seat in the airplane, excitement that we had once known but had long since forgotten.

Once above ten thousand feet, below which no small talk was permitted, we told her she was allowed to talk.

Her first words were superficial and easily anticipated: "You guys have a really cool job."

As was the Captain's clichéd response: "It beats working."

They were both right. It's never a chore to come to work. I loved flying the DC-9, and the night was an especially beautiful night, but it definitely was a job. It was also day six for me, an unusually long stretch, and I value my time above any other commodity. When I got back to Milwaukee, well past midnight, I would get a couple hours of sleep and then take the first flight home to Columbus, Ohio, in the morning. My little baby, Jay, had probably grown an inch during my six-day absence, and my days off with him and my wife would pass much too quickly. Then I would be back in the saddle, feeling like I had only just passed through my home and my life there, which seemed separate from my work life.

The jumpseater probed much further than I had expected, charging well beyond the superficial start of our conversation, what I had assumed was a virtual wall that limited communication with non-flyers. Her twelve-year-old son was actually fascinated with airplanes, and she vicariously assumed his curiosity. She asked us how we got started in flying, what other ways there were to learn, how long it takes, how much money, typical career progression, and whether we would recommend a flying career. Existing in two segregated worlds, one in which everyone flew and my separate home life in which I never thought to even talk about flying, it had been a long time since I had answered, or even contemplated, questions like this, and I was actually surprised by my own answer to her most important question.

It was a moment of revelation for me. I was seventeen when I learned to fly, just a stupid kid, and if I knew then what I know now, I wouldn't have done it. I didn't necessarily regret it, in fact quite the opposite; I love to fly. I love everything about it. I just suddenly realized that I'm not inherently brave enough of a person to have put myself through all that I've endured while chasing the clouds. I was a kid so squarely risk averse that I demanded everyone get their money back after playing cards for pennies and nickels. I was a kid who was intimidated by the challenges involved with earning Boy Scout badges or the honor roll. If I had been offered a safe, effortless, and boring destiny, to never have to face the unknown, I would've taken it and probably never looked back.

I'm not brave enough to enter a profession with so much competition for so few good jobs, especially since you'd likely get furloughed from that job, maybe multiple times. Once you're in the airline industry, lateral moves really aren't practical, because you always start out at the bottom, the bottom of the pay scale, the worst schedules, and the first to be cut as the economy ebbs. You can also never be sure that your career will last through the next checkride or medical exam, tests which are never more than six months away.

There's also bravery in the face of physical danger, with potentially undesirable consequences that I've always wanted to avoid. I've now had too many engine failures to be comfortable flying a single-engine airplane ever again. You become a glider once you've lost your only engine—fine if you're over flat land with plenty of corn fields around, but that doesn't necessarily always mean that you can find a safe, unobstructed surface to land on within your limited glide range. At night, some people have said to aim for a dark spot. Is it a field, forest, or lake? You might get lucky. You might also impact an unseen, unyielding object at seventy miles per hour, and your light-weight aluminum frame won't protect you from it. I've had friends who've guessed wrongly while gliding into an opaque void. I've never been comfortable relying on luck, and I know now that it doesn't all turn out okay. Denial, aided by obsession and youthful ignorance, allowed me to ignore this and other risks when I was young and invincible. Now my keen sense of self-preservation, my fear of an alternate future with crushed metal and bones, won't allow me to do it. Basically, I'm not brave enough.

At seventeen, I was incapable of understanding that someday I would have family who would miss me when I was away. I also couldn't understand how much I would really be away and how much I would really miss. I didn't know how envious I would be of the people who actually get to go home after work, who are lucky enough to hug their wife and kids every day.

You could say that I owe my career to the ignorance of youth. I really didn't understand what I was getting into. Any toughness I may have found along the way certainly came by accident. I may have been told what challenges lay ahead, but I didn't want to hear it. And so I didn't. Certainly no age is immune to ignoring a contrary opinion, but adolescents inherently excel at it. If I had truly been able to hear a warning, I wouldn't have been brave enough to try.

It's hard to say whether it was all a mistake, since I have never decided what I would've done with my life otherwise. My little boys, Jay and Neal, would likely say that it was a mistake, except that they owe their very existences to my career. They weren't fated to become my progeny, just as Dawn wasn't fated to be my wife. A flying job took me to Charlotte, where I met Dawn. Our little boys are the unique result of our union, these loveable amalgams of all of their parents' many neuroses. Genetics aside, these two little boys who I love so dearly will probably always hate this career that regularly takes me a thousand miles from home. To them, the coolest job in the world, my job, isn't cool.

I was initially surprised by how few of my friends' children have followed them into the airlines. I understand now; this is not a family business. This is a business that can break families. I hope that Jay and Neal can be brave enough to try to find their own places in the world and that they can learn to celebrate each day and savor their own journeys and make exceptional lives for themselves.

So far, it has all been a lot more adventure than I ever would have signed up for, because I'm just not brave enough. I've had shockingly less control over my life than I ever would've imagined. When I have made decisions that have helped steer my course, they have often taken me in directions that I didn't even know existed. In real life, the pennies and nickels that are gambled are for keeps in a game with no rules other than gravity, the firmness of the Earth, and the inexorable passage of time, and you never know the outcome until all the cards have been played.

I'm not brave enough to have chosen to enter a contest that we are all ultimately destined to lose, the only entitlement in life being the finality of death. I'm not brave enough to seek out adversity, but here I am, trying to make the best of my fleeting existence, like Jonathon Livingston Seagull, not satisfied with aimlessly marking time, gliding along behind the shrimp boats waiting for the easy scraps.[1]

I don't really know where I'm going, but this is where I've been.

The Ignorance of Youth

I was born on an Air Force Base that defended North Carolina's coastal plain from communist dominos falling into the South China Sea. It was wartime, and many of the base's fighters were deployed to Thailand for combat missions over North Vietnam, but there were still some F-4s at home to thunder over my crib during my first year of life. I couldn't have known what it was back in my infancy, but I've always loved that massive machine, the F-4 Phantom II, unofficially called the Rhino, Double Ugly, Lead Sled, and even Air Defense Diesel, a sleek brute with an angular form more about attitude and meanness than aerodynamics. It's an antique now but still an undisputed master at converting tons of jet fuel into speed and noise.

I've always been obsessed with airplanes. I could never get enough. As a kid I could spend hours looking at pictures of airplanes in books and then more hours drawing my own pictures and building models and dreaming. What would it be like to actually see one of these amazing machines, to touch its polished metal skin, to sit in the cockpit where a pilot can bring the machine to life? What would it be like to watch the world below spread out like a map and to play in the clouds? What would it be like to fly?

Airplane rides were a special treat, the best part of a trip, and I always wanted a window seat. But first I wanted to visit the cockpit to see the pilots, my anonymous heroes, rock stars. They didn't have batting averages, record contracts, or even any fashion sense, just identical short sleeved white shirts, clip-on black ties that seem to hang too short, and abilities that I valued above all others. I hoped I could be one of them someday, that I could know how to defy gravity in those marvelous machines.

When I was sixteen, my cousin Steve flew us from Raleigh to Goldsboro, North Carolina, on a stormy night. It was so stormy that the jetliners at the end of the runway were content to wait until it passed. I sat in the right seat of the Cessna 206, the brawny brute of the single-engine Cessnas, and enviously watched Steve fly through the angry sky. I wished I knew how.

I would soon be old enough for a Private Pilot License, seventeen. My mother arranged for a tour of The Ohio State University's flight school, and I enrolled in the next Private Pilot Ground School. I was definitely not a brave kid seeking challenge and adventure, not Icarus giddily ascending the delirious burning blue.[2] I had wanted to do this, but it was now something that had been set in motion, which would assume a degree of inertia, once an instructor was available.

A couple of months later I got a call from a patient-sounding man named Jim who said he would be my flight instructor. I was very lucky, although I didn't realize it yet. Jim had been out of flying for a while after flying tankers in the Air Force many years prior. Instructing was how he was getting back in. He was not a typical flight instructor, young and inexperienced, only teaching in order to build flight time on someone else's dime. I would get to learn from someone who actually had some experience in real airplanes, which, incredibly, is not the norm.

My first flying lessons were an experience I wasn't prepared for; no one is after living their entire life in a two-dimensional world. I now had to move through a three-dimensional environment while my senses were being assaulted by noise and vibration in the cramped, poorly ventilated cabin that reeked of the stale sweat and undoubtedly even occasional vomit of a thousand prior flight students. Like an aluminum kite with no string, the flimsy little airplane seemed to rock with every gust of wind, and there was no stopping, no time-outs, until you were parked back in the tie-downs. Flying requires planning, staying mentally ahead of the airplane. There is no stopping to regroup, realign your thoughts, or ask for directions as you continually move through the air at a bug-smashing two miles per minute—nothing compared with jet speeds hurtling through a howling jet stream tailwind, when travelling a mile every six seconds is common, but that's for another chapter. With less power and acceleration than a typical family car, there was nothing glamorous about sauntering along in a Cessna 152. The view may have been better, but I was too overwhelmed to even notice yet.

There is a sense of busyness, an imperative to master something quickly that is always present in flight training. This never gets better. In 1987, a Cessna 152 plus instructor cost about fifty or sixty dollars an hour. As your career progresses, airlines pay more than a thousand dollars for each simulator session. By economic necessity, flight training is like drinking from a fire hose. That part never gets easier.

Before you can even get used to controlling this unfamiliar machine in an alien environment with no visible means of support, you are practicing unnatural maneuvers like stall recoveries. A stall occurs when you increase the angle of attack of the wing until the airflow over it is disrupted and the wing quits flying. It's an interesting irony that you learn to fly by getting the airplane to quit flying in midair. You need to be able to fly the airplane through its entire operating envelope, and as long as pilots are going to wreck airplanes in stall-spin accidents, they need to be proficient at recovery.

It's a little frightening to attempt something like this before you can really even positively control the airplane, but it's really fairly docile in a stable trainer like a single-engine Cessna. The airplane buffets a little and then pitches down, which reduces the angle of attack and increases the speed. The airplane practically recovers by itself, unless you're near the ground, concerned about how much altitude you'll lose in the process, and even in a full stall, the airplane doesn't just drop out of the sky. Most airplanes are stable enough that you really have to aggravate a stall, while holding a rudder pedal to the stop, for it to enter a spin and tumble Earthward, but it was still scary to be so close to the edge of that.

There would be no playing in the clouds. That would come much later. This was flying by Visual Flight Rules (VFR), which means you have to stay far away from the clouds and have good visibility. This was just basic maneuvering—maneuvering by ground references, steep turns, slow flight, stall recoveries, simulated engine failures (gliding toward fields or any other place to put it down), and touch-and-go landings. We would fly rectangular traffic patterns around the airport, landing, retracting the flaps, advancing the throttle, and taking off again, practicing about ten landings in an hour, with a couple of surprise go-arounds mixed in.

With maybe ten hours of flight time in my logbook, I was struggling around the traffic pattern, learning how to land an airplane, or trying to, certainly trying to test how robust the landing gear was on the little airplane. If it was this difficult in a single-engine Cessna, I thought I would never be able to do the same thing in a jetliner with a level of performance and complexity that was too abstract to even begin to comprehend. I assumed that airline pilots must've been born with a special talent to be able to perform such an aeronautical feat, guiding a huge jetliner through the same difficult sky with such grace, a talent I may not have the ability to achieve.

As difficult as the activity was, I don't ever remember considering quitting. I was truly feeding my childhood obsession with airplanes. I was actually flying them—or at least trying. When you're learning how to perform an unfamiliar task, you don't have an accurate sense of whether you're any good at it. I never seriously considered the possibility that I could fail at it, but not because I had a seventeen-year-old's excess of confidence; I just didn't know any better.

We never left the traffic pattern for the next couple of lessons, concentrating solely on takeoffs and landings. I knew what was coming up, but I didn't think I was quite ready for it yet. Then, on one especially pleasant autumn afternoon, my instructor, Jim, said we were landing after only a few touch-and-goes. Jim told me to go do three circuits around the pattern, and then he climbed out of the Cessna, leaving me all alone with only about twelve hours of flying experience and a surge of adrenaline to carry me back.

My first solo flight was over before I even had a chance to get nervous about it, which is certainly part of the instructor's plan. Flying is a mental exercise. Three takeoffs and three landings without supervision don't seem like much of an accomplishment, but they are very important exercise in developing a pilot's skill and confidence. It's a small taste of success, an undeniable act of independence for a novice pilot and, in this case, for an adolescent as well. Now I would fly solo for about half of my remaining training flights.

Knowing the big event was imminent, my mother had been coming out to the airport to try to film my first solo flight. She filmed the wrong airplane, and it was also the wrong day.

The ceremonial cutting of my shirt tail and the filming of the wrong airplane actually took place on my second solo flight. My first solo flight had occurred at nearby Bolton Airport the day prior, where the winds were more favorable—that is, absolutely calm. This was forbidden at the flight school, to conduct a first solo at another airport, so we couldn't celebrate it. This also meant I was able to wear a plain white t-shirt to be ceremonially mutilated, a tradition started in noisy, open cockpit biplanes in which the most polite way an instructor could get the student's attention was with a tug on the shirt tail.

I remember well the most difficult part of learning to swim, trusting the then—abstract idea that I wouldn't sink like a rock. Aside from buoyancy, which I also didn't initially understand beyond what can be learned in a bath tub, I didn't trust that only small motions by my hands and feet through a liquid could generate sufficient lift to keep my head above water. Being an invisible substance, it's not inherently obvious to humans that the air that surrounds us and repeatedly fills our lungs does have substance and does share properties with water. Part of becoming comfortable in flight is learning to trust the substance of the air, just as a swimmer must trust an arm stroke through water.

Soon I was learning cross-country flying, which is simply finding your way from one airport to another without help from street signs, mapquest.com, or even Global Positioning System, still years away. All students fear getting lost, which is all too easy for a student pilot to do, especially over the flat, monotonous patchwork of cornfields in the Ohio countryside. You need to learn how to look at Earth as if it was a map, and you need to learn how to find airports. This just comes with time and experience, but a good sense of direction certainly helps. You have to try hard to defy the drift from invisible winds aloft and stay on course until you develop an eye for this, and after a couple of cross-country flights with your instructor, you have to do it alone.

I completed my solo cross-country flights without getting too lost—well, sort of. On the last one I began following the wrong highway out of Indianapolis, realized it wasn't right, and turned to the left and found the correct one. So I guess I wasn't ever lost, more like temporarily confused about my location, if there's a difference. Actually, there is a subtle difference. If you panic while attempting to figure out where you are, possibly even worsening your predicament, you're lost.

I completed my night flights, which were cool, probably in the same indescribable way as fireworks and Christmas tree lights are.

Maybe we share a gene with moths, only manifesting itself as we seek the beauty of lights through the dark. Then I had another chance to practice ground reference maneuvers, slow flight, stall recoveries, steep turns, and simulated engine failures before the next big event: the Private Pilot checkride with an FAA-designated examiner.

A checkride is always the culmination of a training course, the anxious moment of truth when your knowledge and performance is evaluated by an individual by whom you can't help but be intimidated. You satisfactorily pass every required item and the examiner issues a new pilot license, or you fail a maneuver and you are given the dreaded pink slip. There's a lot to worry about. Will your performance meet the examiner's standards, or will you make a silly mistake you never made in training, maybe some little oversight, some small but important detail you failed to absorb during your busy transformation into an aviator? Will he pull the engine in a spot where you don't have any suitable fields to glide to? Anxiety accompanies every checkride, and many pilots say it never gets better, although the source of the anxiety changes. My goal is perfection, but I'm more aware than I used to be about how far I can stray from it and still meet the standards. With experience you also become more confident that you can depend on your skills when needed. On the other hand, the gravity of the event tends to increase. A pink slip for a seventeen-year-old means a few weeks of shame as you prepare for another attempt. Later in your career, a failure can mean getting passed over for upgrade, a lost opportunity, lost money, or maybe even the loss of your job.

My examiner was a nice man who might have been eighty-years-old. He spoke quietly and moved slowly. There wasn't anything intimidating about him—until he saw my written test score. I had taken the Private Pilot written test after I finished the ground school, and I had scored 72%, just two wrong answers away from failure. In retrospect, this really was shocking, considering that the Federal Aviation Administration actually publishes all the questions that you can be asked. I obviously wasn't going to bother myself with looking through a thousand possible questions, which was really just how I had always treated school up to this point. I hadn't even started flying lessons when I took the test. This wasn't a good way to start the oral exam, but after I answered several questions correctly, he commented that I knew the material better than my 72% would suggest.

After he was satisfied with my knowledge, he asked me to plan a cross-country flight. Then we got in the airplane. Finding the first checkpoint of my flight satisfied him, even though it was so obvious it would've been impossible to miss. He asked me to perform all of the required maneuvers, which I managed to accomplish within the published criteria. He pulled the throttle back to idle and told me that I had lost the engine. I turned the gliding airplane toward a nice, long corn field, one he had probably seen before retarding the throttle. Knowing we would easily make it to the long corn field, he gave me back the engine, and we flew back to the airport for a couple of landings. He congratulated me and pulled out the white pad of temporary certificates instead of the dreaded pink pad.

I had a license to endanger passengers, which I regrettably did, first my mother, then my sister, and later friends on a lovely spring morning when we were supposed to be in school, but we all lived to tell about it. I flew my prom date to dinner before the senior prom on my eighteenth birthday, but I was so romantically clueless that even that wasn't enough to get me laid. There was still so much to learn, more than I could even begin to understand, but I still had to get out and get some experience. I had tenuously planted both feet on the first step of an endless staircase that ascended to the stratosphere, I hoped.

Getting Smarter

My parents had set aside some education money when I was young, and it had grown into enough money to pay the tuition at a public university, plus either a dorm room on campus or flying lessons, but not both. I was fortunate to be living a few miles away from a university with an aviation program. My only college application went to The Ohio State University (OSU), which was for some irrational reason treated as the school of last resort by most of the other local college-bound kids, who, I guess, were just anxious to go explore the world, something I intended to do by going to school close to home.

My high school grades were only mediocre until my senior year of high school when I finally decided to start doing homework and studying for exams, so I can't remember now why I was so sure I would be accepted, but I was, and I would major in aviation. I even had a goal; I wanted to graduate with at least twelve hundred hours of flight time and a hundred hours of multi-engine time. I'm not sure how I chose those numbers, other than the unlikely possibility that I must not have tuned out all the advice I was offered. It was more likely that I saw that twelve hundred hours was a charter flying minimum, and I naturally understood that multi-engine time was extremely valuable.

I encountered the first problem when I was enrolling in classes for my first quarter. I wanted to begin working on the next step in flight training, the Instrument Rating, immediately. Obviously, I hadn't taken the prerequisite courses, but in 1988 the scheduling computer wasn't advanced enough to catch that. By the time it was, I had already finished the entire flying curriculum, supposedly faster than anyone ever had at OSU. I eventually got around to taking all the prerequisite courses, and sometimes I would even be in the same class with my flight students.

All through my freshman year I was getting credits for what I loved to do, flying. Since I loved it and genuinely wanted to do my best, attacking the flight labs with obsessive fervor, I excelled in my flying courses. This was quite a change for me, having been a life-long underachiever.

I also quickly figured out how to get good grades in my other courses, the gamesmanship of college. First, you had to show up. Attendance wasn't mandatory, which meant kids who were without supervision for the first time in their lives had to have the self-discipline to show up. This wasn't really freedom; it was just a method that the university used to allow unmotivated students to cut their own throats, academically speaking. Many wouldn't attend until a couple of classes before an exam. By then, they had missed all the hints the teachers had kindly written on the board, things we would definitely see again on a test. If you could just show up and pay attention for forty-eight minutes, three times a day, to people who were very knowledgeable and passionate about what they were teaching, you were probably going to pass the class. Add a little effort, like reading the textbook and reviewing your notes before an exam, and you would do well.

I did well enough to make the Dean's List more often than not, but I should've done better. I should've also taken more classes, but I accrued just enough credits to graduate. I was in a hurry to check all the boxes so I could get out into the world. Education is wasted on the youth, who are incapable of fully appreciating the opportunity they are being given.

My flight education was the part of my curriculum I truly took advantage of, but not necessarily due to my work ethic; it was what I wanted to do, my hobby, my passion, and, I hoped, some day my career.

The second step in flight training, after acquiring a Private Pilot License, is the Instrument Rating, which allows you to fly an airplane without any visual references beyond the flight instruments. When you are in the clouds or have no discernible horizon, your inner ear will lie to you. You have to completely disregard your visceral cues for your equilibrium and only trust the flight instruments, especially a three-inch-wide artificial horizon, which is the central point of your instrument scan.

Instrument navigation means tuning navigation radios, setting courses, and then following wandering needles on the instruments. Instrument approaches take this form of navigation a step further by allowing you to descend to lower altitudes at certain points in order to find the airport or, even better, giving you an electronic glide path to follow to a runway you can't see. Learning all this was so mentally taxing that once during an instrument approach, my instructor told me, "Don't forget to breathe."

One of the requirements for the Instrument Rating is fifty hours of cross-country flight time. My Instrument Instructor was dating a Naval Flight Student, so other students and I would put the cross-country requirement to use by flying our instructor to Pensacola, Florida, on the weekends. I wasn't living in a dorm, but I was starting my freshman year with a different kind of freedom than the typical college student, with regular weekend trips to Florida.

Immediately after taking my Instrument checkride, I began working on my Commercial Pilot License, which has nothing to do with a commercial airline. This is simply a basic license to allow you to get paid to fly, although at this point you don't have enough experience to be employable for much beyond traffic reporting or banner towing. This entails practicing maneuvers just a little more complicated than those required for the Private License, as well as flying complex airplanes, airplanes with retractable landing gear, controllable propellers, and retractable wing flaps, although nearly every airplane now has flaps.

Complex airplanes eventually lead to multi-engine airplanes, which add new aerodynamic challenges after the loss of an engine. This is an additional rating on your pilot certificate, requiring yet another checkride. Every new privilege requires another checkride.

After my Commercial Pilot checkride, I was assigned to a legendary old semi-retired instructor named Marv for my Flight Instructor training, which is an additional certificate, with yet another checkride, the scariest of them all, because at the time it had to be with a Federal Aviation Administration (FAA) inspector, not just a designee. The flight training was just the same maneuvers as before, but from the right seat instead of the left, plus spin training on nearly every flight. Marv truly understood, probably more than anyone I've met, the fundamentals of how to fly an airplane, and he also understood how people learn. Marv was unquestionably the best instructor I ever had, and at exactly the right time, when I had to put together all I had learned so I could passably teach it.

I gave my first flying lesson three days after my Flight Instructor checkride. I had to dodge an airplane and then a helicopter that I accidentally got too close to while thoroughly engrossed in my first hour of teaching. This was all see-and-avoid flying, so this can happen when you're maneuvering in busy airspace, but luck can be unkind to rookies, a cruel form of karma that stalks the inexperienced. I would encounter this phenomenon throughout my career, and although mysterious, it wasn't a malevolent supernatural force—just bad luck influenced by all you don't know and all you're not ready for about that next step on the grand staircase into the stratosphere.

I didn't realize it yet, but fate hands you two bags when you get a new license. One bag is empty, but that's where you put your experience as you acquire it. The other bag is full of luck, you hope. The trick is to fill up your experience bag before your luck bag is empty. You think you're prepared, but in reality, you don't know what you're doing until you've bagged a substantial amount of experience.

The only lesson really learned from that first hour of flight instruction, by anyone, is that basic survival is more important than the mission.

To achieve my flight time goal of having enough experience to be marketable, I would need other people to pay for my flight time. The problem is that you can't get a job without experience, and if you don't have experience you can't get a job. To help give a leg up over this seemingly insurmountable hurdle, at OSU, when aspiring flight students got a Commercial Pilot License and a Flight Instructor Certificate, they would be given a couple of flight students to train. If they did a good job they would get more students. This was a good opportunity for a commercial pilot without any experience, but it also means that the next generation of pilots is always being taught by the least experienced pilots imaginable, who are often barely more than a lesson ahead of their students. I became a flight instructor when I was just nineteen, which meant that I didn't have much life experience either, although I was too young to realize that.

Three things helped me to overcome my lack of experience. Although I wasn't ever the life of a party, I found I could get along pretty well with almost anyone, and I had some common sense, but probably the most important component of my early success was my neurotically unhealthy obsession with flying. Teaching wasn't just time-building for me. I put everything I had into it, because airplanes were my whole life.

Common sense would help me solve the first challenge I encountered, which was with a student who would get hopelessly lost as soon as the wheels left the runway, even if the runway was practically pointed toward the destination. The guy must've had some sense of direction, since he found his way from campus to the airport, so I guessed he was just getting lost in all the extraneous calculations.

I decided to keep it simple, to try to emphasize what was really important while filtering out the noise. Before we even got in the airplane, I would ask the student to point toward the destination, which was easy to do since there was an east-west runway right in front of the flight school and all the airplanes pointed to north in their tie-downs, two rows of identical aluminum compass roses. Then I told the student that if we flew in the pointed direction, we would find the destination. If we went any other direction, we wouldn't. No matter what tools and methods you used for navigation or how much calculating you did, the problem was as simple as that. Then we climbed into the airplane with nothing but a map in hand and flew from point to point across the Ohio countryside. It worked, and I was accidentally starting to get noticed as a good instructor.

The Chief Flight Instructor decided to challenge me with a student who had been unable to solo after well over a hundred hours of instruction. Typically, a student is ready to be kicked out of the nest, to fly solo, after about ten to fifteen hours of instruction. The student was a smart guy, a professor of aviation management. He just couldn't learn how to land the airplane. All of his instructors, and he'd had a few of them, were stumped, almost to the point of recommending he take up chess instead of flying.

The professor maneuvered the airplane around the traffic pattern perfectly, which should only have been expected from a hundred-plus hour student pilot, but then each trip around the pattern ended with a bone-jarring collision with the runway. The landings could've been just as good with his eyes closed. Maybe that was the problem, sort of. He had a short stature and terrible posture in an airplane with less than ideal visibility and no vertical adjustment for the pilot seats. Maybe he was losing sight of the runway ahead during the landing flare. If this was the problem, we needed to fix it quickly, because we were both getting shorter with each spine crushing arrival.

He had indeed been losing sight of the runway during the landing flare, and it had never occurred to him how that might impact the landing (pun intended). This isn't as dumb as it might seem. There are some tail draggers, including some famous fighters from World War II, in which you can't see over the airplane's nose when it's perched on all three wheels. None of his instructors had noticed that he was losing sight of the runway, but remember, flight instructing today is too often a clumsy exercise of the blind leading the blind.

I made him sit on a phone book the next time we flew, and those two extra inches of height were all he needed. Now he could see the runway ahead through the entire flare, and he could land the airplane. I was able to send him up solo immediately. It was actually the most comfortable I would ever be for a solo endorsement, normally a nerve-wracking event for a flight instructor, but that was because he had nearly half as much flight time as I had.

This was a very high-profile success, since it involved an aviation professor who had not progressed with the department's star instructors. It would teach me an extremely important lesson; when your boss thinks you do something well, you're asked to work harder at it than everyone else. I was now doomed to work with all the problem students who were being given a last chance before being shown the door.

Luckily, I also had a small contingent of superb students who would request for me to be their instructor. The manager of the academic flight program would do his best to honor these requests, even if it meant double scheduling my time slots, which he wouldn't ordinarily do. He knew I would get all of my students finished. He wasn't necessarily complimenting my work ethic; he was acknowledging that I had absolutely no life outside of an airplane.

I became a regular award recipient at the Aviation Department's annual recognition ceremony, including the big one; the exclusive Outstanding Student Flight Instructor Award, which was accompanied by a one thousand dollar scholarship. I was young and green—much more so than I was capable of understanding—but in this rather limited context, I had become the very best. I was on top of the world, in control of my own destiny, so I thought, except that I only had a vague idea of what that destiny looked like. I knew it involved airplanes, but I couldn't truly imagine what lay beyond the next week's flight schedule.

I added Instrument and Multi-engine ratings to my Flight Instructor Certificate, which required more training courses and, of course, more checkrides. Then I was qualified to teach every flying course in OSU's curriculum, a distinction few achieved. The university's insurance policy required multi-engine instructors to have 100 hours of multi-engine time, a prohibitively expensive block of flight time at $260 per hour, but I had more than enough after my six-month internship as co-pilot in the University's Air Transport Service King Airs. From then on I would teach half of the university's multi-engine students in a pair of antique Piper Aztecs, growling fat-winged brutes so ancient their airspeed indicators were marked in miles-per-hour instead of knots, but the multi-engine experience was like golden ink in my thin logbook.

I was also selected to be a check airman, which meant I would give students checkrides to allow them to move to the next phase of training. This is something I had wanted, mainly because it would add a little more flight time to my logbook. I just wasn't very good at it, because I didn't want the students to fail. I was just supposed to be checking students, but I would always end up giving a little remedial instruction and very long debriefings. There were only a few times I wasn't able to re-train an unsatisfactory maneuver during the flight. I hated telling a student they had failed. Actually, I don't think I ever did. I would just say, "I think we should go do that maneuver again."

It didn't take long for the other instructors to catch on that I was a Santa Claus examiner and that I was also willing to go to the airport twenty-four hours a day, seven days a week. I didn't mind my new reputation; it actually meant more business. I wasn't passing students who shouldn't pass. We would just stay out there until they knew how to do it right. I never have liked the ceremony, anxiety, and inevitable black-and-white judgment of a checkride. Even more absurd was that some examiners thought they needed to maintain a certain pass/fail percentage. A percentage would have to fail, whether they deserved it or not, just so the examiner could maintain a desired self-image as a bad-ass. I just wanted to know if the student could fly the airplane. Besides, students would actually learn something from me, and that's really the purpose of training.

The newer flight students who didn't know the other instructors yet were never as confident as their instructors were when they would schedule a stage check with "The Butcher," which should really only be a frightening name for a surgeon. There was an especially gruff-looking guy who was an outstanding instructor and, like me, a permanent fixture at the airport. He was an older guy, a former diesel engine mechanic, who had a barrel chest, a gray flat-top, bushy gray mustache, and an intimidating scowl. He was a nice guy, very smart, and he would deservingly go on to become the Chief Flight Instructor. He did tend to abuse his students by making them memorize the lift equation ($L = \frac{1}{2}\, \rho v^2 A C_L$), while I was more concerned with whether they understood that when you pulled back, the houses got smaller, and if you kept pulling back, the airplane would eventually quit flying. A few anxious students told me with relief that when they heard they were flying with The Butcher, they thought it was him, an appropriately intimidating name for an intimidating persona. So they were telling me I couldn't scare anyone unless they mistook me for someone else. I failed those students.

The check airmen were especially busy during finals week, as students were finishing their flying courses and those who weren't finished would still need a checkride for a grade in order to get credit for the course, an all too common occurrence (except with my students). That meant I was too busy to study for my own finals, since I was still a full-time college student too. This was probably the difference between a B+ and an A—average for me. I could have done better, but at least I got an education. When I began incorporating geology into my explanation of compass errors, or psychology into my explanation of visual illusions while night flying—basically when I started to see how everything in the world is inter-related—I knew I had an education. I would also acquire an audience on the dreary days when none of the airplanes were flying and I could lecture uninterrupted for hours, lectures that I gave for free.

Soon after I had taken my last exam on my last day of college, I heard the news about John. I knew him because he taught the King Air ground school that I had to take before I was an intern/co-pilot in the University's two King Airs, which was also the only time I ever took a prerequisite course when I was supposed to. John had flown a King Air for a local corporation until they sold the airplane and laid him off. In a bad job market, he had recently taken some dangerous jobs to pay the bills. He flew a Baron in and around thunderstorms, testing weather-avoidance equipment for an avionics company. He also did some crop dusting, and on that fine day when I finished college, it killed him.

John was the first person I knew who died in an airplane. He would be the first of many. It was easy to say he had been asking for it, boring holes in thunderstorms and spraying crops from ten feet off the ground. It was easy to say it wouldn't happen to me. I wasn't doing anything as dangerous as John was, except occasionally flying single-engine airplanes at night, even crossing the Appalachian Mountains at night. No pilot goes to the airplane thinking that they'll screw up, that crushed metal and torn limbs and flesh are their fate. John was too good of a pilot for it to happen to him. He certainly thought he was too good of a pilot to snag a power line on a peaceful, sunny afternoon in May.

I exceeded my flight time goals, graduating with fourteen hundred hours of flight time, with more than two hundred hours of extremely valuable multi-engine time. I was only able to accomplish this because of the head start I got in high school, because I completed the academic part of the aviation curriculum backward, and because I taught a full load of flight students for over three years. If I had completed the program as it was planned, I would've graduated with a Commercial Pilot License, a Flight Instructor certificate, and about three hundred hours of flight time. No one ever tells you that you'll graduate from the flight program totally unqualified to enter the industry. I'm not even sure how I figured it out.

Common advice given to aspiring professional pilots is to major in something else and learn to fly on the side so you'll have something to fall back on, if you aren't smart enough to just stay away from the industry altogether. OSU made that very difficult. The aircraft systems majors, who were the people putting all of their eggs in one flimsy basket and then handing that basket to the bag smashers at the airlines, had priority for flight training time slots. If you were smart enough to major in something else, you couldn't depend on even getting a flight training slot from one quarter to the next. OSU, and I believe all of the other collegiate aviation programs too, was producing flight students who weren't yet qualified to enter the industry and often weren't qualified to do anything else either.

I was enjoying what I was doing. I was even pretty good at it. I just wouldn't make any money. Upon graduation, I got a dollar per hour raise: seven dollars an hour for teaching people how to fly airplanes, and that's just for the billable hours. In reality I had been putting in full-time hours for about thirty-five hundred dollars per year. With my raise and without a course load of my own, I might exceed four thousand dollars a year.

I needed to move on, but in 1993, there weren't many places to go, especially not for someone as inexperienced as me. Yes, ascending to the top of the flight school still left me at the bottom of the industry.

I didn't realize yet how cyclical hiring is in the airlines, which is just further proof of the ignorance that had started me down this turbulent course. Aviation tends to be one of the first industries affected by a receding economy and one of the last to recover. There may be industry-wide hiring for a couple of years, and then all of the doors will slam shut. After the hiring stops, the furloughing begins, sometimes on the same day and maybe even affecting all the pilots hired during the last hiring cycle. There is intense competition for very few vacancies industry-wide, and airlines can't hire again until all of their furloughed pilots are recalled to work. Timing is everything, and my timing wasn't good.

The recent demise of Eastern, Pan Am, Braniff, and Midway flooded the job market with experienced pilots, plus each of the surviving major airlines had furloughed several hundred pilots. I certainly wasn't qualified for the same jobs the airline furloughees would fill, but stagnation in the major airlines freezes hiring all the way down to the entry-level jobs. Plus, most companies were still trying to recover from the surge in oil prices that had accompanied the most recent war to keep the oil taps flowing, an ironic, unintended consequence that we stubbornly refuse to learn from (well, maybe it is intended, but that's for another chapter).

There was still a little hiring in the commuter airlines, the small turboprops that wore the paint of the trunk lines that they fed, and these companies took advantage of the poor job market by passing the training costs along to their new hires. A pilot would have to pay ten thousand dollars to get a job that may only pay twelve-thousand dollars per year. You couldn't expect to break twenty grand until you upgraded to Captain, and with stagnation in the industry, upgrade times were indefinite.

I sent resumes to the few remaining commuter airlines that didn't make you buy your job, but I can imagine now that they probably laughed as they crumpled and round filed my thin resume. I sent resumes to every corporate flight department I could find that had a King Air, since I had some King Air time from my internship with the University's Air Transport Service, but you generally need to know someone to get a corporate flying job.

Three instructors from the flight school went to Alaska to be bush pilots. No matter what is happening in the industry, operators in Alaska perpetually need a steady stream of eager young pilots. When these companies talk about attrition, they don't mean losing pilots to the airlines; they mean mortality. Even in 1993, another bush pilot was dying in Alaska every nine days. I wasn't desperate enough to resort to that yet, and really, I wasn't brave enough.

I got a few rejection letters, but mostly I heard nothing. I just continued to go out to the airport every day to teach.

One day I ran into Sam, a good friend and former student of mine. It was the first time I had seen him since he was fired from the flight school. He was a sharp guy and a good pilot. He was fired because one of his commercial students had ground-looped an airplane during a crosswind landing on a solo flight, smashing a taxiway sign but not even scratching the old airplane. They fired Sam because he had let his student fly to an airport where the crosswind had exceeded the flight school's limit by a knot.

Sam's student was assigned to remedial crosswind training with me, since they still had too much faith in my ability to solve their problems. There was no problem to solve. We waited for the windiest day and then did touch-and-goes on the least favorable runway, truly approaching the airplane's maximum demonstrated crosswind component. He did a fine job. We would keep the airplane in a side-slip, trying to complete an entire landing and takeoff with just the upwind main wheel touching the runway. He could do this, and he had now controlled the airplane in crosswinds that most of the other well-sheltered flight instructors had never even experienced. He had just let the airplane get away from him for one brief moment, which triggered a chain of events that would actually lead to a job for me.

Sam landed on his feet, so to speak, finding an instructing job in the in-house flight school at a night freight airline based in Columbus. The company had started their flight school with hopes of having an organic source of pilots for their airline. The plan was to train a brand new student, from zero time through to a Commercial Pilot License with multi-engine rating. Then the low-time pilots could pay to sit in the right seat of the company's light twins on freight runs, eventually buying their way into a job once they had twelve-hundred hours of flight time, the minimum experience requirement for that kind of flying.

Sam had previously betrayed the University by going to this new flight school to get a multi-engine rating, since they charged twenty dollars an hour less for their old Baron, the blue bomber, than OSU did for its antique Aztecs. He obviously did well in his training, because they offered Sam an instructing job after he was fired from OSU.

I told Sam I had sent the company a resume, but they sent me a postcard saying they weren't hiring. They were one of the few companies to even give me the courtesy of a rejection, but apparently they lied to me. They were indeed hiring. He told me to send them another resume and he would make sure they looked at it.

The company invited me to an interview a few weeks later. Through hard work, you can supposedly achieve anything, but only if you know the right people, which didn't seem fair to me, knowing so few people out in the industry, but this was my first break.

I was obviously nervous for the first interview of my career, and even more so when I learned the other pilot who was interviewing that day had over three thousand hours of flight time and was already out in the world, flying for a charter company. I naturally assumed that this guy, who had twice as much flight time as me, must really know what he was doing. I assumed that if this was a competition, I wouldn't have a chance.

We took a written test, and then we waited for the director of training to summon each of us for a short interview. While we waited, the other guy was complaining about the questions on the test. I thought it was easy, but I kept my mouth shut.

The interview and the simulator evaluation were strictly technical, basically just a multi-engine checkride. He asked some questions about multi-engine aerodynamics. I flew a couple of instrument approaches and handled an engine failure in the generic multi-engine simulator. This was the stuff I taught every day. I knew this stuff inside and out, even upside down, which is what happens to you if you get too slow in a multi-engine airplane after an engine quits. This was easy, but I still assumed everyone else was more qualified than I was.

The Dark Side

I received the letter the next day. They must've mailed it as soon as I walked out the door. I was selected, along with five other pilots, to be in the company's next training class. The company wouldn't actually hire us until we graduated from the class. I would leave my instructing job for a month of unpaid training so that I could begin my career as a freight dog on the dark side of the planet, the dark side of the industry.

Our indoctrination into the dark side of aviation began with an explanation that if we didn't make our deadlines, our customers didn't have to pay for their shipments. Gas was cheaper than time, and we would fly every leg as fast as we possibly could, which would require much more aptitude than simply pushing the throttles forward. There were signs in the building that said things like "You are handling the nation's payment mechanism," trying to inspire a war-like sense of urgency in what was really just flying slips of paper, cancelled checks, around in the middle of the night, literally risking our lives for money, someone else's money. They were planting seeds in a receptive audience. We were all young and invincible and thrilled that someone would pay us to fly their airplanes. That's exactly how they wanted us to be.

They told us that fixing airplanes at outstations was expensive, so it was helpful when airplanes only broke on their way back to maintenance bases. They weren't necessarily telling us to fly broken airplanes, but we got the hint. They were also making sure we understood the imperative to always get the job done, no matter what happened along the way.

They pointed out that most airplanes can fly just fine well above their legal maximum takeoff weights. They weren't actually telling us to fly overweight; they were just making sure that we knew it was possible. Completing the weight and balance before a flight, like you're legally supposed to do, is time consuming. There would be time to do it enroute, unless a fed was giving you a line check, an unlikely occurrence during the darkest hours of night.

It was illegal to depart to an airport when its weather was below minimums, but they said we could do it by filing a flight plan to a different airport and then changing your destination back once the weather was good enough to fly the approach. This would never fool the controllers, since the company had a scheduled network, but they apparently let us get away with it. It probably helped that we were encouraged to bribe the controllers with pizzas and doughnuts. The company would reimburse us without questions. We probably could've expensed hookers for the controllers if it got us priority handling.

They never told us to avoid thunderstorms, because deviating would cost time. Instead, they told us the best way to penetrate a thunderstorm, usually to try to go under it. All of the airplanes had holes burned into them from lightning strikes, paint buffed right off the leading edges of everything from countless hours of pounding rain, and the old airframes had certainly been weakened by the violent turbulence they had endured.

Some of the airplanes weren't certified for flight in icing conditions, but they told us we could fly an airplane that wasn't fully certified for it, through known icing conditions as long as we stuck our fingers in our ears and hummed while another pilot was reporting icing conditions, because if we didn't hear it, it wasn't known. Well, not exactly, but they did have a rationale that I've long since forgotten.

They were trying to get us to operate in the cracks between regulations, much cheaper and more productive than remaining safely, legally, in the middle, but we were the ones who would bear the legal burden. A violation isn't like a speeding ticket; a violation could mean a sixty-day suspension, or even a revoked license, and a permanent stain on your record that would likely keep you out of a good job. They justified this philosophy by saying that it was much better than it used to be, which has since become a warning sign for me. Whenever someone says "It's better than it used to be," or "They've never had it as good as they do now," or any similar variation, then they know damn well it's wrong. They're just offering a lazy justification for why they aren't going to do anything to fix the problem. "It's wrong, but it's a little better, so it's good enough." I was naïve enough to believe it. I hadn't yet realized that nothing ever gets better unless someone rocks the boat.

Then an instructor got out the book of Federal Aviation Regulations, and read, word for word, Chapter 1, definitions, to our class. He was literally reading the dictionary to us, just the vocabulary that we use every day. This was the most absurd lecture I had ever witnessed. He had just told us numerous ways in which it would be helpful for us to risk our lives and careers by bending and stretching the rules, and then he acknowledged the regulations by reading the least relevant chapter, in its entirety. As absurd as this was, if I was a good student and just kept my mouth shut, they might pay me to fly their airplanes. I kept my mouth shut.

What cargo was worth this war-like sense of urgency and total disregard for the intent of the regulations? Money, except we weren't even really flying money; we were just flying a day's interest on a day's cancelled checks. This was just money that banks were skimming off every transaction they processed.

The company hauled other cargo as well, all time-critical and much of it hazardous. As bad as it all seemed, I also knew just enough to know that the company was actually one of the best ones in the night freight industry, for quality and airworthiness of the equipment, dedication to following the rules, and even pilot pay and career expectations. I had truly entered the dark side, the dark side of aviation, on the dark side of the planet.

Competition could be fierce, as new operators bought old airplanes and tried to break into the business. Speed and completion were everything. When two companies were competing on a route, it wasn't unheard of for a pilot to sneak up on the competition and chock their wheels as the other pilot was starting the engines, then jump in their own airplane, and win the race to the destination by a minute.

One of my classmates fell asleep in class one day, which is perfectly understandable when you're having the dictionary read to you all day. During the next break the instructors pulled him aside, and we never saw him again. He was the most experienced pilot in the class by far, but he had committed one of the worst sins a freight pilot could ever commit: being human.

Then we found out that our class would be the first class hired under a new pay scale. We got base pay, plus an hourly pay rate, which was now based on a forty-eight hour work week instead of the standard forty hour work week, which was only legal because the Railway Labor Act excludes air carriers from the Fair Labor Standards Act. Depending on the schedule you ended up with, this either meant they were getting eight hours of free work out of us each week or paying us two-thousand dollars less per year than the pilots in the previous class. Overtime would be paid at five dollars per hour, which is really just incentive to not work more than forty-eight hours, although we would never have a choice. I guess we did have a choice; we could get up and leave. I wasn't brave enough.

The owner of the company was an avid glider pilot, so they gave us glider training before they checked us out in Barons. It was a fun diversion, but I'm just glad he wasn't into sky diving or bungee jumping or group sex. The instructors made a point to tell us that this was the only no-jeopardy portion of our training, the only time we wouldn't be fired on the spot for not making the grade, but it was actually very relevant to check hauling. Whether you choose to fly an airplane as fast as possible or as efficiently as possible, you have to understand energy management. Speed is like money in your pocket, and altitude is like money in the bank. Without an engine, flying a glider requires the ability to manage these forms of energy, a skill that we would eventually master on the line, elevating our trade to an art form.

Something else I didn't understand at the time was that they weren't expecting all of us to make the cut. We all did, except for the guy who fell asleep in class. In the coming years, as industry-wide recovery absorbed more of the talent available, there would actually be indoctrination classes with only one graduate or maybe even no graduates at all, but that's for another chapter.

Our seniority within the class was determined by our flight time. The 1,566 hours of flight time I had worked so hard to acquire ranked me last in seniority by a couple-hundred-hour margin. I would be the last person in class to be assigned a position and a number on the company's seniority list. Unfortunately, we discovered the company trained new pilots for forecast need and there were currently only two vacancies to fill. The rest of us were trapped in some ambiguous state between unemployment and slavery, which I didn't understand before I started. If I had understood, I'm not sure I would've left the flight school for such uncertainty, because I'm not brave enough.

While we waited, the company encouraged us to ride along on revenue flights. They even paid us four dollars an hour for flight time, which I think may have been less than minimum wage then. I had no problem riding with line pilots who could show me the ropes—in fact, I wanted to learn all I could from the veterans—but it was actually insulting for them to pay me four dollars an hour. I guess they had to do it so they could justify to the feds that I was actually a crewmember, even though they didn't want to officially hire me until they knew where they were going to put me.

I found I couldn't even ride along out of Columbus because of the low-time co-pilots from the ab-initio program. Their class dates were earlier than mine, so they had seniority over me. Unlike them, I was actually qualified, and I couldn't even ride in an airplane because of the unqualified pilots who were buying their way in. I had to go stay with my sister in Chapel Hill for two weeks just to complete my initial operating experience in a Baron on the company's Raleigh-based route.

I would've loved to have had the Raleigh route, but the Raleigh-based pilot, Fred (not his real name), wasn't going anywhere soon. Even if he did, I wouldn't have the seniority for it. He flew to Greensboro, Charlotte, then maybe Atlanta, back to Charlotte and Greensboro, and then he was home at a reasonable hour, maybe three in the morning, I can't remember exactly.

Fred was a little bored, flying so little and always to the same places, and I think he enjoyed having someone ride along. On the first leg of my first night flying with him, a small thunderstorm churned the night sky just to the right of our course near Greensboro. Fred asked me if I had ever flown through a thunderstorm, knowing very well that my answer would be no. Wanting to educate or haze the rookie, or maybe just out of boredom, he said, "Let's fly through that one," and he keyed his microphone to ask the air traffic controller for a deviation, a deviation to fly through a thunderstorm, exactly the opposite of what every other sane pilot would ask for.

We were already down to three thousand feet, so we only went under it—just some heavy rain to wash the smashed bugs off the leading edges, and maybe a little more of the already peeling paint, a few jolts of turbulence, and a few flashes of lightning, though we didn't get struck. It was just a small southeastern thunderstorm, just an annoyance, or, for Fred, a little sport on the dark side.

It would get worse yet. I was finally next to get a seniority number, and there was a vacancy. I knew I would finally be unambiguously employed. But they gave the route to a co-pilot who had just reached the legal minimum of twelve-hundred hours. I was pissed, not just because what I thought was mine had been taken by someone who essentially bought his seniority number, but because I could potentially stay in that state of limbo forever as more co-pilots accrued their twelve-hundredth hour of flight time.

The explanation I was given was that their class dates were earlier than mine. It didn't matter that they weren't actually qualified when they went through class, or that they probably couldn't even legally log co-pilot time in a single-pilot airplane, not that legality is much of a concern in the dark side of the industry.

The Chief Pilot was surprisingly sympathetic to my complaints, and decided to go ahead and give me a seniority number. He would just use me as a Captain out of Columbus until I could bid a vacancy.

I got my seniority number just in time. On my first night of unambiguous employment, flying one of the Columbus-based runs, I had a co-pilot who was within a couple of hours of becoming qualified, which he would likely achieve that very night. He would have gotten the next vacancy in front of me, and it turned out to be the last vacancy for months. But instead he had to crank my landing gear down by hand, fifty turns of an inconveniently placed crank, because the old Baron's landing gear motor failed on my very first flight as Captain, a little of the bad luck that was always waiting for a rookie like me.

They decided to check me out in the Aerostar right away, a sleek, demanding machine that killed unsuspecting pilots at a rate that far exceeded every other light twin in existence, about three times the fatal accident rate of the Baron. I had an exhausting night of ground school on the airplane, and then, after being in class all night, they told me I would probably have to fly a Baron up to Utica, New York, to pick up some of our pilots who were stranded there. The runway was icy and one of our Aerostars had slid off the side in a stiff crosswind. The company's two Learjet instructors were flying by there, had dropped in to Utica to pick up the Aerostar pilot, and the Learjet had slid off the side of the runway too. So they told the most junior pilot in the company that he would need to go up there and fly everyone back. Then someone exercised a rare moment of restraint and decided not to risk wrecking a third airplane in the same location that night, probably because the freight had already missed the deadlines anyway.

The next night they called me in a little early. I would fly to Erie, Pennsylvania, with an instructor, and he would check me out in the Aerostar on the way. Then we would fly it to Pittsburgh, Cleveland, and back to Columbus. It was a difficult night. We were in a hurry, flying a scheduled run with deadlines to be made while training in a new airplane. The instructor had little patience for anything less than perfection, which I was too green to deliver, especially in an unfamiliar beast of an airplane.

A half hour after finishing my on-the-job training, before I could even put my Aerostar time in my logbook, they told me to fly one particularly grizzled Aerostar to Buffalo and back. The Aerostar was a slick airplane with a reputation, but this particular airplane, "One-Two-Sierra" (shorthand for its registration number) was known by our pilots as "One-Two-Suicide." This was one of only three of the Aerostars in the fleet that didn't have an autopilot, and it wasn't stable enough to take your hands off of it. You couldn't take a break from this beast until you got it back on the ground.

I had already had a full night of flying, and now, at five in the morning, it was far from over. I was nervous as I taxied out alone on this dreary morning in this airplane I barely knew. The Aerostar accelerated briskly down the soggy runway. With a slight tug at the yoke, the sleek monster leapt into the dark gray void. The world below disappeared, making me feel more alone than I had ever felt in my life. I felt like a kid who was learning to swim by being thrown in a murky, churning river, and I was in over my head. I trusted the little three-inch-wide horizon on my instrument panel, which represented the world I couldn't see. The little gyro, and my instrument flying skills, didn't fail me. The infinite gray eventually yielded to the approach lights leading to the runway in Buffalo, the first view I'd had of anything at all since I'd left the runway in Columbus.

I taxied across the icy ruins from last night's freezing rain to the UPS ramp, the only part of the airport that was open (the freight always goes). My courier and I had to haul seven-hundred pounds of canceled checks across a hundred feet of ice glazed with a slippery film of water. I slipped on one of my trips back to the airplane. I was flat on the cold hard ground before I realized I was falling. I didn't think I was hurt, but my pants were wet from the film of water on the ice. The cold, drafty cabin of the Aerostar would have no sympathy for a rookie, me. The leaky door seals would blow cold air onto my wet left knee the whole way back to Columbus.

It was a long trip back in the wake of the powerful winter storm. Even down at three thousand feet, I was flying into a seventy-knot headwind. I hadn't planned for this long of a trip, and I hadn't been able to get fuel in Buffalo because the fuel trucks were iced in on the other side of the airport. I had the benefit of a seventy-knot tailwind on the way there, but I was exposed to the headwind for much longer than I was exposed to the tailwind; with any wind at all, an entire trip takes longer.

Nearing Columbus, with my wing tanks dry, I just had the Aerostar's small fuselage fuel tank left. As the airplane rocked in the bumpy air, the low fuel light would flicker as fuel sloshed in the tank. I had a legal reserve, but I was used to having a much greater margin in the sheltered world of flight instruction. Now I was in the real world, and it was much more demanding, and frightening, than I had imagined.

My fourteen-hour work day was finally over. I was exhausted from learning to fly the Aerostar and from the eight hours of hard-core instrument flying inside the thick, gray clouds of the winter storm without relief from an autopilot or even a glimpse of a horizon. I was numb from the wet and cold, fatigued to my core from the unrelenting turbulence and a long cold night of shivering, eight hours in a paint shaker, and sore from my fall on the ice. Absolutely beat, I fell into bed at ten in the morning, but only managed a few hours of restless daytime sleep to prepare for my next all-nighter. I wondered if all nights would be as difficult as this one. They couldn't be. I didn't think I could continue to do this job if they were.

The next vacancy was in Buffalo. I would be based there and fly the same route four nights a week. I had actually just flown parts of my new route during my first night in the Aerostar.

With very little notice, I drove to Buffalo, a place that had made a painful and exhausting first impression on me. I arrived in the eerie darkness of the earliest hour of morning. Sparse snowflakes drifted, almost in slow motion, downy feathers falling from the heavy sky, glazing the lonely road ahead with a thin blanket of slush that had not yet been cut by tire tracks. I wasn't just driving to Buffalo; I was driving into the uncertainty of my future, truly alone for the first time in my life.

I felt like a mouse in a maze while driving around Buffalo looking for an apartment. Snow was piled up so high I couldn't see around corners. The streets were slick with snow from the lake-effect snow showers that can last for days, until the wind finally shifts, but in Buffalo the wind can blow from many directions and you'll still be downwind of a lake.

I had been told that Buffalo has the ability to handle snow. That's true, but the streets always seemed to be covered with the perpetual snow, in what was to become an unusually snowy winter. It may not take long for the fleet of snow plows to clean every street in town, but every one of those streets would have another inch of snow an hour later.

I found a cheap apartment in an old hotel that had been converted to studio apartments. It had the potential to be nice, but it wasn't. The price was right, and I was planning on bidding almost any vacancy to get out of the snow, thinking it wouldn't be long, hoping it wouldn't be long.

I asked the landlord if it was quiet, since I would be going to bed at eight every morning, always struggling to put together a day of restless sleep.

The landlord lowered his voice, as if saying it quieter made him somehow less of a bigot: "I put all the blacks in the back building. You'll be in the quiet building."

That wasn't quite the answer I expected. I've never seen a black person play the bagpipes. Actually that's not fair, because I've maybe only seen one person play the bagpipes. What little I did know about bagpipes was they were ear-splittingly loud. I should have asked him if there were any bagpipe players in the front building.

He asked me how long I would be staying. I told him I didn't know. I already wanted out of there. My perception was already poisoned by that exhausting first night in the Aerostar, and incalculably massive amounts of snow. He sighed and then said, "You seem like a decent kid; you can just go month to month." I wondered if he made the people in the back building sign leases. I would think so?

I had grown up in a homogenized Midwestern suburb, in the era of the angry white male, the natural backlash from what, in our collective ignorance, seemed like a legislated hand up for everyone but us, the young white males. My conversation with the landlord, really my first brush with anything more substantial than angry rhetoric, had left me vaguely uncomfortable, knowing the bigot had given me special treatment for the color of my skin, or lack of, which was simply an accident of birth, an irrelevant condition from which there was no escape. It was an old prejudice, even spelled out by the nation's sacred Constitution, which stated that a back-building resident was really just three-fifths of a person. Even women were only made constitutionally whole within my grandparents' lifetimes.

I would become even more uncomfortable once I realized that even professional pilots were stratified into different social classes and that I could encounter discrimination because I had just joined the lowest tier, the freight dogs.

What would you think if you saw a black man standing next to an airplane at two in the morning? Airport police naturally assumed he was a criminal (a black freight dog?), so they handcuffed him and threw him in a police car. It took an hour to convince the police he was one of our pilots. We had company ID badges, but pre-9/11 in the middle of the night, no one ever wore them. He probably had to sign a lease for an apartment too, but at least he'd be in the back building, where he wouldn't have to be inconvenienced by my annoying bagpipe lessons while struggling to sleep in the middle of the day.

As Lake Erie froze over, the lake-effect snow finally subsided, except for a perpetual snow shower tethered just downwind of the open water at the mouth of the Niagara River, quite often hovering right over the Buffalo airport.

I was getting more comfortable with the airplanes every day. I was getting more comfortable with the tight schedules and with what I had to do to make the deadlines.

I was learning quickly, but I still knew how inexperienced I really was, and that's a difficult realization, because when you don't know, you especially don't know how much you don't know.

I knew a lot about weather, but until now that was mostly weather theory, abstract in the sense that in flight training we talked about it, but we were never actually in it. In the sheltered environment of training, you just cancel and try again the next day. In night freight, you have to make the deadlines, and the weather almost never gets bad enough for you to cancel. My new colleagues and I, all former flight instructors, would joke that we used to teach our students how to make a "go, no-go" decision. Now we were expected to make a "go, go-now" decision. We were doing things we had always told our students not to do. We were really just novices testing the limits of what was possible, out in the desolate margins where only well-seasoned professionals should tread, although they were wise enough not to. We were getting the job done, on schedule, in spite of the thunderstorms, ice-laden clouds, gale-force winds, freezing rain, blizzards, and blinding fog, and we were each doing it alone. We had to either climb this steep learning curve or quit.

We would actually sometimes have to fly more on the very worst days, when the roads were too treacherous for couriers to make the deadlines of shipments that were ordinarily driven, such as an early morning delivery from Columbus to Charleston, West Virginia. In time I would frequently find myself on ice-covered runways on Charleston's mountain-top airport, where sliding off the runway could mean a trip down the mountainside. In fact, the only times I would go there would be when the weather was that bad, an absurdity that was probably unique to night freight.

It wasn't just the weather's limits that we were testing. We were regularly operating our old airplanes and our exhausted bodies at their limits. What I didn't realize yet was how good at it I was actually getting, quickly. There was too much uncertainty about what I would encounter next, and whether I would be up to the challenge, to ever get cocky about it.

When I pulled off a successful circling approach into Lakefront Airport in Cleveland during a snowstorm, I knew I was straddling a fine line between perfection and losing control. A circling approach is an instrument approach that doesn't line you up with the intended runway, because of obstacles or unfavorable winds, and requires low altitude, low visibility maneuvering to line up with the appropriate runway after emerging from the clouds. You had to know exactly where you were at all times, with limited visual reference in a raw data airplane, and most importantly, you had to know exactly how much room you needed for maneuvering, with winds of magnitudes that you'd never previously needed to consider, and with that extra speed you're carrying to compensate for the ice on your wings that you couldn't shed (de-ice boots don't often give you a perfectly clean wing). This was truly hard-core flying, turning out over the utter blackness of Lake Erie at low altitude and then turning back in at the right moment, knowing a fierce Arctic gale would whip you toward the skyscrapers in downtown Cleveland. Then you would have to land the airplane in a crosswind that was at the airplane's limit on a runway slickened by snow and the freezing spray from the giant waves crashing into the sea wall next to the airport. I was certainly satisfied with my accomplishment as I walked to the terminal through the frigid darkness on wobbling knees, with sweat freezing to my brow, but I also had the sense that I had just gotten away with another one. I was never sure how it would turn out the next time, only that there would indeed be a next time.

Mundane items on a checklist performed repeatedly every night can hide as much danger as a tense, night-time circling approach in a snowstorm. The Baron's simple fuel system never required attention in flight, except checking that you had enough fuel. Through endless repetition, it became an item that was easy to neglect. But there was one bastard Baron that was completely different, 40Vicious, the blue bomber, an oddball that required you to physically switch fuel tanks.

On a rare night that I was actually in the blue bomber, I didn't remember, and I mentally bypassed the mundane checklist reminder that never applied to the other Barons. I landed in Columbus at four in the morning, turning off the runway and straight toward the company ramp. The right propeller quietly stopped beside me as the starved engine quit. I realized my omission and switched fuel tanks before the remaining engine drank its last sip of fuel from a nearly empty tank.

That was a close one, with starvation of one engine occurring mere seconds after landing, although I still had plenty of fuel in the tanks I wasn't using. It was a valuable lesson about discipline, complacency, and attention to detail, and I was lucky enough to learn it without hurting myself. Countless pilots haven't been that lucky, and our procedures and methods are now written with their blood.

On the dreariest of nights, when a precisely flown approach to minimums was required, we knew we had all earned our way into the airport. There seemed to be a mutual shroud of respect that hung in the air as thickly as the dense fog that had obscured the runway. We were all doing the same job, in the same tired airplanes, through the same miserable weather on the dark side of the planet.

I had always believed the American rugged individualists myths, including the idea that a seniority system would encourage, or at least allow, mediocrity. My career had been a competition until then, with whom or what I'm no longer sure. Now I was getting used to my place on the seniority list, a long list of competent professionals who were always giving their best, where you would do your job and wait your turn. It wasn't an easy adjustment for me, especially since I held the last number on the list for two agonizing months. Now I knew I was in good company there. Some were certainly better than others, but there was no mediocrity; the demands of the job didn't allow it. There also wasn't any office politics, backstabbing, or brown-nosing your way to the top. Without a seniority list in a challenging environment with a tremendous financial imperative for mission completion, dangerous flying is potentially encouraged as pilots do anything to make sure the job always gets done and to make sure they get promoted. Conservative decisions cost money and productivity and mark a pilot as one who is unwilling to sacrifice for the team, more furlough fodder than upgrade material.

The airplanes worked hard, and they had been abused for years. Maintenance wasn't a problem. If you told them to fix something, they would fix it, but first they would always ask you if you could get it back to a maintenance base. No one wanted to be the guy who was always making them fix airplanes at an outstation because that cost more and marked you as a troublemaker, that selfish type (as well as safe, legal, and reasonable) who was unwilling to take one for the team, an expensive liability to a company that wanted to fly airplanes for cheap and still get the job done. This is part of the economics of safety, and my company wasn't necessarily any worse than others in the dark side of the business.

There also wasn't always a black-and-white distinction between working and broken. More often something was just impaired in some way or required just the right tinkering to perform, and many pilots would just accept these little problems in order to keep an airplane they liked. My route was one of the conduits for getting airplanes back and forth between Columbus and the East Coast, and I would often find a month's worth of accumulating problems as I would bring an airplane back. Some airplanes had illusive problems, which were more like personality flaws that the mechanics were genuinely trying, but never quite succeeding, to correct.

I learned you couldn't judge an airplane by appearance. Often the ones with the best paint jobs were among the most abused. The airplane had probably only been sent to the paint shop because the director of maintenance was becoming embarrassed by how nasty it was looking, or maybe it had just been repaired and repainted after an accident. There were many accidents.

The airplanes had big, air-cooled, hard-working engines, and most of the pilots tried to take care of them. Our lives depended on the engines, because light twins aren't required to have much, or any, single-engine climb performance, and we were usually very heavy. Before landing, you had to reduce power very slowly so you wouldn't shock cool the engines. It would actually take about eight minutes to reduce power for landing, which meant you were starting this gradual power reduction about twenty-five miles from the destination (reducing power by one inch of manifold pressure per minute). This also meant you would begin slowing down, and we were always supposed to be going as fast as we could. I would plan my descents so I would be trading in a little more gravity every time I squeezed the power back some more, and I could maintain cruise speed all the way to the traffic pattern. Energy management was an art, an art I would get to practice five times per night.

All the airplanes were drafty and cold in the winter and hot, musty, and stale in the summer. There didn't seem to be much in between, and they were always deafeningly loud. To turn the airplanes into freighters, their interiors and insulation had been pulled out, leaving just a noisy aluminum shell. The airplanes had combustion heaters, which would actually burn gasoline in a little combustion chamber in front of your feet, something I was never comfortable with, but I also wasn't going to freeze to death. Ram airflow over the combustion chamber was our only heat in the airplane, and it couldn't compete with all the drafts and leaks in our stripped cabins. There was a little fan that blew air over the heater for when you were on the ground, but it wasn't enough airflow to prevent the combustion heater from overheating. If it overheated, it would trip a circuit breaker that we couldn't get to in flight. You couldn't let that happen, so you wouldn't turn the heater on until you took off, and you had to give it a chance to cool down before you landed. I wore multiple layers, long johns, hat, and gloves, and the ink would still freeze inside the pen in my pocket. I wouldn't get warm until I got to bed in the morning.

Barons were stable and easy to fly, but there was absolutely no standardization in the cockpits, and I'm sure the company didn't have two that were alike. This lack of conformity was exacerbated by the Baron's unusual control column, which actually hid many of the switches. Some had radars, good navigation equipment, and autopilots, and some had nothing extra at all. The throttles and propeller controls were even arranged differently than in any other light twin. This has supposedly been corrected in new Barons, but new airplanes don't haul freight.

All of the airplanes had deicing equipment, but some were certified for flight into known icing conditions and some weren't. They all could've been certified, but why should they spend the money to upgrade them when they employed a bunch of kids who would willingly fly the airplanes through anything? The airplanes that were certified had, among other things, a small, square hotplate in the middle of the windshield. That little square would be free of ice, but it wasn't very useful in the middle of the windshield; it needed to be in front of the pilot's seat.

The airplanes that weren't certified had a piccolo tube that sprayed alcohol at the base of the windshield, right in front of the pilot's seat. You couldn't use it continuously, because you'd run out of alcohol. You had to let ice form during the flight with the hope that the alcohol would melt some of it off later. You also had to shut it off as you were nearing the runway, because you couldn't see through the alcohol.

Barons had simple fuel systems but tiny fuel gauges with questionable accuracy. You only really knew how much fuel you had when you had topped the tanks, but then you couldn't load the airplane down with freight—well, unless you just flew overweight. Two of my friends ran out of fuel in the middle of the night, in one of our newer Barons that was still indicating a quarter tank of fuel in each wing. They aimed for a dark spot and got lucky, sort of. They injured their backs and destroyed the airplane, but they survived.

Most of our Barons didn't have shoulder harnesses, because the airplane was certified before they were required in airplanes. Adding a shoulder strap was a cheap way to make the airplanes safer for us. At the very least it would prevent us from having to pick little shards of glass from the flight instruments out of our faces after a minor accident. The company agreed and began retrofitting the airplanes, at the rate of about two per year. That made it a twelve-year project.

The Aerostar has a reputation as a dangerous airplane, and although that reputation was fed by the blood of a lot of dead doctors (or any other amateur with more money than skill), I think it's undeserved, except for the statistical problem that it has three times the fatal accident rate as the Baron. It's a hot little airplane, maybe too hot for the weekend pilots who were getting into them. It's fast and maneuverable, and it's a great airplane if you fly it correctly and stay current, possibly just less tolerant of sloppy handling.

Aerostars had a bad habit of rolling over when the wing stalled, which is normally undesirable, especially when you're about to land. There's an easy solution to this problem, something fundamental that every pilot does on every flight, regardless of the type of airplane; you just don't let the airplane get slow enough to stall. That wasn't good enough for the feds. They required all of the airplanes to be modified.

The manufacturer's solution was to extend the rudder beneath the tail to give the airplane more controllability. We called this a water rudder, and it was the best solution.

Since the company had old airplanes, most of our airplanes were modified with a Machen kit, which consisted of a strake on the left side of the nose and about a hundred vortex generators strategically placed on the wings and tail. Vortex generators are little metal vanes placed at angles to the airflow. They create little vortices that actually help airflow stick to the control surfaces to give the airplane more controllability approaching a stall. Aerodynamics isn't just math, physics, and slide rules; it's compromises. If you want something, you have to give something up. The Machen kit gives up too much in drag. A hundred little metal vanes, creating a hundred little tornados, caused these airplanes to cruise at least twenty knots slower than the few Aerostars we had with water rudders.

I never adapted to staying up all night. I think I just got used to always being fatigued. Day sleeping is unnatural for a diurnal species, and it cannot be offset with caffeine and artificial light through a long winter's night. I tried to trick my body by darkening my room, but my body knew better if there was even a tiny sliver of daylight peeking through a crack. I found sleep masks to not be much more effective than my own eyelids. I tried to drown the daytime noises with a fan or by wearing ear plugs, but I would still hear the lawn mowers, delivery trucks, and construction equipment.

I was flying the same route every day, but I was getting paid for what I loved to do, and fortunately the scenery was always changing. Within my exhaustingly long workday I was always treated to a sunset and a sunrise, and no two were exactly alike. Moisture or the utter lack thereof gives the sky its character. Whether you are above, below, or between the clouds, the density and texture of the clouds and whether there is any precipitation can totally change how the first or last rays of the sun paint the sky. Sometimes you can even be in the middle of it, surrounded by glowing clouds.

One particularly memorable stormy morning, I flew through a narrow canyon of clouds with purple walls seven miles high, which framed a bright orange glow spilling over the predawn horizon ahead. Occasional great veins of electric blue lightning illuminated the canyon walls, a spectacular cloudscape that no one else saw and no one will ever see again. And on that fleeting and unrepeatable early morning, it all belonged to me.

Goodbye, Friend

As I entered my fourth season in Buffalo, I learned my time there was nearing its end. My route was being broken into two new routes. One part would be flown out of Utica, New York. The other part would probably be flown from Pittsburgh, but they weren't sure yet. They displaced me to Utica. I had spent my entire time in Buffalo as a transient, certain that at any time I would be able to bid something else. It never happened. Now I was finally leaving Buffalo because they kicked me out.

My first trip to Utica had been the prior winter; right after Utica got thirty-three inches of snow in a twenty-four-hour period—another troubled first impression and winter weather unlike anything I had ever seen. I wasn't familiar with the airport, but I did know that only one runway and one taxiway were open. Everything else was buried in snow, including the runway lights, which were under six-foot snow banks. With an ILS (Instrument Landing System) approach, I could do without the lights; nighttime in a snow-covered landscape is rarely black.

I landed between the snow banks, on a fluffy carpet of virgin powder, and rolled all the way to the end of the runway, looking for the open taxiway. It wasn't as clean as the runway. My Aerostar's wheels got stuck in deep snow as I neared the terminal. I tried to power my way through it, but all I accomplished was to envelop my Aerostar in a swirling cloud of white powder. A tug had to pull me the rest of the way.

Now I was back in Utica in autumn. New York is beautiful at that time of year, dressed in autumn colors and with long shadows snaking across a landscape subtly shaped by continental glaciation. It was beautiful and serene and probably the first time in my life that I truly appreciated this transitional season, but I really didn't want to move there. I wouldn't need to. On my second day in Utica, we got a new bid sheet, and I had the seniority for three of the vacancies. I chose Columbia, South Carolina, but it would take a while until they could move me.

I was a lot more comfortable with the job now. In Utica I was flying four legs every day, but with seven hours of duty, my work day was only half as long as it was in Buffalo. It was still a lot of flying, and hard-core flying at that—single pilot, often without an autopilot, raw data, all weather, and tight schedules, and the lake-effect snows were already starting back up. Everyone who does this kind of flying for very long gets very good at it. Still not cocky about it, although certainly proud, I was beginning to realize I had elevated my skills to another level as a lowly freight dog.

The air traffic controllers knew we were good too. One night I was complimenting a controller in Columbus for how well they moved us in and out during our busiest hub. His response was, "You guys deserve the credit. I just aim you at each other, and you guys do the rest." Unless you're following a joker who turns off his lights and slows to the edge of a stall right after you report him in sight, relieving the controller of responsibility for separation. We had a couple of those.

One foggy morning I was watching a friend leave Utica in an Aerostar after a quick-turn. As soon as he shut the door, one of the propellers began turning. The Aerostar began rolling toward the runway as the other engine roared to life. Almost immediately, the still, morning air was filled with the scream of two Lycoming IO-540 engines as the sleek airplane accelerated through the fog. My friend's hands had moved from one switch to the next in a precisely choreographed performance that had started less than a minute earlier. This was flying elevated to an art, as if one fluid motion was performing the complex task of beginning a flight in an Aerostar. A mere technician would've clumsily needed several hands and a lot more time to accomplish the same feat.

It was too efficient. In the controller's haste to allow my friend to depart, he had forgotten about the Navajo that had already been cleared to land on the crossing runway. Like a ghost, the Navajo emerged from the fog, racing the Aerostar to the intersection. Both pilots were focused on their own tasks, straight ahead, on a collision course, each going well over a hundred miles per hour. In the blink of an eye it was over. Watching from some distance, I couldn't even tell who made it through the intersection first. My friend thought the Navajo did, but even he wasn't sure, and he was actually there.

For some reason these events are called near misses. This was a near collision, missing by a matter of feet. After the near collision, the controller saw his error, and said, "Sorry," into his microphone. No one reported the incident. My friend had straddled that thin line between perfection and losing control, and then the controller made a mistake. No one got hurt, that time.

Toward the end of my first week in Utica, the flight department called and asked me if I wanted to go back to Buffalo until they could move me to Columbia. They were already starting a new route there, and it was grueling: fourteen hours of duty and eight hours of flying, five days a week. I told them I had already closed that chapter in my life. I would just hang out in Utica until they could move me. I couldn't have known it then, but I had just decided the fate of one of my best friends.

They sent my friend Sam to Buffalo, the guy who helped me get hired. He had left the training department a few months prior to fly the line, and now he was also waiting for them to move him to his new base, Cleveland or Detroit, I can't remember now which.

Sam would have a long layover in Utica every day before I would show up for work. I was staying at a hotel right at the airport, so we would go to dinner every night. It helped break up the lonely wait for both of us as we were both transients, waiting to get on with our lives.

When they finally let me move, I told Sam I felt like I was abandoning him since he didn't know how much longer they would make him wait in Buffalo. He just said, "You are." I would never talk to my friend again.

A week later, as Sam's Aerostar was cruising a mile above the dark New York countryside, it suddenly plunged into the earth. There was no distress call. There was no good-bye. Sam was here, and now he's gone. He had just proposed to his high school sweetheart. He had his life ahead of him.

The accident investigation found that Sam had been on duty for sixty-six hours and had flown thirty-seven-and-a-half hours during the five days prior to the accident. If you include the crew resource management ground school that he attended during the prior weekend, he was on duty for eighty-two hours during the seven days prior to the accident, and immediately prior to that was another sixty-six hour work week. The Director of Operations acknowledged that Sam had told him that the new route had too much flying and that he would quickly exceed the FAA's (Federal Aviation Administration) cumulative flight time limitations, which were actually quite liberal for this kind of flying. On the night of the accident Sam had even asked someone to fly with him just to help keep him awake.

Sam and I had talked a lot about how hard it was to stay awake at the end of the night. I mentioned that sometimes it was easier to stay awake if you were concentrating on hand flying, rather than monotonously watching the autopilot fly and occasionally dozing off. Or was it Sam who mentioned it? I can't remember now. We both certainly agreed. That's a conversation that could only occur between invincible, ignorant kids who didn't yet understand that people really do have limits, and we were regularly operating much too close to them. Sam reached his limit on the last leg of the last night of a very long week, and his hands were on the controls as he fell into a sleep from which he would never awaken while the unguided Aerostar spiraled toward its doom.

First I made a decision that sent Sam to Buffalo, and then I had a conversation with Sam, maybe even a couple of conversations, that would directly lead to his death. It's hard for me to not hate the naïve kid I was, the invincible, ambitious, loyal young punk who feared the shame of not getting the job done. There would've been no shame in saying you could go no further; in making the banks float a day's interest. There's no shame in staying alive.

The company was quick to blame Sam for not getting enough rest. They published a memo reminding us of the obvious, how important it is to report for duty well rested, and the feds were satisfied. Another young pilot took an airplane to Buffalo, undoubtedly giddy to be getting paid to fly. And nothing ever changes.

Hundreds of thousands of years of evolution made us into creatures of the day. When we resist, we sleep restlessly during the day, unable to hide from the sun and from a society awake. All night you struggle to resist the natural urge to lay your head down and succumb to sleep, and no amount of caffeine, adrenaline, or artificial light will suppress your biology. You never get used to nocturnal life, although you do, to some degree, become accustomed to chronic fatigue. Every year spent enduring this abuse is supposedly a year that can be subtracted from the end of your life. In Sam's case it was considerably more.

I realized, for the first time in my life, that I was expendable. If my future led me into a deep, smoking crater in a K-Mart parking lot in Albany, New York, I would become a liability that the company would try to separate itself from. They would find a reason to blame me and then distribute a memo to the other pilots, reminding them not to make the same mistake. That would satisfy the feds that the remaining pilots had been trained and that it wouldn't happen again. Banks would have to float a day's interest on the checks incinerated in the post-crash fire. An insurance company would cut a check for an airplane that was getting too old and ragged anyway. Then everyone would be able to return to their business as if I had never existed. I was bitter about this revelation, that Sam had given his life for nothing. Suddenly and unexpectedly disillusioned, I was sure then that there was no cause worth dying for, not for god or country, and especially not for hauling money on the dark side of the planet.

Moving On

I was driving into the unknown again, on the dark side of the planet, of course. A black wall of pine trees stood on each side of the highway, with a crisp starlit sky above. I arrived after midnight on Sunday, and all of Columbia, South Carolina, was asleep, except for a few stubborn crickets who hadn't yet accepted winter's arrival.

I gave up any possibility of overtime to fly an easy route in Columbia, but it was worth it. Overtime under the Railway Labor Act wasn't worth it anyway; five bucks an hour in excess of forty-eight hours. Regardless, the flying was easy. I flew to Charlotte, then Richmond, where I played ping-pong and billiards for an hour with other freight dogs and then flew back to Charlotte where I would sleep for three hours before flying home. I would be in bed by eight, and sleep until noon. I actually had half a night of sleep while at work, at night even, and some free time on work days, which were both novelties after the exhausting schedule I had in Buffalo. I would even finally have time for the bagpipe lessons I had wanted to take to annoy that bigot landlord in Buffalo.

Winter was mild and brief and yielded to an early spring that wasn't necessarily distinguished astronomically or meteorologically but by an explosion of color. Columbia was suddenly ablaze in the hot pink, lavender, and red of azalea blooms. They were soon joined by the handsome white dogwood bracts and the enormous magnolia blooms.

Sex was much messier for the wind-pollinated pine trees, and this was an especially messy year. The sticky grains of pine pollen that drifted on the wind stung my eyes and throat and coated every surface in my apartment when I opened my windows to a pleasant spring day. Even the oil stains in parking lots glowed yellowish green with thick films of trapped pollen, as if they were the subjects of an Andy Warhol silk screen.

My nap in Charlotte was in the pilot's lounge at Signature Flight Support, the only Fixed Base Operator (FBO, general aviation) on the field. Unfortunately, Signature just happened to be escalating its harassment of the lowest social class in the industry, the freight dogs. Most FBOs liked to segregate us from their favorite customers, corporate pilots, but Signature's war on freight was a little silly.

We wore blue jeans and sneakers to work, and if we had pizza sauce on our shirts or occasionally missed a shave, it was only because we knew no one would notice in the middle of the night, but we were also the FBO's most lucrative customers. We were Signature's largest fuel customer, plus they charged us a fifty dollar handling fee for every airplane that passed through and they never actually handled us, except to pump fuel. We were the reliable customers in a fickle industry. We flew four days a week, regardless of the ebb and flow of our cyclical economy, and we normally carried heavy loads of freight, which meant we would buy fuel almost everywhere we went. If there had been another FBO on the field, we certainly would've gotten a bit more respect as they fought over our business.

Corporate pilots had shinier shoes, but they often wouldn't even buy fuel because they would try to fuel their planes for round trips back to base. While they waited for their passengers, they often required a lot of handling.

One morning I had to walk past a shiny Falcon 50, a multi-million-dollar three-engine business jet, to get to my battered, antique Baron. The Falcon pilot was standing outside admiring his airplane and supervising the linemen who were doing his work, carrying coffee and ice, and catering to his airplane. Then the Falcon pilot rudely stepped into my path and asked, "Where do you think you're going?" I told him I was going to my airplane. He chuckled as he smugly said, "No, that's my airplane." If it looked like I was walking toward his plane, it was only to step out of the way of one of my company's trucks—very important if you value your life. I half-heartedly pointed to my grizzled old Baron as I stepped around the prick, never looking back.

How I wished I could have that one back. If I could relive that episode, I would grab that arrogant jerk's arm and . . . beg him to give me a job.

When the freight pilots started filtering into Signature's pilots lounge, around nine or ten at night, the pilot's lounge would already be trashed with a day's worth of coffee cups, soda cans, newspapers, and even popcorn smashed into the carpeting. It was such a disgrace that we would actually clean the place up when we got there, but any mess would be blamed on the freight pilots.

There certainly were some miscreants on the night shift, but they weren't necessarily even freight pilots. One night I stirred from my nightly nap in the pilot's lounge to see a plump, undulating sleeping bag on the sofa, its two occupants, at least one a local ground courier, engaged in some kind of intimate activity, or maybe wrestling. I was too tired to care, my mind still clouded with sleep inertia, and besides, this was the night shift, the dark side of the planet; I was not surprised by anything anymore. I gave them back their privacy, not that they seemed to care, by shutting my eyes, my earplugs drowning any noises, and drifting off again.

The FBO wouldn't let freight pilots use the crew car, and for a while they even locked the pilot's lounge during the night. Then they opened the pilot's lounge back up but tried to freeze us out of it, turning the thermostat down to fifty degrees with a locked thermostat. They claimed the pilot's lounge would get too warm during the day unless its starting point was fifty degrees. We would just take our naps in the cold, although my knees would ache after sleeping in that cold of a room. Then they took the recliners away, but that didn't last long since corporate pilots also value a good nap.

By June my route had been changed to just three round trips to Charlotte every night. Not including the gas I would buy there, I was generating one hundred and fifty dollars in handling fees for Signature every night, and all I wanted from them was to be able to take a nap from three until six in the morning!

Only flying between Columbia and Charlotte was getting monotonous. It was even getting hard to keep track of what day it was, even though I only flew four days a week. There was a whole world out there, but I was now confined to just seventy-six nautical miles of it.

The suffocating heat and humidity of summer in Columbia also felt confining, making it hard to be outside. The hottest temperatures in the Southeast often occur along the border of the Piedmont Plateau and the Coastal Plain, which included Columbia. Plus, there was the heat island effect from being in a city with endless miles of pavement. There was little relief at night because of the tropical humidity. I would become drenched in sweat while tossing bags in and out of the stuffy cabin of my Aerostar, and I would remain uncomfortably damp for the rest of the night.

The humidity created plenty of foggy nights as well. I think I'll always remember the terrifying anxiety of flying my first solo ILS (Instrument Landing System) approach to minimums, to within two hundred feet of an unseen runway during my first couple of months in Buffalo. Now flying an approach to within two hundred feet of an unseen runway seemed normal. So did flying in circles in a holding pattern over Columbia, waiting for the visibility to increase to landing minimums. At one point I realized that following my instruments into the gray void where the unseen runway was supposed to be wasn't even increasing my pulse anymore.

On one particularly steamy night, I was sequenced behind a Seminole on a training flight during my second return flight to Columbia. It was unusual enough to see a training flight at one in the morning, but it was really strange for a trainer to be flying in such heavy fog. Flight schools normally have strict weather minimums, and for good reason. Being in a twin-engine airplane, the student and instructor were relatively advanced, but undoubtedly inexperienced in weather flying. I knew they would fly much slower than I would, and this was my tightest deadline of the night. I was pissed. I actually had a job to do, but I was going to miss a deadline because I was following a trainer that had strayed into the real world, a place where they didn't belong yet.

The air traffic controller sensed my frustration and tried to appease me by asking the Seminole pilots to keep their speed up. Being dutiful young men like myself, they tried to do what was requested of them. That meant they would need to use a higher power setting than they normally did on an approach or else they would descend below the glide slope while chasing a higher speed, neglecting one little drifting needle on their instrument panel indicating their imminently fatal deviation below the glide slope. Inexperienced pilots tend to get too wrapped up in profiles and power settings, like novice cooks consumed by measurements in a recipe. An experienced cook just intuitively knows the progress of a dish from aroma, sight, and sound and knows exactly when to add more stock, when to adjust the heat, and when to give it another stir. A pilot who understands the art of flying doesn't necessarily use a recipe to maneuver the airplane; it becomes like another sense. These pilots hadn't reached that level of competency; there's no way they could've until they've had lots of time to practice out in the world.

Soon after I watched their lights disappear into the thick fog below, they crashed into the dark pine forests, a half mile short of the runway.

The airport was closed until the wreckage could be located, and that took a couple of hours on this dark, foggy night. Now instead of getting delivered a few minutes late, the checks didn't get delivered until morning.

The National Transportation Safety Board wrote that the probable cause of the accident was the pilot's failure to stay on the glide slope and descending below the decision height. But when I read in the accident report that the pilots had just been told to maintain their maximum speed on the approach, it was obvious the accident investigators considered this request to be significant. The investigators had undoubtedly heard the impatience in my voice on the air traffic control tapes, and although I didn't kill them, it felt like the investigators were pointing a finger at me.

I thought I was a patient person. What had happened to me? I wished I could do it over but this time hide my impatience. Or better yet, to just not be impatient with a 380-hour pilot who needed help on a challenging night. I had let myself become corrupted by my company's objective to allow the banks to save a day's interest on other people's money. I felt like I had become a tool to the same kind of raw capitalism that had killed my friend Sam, trading lives for money. To undo what happened, to bring these two guys back to life, would be the only way to assuage my remorse. That was impossible. More lives wasted for nothing. I wanted to be loyal to humanity, not to banks and their money.

Soon the first Arctic air mass of autumn spilled into the Carolinas, brightening the skies but not curing my malaise. I needed to get out of Columbia. It wasn't my home, not that I was looking for a home anymore. I wanted to see the country, which ironically meant I needed to go back to Ohio. I was closing in on two years with the company, and I knew I'd be able to hold one of our nine Columbus positions once one opened up. These were coveted positions, because along with variety, these pilots usually earned extra money.

Travels

The Columbus-based pilots were responsible for flying the three daily routes based in Columbus and flying for the out-based pilots when they were on vacation or came in for training. Any pilots left over were put on standby, which was basically just hot reserve all night at the airport. This was the least desirable assignment, because you weren't flying or making extra money. That's what I would be doing initially, just hanging out at the airport waiting to get paged. Not exactly what I had wanted to do, but I didn't have the seniority to choose. I would rather have a known assignment, even if it was not as good, rather than to depend on the unknown. That's my risk-averse personality, because I'm just not brave enough.

On what was to be my first night of standby in Columbus, they called me at home a couple of hours early, telling me to get an airplane down to Raleigh in time to fly the Raleigh route. More good luck followed when they sent me to Birmingham and back to Raleigh again. I was still always flying routes that went through Charlotte, but at least I had strayed outside of the seventy-six miles between Columbia and Charlotte. I was also making extra money, because they paid us considerably more when they sent us out on the road.

On one of the rare nights that I was actually sitting around the airport, they decided to check me out in the Navajos, the newest additions to the fleet. A larger airplane, the Navajo didn't have the sharp, responsive handling of the Aerostar, but it was a great airplane to fly. It was solid, stable, and actually had some elbow room in the cockpit.

I'm definitely not a gear-head, but I do love the mechanical hum of the Navajo's turbo-supercharged Lycoming engines. A lot of guys like the un-muffled popping of the Baron's Continental engines because they remind them of a Harley Davidson motorcycle. It doesn't do anything for me. In fact, I wore ear plugs under a noise attenuating headset when I flew. But there was something pleasing about the sound of a Navajo. I had flown a little in a Navajo in Goldsboro, North Carolina, when I was a hundred-hour pilot. That was the first time I had heard those engines, and I was probably just nostalgic for all the good times I had on trips to Eastern North Carolina while growing up. I've also always longed for a connection to Goldsboro, the place of my birth but never my hometown.

Navajos actually had the same 540-cubic-inch engine block as the Aerostars, except that the Navajo's turbo-superchargers tricked the engine into thinking it was breathing dense air equivalent to fourteen thousand feet below sea level. This boosted the power, and you could maintain that power through twenty thousand feet, but there was a price to pay. Just as with aerodynamics, power was about compromises. The Navajo used considerably more fuel, plus it needed a little excess unburned fuel in the exhaust stream to help cool the turbo-superchargers. Even still, the exhaust manifold leading to the turbo was so hot that at night you could actually see the pipe glowing red through louvers on the side of the engine cowling. You also needed to make sure the turbos weren't still spinning when you shut the engines down and eliminated oil and fuel for lubrication and cooling. Because of how much harder these turbo-supercharged engines worked, they only lasted a little more than half as long between overhauls as the normally aspirated models. Besides the high-altitude performance, these overworked engines only produced a measly sixty extra horsepower each, which was just 20 percent more power. With all this in mind, I've never understood why someone would want to put a turbo in a car unless they regularly drive on the Tibetan Plateau.

There was also a high degree of standardization in the Navajos, so you were never looking around in the dark for switches like you were in a Baron. All the Navajos were equally well equipped, with GPS navigation, radars, autopilots, flight directors, heated windshields, windshield wipers, and even supplemental oxygen to take advantage of the airplane's high altitude performance.

On a Wednesday the company announced it would be starting a new route for a new customer, the Bank of Mississippi, the very next week. The chief pilot had already written the schedule for the Columbus pilots for the next week, and as the junior pilot, I was relegated to standby. Luckily for me, that meant I would be getting the best assignment of the week, starting a new route in the Deep South while winter settled onto the rest of the country. Even better, this was an extremely rare daytime route.

On a sunny Sunday afternoon in December, I flew an airplane to Birmingham to start the new route the next morning. Something like this was what I had hoped for when I moved back to Columbus. Ironically, if I was senior to just one other Columbus pilot, I would've chosen to fly one of the Columbus-based routes, just so I would know my schedule in advance and how much money I would make doing it, a whole six bucks extra per night. But I didn't have a choice and this fell into my lap.

The Bank of Mississippi had just fired a company who had been flying for them because they weren't making the deadlines. They were apparently a very difficult company to please, and I'm not sure why we thought we could do any better.

We almost screwed up on the first day. I was suspicious that my company had listed the wrong airport in Hattiesburg on the trip sheet, but they insisted it was right. I still didn't believe them. The deadline was tight enough that it would be hard to absorb a trip through a wrong airport, which would make us late on our first day.

When the checks arrived in Gulfport, I flew as fast as I could to Hattiesburg. I was going to land at the airport they told me to go to, but if the courier wasn't there, I would immediately fly across town to the other airport. As I suspected, the courier was waiting for me at the other airport in Hattiesburg. I threw the checks on the plane and departed for Jackson. I made the deadline in Tupelo, but I wouldn't have if I had wasted any time waiting at the wrong airport wondering where the courier was.

Now that I knew which airports I needed to fly to, I was able to enjoy the rest of the week. I was flying during the day, getting a good night of sleep every night, seeing a state I had never seen before and undoubtedly would never choose to, no offense intended to the good people of Mississippi, and making more money than I had ever made in my short career. I also never saw another company employee to remind me for whom I worked. It was like I was on my own, on a little private adventure, flying over the pine forests and black-water swamps of the Deep South.

I was still enjoying cloudless skies by Thursday. It had been an enjoyable week, and I would have a quick and easy trip home on a company Learjet. When the courier in Gulfport said, "See you tomorrow," I thought nothing of it, just a polite parting. Even with a four-day work week, it's sometimes hard to keep track of what day it is. When the courier in Hattiesburg said the same thing, I began to wonder if they knew something I didn't know. When the courier in Jackson said the same thing, I ran for a phone to call dispatch. The company's normal route system only flew four days a week, but this wasn't a part of that. This was basically a daily charter for a single customer. Dispatch assured me that the route did not fly on Friday. They were even more certain of this than they were of what turned out to be the wrong airport in Hattiesburg. I insisted, "You really need to ask the salesman."

I called them again from Tupelo. They still didn't know. "You need to find the salesman before I get on a flight home." They found him by the time I got back to Birmingham, although I'm not sure even he knew the answer at first, and he sold the route to the bank. I would need to stay and fly the route again on Friday. I should've asked for a percentage of the profits, since I had saved the company from two fairly serious mistakes with a new customer that was hard to please. Actually, there probably was no profit, since the price the salesman quoted to the customer would've only included operating costs to fly four days per week and the operating costs had just unexpectedly increased by 25 percent.

The next week I found myself flying over the snow-covered mountains of New England. As I got out of the airplane in Burlington, Vermont, I was greeted by enormous fluffy snowflakes so big they almost seemed to defy gravity as they slowly and delicately settled to Earth.

The next day I walked through knee-deep snow in a forest of bare-limbed dormant trees to reach the shore of Lake Champlain. The mysterious gray water reflected the gray December sky, accented by sparkles of distant sunlight occasionally peeking from beneath the clouds. Small waves lapped against tiny slivers of ice on the shore, creating a faint rhythmic jingle in the otherwise silent landscape.

I hadn't realized how much I had missed winter. Of course, I was only thinking about last winter's absence in Columbia, forgetting about my seemingly endless winter in Buffalo two years prior. It was still early in the season. I'd remember soon enough.

Standby was actually turning into a good gig for me. I started the next week flying the Nashville route and then ended the week flying one of the Milwaukee routes. So far I hadn't done much sitting around the airport, and I was making a lot more money than if I would've just flown one of the Columbus-based routes, easily 50 percent more.

The next week I would earn the extra pay in Portland, Maine. The Portland route was about fourteen hours of duty, with seven legs through the busy airspace of the Northeast. A major winter storm was approaching, which would dump more than a foot of snow across the entire Northeast.

Winter storms can be punishing in so many ways that it's easy to think of a storm as a vengeful being. The demon is actually within us. The storm is just frigid unstable air loaded with moisture, drifting indifferently across Earth, leaving a trail of snow and ice in its wake. It's quite beautiful, when viewed through a window from inside a warm room with no place you need to go or nothing you need to do. Our stubborn allegiance to the clock, foolishly trying to keep our schedules, is when we face the storm's unrelenting wrath. We aren't battling the storm; we're battling our own defiance of the natural world. Airlines may cancel flights by the dozens, or even hundreds, but the freight always goes, especially when the cargo is money.

On the Portland route I flew through Boston three times a night as Boston struggled to keep a runway open amid the relentless snow. The taxiways were in terrible shape, with a couple of inches of packed snow and ice, cracked and cratered from the massive weight of the passing heavy jets.

Even taxiing at a crawl, I was afraid the punishing jolts would be too much for my Baron's landing gear. It was. As I climbed away from the runway in Boston, the landing gear refused to retract. The squat switch had broken, so the airplane couldn't recognize that it was actually in the air. I would have to fly the airplane to Hartford, which did happen to be a maintenance base, with the landing gear down.

The minimum speed in icing conditions for a Baron is 140 knots, because any slower and the ice will actually form beneath the wing, behind the de-ice boots, where you can't get rid of it. (De-ice boots are inflatable rubber chambers on the front of the wings and tail that are used to break off ice accumulations.) I probably wouldn't be able to go much faster than that because of the extra drag from the dangling landing gear. Fortunately, there wasn't much ice in the turbulent clouds; there usually isn't much ice when it's actually snowing since the moisture is already frozen. The ice I did get was mixed ice, which is so aerodynamically offensive that it's easy to shed when you inflate the de-ice boots, although I was certainly accumulating ice on the landing gear struts and tires, about which I could do nothing.

I discovered where some of the drafts emanated from while sitting in the cold, on the slow plane to Hartford. Frigid ram air was filling the nose wheel well through the open gear doors, forcing air through every seam, too much for the little combustion heater to battle.

About a month later, the same airplane had the opposite problem when the slush-covered landing gear froze into the wheel wells. The pilot tried to dislodge the frozen wheels with the manual gear extension crank, but that only sheared the shaft. The airframe was written off after the gear up landing, but the pilot wasn't hurt.

I was back in Birmingham the week after fighting the winter storm from Portland, Maine. The prior week had more than satisfied my longing for winter, so I was glad to be back in the Deep South. The route had just expanded, and it was now a solid eight hours of flying per day. After dropping off the checks in Tupelo, I would pick up medical lab samples in Shreveport and Monroe, Louisiana, and in Jackson, Mississippi, and take the boxes to Birmingham. I'm quite sure the salesman remembered to include five days' worth of operating costs when he quoted the price for this new service.

On my second day, I arrived over Tupelo to find it was too foggy to fly the approach. Air Traffic Control put me in a holding pattern. A thousand feet below me was a commuter turboprop, also holding, waiting for the visibility to increase to landing minimums. Since Tupelo was a non-towered airport, once the visibility reached landing minimums, the turboprop would have to leave the hold, fly the full approach procedure, land, and then cancel their clearance before I would even be cleared out of my holding pattern. It could be a while, and we didn't know when or if the visibility would get better.

I decided to divert to Memphis for more fuel and then come right back to Tupelo. As I walked into the FBO in Memphis, I saw Jim, my first flight instructor. Even though I hadn't seen Jim in eight years, a small part of him flew around with me every day. Our companies give us procedures to follow, but within those procedures everyone has their own style. Your individual style is an amalgam of the styles of the other pilots you've flown with and the experiences you've had. Jim was the first pilot to leave his imprint on me, and I considered it a good one.

The unexpected reunion made my fuel stop a couple of minutes longer than it needed to be, but soon enough I was over Tupelo, flying the instrument approach. The checks were a little more than an hour late. The bank would have to float a little interest, although I'm sure they still had time to process part of the load. The operations manager at The Bank of Mississippi was pissed. We weren't able to do a better job than anyone else. They didn't fire us though—probably because there weren't any companies left who hadn't already been fired by them.

I still had to face the scrutiny of my company. I had made a conservative decision by diverting to Memphis immediately. I had some holding fuel, but with an airplane in front of me, and no idea when or if the visibility would get better, I was going to miss the deadline anyway. Their first question was, "Why didn't you have more holding fuel?" We're supposed to buy fuel where it's cheaper, and the forecast hadn't predicted visibility that low. If every day I bought thirty or forty gallons of fuel at an airport where fuel costs thirty or forty cents more per gallon, even though I never needed to use it, I would certainly be criticized for spending too much money. Now on the one day I diverted, they wondered why I hadn't done just that. I work in an environment that is too dynamic to always have a right answer, especially while being scrutinized by someone in an office far away who always has the benefit of retrospection. Aside from a moment to vent their anger, I never heard another word about it.

Two days later a storm was approaching the South, with a forecast of heavy freezing rain. The medical customer had already cancelled the lab shipments for that day, but the money always goes. In the morning, I called all of the FBOs to make sure they had de-ice trucks.

Otherwise it was just another day at work, except without my trip across northern Louisiana, and if I was lucky I might even beat the freezing rain.

I shared the van ride from the hotel with a bunch of ladies who were going home from a religious conference. They asked where I was flying to. I listed a bunch of cities in the path of the storm. A lady said, "We'll pray for you," and handed me a little gold charm stamped with an alleged image of Mary. I would need all the help I could get. I thanked her, and, although I'm not religious or superstitious, I dropped the charm into my pocket, where it traveled for a year or two until I eventually misplaced it. I was still young enough to hope there was an unseen benevolent deity looking out for me, although I'd already been on the dark side long enough to know there wasn't.

I made it through Gulfport, Hattiesburg, and Jackson ahead of the freezing rain. I cruised through rain at seven thousand feet, above the temperature inversion. Freezing rain was already falling in Tupelo, where I was going. I reached the freezing level as I descended through about thirty-five hundred feet. Clear ice began forming on the leading edges of the airplane as the cold raindrops turned to ice. This is the worst kind of ice. It builds quickly, and in order to get rid of it, you need to accumulate the right amount before you inflate the de-ice boots. It also supposedly has enough plasticity that, if you inflate the boots too early, you might mold the ice into a bridge and you'd never be able to break it off. If you have too much ice, it might be too hard for your boots to break. The only real solution is to climb into the warmer air, because to have freezing rain there must be warm (above freezing) air overlying cold air.

I descended rapidly to minimize my time in the clear ice. My windshield alcohol was keeping a small patch free of ice, but I would still need to shut that off so I could see to land. I hadn't accumulated much, but I inflated the boots once to shed some ice while I still had enough speed to shuck it off.

Safely on the ground, the freezing rain was quickly glazing my Baron with ice. I told the lineman, George, that I needed to get de-iced. George grabbed an unheated five-gallon garden sprayer of glycol. That was not what I had in mind when I called them this morning to ask if I'd be able to get de-iced. This was not going to work, but George said there would be room for the Baron in their heated hangar. I can't imagine why Tupelo even had a heated hangar, but that would be my ticket out of town.

As slabs of ice began loosening on the airplane, I pushed them off with a push broom, undoubtedly with some more of the old airplane's paint too. With the ice gone, George sprayed some cold glycol on the Baron with the garden sprayer to try to prevent more ice from forming. I climbed in the airplane and then George pulled it out of the hangar. As soon as George released the tow bar, I started the engines. I was in the air about a minute later, climbing toward the freezing level.

It was a long, slow climb, and I'd be accumulating ice the whole way. Chunks of ice banged into the side of the airplane as the propellers shed their icy burden. Every propeller-driven airplane that works for a living has dents in the side of the fuselage from this. It was time for the de-ice boots. Nothing. They had worked on the way in to Tupelo. Maybe the ice was already too thick. As the Baron was slowly clawing its way aloft, I remembered the sarcastic nickname of the one I was flying, "69Quick." Quick, it was not. In fact, it was the slowest Baron in the fleet, maybe just a little crooked after surviving an accidental gear-up landing ten years prior. I had to get to the freezing level, and I was in the worst airplane in the fleet to get me there.

I was getting desperate. I was furious at myself for getting into this situation, knowing very well that it might end badly. I suddenly realized why an angry invective is often a doomed pilot's last word before the impact breaks the tape in the cockpit voice recorder. It might be my last word too, but since Barons don't have cockpit voice recorders, no one would even get to hear it.

There was only one thing left to do: trade some airspeed for altitude. There was no reason to maintain the 140-knot icing speed anymore, since for some reason the de-ice boots weren't working anyway. My wings had enough ice that it had certainly changed the stall speed of the wing, but it was a smooth layer of clear ice, and a Baron wing can actually fly pretty slowly. I only needed to move the thermometer a needle width closer to zero degrees Celsius. I could probably trade some more airspeed for altitude, possibly enough to reach the freezing level.

It's truly amazing how quickly thirty-three degree rain can de-ice an airplane. Whole slabs of ice began peeling off the airplane, some smashing into the tail and horizontal stabilizer. With its burden gone, 69Quick began accelerating, as best that the slow airplane could. I didn't want to do that again.

Poor old 69Quick would have its last adventure the next week in Buffalo. It would become the other Baron to have its landing gear freeze into its wheel wells during a two-week period. Just as in the other recent accident, the airplane was destroyed, but the pilot was not hurt.

The next day parts of the South were glazed with as much as an inch of ice. Tupelo was hit hard and not equipped to handle it. I knew the runway would still be covered in ice, but it was long and there was no crosswind. I wouldn't have any extra speed when I touched down, and just let the airplane roll to a stop without using my brakes. This I knew how to do. Every freight dog who had mastered energy management and cut their teeth in the icy North knew how to do this.

I lined up with the runway and slowed the Baron to about eighty-five knots (about a hundred miles per hour) just as my wheels met the ice-slickened runway. The airplane decelerated nicely on the subtly textured ice. I turned off about two-thirds of the way down the runway, and taxied very slowly to the FBO.

All of Tupelo was closed, except the bank. The money always goes. The courier company that delivered the checks to the bank refused to drive. The operations manager from The Bank of Mississippi, the same short-tempered man who has fired every other freight airline, came out to the airport with one of his sidekicks. Since the FBO was closed, I had to lob the six-hundred pounds worth of thick, canvas bags over the top of a barbed-wire fence while trying to keep my feet under me on the ice.

The operations manager remarked, "Wow, that looked just like a normal landing" and made some compliments about skill and bravery or some other bullshit. I didn't say much. I didn't tell him that it actually was just a normal landing. The wheels just hold the airplane up when it isn't flying. The airplane doesn't care if it's on a slick surface; you just need to plan ahead so that you can stop. I didn't tell them that every freight pilot with wintertime experience would've done the same thing. That was easy. The day before had been hard—too hard, I know now.

The next week the salesman who had sold this route called me to say that the operations manager from the Bank of Mississippi wanted to take me out to dinner to thank me for flying when the whole town was shut down. I had apparently become his hero, completely by accident. I wonder if he realized I was the same pilot who missed the deadline earlier in the week when I diverted to Memphis. The good and the bad, it was all an accident. I just happened to be there.

I was getting a lot of credit for that one landing, so the company asked me if I would stay down there for a while to keep our short-tempered client happy. I stayed for six more weeks. I had seen the last of winter for the season.

Since the route started with an empty leg from Birmingham to Gulfport, I would just fly the airplane to Gulfport on Saturday and spend the weekend at the coast.

Gulfport was still crowded in the winter, but I always had the beaches to myself. Gulfport's beaches weren't extraordinarily pretty, but I do love the solitude and the low angle of the sun on a winter beach.

The parking lots at the casinos were always full, no matter when I drove past them. This is something I'll never understand, but then again I was the kid who wouldn't part with pennies and nickels in a card game. I don't mind paying for something I need, but I don't want to just throw money away with the luck of the draw. Just living is big enough of a gamble for me. I guess some people see it as entertainment, but for some others it's foolish hope. Slot machines are programmed to manipulate you with small payouts and the mistaken belief that you just missed the jackpot. In the end, the house will win. Otherwise there would be no house.

One pleasant afternoon I was startled by a man who walked up to me and asked for fifteen dollars. The last time someone asked me a question like that, the guy was just about to rob me, but I had somehow gotten away from him before he could. This time there was no one around, just a casino a half mile down the beach in the direction from which he came. I suspected he had either gambled away his gas money to get home or else a machine had teased him into thinking that, with just fifteen more tries, he'd have a chance at some mythical gazillion dollar jackpot. The man actually argued with me, but I didn't want to donate my fifteen bucks to the gaming industry or pay for his gas because he just had.

That guy didn't rob me, but a maid in Birmingham did. I had just gone to the gym. I didn't think the maids would clean my room right then, and I also didn't think they would go through the pockets of a pair of jeans folded in the top of my suitcase. I only knew because my wallet was folded the wrong way. She took most of my cash but not my credit cards. She left enough small bills so that I might not have noticed anything was missing until I was far from Birmingham. That was clever, but she should've known I wasn't going anywhere; except for the weekends, I'd been staying at the hotel for so long my colleagues thought I was based there.

I reported the theft to the police and the hotel manager. The manager decoded the electronic lock and found out exactly which maid unlocked the door. The spineless manager wouldn't do anything, and the police couldn't do anything. That was the end of it. I just hope the maid didn't blow her windfall on slot machines or crack. Maybe she used the hundred bucks for something good, like to feed her kids, or take bagpipe lessons, but I doubt it. Definitely not bagpipe lessons.

Crime goes unpunished in the land of liberty and justice for all, but I did have an idea to recover my loss. I had already accrued a few free stays at the hotel that I would never use, and I wasn't going to give them to my company either. I couldn't redeem them anywhere else, since this was one of the last independent hotels left in the country (probably why I liked the place so much). I asked the spineless manager if he could make good for one of his best customers by allowing me to trade in my free stays to replace my lost money, which had probably already gone through his maid's crack pipe. He agreed with my proposal.

My courier in Monroe drove a different car to the airport every night, the back seat always crammed full of big white boxes containing various bodily fluids and excreta. I remarked to him once that he seemed to have a lot of cars. He gave me an irritated sideways glance, and said nothing. Later I learned that the courier owned a body shop and he had been delivering biohazard shipments in his customers' cars. It would be wise to check your odometer and vaccination records before you drop your car off at the shop in Monroe.

My hotel in Birmingham was the local crew hotel for a major airline, and my friend Doug (not his real name) had an overnight there during my long stay. Doug was one of my star students, and I helped get him an interview at my company when he had about a thousand hours of flight time. He was accepted, although he would have to sit in the right seat of a Baron for two hundred hours to become qualified for Part 135 flying. While he was waiting for his class date with my company, a major airline had invited him in for an interview, and now he was a 737 First Officer for that airline.

Doug had gotten his interview because he had completed a college internship with the airline. I had been offered the internship too, but I did the University's Air Transport Service internship instead. I thought that actually serving as co-pilot on the University's King Air 200s, twin turboprop executive transports, would make me more qualified to be a professional pilot than being an office slave for three months at an airline. I couldn't have been more wrong. During those three months of stuffing mailboxes in Chicago or Denver, I wouldn't be accruing any flight time, getting any closer to graduating, or even earning a dime with which to pay for temporary living expenses. Unfortunately, I only knew how the world should work, not how it actually worked. This was a missed opportunity because of the ignorance of youth.

All through dinner, Doug's Captain kept telling me, "Don't be stupid; get into the airlines now."

I think we've already established that I was stupid—well, maybe not exactly stupid, but certainly naïve. The airlines were just starting to hire again, but with all of my multi-engine piston time, no jet time, and no experience stuffing mailboxes as an office slave at a major airline, the only airline job I could realistically expect would be at a commuter airline, making seventeen thousand dollars a year in the right seat of a turboprop or in the new innovation in the airline industry, the regional jet. I wasn't going to do it.

I would have the seniority to get in the Learjets soon enough if I stayed where I was. I was finally making decent money, and I was young and free, something I was only beginning to understand.

I knew I was getting very good at my trade, although I wouldn't understand just how good until many years later. I didn't realize yet that check haulers had among the best stick-and-rudder flying skills in the industry, but I also didn't realize yet how little that actually mattered.

Mississippi was extremely foggy for a few days, giving me several opportunities per day to use my stick-and-rudder skills, hand-flying raw data approaches to minimums in my sparsely equipped Baron, except in Jackson. Jackson had one runway closed for construction, and the only ILS (Instrument Landing System) approach to the other runway was broken. That left Jackson with a non-precision instrument approach that could only bring an airplane down to about five hundred feet, and you would need at least a mile visibility to land. Jackson was much foggier than that and was staying foggy around the clock. I was supposed to land there twice a day, but all I could do was pass by.

What is one to do to quickly acquire replacement parts so air travel could re-commence in Jackson? The components were being shipped by overnight air freight. The freighter carrying the replacements couldn't land there, and it was apparently impossible to locate the package among all of the other freight in the back of an idle 727, not far away in Memphis, and just drive it the rest of the way. It was a couple more days before the fog lifted and the parts could be delivered. Of course, once the ILS was repaired, we didn't need it anymore since the weather was good.

When I finally got back to Columbus, three pilots asked if I was in for training. Everyone thought I was now based in Birmingham.

It had seemed like I had just dropped out for a while. I was flying during the day. I was always well rested. I was flying my ass off, more than 120 hours in February alone, 120 hours of raw-data hand-flying, but that's what I loved to do.

The company name had changed while I was away, and I hadn't even known about it. Now everyone unfamiliar with the company, which was pretty much everyone else in the world, except for banks and a handful of air freight brokers, assumed we were a cell phone or computer company, confusion you don't want unless you're a covert government contractor, which would actually be a logical future once the checks could travel through the internet, an inevitable future about which I was still in denial.

Management wasn't in denial about the tenuous future of our primary cargo. Our daily route network was a little faster than the big overnight freight companies, so the company wanted to leverage that slight speed advantage and become the freight airline to use when an overnight shipment was just a couple of hours too slow. They paid someone a lot of money to confuse all of those potential new customers with a strange new name. Another freight airline had already proven that the brand confusion exercise wasn't necessary at all, starting out as an express air courier service for the Federal Reserve Banks but keeping the Federal Express moniker even after the complete diversification of their service.

My company's name change had been part of the strategy to participate in the IPO boom, the stock price manipulation bubble created in part by the de-regulation of trade commissions. Going public was supposed to raise capital for expansion, but that never happened, except for the purchase of a small air freight airline that had been the most recently fired company by the Bank of Mississippi and the purchase of a bicycle courier service in Manhattan.

The company threw stock options around by the thousands, along with a lot of hot air about a new economy in which we now owned a part of the company's future. I didn't understand the scam yet, so I didn't realize we wouldn't get to own anything. You either flipped right away for a quick buck or your options would be underwater forever, as useless as the paper checks we flew.

While the CEO was on his road show, selling the illusion of investment value, really just a redistribution of wealth from the pockets of the suckers to the pockets of the insiders who understood the scam in their dying business, I was busy with my own road show, actually generating shareholder value, finding my way through the country as well as finding my way through life. I flew to Cleveland, Ohio; Richmond, Virginia; Charleston, West Virginia; Pittsburgh, Pennsylvania; Grand Rapids, Michigan; Nashville, Tennessee; Evansville, Indiana; Louisville, Kentucky; Indianapolis, Indiana; Charlotte, North Carolina; Atlanta, Georgia; Birmingham, Alabama; Columbia, South Carolina; Detroit, Michigan; Philadelphia,

Pennsylvania; Baltimore, Maryland; Buffalo, New York; Chicago, Illinois; New Orleans, Louisiana; Fort Wayne, Indiana; and Rochester, Minnesota.

I was now seeing the country, and what I was seeing was that every place was starting to look the same: the same restaurants with the same menus, the same airports, and the same hotels. There are variations in geography, topography, and the local flora, but all of that is being bulldozed to make room for sprawling plastic suburbs with their treeless, toxic lawns and the new discount Super-Center at the edge of town. There is still local character, but it remains hidden from transients like me and likely from many of the natives as well, deep beneath the homogenized façade of everywhere, or, perhaps more appropriately, nowhere. Like adolescents desperate to conform, we have suppressed the very thing I sought in my journey, authenticity of place. My superficial passage through night sky and airport hotel only, maybe somewhat paradoxically, deepened my curiosity and my disillusionment at the same time.

Places that depend on tourism can even succumb to an unusual dichotomy of simultaneously being unique and artificial. The identity that the tourists seek, even when it is authentic, inevitably becomes a commodity to be manufactured, packaged, and sold. To find authenticity within any place is a quest for the unexpected, and requires the patience and curiosity to explore deep time.

Arriving at Lakefront Airport in New Orleans, which juts out into Lake Pontchartrain, you pass through enormous gates to enter a walled city. These walls don't protect the city from barbarian raiders; the wrought iron bars over the windows and doors of the handsome little ranches in the tidy neighborhoods near Lakefront Airport do that. These walls keep out a much more ruthless enemy, one that never relents. It is never intimidated by our resistance to it, and it will never negotiate away the pounds of pressure that it exerts on these walls. Standing at the edge of the French Quarter in 1996, relatively high ground in the precariously sinking city, I was actually uncomfortable gazing across the dark muddy water of the Mississippi River, nearly at eye level with me, water that was relentlessly pushing on that wall, pushing toward me with unimaginable pressure.

I first learned that America was a cultural melting pot in my Midwestern middle-class suburban school, a strikingly obvious irony that was somehow lost on me and the other students, and probably the teacher as well.

New Orleans displays and actually celebrates its diverse cultural heritage with gritty revelry, a melting pot rooted deeply into the soft alluvium on which the city was built. Appropriately, this is land that exists only because of the continental ooze brought here by the great river, earth eroded away from thirty-two states and two Canadian provinces, a geologic melting pot. There is no land here that wasn't borrowed from another place. Unnaturally channeled, the river is now unable to replenish the oozing land that it built, land inexorably slipping into the sea at a rate of about thirty square miles per year.

I would eventually, many years later, fly a lot of New Orleans trips and spend a lot of time there, always staying at the edge of the French Quarter, never as a tourist, just a pilot on an overnight soaking up the authenticity. I spent a lot of relaxed mornings in the shade of the Café du Monde's green awning at the corner of Jackson Square, taking in beignets and jazz and some chicory in my café au lait, an obligatory tourist's experience but still authentic. I had cynically assumed the musicians got a kick-back from Café du Monde, staged to bring in tourists, but then I talked with them during an intermission and found that this was wholly organic entertainment. Jam sessions evolve as musicians come and go throughout the day, and all that is scripted is simply a common knowledge of some jazz standards.

In July I returned to Birmingham. I was glad to be back, except that it was July in the Deep South. Our Barons were flying greenhouses that had no air conditioning and only minimal ventilation. How can an airplane that is so drafty and cold in the winter be so stiflingly hot in the summer? The short flights on this route confined me to the hot, humid, turbulent low altitudes. The only shade was that offered by the rotation of Earth, and by then my long work day was almost over.

Soaked with perspiration, I climbed into the airplane in Hattiesburg. The left engine roared to life as I was settling into the soggy seat. I moved the switch to engage the right engine's starter. Nothing happened. The right engine's starter motor was dead. I shut everything down and headed for a telephone to call our maintenance office in Columbus. The mechanic agreed with my diagnosis, but he said there was one more thing I could do to troubleshoot. Asked if

I knew what the starter motor looked like, I told him I did. He then asked me to take the cowling off the engine, put a wooden chock up to the side of the starter motor, and beat the chock with a hammer. He said if I couldn't find a hammer, I could just beat on the starter with the wooden chock. So that's how we fix airplanes? I told him I would rather just wait until a local mechanic could look at it.

The local mechanic examined the starter, but I never saw him reach for a chock or hammer. He laughed when I told him what I had been asked to do. I could have beaten the starter until the chock was reduced to splinters, but it wouldn't have changed my fate. I would be stuck in Hattiesburg until another starter could be shipped in. Even when you're only going out for a day-trip, you should always take your suitcase with you. You never know.

The FBO set me up at wonderful local hotel, and they even let me take the crew car overnight.

The Bank of Mississippi didn't fire us. The short-tempered operations manager there was probably now a stockholder in my company. Welcome to the new economy.

I stayed in Birmingham for the weekend so I could sail with my friend Randy, a veteran freight pilot who lives about an hour east of Birmingham. We put two boats in the water. Randy put me in a Buccaneer, a sporty little sailboat, with his friend Rick, a Flight Service Station briefer who often gave me my morning weather briefings over the phone in Birmingham.

We sailed swiftly through the cool breeze from the outflow of an afternoon rain shower. When the tiny shower moved on and our wind died, we rafted the boats together and spent the rest of the afternoon swimming and lounging on the calm lake.

I told Rick about how I was hoping to sail my aunt's sunfish on vacation in a couple of weeks. Rick was supposed to be racing his boat in the Buccaneer Nationals on the Chesapeake Bay that week, but his crew had just cancelled on him, so he asked me to sail with him on the Chesapeake.

I warned Rick about my inexperience as a sailor. I've never even had lessons. I learned by reading a book and then putting a boat in the water. He had probably already figured that out; competency in any task at all is impossible to fake. He needed someone to trim the jib and hoist the spinnaker, and I could do that, with some instruction from Rick.

There were only thirteen boats in the race (the Buccaneer isn't a very common boat). We raced three times a day, and although the races were very competitive, the sailors were not. We lost nearly every race, but every race was followed by an exhilarating broad reach back to the yacht club through a cool sea breeze. Then we would just relax with good company in a beautiful place until it was time to take the boats back out.

It had all happened by chance, which was something I wasn't used to, or at least not used to recognizing yet. I was still naïve enough to think I actually controlled my life. It reminded me of something a college professor I had flown with quite a bit had once told me; "When you meet someone, you don't know how that person will affect your life, so you need to be true to everyone."

After my vacation, I went to Tulsa to start another new route for the company. It was another daytime route, which meant I would roast in the August skies above Oklahoma and Texas, but at least I was well rested. It also meant I could see the unfamiliar countryside, which was lovely, pastoral and sparse and much more open than any place east of the Mississippi. Flying south from Oklahoma City, the rusty brown water of the meandering Canadian River was accented by cream-colored sand bars and bright green grass, studded with occasional dark green trees.

I finished the third quarter in Birmingham. My friend who had been flying eight hours a day, five days a week was legally timed out. He got some free vacation time, and I got to go sailing again in Alabama.

In the ten or so weeks I flew the route that year, I never once felt sleepy in the airplane, and it was a brutal route. The route flew as much as the grueling route that killed Sam, but flying during the day, when your body wants to be awake, was much different than struggling to stay alert all night, occasionally failing, and dozing off. The regulations list flight-time and duty-time limits, but those numbers seem completely arbitrary compared with whether or not those hours are flown on the dark side of the planet.

On the dark side of the planet, even after an honest attempt at daytime sleeping and a cup of coffee at every stop, sometimes you still can't resist your body's urge to succumb to sleep with the steady, monotonous hum of the engines through smooth air in the dark of night. I no longer invincibly think I can fend off the sandman by stubbornly muscling through my diurnal biology and hand-flying the airplane. When I was feeling tired I engaged the autopilot and tried to make myself as uncomfortable as possible, so that if I drifted off, I won't—I hope—be out for very long. They're usually just unstoppable micro sleeps, but once, peacefully cruising to Chicago in a Navajo at four in the morning, I was suddenly sleeping so soundly that I forgot I was in an airplane. I woke with a surge of adrenaline as both engines sputtered as they slurped at the empty outboard fuel tanks. I switched to the inboard tanks and the starving Lycoming engines roared back to life. I finished the trip in a strange state of wired exhaustion, uncomfortable enough that my daytime sleep was even more restless than usual. I knew the next night would be another difficult one, but I would be legal.

I would finish the year by splitting my time between Willow Run Airport and Teterboro Airport.

Willow Run Airport was a decaying but, at that time, very busy airport just outside of Detroit. Bombers were mass produced there during World War II. Airplanes of every size and description flew through there, but they generally had two things in common: they worked hard supplying just-in-time inventory for the auto industry, and they were old. Some were very old, retired from airline service long ago and now relegated to anonymously hauling freight through the darkness of night.

Lots of pilots have passed through Willow Run, flying metal that belonged to prior generations: young pilots building time, furloughed pilots trying to salvage their incomes and stay in the business, and, as the end of the line for some, pilots with stains on their records that prevent them from going anywhere else.

Teterboro Airport, just across the Hudson River from Manhattan, was also very busy but otherwise was the antithesis to Willow Run. A lot of pilots passed through Teterboro too, but they were usually crowding the little airport full of shiny new business jets. And wherever there was money, specifically, obscene amounts of money, the check haulers crowded the airport by night.

I was intimidated by the size and pace of New York City, and whenever I was near it I would have the totally irrational fear that we would suddenly pump our last gallon of dinosaur juice from the ground and I would be trapped there with several million people.

The airspace over New York was ridiculously crowded, with Teterboro, Newark, La Guardia, and Kennedy Airports all overcrowded and all very close to each other. This meant delays, and in my job time was money. A lot of our prop pilots would fly by visual flight rules (VFR) when the weather was good to avoid delays and all the extra miles the air traffic controllers would require the rest of the airplanes to fly. I never did this. I wasn't brave enough. I always flew by instrument flight rules (IFR), even when my clearance would nearly double the length of my flight. There were too many airplanes to watch out for, and there was too big of a risk of straying into airspace where you didn't belong.

On one of those nights spent traversing the busy airspace of New York, a TWA 747 blew up, showering the ocean just off Long Island with flaming wreckage, an accident about which conspiracy theorists are still arguing. While I didn't actually see the explosion, it suddenly seemed like I was always near these tragedies. I was flying from Erie to Pittsburgh when a US Air 737 had an uncommanded rudder hard over, and spiraled into the earth. I remember watching as helicopters frantically circled beneath me, filming the crash site, without realizing what had happened just moments prior. A few months later I was punished for hours by the winter storm that claimed an American Eagle ATR-72 in Indiana.

It was already winter again. I had been flying freight for three years. These were quick years, not anything like the years I remember growing up, when summer was always impossibly far away.

The industry had changed in those three years. Airlines had been recalling their furloughed pilots and now were actually hiring again. This meant that suddenly everyone was hiring. The commuter airlines that had been making pilots spend ten thousand dollars to buy their crappy jobs just a few years ago had to drop their training fees in order to attract enough applicants. Young pilots who spent six months to a year hauling freight could pick which commuter they wanted to work for, and they were leaving faster than they could be replaced.

Even though the commuters were now getting shiny new regional jets (RJs), I still had no interest in leaving for a twenty thousand dollar per year job. So I didn't ride the wave that was carrying our prop pilots toward further exploitation in the commuters, but at least I finally had a good excuse. I had the seniority to hold a Learjet co-pilot position in Columbus, but because of our chronic shortage of prop pilots, it would be a while until they trained me in the Learjet. I could wait; I loved what I was doing.

One of the many routes left vacant by the exodus was my old route in Columbia. I now had the seniority to pick my assignment, so I requested to go fly in Columbia until they could move a new-hire there.

The route no longer resembled the monotonous Charlotte shuttle that drove me away. Nothing ever stays the same. I was coasting through another winter in the South, and I was coasting to the end of my career in the props at the company. It was a sentimental return for me and actually bittersweet.

I was excited to be getting in the Learjets soon, but I knew I was nearing the end of another chapter that I had thoroughly enjoyed, an adventure that had permanently changed me. Yes, I had always wanted to fly jets, but I was still leaving something that I loved. I was good at it, too. I had learned a lot in thirty-nine months. Some of that experience, like the art of how to operate the temperamental reciprocating engines, would be lost. I knew I was eventually taking a great step forward, finally joining the jet age, but I knew I would have fond memories from my time spent flying alone in the props.

While I was in Columbia, I received a bid sheet for our Charlotte Learjet co-pilot position. This route would be much more interesting than the flying I would do in the Lears in Columbus, mainly flying the Columbus Lear routes, mainly night flights to and along the East Coast, but I really didn't want to move if I didn't need to. Moving was too much trouble. I knew that two pilots senior to me wanted it, so I went ahead and bid, knowing with a high degree of certainty that I wouldn't get it.

One evening the Chief Pilot called me as I was passing through Charlotte. He said I had the Charlotte Lear co-pilot position if I wanted it. Surprised, I asked him if I could have time to think about it. He tersely told me "No," so I told him I would take it.

I hated moving, and I wasn't even going to have to move to fly Learjets. If I had been given any time to think about it, the rest of the evening, or maybe even just a few minutes, I'm sure I would have talked myself out of moving to Charlotte. It was too late now. This was probably the most spontaneous decision I had made in my life. Actually, it was the only spontaneous decision I had ever made, and unexpectedly the decision accelerated me to the front of the training schedule and I suddenly left that bygone era of long, cold nights and cantankerous old piston engines greasily thrumming through the tumultuous low altitudes and entered the jet age.

Travels with Wilbur

My career was about to ascend to new heights, specifically way into the stratosphere. Learjet is a name that many people know, but it is often incorrectly used as a generic term referring to nearly any business jet. It's actually a brand name, descended from Bill Lear's grand ambitions, sleek, strong, and powerful, as fast as a rocket on roller skates, an unmistakable presence respected by all, even by the air molecules that its rocket-like nose and tip tanks threaten to pierce at transonic speed. Learjets are machines like no others, which was exactly why they were the backbone of our fleet. You can pack the Learjet's cabin full of the heaviest freight imaginable, fill the fuel tanks, and send it hurtling effortlessly through the heavens with unmatched style and grace.

I had already completed the company's Learjet ground school, if you could actually call it a school. It went from about nine at night until six in the morning on Friday and Saturday. For me, the two sessions were separated by a month because I unexpectedly had to fly on a Friday night when I was first scheduled for the class. So prior to both sessions, I had flown all night and then airlined back to Columbus. By the time each session was over, I had been awake for more than thirty hours, not counting a few inevitable micro-sleeps. The class should have lasted a week with an alert, receptive audience, but instead it was a shotgun blast of information into minds too fatigued to retain anything of significance.

The only thing I can say I actually learned is how to not run a ground school—that is, if the intention is for real learning to occur, which, as it turned out, they seemed not to care about too much.

I was obviously excited that I would get to fly a jet, but I also had the anxiety that always accompanies learning something new, and from knowing I was a zombie when I was supposed to be absorbing information about my first jet. Training costs money, and no one wants to spend a penny more than required. We would be training in the airplane, which is very expensive. I knew it would be intensive and I would be rushed into a checkride I'd barely be able to pass.

Training was more like a hurried introduction, and before I knew it, it was done. After a one-hour training flight in a Lear 35, which also served as my checkride, I was qualified, on paper at least, as a Learjet co-pilot. Although he never actually grabbed my wrist, the main evaluation criterion for the instructor was undoubtedly whether or not I had a pulse. If my Captain wanted me to be more than a glorified passenger, he would have to teach me everything himself.

I had known the Charlotte-based Lear Captain, Wilbur, for a few years, but I didn't know him well. I warned him I considered myself to be essentially untrained, but he already knew. He had been through the same pencil-whipped training a few years prior when he first got in the right seat of a Lear.

Wilbur had already decided I would be flying the first leg, from Charlotte to Columbus. That was the easy leg. The next leg was to Denver Centennial Airport, with its narrow runway and high-density altitude and accompanying higher true airspeeds on landing. Then we would go on to Burbank, California, with its two short runways and mountainous terrain.

Wilbur and I climbed into our seats in a Lear 25, an older model of Lear in which I had never been but was now somehow qualified to fly. None of the switches were where I expected them to be, not that my hour in a Lear 35 made me an expert. I would learn that every old Lear was practically a homebuilt, with different switches located almost anywhere.

This total lack of standardization stems from the very history of the Learjet. Bill Lear took a pair of CJ610 turbojets, which are just the J85 engines on F-5 fighters and T-38 trainers, except without afterburners. He took the wings from a Swiss fighter that never went into production after two of the first three prototypes crashed, reminding the Swiss that they shouldn't question their nation's military neutrality (the accidents were actually caused by inexperienced test pilots). It was really after the first Learjet was assembled that they decided to think about how to get fuel to the engines and how to get electricity to the flight instruments and radios. These systems would continue to evolve every few serial numbers, especially with the early 20-series Lears.

Wilbur waited for me to start the engines, which I had never done. I didn't even get to start the engines on my training flight, but that was a Lear 35, with different engines anyway. We probably talked about the start sequence in ground school, but that was just a waste of everyone's time. Poor Wilbur had a lot to teach me.

Taxiing the airplane was the next lesson, since I didn't get to do that either on my brief training flight. Old Lears have one of two different nose wheel steering systems, depending on whether it's an early or late model, and later Lear introduced a third steering system. Regardless, if you don't know how the systems work, you probably won't even be able to keep the airplane on the pavement. It's really that difficult; just one of the things that makes a Learjet a unique machine. This was undoubtedly also covered in ground school.

Fortunately for Wilbur's infamously fragile patience, we soon found something I knew how to do. I pushed the power levers forward, and the Learjet raced briskly and smoothly down the runway. When Wilbur called "rotate," I gave the control wheel a gentle tug and the Learjet eagerly leapt toward the black stratosphere. Only a couple of minutes were required to pass through the low altitudes where I had, until that moment, spent my entire career. Small nudges to the control wheel and trim switches were all that was required to keep the responsive airplane climbing like a homesick angel, toward the infinite blackness of space and, ultimately, Columbus, Ohio.

The Learjet abides by the same laws of physics that govern all airplanes, but taming it, that is, combining positive control with smoothness, definitely requires extraordinary skill. The editor of an aviation magazine once wrote that the Learjet couldn't get certified today because it's too hard to fly. I think that's a stretch, but it certainly doesn't tolerate sloppy handling. It absolutely requires finesse and a sharp instrument scan. It'll immediately go where you point it, so you'd better know exactly where you need it to go.

My job actually got a lot easier when I began flying a two-pilot airplane. One pilot runs the checklists and the radios so the other pilot can fly the airplane without distractions.

My greatest fear during my career on the dark side had been falling asleep in the airplane, and no matter how scared you are, your fatigued body will not be denied its rest. I can't even guess how many times I had dozed off in an airplane, but now, with another pilot, I no longer feared it. Although naps are illegal, a two-pilot crew can coordinate their efforts to make sure one pilot is always alert. And this was the reason for Wilbur's uncharacteristic patience with me; the sooner I was trained, the sooner Wilbur could trust me enough to allow himself to doze off.

Our nearly three-hour flight to Denver at five in the morning was probably one of the worst legs in the company for trying to stay awake. The peaceful trip was flown in the semi-darkness of a dawn that would last for two hours as we raced away from the rising sun at 80 percent of the speed of sound. The tranquility of the stratosphere, the smooth steady hum from the engines, and the soft lights in the cockpit framed by a pastel early morning sky slowly creeping up on either side of us could cure any insomniac, even Wilbur. If Bill Lear had been successful in getting Learjets certified as single-pilot airplanes, Utah would undoubtedly be littered with Learjet wreckage as my company's Lears glided to Earth with unconscious pilots and empty fuel tanks, having over-flown Denver on the sleepiest leg in the entire company.

Our westward journey was far from over when we arrived in Denver. We would stay there just long enough to stretch our legs and catch a fleeting second wind that would already be fading by the time we got back in the airplane for the two-hour flight to Burbank. Still feeling like crap, this leg was a little easier, since the sun had already risen, but if we both fell asleep on this one, we could've ended up out over the Pacific Ocean.

We would finally check into our hotel rooms at about noon Eastern Time, with exhausted, thoroughly disoriented bodies that still would not sleep easily. Wilbur and I modified all of the suites on the honors floor at the Burbank Airport Hilton for day sleeping, trying to block any sunlight from contaminating our rooms. We would back a screw on an air intake out about a half inch and tuck the edge of the curtains behind the intake. Ironing boards and other loose articles would seal out the remaining leaks of sunlight. I would sleep, although never restfully, usually just a day-long series of short naps. Wilbur complained that he would barely sleep at all.

Wilbur brought a tremendous amount of experience to the job, at that time around twelve thousand hours of flight time, plus an unquestionably unique personality. Wilbur inherently had the discipline to perform the most mundane tasks exactly the same way every time; great protection from the complacency that can lead highly experienced pilots into mistakes. This predictable kind of discipline would seem natural for a very dull person, but Wilbur was anything but dull. Flying with him was certainly never boring. Wilbur combined boundless nervous energy with a social ease that allowed him to strike up an animated conversation with nearly anyone, and absolutely no topic was ever too controversial for Wilbur.

Charlotte was a unique move for me, because I actually knew people there. Wilbur just happened to live one apartment building away from my cousin and her husband. I rented a nice apartment with a wooded view, partially shaded from the daytime sun, down the street from them.

I moved to Charlotte knowing I was only passing through. I never thought I would grow roots there, but I was also in no hurry to move on. I was finally content with simply existing, without needing to search for where or how I was supposed to fit into the cosmos, freed from the notion that I needed to find a specific place to call home.

It was comforting to be in a city that had grown so much in the two prior decades that a significant percentage of the population was from elsewhere. I was a non-native among non-natives, but it was much more than that. I felt like I had dropped out of society, and I liked it.

I had a sense of freedom I had never imagined I would experience. With just two round trips to the West Coast per week, I felt like I had a part-time job, and I loved my job flying Learjets anyway. I essentially had a four-day weekend, and my eighteen hours off on Wednesday between trips seemed like a day off in the middle of the week. I was young enough to endure sleep deprivation, and I could always get a nap in the airplane—well, at least if I happened to fall asleep, it would be okay if Wilbur was still alert. I never needed to set an alarm clock. Late in the afternoon after getting out of bed, with a book, a steaming cup of coffee, and a Zen-like feeling of peace, I knew most of the working world was fighting rush-hour traffic with fists tightly clenching their steering wheels, a kind of stress I never had. I felt like I had suddenly taken ownership of my life and found my place in the world.

Before I knew it I was comfortable in the Learjet and with the Learjet's performance. Flying is flying. Performance is measured by numbers, and numbers are relative. I was seeing higher numbers than I had ever seen, but once I was used to seeing them, they were never high enough. We would be struggling into the stratosphere in a heavily-laden airplane, and I would find myself disappointed by the airplane's climb performance. Or I would be disappointed by our groundspeed, because I was expecting more tailwinds, even though we were travelling more than six-hundred miles per hour. The Learjet, a machine that had so recently seemed so extraordinary, had become normal.

During my last year at OSU, one of the instructors flew a Cessna to San Diego and brought back an account of how desolate and boring the trip was west of Amarillo. When I flew a Cessna to Scottsdale, Arizona, with a student later that year, I was absolutely enthralled by the scenery, which only got more interesting and more exotic past Amarillo. I agreed it was desolate, but the colors and textures of the desert were anything but boring. Or does that just make me boring? I had wanted to see the desert again, and the scenery on the Denver-to-Burbank leg was one of the reasons why I had bid this route. It did not disappoint me.

Just west of Denver the short grass prairie, what's left of it at least, gives way to the jagged gray peaks of the Front Range. The Rocky Mountains were much more impressive than I had expected, because they filled the vast landscape all the way to Utah.

Leaving the mountains, we entered the exotically colored and sculpted canyon country. The Colorado Plateau is arid land, but the canyons, cliffs, buttes, and mesas were all carved by water, revealing a full palate of earthy and rusty hues.

Civilization is noticeably absent from these rugged lands, probably because we haven't figured out many ways to exploit them yet. The exception is the deep blue water of Lake Powell, which drowned what was once one of the most beautiful canyons in the area, Glen Canyon. Although John Wesley Powell advocated limited irrigation in the west, he also advocated conservation. He probably wouldn't have approved of giving his name to a reservoir that forever flooded such a beautiful wilderness that he, and so few others, had the opportunity to see.

Soon Earth opens up on the left side of the airplane. The Colorado River disappears into the shadows, deep inside the grandest canyon in the canyon lands. The surreal width and depth of the Grand Canyon are best appreciated from an overlook on the rim, but only from the air can you truly understand the immensity of this 277-mile-long gash in the Earth, and I would fly the entire length of it twice per week.

The Colorado River leaves the Grand Canyon and fills a few more unnatural reservoirs in unlikely arid places. The mighty river which carved this beautiful landscape no longer reaches the sea.

West of the Colorado Plateau, the Mojave Desert is defined by the presence of Joshua trees, although you can't see them from 35,000 feet up. The geologic antithesis of the eroded canyon lands to the east, this is a parched, brown land of deposition, dry lake beds, sand dunes, and alluvial fans punctuated by the jagged remnants of tectonic cataclysm.

Los Angeles is paradise, or it would be if not for the crowded sprawl. Barriers of steep mountain ridges surround the city, keeping the desert out and the stabilizing influence of the cool Pacific Ocean in. Hot desert winds do occasionally breach the mountains in the summer, and there's occasional rain and fog in the winter, but otherwise the climate is dependably stable, with seventy-degree temperatures year round. Unfortunately, the same geography that created paradise tends to trap a noxious brown cloud, exhaust fumes from a car-crazy culture.

Geographically, Los Angeles is actually on a different tectonic plate than the rest of North America, and it's slowly migrating north. Earthquakes are inevitable. One even occurred when I landed one morning. My landing didn't cause the earthquake, I don't think, although I was pretty tired. There are actually about ten thousand small tremors per year in the area, most imperceptible without a seismometer, so I wouldn't be surprised if a few of those were really just firm arrivals from very tired pilots.

My Tuesdays and Thursdays in Burbank were a nice diversion, not that I really needed it. It was an escape from summer, an escape from winter, an escape from my apartment, a change of scenery, exotic scenery that was much different than anything in the East, and no, I'm not just talking about the work of the geographically abundant plastic surgeons. Well, there was a lot of that too.

The employees at the Burbank Airport Hilton knew us and treated us well. It was my second home. They would check us in before we arrived, in suites on the honors floor with breakfast vouchers. The hotel also took care of a day sleeper's most important need: to be left alone. This was not as easy as it should be. Hanging a "Do not disturb" sign on the doorknob usually prevents a knock on the door, but sometimes an overly ambitious housekeeping manager will just call your room instead. While I appreciate their concern, for those of us who work on the dark side, it's like having a telemarketer call at three in the morning, except that day-sleepers probably won't be able to get back to sleep after the call.

Wilbur and I would fill out comment cards, complimenting the staff for their superb service, which led to promotions for several of our favorites. This meant we were periodically training new people for our specific needs, which was very important since there was always a long line of people checking out and we were too tired to wait, almost noon Eastern Time after being up all night.

Wilbur and I had a predictable dinner routine in Burbank, eating at California Pizza Kitchen on Tuesdays and Chevy's on Thursdays. I know it sounds boring, but the San Fernando Valley isn't exactly a glamorous part of Los Angeles. We were close enough to Hollywood to have our pizzas served by aspiring actors and actresses. They knew us as regulars, and Chevy's fresh salsa and fajitas were hard to beat.

We would browse the bookstore after dinner and walk through a neighborhood that we probably shouldn't have walked through, breathing air we probably shouldn't have breathed. People would always ask me what exciting things I would do in Southern California. To do anything exciting would've meant sacrificing sleep, and I never wanted to do that after enduring the exhausting trip out. My only desire was to get in bed, even if sleep was just a daylong series of restless naps.

The trip back was much easier, although the leg from Burbank to Columbus was probably the most important single leg in the company. At nearly four hours, this leg stretched the range of a Lear 35 (at high speed cruise, the company's only cruise speed, especially on this leg) and the capacity of its pilots' bladders; no coffee on Tuesdays and Thursdays. This was the last flight into the last hub of the night in Columbus. About three dozen airplanes would await our arrival, each with tight deadlines to make, some even meeting other airplanes at their destinations. Time was so critical that three Bell 206 helicopters would fly the checks from the rooftops of banks' operations centers in downtown Los Angeles and park right next to our Learjet.

We normally carried about 2500 pounds of checks out of Burbank, mostly in boxes. We had to stack the boxes just right to make it all fit, and we had to do this very quickly. Then we would fly the Learjet as fast as we could, while still retaining a safe margin of fuel in the tanks. This was easy when we had some tailwind, but it was very tight when we didn't.

The banks were always running behind schedule, trying to process as many checks as possible before they sent them to the helicopters. We couldn't absorb their tardiness without a healthy tailwind. As the winds aloft died in June, Wilbur warned the company that we had to leave right at departure time.

Wilbur was true to his word on a windless night when we would have a full four hours of flying ahead of us, our dramatic exit fueled by Wilbur's high-strung temper, reminiscent of the last flight out of Saigon prior to the fall of the besieged city. With screams of angry invectives even louder than the screams from the Lear's big Garret engines, Wilbur flashed the taxi lights at the small crowd of people who were standing in front of the airplane and released the parking brake. As the Learjet, a sleek-winged missile of an airplane, lurched forward, the spectators scattered in all directions. Four hours later, we learned the suited spectators who scurried from our path like scared rabbits were executives from the bank that was making us late and they were pissed that we left a minute before their last helicopter arrived, although it would've taken a few more minutes to load the cargo.

We left behind $450 million that night, and the bank claimed they lost $150 thousand in interest, to which our Vice President responded, "I guess that means we aren't charging you enough."

The Chief Pilot was the first person to get in the airplane as we parked in Columbus. His first words were, "What the fuck happened out there?" He vented some of his own anger while being hit by flying boxes as the cabin was being frantically dumped by the designated star loader of the night, but he couldn't punish us for doing what Wilbur had said all along we would need to do to stay on schedule.

The helicopters arrived on time for the rest of the month, which seemed to be the limit of the bank's memory as they eventually reverted to their typical tardiness.

Except for occasionally cursing air traffic controllers when they wouldn't clear us directly to our destination (we're not even to Nevada yet, Wilbur), without keying the microphone of course, I only saw Wilbur really get angry a couple of other times.

Once when Wilbur and I were coming back from Burbank at forty-one thousand feet with two jumpseaters, a foul intestinal stench wafted forward. In the tight confines of a pressurized cabin, this was an offense that ranked up near making inappropriate disparaging remarks about someone's mother. Wilbur and I looked at each other in disgust as he reached for the cherry picker, a little switch with a red ball on the end that manually opens and closes the outflow valve, a valve that operates automatically to meter the air leaving the cabin to keep us pressurized. A quick tap on the cherry picker is usually enough to expel an odor, and make your ears pop, but the way Wilbur's face was curled in anger, I knew he wouldn't be able to let go of it. As our air was rushing overboard into the stratosphere, I watched the cabin altimeter climb as my ears popped; six thousand, seven thousand, eight, nine, ten. By now the emergency pressurization valves opened automatically, dumping massive amounts of hot, noisy, raw bleed air directly into the cabin in a desperate attempt to keep the airplane pressurized.

Wilbur finally released his grip on the cherry picker. With the cabin altitude descending back into breathable range, I reset the emergency pressurization valves. Now that the cabin was quiet enough to talk again, Wilbur turned toward the jumpseaters, raised his hands, and hesitated, obviously still furious. Then he barked an angry reprimand to our jumpseaters: "Look, we have a dual responsibility here; you guys don't stink up the cabin, and I won't have to dump it again." One of the passengers admitted to the offense and promised to keep his sphincter cinched tight for the rest of the trip.

On a rainy morning in Columbus, Wilbur and I were hurriedly moving our stuff from one airplane to another when Wilbur realized his wallet was missing. We tried to retrace our steps across the flooded ramp and through the building, but we couldn't find it. Wilbur was not happy. I made yet another trip along his probable path and saw Wilbur repeatedly slamming the airplane's traveling log, an aluminum binder with lots of important papers, onto the jumpseat of the airplane we just brought in from California.

After he left, stomping away with long angry strides, I looked in the airplane again and found Wilbur's wallet between the seat and the wall. The traveling log was lying on the floor of the cabin, bent to hell, with all the pages ripped out.

A few minutes later we were in our seats, ready to leave for Charlotte, Wilbur now just quietly fuming. I broke the silence by asking Wilbur if he knew what happened to the traveling log in the other airplane.

Wilbur stared out the windshield as he calmly asked, "Did you see me throw it?"

"No."

Wilbur hesitated as he continued to stare out into space, and then, with a perfectly straight face, said, "Well, I don't know what happened to it then."

It probably took a mechanic half a day to put it back together.

Several pilots exercised the open and free communications policy, which was one of the company's stated "core values," by asking for a pay raise. Our pay scale hadn't changed since it was adjusted downward four years earlier. Adjusted for inflation, the pilots' wages were lower than they had ever been in the company's twenty-five-year history. The company was still profitable, and they had a virtual monopoly in their niche, so it seemed like a fairly reasonable request.

The company always tried to conform to the latest managerial fads, so they set up a committee. This was just as much of a fraud as the core values, calling us team members instead of employees, and all the other gimmicks from the latest business theory books, but several pilots gave up their weekends to fly to Columbus and participate in a cheap substitute for a negotiating committee, a committee with no teeth, without even a splash of Kool-Aid.

Our CEO, Jimmy (not his real name), opened the meeting with a speech about how there wasn't a budget for pay raises and how by asking for anything we were asking too much. He told them he would never be able to face the board or the shareholders if he gave us so much. He was the largest shareholder, so he apparently couldn't face himself. Then he left. So this was the new economy he was so excited about when he took us public?

I used to trust the propaganda and appreciate that Jimmy's entrepreneurial spirit had created the company that gave me a job. We had all heard the mythical stories about how our hero Jimmy mortgaged his house to save the company and achieve the American dream for all of us. He was never going to end up in the gutter if his business failed. The company wasn't even his idea. Jimmy's father golfed with a bank executive who needed someone to fly payroll checks around the state of Michigan for some large client corporations. I guess golf actually does have a purpose. Jimmy just happened to be a twenty-two-year-old kid with his own airplane, not a common possession for a kid, and the company was born. Whenever new companies would invade his niche, he would just buy his new competitors. Technically, Jimmy was an entrepreneur, but his biggest risk in life was choking on his silver spoon.

Now Jimmy gave himself a two million dollar salary, which was nothing compared to the value of his stock and stock options, and four of the company's executives were among the top ten executive salaries in the state of Ohio, clearly reaping the benefits of the new economy. He could justify *that* to the board and the shareholders, but not a cost-of-living adjustment for the employees who nightly risked their lives at 80 percent of the speed of sound to generate the company's revenue.

To my surprise, the jet pilots did get a respectable pay raise. They had to appease the jet pilots, because we would be the pilots who were jaded enough to bring in a union; we had been on the dark side for too long.

The company used to be a better paying alternative to the right seat of a turboprop at a commuter airline, but the industry had suddenly changed. The prop pilots were now seen as transients, so they got indentured servitude and lost a week of vacation too. Fifty-seat regional jets (RJs) had just hit the market in huge numbers, and airline pilots let these little "Barbie jets" go to their commuter affiliates, which would eventually prove to be an enormous mistake for the entire profession, but that's for another chapter. There now seemed to be no end to the supply of low-time pilots willing to sit in the right seat of those big shiny jets for twenty grand a year, including many of our prop pilots. The prospect of becoming one of the sharpest sticks in the industry, while waiting for a chance to fly a Learjet, was no longer enough incentive to keep them.

To reduce turnover in the props, the company started forcing new-hires to sign a one-year training contract. A pilot would owe the company seven grand if they left before their year was up, non-prorated, but if they stayed for a whole year they would be rewarded with a five hundred dollar bonus.

Minimum experience for a Part 135 (the chapter of the FAA's regulations that governed charter flying, small airliners, and small freighters) Baron Captain is twelve hundred hours of flight time, and that's exactly what our new-hires would have, and I wouldn't doubt that sometimes some of that time was pencil-whipped. Solid multi-engine experience, which had previously been essential, was no longer even a consideration. If an applicant had a multi-engine rating, they were hired, even if they had only completed a five-hour budget multi-engine course from a pilot factory. Pilots were being rushed through training and then barely had a chance to learn the ropes from the line pilots who had been around for a little while. I was worried that there would be more accidents. Young, inexperienced pilots and their inherent eagerness to please a company that expects a lot from their pilots in a difficult environment was a dangerous combination. It always was, but the company had previously always had access to more talent than they did now.

Wilbur had a pained look on his face as he checked in with dispatch from the Burbank Airport. I couldn't hear what dispatch was saying, but I knew it was bad. When Wilbur hung up the phone, I asked him who died. His name was Mark, and it was his first night alone in a Baron.

Mark was running late, which was only to be expected of someone new to this kind of flying. Mark was undoubtedly trying to save every moment he could, flying a high-speed approach (we were told that every approach needed to be a high-speed approach) and landing on the edge of the pavement so he could exit the runway at the first intersection, which in this instance led straight into the company's ramp.

Unfortunately, Mark was following a Boeing 757, an immense machine that generates especially nasty wake turbulence, the invisible tornadoes that trail from an airplane's wingtips. All you can do when told that you're following a 757 or a heavy (basically any airplane larger than a 757) is to slow down, stay above the preceding airplane's glide path, and arrive a little later, and in this case have a couple of extra minutes of taxi time as well, but Mark's ambition betrayed him as he descended into the invisible vortices spinning in the 757's wake. Mark's Baron rolled violently and slammed into the runway, inverted, right in front of the company's headquarters. Mark wasn't even lucky enough to die instantly. He suffered for a few hours, badly burned with his chest ripped open.

Another pilot needlessly gave his life. There's a little girl out there who grew up without her father. There was another memo stuffed into every pilot's mailbox, about things we already knew. But nothing really changed.

Soon another pilot on his first night alone accidentally landed his Navajo with his landing gear up. Fortunately, you don't die from that, but it was still another airplane wrecked because the company didn't want to spend the money to attract and retain more experienced pilots.

I was worried about the safety of regional jets too. As the RJ boom absorbed more airline flying, the regionals were hiring pilots with as little as 250 hours of flight time to sit next to a brand new, low-time Captain with no prior jet experience. It was the next phase of the blind leading the blind, but this time with you in the cabin, completely unaware you had bought a ticket on a training flight. Yes, you should be scared; I was. I knew there would be accidents, needless accidents that could be avoided if only there was an experienced skipper at the helm, but that's for another chapter as well. It didn't have to be that way. There were experienced pilots out there, but they weren't going to take twenty thousand dollar per year jobs.

I watched more and more experienced, disciplined, highly skilled pilots who flew high-performance jets every day get rejected by the major airlines. Too often, I was seeing the wrong people get the good jobs, at least not the best people. The airlines weren't necessarily evaluating pilots by skill and experience. It seemed to be more of a beauty contest instead. I became disillusioned by the unfairness of it. My friends were flying jets every day, honed to the very edge of perfection, just hoping for a break that never seems to come, like the actors and actresses who served my pizza in Burbank.

An entire industry developed to fleece pilots wanting to move up to the next level. One airline discovered they could still get ten thousand pilot applications even if they charged a fifty dollar application fee, so another airline decided to charge one hundred dollars. Then another decided to charge a hundred and fifty dollars, and they would charge another sixty dollars just to update your application. One airline even made you buy a 737 type rating, which at that time was about ten thousand dollars. The airlines were figuring out that they could get new pilots to pay recruitment and training costs, even though an industry-wide hiring cycle was apparently just beginning. Jobs allegedly weren't scarce, but pilots were still willing to do almost anything to fly airplanes.

Companies would sell interview gouge for all the airlines or coach you for the interview for a very large fee. If you really wanted to make yourself competitive, you could buy the simulator profile and a few hours in the type of simulator you'd fly—that is, if the airline even evaluated your flying skills. Some didn't, since flying skills weren't necessarily what they selected for.

One airline even tried a bizarre slot system for inviting pilots to interviews. For every three interviewees, one would be an experienced pilot, one would be a low-time pilot, and one would be a woman or minority. I would want to hire the experienced pilots, but whoever thought of this scheme, some human resources guru who has never flown a transonic jet, probably hired the charming one who paid a thousand bucks to be coached for the interview and the simulator evaluation. And why are inexperienced pilots a minority group worth protecting? Every future pilot is born equally unqualified. Why shouldn't they go out in the world to learn the craft like the rest of us before they're entrusted with hundreds of passengers' lives?

I had once believed that perseverance and hard work would be rewarded with success. After all, this is supposed to be the land of opportunity. Flying is a professional skill on which people's lives depend, but it seemed like a beauty contest that people are willing to whore themselves for, and the only way to truly preserve your dignity is by staying out of the game. I opted to keep my dignity, to keep going to work, anonymously, on the dark side of the planet, to keep developing my skills and experience, and to upgrade to Learjet Captain when the opportunity arose.

I was checking the weather for the flight to Denver, with an unfamiliar guy looking over my shoulder at the weather computer. He had just interviewed for a pilot position and was waiting for his flight home. I asked him how it went, although I already knew by the excited glow on his face. The company was so desperate to fill vacancies that they were no longer waiting for acceptance letters to travel through the mail. They had already given him a class date, and he was obviously excited that he was going to get paid to fly airplanes.

There was something else about this guy. He was probably the most innocent-looking person I had ever seen, or at least the most innocent-looking person you can ever see at four in the morning. He looked uncorrupted, like he still had his dignity, and he still had hope, and he undoubtedly had never imagined he might lose either of them. The poor guy was about to leap into the dark side.

The guy asked me what it was like to fly for the company. I thought about his unanticipated question for a minute, and then I realized I couldn't crush his dreams with the cynical view of the world I had acquired from five-years of hard-core flying in the dark side of the industry, on the dark side of the planet. I couldn't tell him that he would be rushed through training and into a world he was not ready for, being pressured to do dangerous and illegal things for some banker's profits. I couldn't tell him that every year the company, and the rest of the industry, would find new ways to cheat him since there were pilots willing to do virtually anything for a chance to fly airplanes for a living and management was well aware of that. I couldn't tell him that he would face discrimination because he would be labeled, possibly unfairly, as a reckless freight dog. I couldn't tell him that he would consider his own fragile mortality while he was still young and that he or one of his friends may needlessly give their life to move paper through the night sky.

The most coherent thing I could think to say was, "I've been comfortable here." And I warned him not to be a hero if he was just too tired to go any further. This guy, and all of the rest of us too, deserved something better than what I'd seen so far here on the dark side. It was a haunting experience, because I almost felt like I was going back five years in time, trying to figure out how to warn myself what I was getting into.

I had a comfortable life. I'd just gotten a big pay raise. I had an easy job and a great schedule, although I had to stay up all night. I wasn't whoring myself in a job market that defied reason. I didn't really even have to deal with the company. That was the Captain's job, and Wilbur worried more than enough for both of us anyway. My body traveled to California and back twice a week, but my mind was free to go much further. I knew my life would probably never be as easy as it was right then, and I knew I needed to appreciate the moment.

I had already met the girl I was going to marry, Dawn. Although my short thirty hour trips to the West Coast and back seemed like an unbearably long time to be away from her early in our romance, I rationally understood that I would never be able to spend as much time with her as I did right then and we were both spoiled by it. I tried to tell her it would only get worse. Even I had no idea how much worse it could actually get, but that's for another chapter.

No office had a better view than mine, and not just the hundreds of miles from horizon to horizon; there were little things too. I saw lots of St. Elmo's fire while flying the props through lake-effect snow showers, but it can be spectacular on a dark night in a jet, with bright blue and purple sparks dancing across the windshield against the blackness of space. Before electricity was understood, sailors saw the blue sparks on their mastheads as a sign from their patron saint.

Every northern culture had a different explanation for the Northern Lights, but now we understand the Aurora Borealis to be charged particles deflected to the poles by the magnetosphere. This is a rare treat at the mid latitudes, but from forty-one thousand feet up, I was lucky enough to witness dozens of truly spectacular light shows.

On one particularly good show, Wilbur switched seats with a passenger who had never seen the Northern Lights. Wilbur preferred the newspaper, which he diligently read from cover to cover every day, every word of it. The passenger and I stared as pulsating curtains of green, yellow, and red lit the night sky. It was spectacle enough to inspire new myths, had we not understood what was happening.

Far to the southwest, we were beginning to see a different kind of light show, dim flashes partly obscured by high cirrus clouds. Our passenger asked if it was heat lightning or real lightning, another meteorological myth that won't die, even in the age of geosynchronous weather satellites and Doppler radar. Heat lightning was an ancient attempt to explain the mysterious night-time flashes from storms too far away to be seen or heard. I pointed to a cluster of colors on the airplane's radar screen, telling him that they represented the distant thunderstorms that were producing the lightning. We would eventually pass close enough to the weather to see great veins illuminate whole thunderstorms eight miles tall.

The passenger asked me if I ever got tired of this. "No." I may have acquired a cynical worldview from that seat many miles above the dark side, but I was doing what I loved to do.

Wilbur and I had to start a little early one night and flew to Orlando before making the trip to the West Coast. During the trip south, we watched the moon rise from the Atlantic Ocean, and later we watched it set in the Pacific. Even though I was only hauling money, I felt like I was accomplishing something in that I crossed the continent with each work day.

I had lost part of my identity when I became a Learjet co-pilot. The Captains got all of the respect at the company. I had a name when I was a Captain in the props, even though I belonged to a lower stratum than the jet pilots, but now I was just Wilbur's co-pilot. One friend even called me Orville, because of my association with Wilbur. It is implied that a co-pilot is the Captain's servant, an apprentice, something less than a real pilot.

I had a happy childhood, but even as a child I knew I was a person. I felt disrespected whenever someone treated me as less than a real person because I was only a child. That is how it is to be a co-pilot for this company.

One night in Charlotte, three company employees were squabbling over who would get the last two jumpseats out of town. Wilbur and I were already seated in the airplane, trying not to get involved in a dispute that was going to leave one person behind. One of the passengers asked Wilbur if the co-pilot had to go. Wilbur, who was seated a foot away from me, said with a clearly irritated tone, "Yes, he has to go." I just sat quietly, like I didn't exist, the bastard stepchild who was preventing some freeloader from going home.

On a foggy morning in the San Fernando Valley, Wilbur, ever talkative, told our passenger we weren't going to see the runway until we were about two hundred feet above the ground.

I was in the left seat, flying that leg, and our passenger was suddenly almost in a panic. "Are you actually going to let the co-pilot land the airplane?"

Wilbur and I tried to reassure the passenger that I was qualified and able to fly an instrument approach and that I had done so more times than he could count. I had more than six thousand hours of flight time, with two thousand hours in Learjets, twice as much flight time as most regional airlines required for upgrade in their Barbie jets. I flew half of the legs every night, and this guy had even seen me fly several times. He was thinking that the co-pilot was some kind of student pilot. Wilbur and I together had nearly twenty thousand hours of flight time. That was probably more flight time than an Air Force One crew or Space Shuttle crew.

Safely on the ground, if the ground is ever truly safe in earthquake country, our still anxious passenger said, "Good job. Is that the foggiest weather you've ever flown in?"

Not even close. This was my damn job, and had been for years, with opportunities to practice my trade several times a night. Fog was just part of my world. I knew the Learjet, and I could fly the hell out of it. I was a professional, not a student pilot. My number was almost up. I would be one of the next to upgrade, and I had been preparing for it, preparing to regain my identity.

I had moved up two numbers because the company had recently fired a fairly new Captain and his co-pilot after they wrecked a Lear in Kansas City.

It was a rainy night with a stiff north breeze. This was a dangerous situation at Kansas City Downtown Airport. Because of several tall towers and the buildings of downtown Kansas City, the only good instrument approach to the north is to a runway that is often too short for a heavily laden Learjet, especially when the runway is wet. That leaves two options: fly the approach to the short runway and then, when you get the airport in sight, do a potentially dangerous circling approach to the longer runway, without hitting the towers just to the east of the approach, hidden in the mist; or just land on a ten-thousand-foot-long runway with no nearby obstacles at Kansas City International, ten or so miles to the north, because sometimes you just can't get the job done.

They chose to land on the short, wet runway. Not only were they too heavy for the short runway, apparently they were above the airplane's maximum certified landing weight too. They didn't use the drag chute, but by the time they realized they weren't going to stop, they would've already been too slow for it to even deploy. (The drag chute has to be planned in advance; it's not there to save a pilot from his mistakes.) They sliced through a parked Navajo and a Cessna like a hot knife through butter and then pierced a hangar door.

The accident demonstrated the need to respect an airplane's limitations. There are a hundred and fifty pages of performance charts in the Lear's Flight Manual for a reason. It also demonstrated how goddamn strong a Learjet is. They left a trail of destruction, but the only injuries that rainy night were to their careers as professional pilots.

I effectively moved up two more numbers when two co-pilots were sent home from upgrade training as punishment for not coming in fully prepared to pass their checkrides. Those two guys would get passed over for the next vacancies. There would be no real training; that cost time and money. We were supposed to have taken the initiative to learn everything on the job as co-pilots. If I didn't want to get sent home and passed over, I would have to essentially show up ready to pass a Learjet type-rating checkride.

Dawn was preparing for my upgrade by putting her house on the market and by figuring out the cost of living in all of the cities where we based Learjets, part of her professional expertise. I was grateful for Dawn's support. I knew people who either didn't upgrade, or had to commute, because their wives had been unwilling to move.

Dawn had immigrated to Charlotte also, except that she moved there without a job offer. She just knew she would have better luck finding a job there, in a prospering Sun Belt city, than back at home, in rural Northwestern Pennsylvania, a bold move for a twenty-two-year-old girl. Dawn had done well for herself in Charlotte, and now she was about to take another big risk with me. We weren't even married yet, although we did have plans. Lots of people had plans though. Society is littered with the ruins of broken dreams. I intended to not let her down.

The industry has a high divorce rate. Many spouses are let down. It takes a special kind of person and a strong relationship to endure the unusual lifestyle of a tumultuous career spent traveling and still be supportive after countless disappointments. Dawn would inevitably endure enough, but that's for later chapters.

Upgrade

The next bid sheet had four Lear Captain vacancies, which included two new routes in Kansas City. Except for the possibility that an existing Captain might bid a new base, I would likely have my choice.

My easy life in Charlotte was nearing its end. I knew I would be making sacrifices, but I needed to have some jet Captain experience (jet pilot-in-command time) in order to advance my career. Wilbur and I had already contemplated the end of the good life when he heard a rumor that they might close the Charlotte base. Never trust rumors in aviation; the good ones never come true, and reality always becomes a lot worse than what you hear in the bad ones. All things must come to an end, and this time it would be my choice, with help from Dawn. I needed her help to be brave enough to re-enter the world I had dropped out of when I moved to Charlotte, that unique time when I was free.

We chose Kansas City because it had the lowest cost of living of our choices. Dawn and I believed in some unpopular and possibly even un-American ideas, like saving money and not burying ourselves in debt. We saw other people doing just that in an era of fashionable greed, and we never imagined that someday we might have to pay for the irresponsibility of others, but that's for another chapter.

Dawn and I flew to Kansas City for the weekend to explore the city and find an apartment. Neither of us knew anything about the city. To me, Kansas City had always just been a sprawling cluster of lights in the middle of the continent, far beneath me.

Dawn was having no luck selling her townhouse, and her realtor, a guy recommended by one of her colleagues at work, didn't seem to be even trying to make a sale. When Dawn asked her friend about the inept realtor, her friend admitted that he didn't try very hard, but he was a nice guy. Dawn had wanted a recommendation for a competent realtor to sell her house, not charity for a friend of a friend in a good-old-boy network.

Dawn somehow sold her house just in time, freeing us from the strange dichotomy of property ownership, self-imposed slavery in the land of the free.

The rest was up to me. I still had to earn an Airline Transport Pilot License with a Learjet type rating. This would be the biggest checkride of my career, and I had the anxiety to match.

Upgrade training was just what I expected. We sat down in a classroom, and the instructor opened a Learjet flight manual. He asked me every limitation in the manual. He asked me to diagram a schematic of every system from memory and explain how they worked. I even had to know the amperage of all the little current limiters and circuit breakers, not just the two big ones.

For three nights we were interrupted by having to ferry airplanes or fly routes that went through Columbus. During these flights I was able to demonstrate all of the maneuvers and emergencies that would be required on a checkride. It was three days of evaluation, and the instructors thought I was ready.

The Learjet examiner was also our Director of Operations (DO), a colorful guy full of tall tales, but his most interesting stories were actually the ones he never told. He had been based in Miami at the beginning of the cocaine boom, when there was lots of money to be made flying illicit cargo out of South America. He was never caught, but his business partner was, his co-pilot in the Miami-based Lear, a guy Wilbur and I knew. He was another legendary character who did his time but never ratted on his partner in crime, allegedly our DO. When he was released from prison, the DO created a new job for his old friend, a gift for his friend's silence.

The examiner asked me a few questions, including a couple he knew I wouldn't know the answer to, and I didn't. I flew the airplane, performing every required maneuver with ease. He congratulated me and typed up my Airline Transport Pilot License with Learjet type rating. I handed him a bottle of Jack Daniel's whiskey, as I had been told to do.

I think the instructors had already given their approval, so the checkride almost seemed like a formality, relaxed and actually kind of fun. The examiner was more interested in being a test pilot, to see if he could get the Learjet to actually stall before the stick pusher could prevent it, trying to recreate the conditions of another recent accident in the company. One of our crews had just wrecked a Learjet while landing at Chicago's Midway airport. The DO thought they may have stalled the airplane in the landing flare, maybe suddenly running out of airspeed, altitude, and answers at the end of a dead-stick approach to a short runway. The airplane rolled to the right and its tip tank striking the runway so hard that it actually bent the wing. They were very lucky the airplane didn't cartwheel, which would've killed them.

To try to replicate the accident, we had put the airplane in the landing configuration, landing gear and flaps down, but at ten-thousand feet; far above the unyielding pavement they crashed into. At idle power, as if I had dropped anchor, our speed bled off toward a stall and then, an instant before the stall, I jammed the throttles forward while pulling fully aft on the control yoke. The airplane buffeted in a stall, rolled abruptly to the right, and then, a moment too late, the stick pusher shoved the nose forward, trying to prevent a full stall that had already occurred. You should never actually do this in a Learjet, even at ten thousand feet, where we were. Undesirable stall characteristics are why the airplane is equipped with a stick pusher. I wouldn't have done it if he had briefed me ahead of time, but he didn't, so I did and took a wild ride that few have experienced in a Learjet.

Dead-stick approaches were something we all did occasionally, amusing ourselves while honing our skills, pulling the throttles back to idle at 41,000 feet and gliding the Learjet all the way to the runway without touching the throttles again, trading pitch and airspeed to keep the airplane on a trajectory initiated eighty miles distant. Now that requires extraordinary skill, and I'll admit that it's satisfying to know you threaded a needle at five hundred miles per hour from eighty miles away. The dangerous part is at the very end, when you drop anchor, add that last notch of flaps, and your speed rapidly decays as you enter the landing flare. If you don't plan that just right, you can get yourself into trouble before you have time to jam the throttles forward. It was a fun brush with perfection, but the risk in those last couple of seconds isn't worth it.

I now had my first rule as Captain: to be stabilized, with full flaps and the engines spooled up, for at least the last five hundred feet of an approach, just like the Learjet flight manual requires (in visual meteorological conditions). We can dead-stick to there, but no further. It may not be as cool, and it may cost me a few seconds at the end of the flight, but it's certainly much safer, in many more ways than I'll mention here.

There was no time to celebrate after my checkride. It was moving day. I didn't think I needed to celebrate anyway. I knew a lot about Learjets and I could fly them well, but the primary reason why I had upgraded was because I had the seniority for it. I had taken a number and patiently waited for my turn.

The following Monday I showed up for work in Kansas City as a Captain. I still had some anxiety, because I knew very well that I didn't know all there was to know about flying Learjets. I knew I wasn't ready for everything; no one is. For the past two years, I had flown with someone considerably more experienced than I was. Now I would be the one to bring the skills and experience to an emergency. With only 6,200 hours of flight time, which I no longer considered to be very much, I knew there was still so much I hadn't seen.

I took off and turned the Learjet to the east. The brown waters of the Missouri River slithered across the broad floodplain beneath me, disappearing into the distant horizon. Soon enough, the sprawl of Saint Louis began spilling over the same horizon. My wheels met the runway there with an unsatisfying thud. I had better landings when I was a co-pilot. I had not magically achieved a new level of skill just because I had signed for the airplane.

As I settled into my new position, I found myself worrying about all the things that Wilbur used to worry about when I flew with him. After two years of flying together, I guess I shouldn't have been surprised by his influence on me. Our crews would spend more time with each other than they would spend with their wives. I figured that if I expected and planned for the worst, then whatever happened, I should be safe. Having blind faith that everything will turn out fine can be lethal if you aren't prepared. Pessimism is much safer.

I decided I was no longer flying for the company; I was flying for myself. I didn't want any heroics on my plane. There would be no shame in not being able to complete the mission.

Wilbur gave me some parting advice as I was leaving for my new and immensely challenging assignment: "The two most important things that a Captain must know how to say are 'no' and 'fuck no'."

I would use Wilbur's advice during my second week as Captain.

During your first hundred hours as Captain of a turbine-powered aircraft (jet or turboprop), you have to add a half mile visibility and one-hundred-feet to the landing minimums for an instrument approach. I knew this would be a problem in Columbus that night because of heavy snow. Dispatch was aware of it too, and we were all thinking the same thing. In Saint Louis I could switch places with another Learjet Captain I met there. I would go to Chicago instead of Columbus, and then I would pick my route back up there. It was an easy remedy, so that's what we did.

By the time I arrived in Chicago, it was snowing heavier than forecasted there too, up to the edge of my high minimums. They unloaded my plane, but then they started to load more freight. I knew I was the only Lear Captain there, so I guessed they wanted me to fly. I checked the Columbus weather before I called dispatch. Columbus was still at minimums, below my legal minimums.

The dispatcher said that because of the weather, two props had missed their connections with the last Lear from Chicago to Columbus. They needed me to fly the misconnected freight to Columbus. I told the dispatcher I still wouldn't be legal to land there since I needed high minimums.

He said, "Well, you're our only hope."

With one sentence, he summarized the operational philosophy at the company. They're glad to follow the rules, especially when it's convenient. There are an infinite number of variables that can make doing things correctly, legally, and safely inconvenient. I reminded him that they couldn't have it both ways.

I stayed in Chicago. I was just not a company man anymore. I probably hadn't been for a long time, but it was easier to keep a low profile as a co-pilot while Wilbur was fretting over the complex and dynamic dance of getting the job done but still doing it correctly. At one time I would have done it, having started this job as a naïve, loyal kid. I wouldn't have been caught. There will never be a Fed out in a snowstorm at five in the morning unless they've had to come out to investigate a smoldering, crumpled pile of aluminum that used to be one of our planes, which did happen a lot—so often that it was getting hard to mentally keep track of which airplanes had been wrecked and by whom.

I expected to hear about my conservative decision to follow the regulations instead of taking one for the team. I was never asked about it, but I'm sure it didn't go unnoticed. I had now officially gone to the other side, a troublemaker. If I kept finding myself in situations in which my insistence on following the rules cost the company money, they would get rid of me any way they could. They could give me a checkride that no one could pass or just wait for me to make a small mistake. This is a business, and we don't make money unless we keep moving the money faster than anyone else can. This is why I realized our pilots needed union protection—not because I wanted to get rich or be lazy; we were naked without it. Ballots would be in the mail soon. I would be voting yes.

My first hundred hours as Captain passed quickly, but even without the high minimums restriction, there are never guarantees that the weather will be good enough. Des Moines wasn't forecasting fog on one particular morning, but the densest fog, the kind that shuts an airport down, sometimes occurs on the cool clear mornings when it isn't predicted. This morning Des Moines was reporting a one hundred foot ceiling with a thousand feet of runway visibility. A thousand feet may seem like a lot of visibility, but it's not. That's the point at which the transmissometer light fades from a barely perceptible dull gray to invisibility. Slowed all the way to landing speed, that's a distance I covered in only four seconds, while fatigued from being awake all night. I would need eighteen-hundred feet of horizontal visibility to be able to fly the approach, a rule that applied to every air carrier, enforced by the air traffic controllers who had to clear you to fly the approach.

I had enough fuel to hold for a little while, but I thought it was silly to fly in circles over Des Moines, squandering my fuel, when the weather was still good in Omaha and Kansas City; I was carrying time-critical freight for both cities. I decided to go to Omaha, then Kansas City, where the freight would still arrive on time. One of the props could fly the freight to Des Moines once the fog lifted.

On the way to Omaha, a sudden loud bang, followed by an extremely loud vibration, shattered the early morning peace. It was a Garret grenade, a catastrophic failure in the hot section of one the engines, and now severed turbine blades were falling across the Iowa countryside, a shower of titanium knife blades.

The vibration subsided somewhat when we pulled the right throttle back to idle, so we shut down the right engine.

Engine failures in training are always black and white. The equipment works or it doesn't. This one wasn't like that. The airplane didn't lurch violently with a sudden, complete loss of thrust. The engine gauges were still relatively normal. The crippled engine was undoubtedly still making some power but continuing to further damage itself with imbalance induced vibration. The worst thing we could have done would have been to hurry and accidently shut down the wrong engine. We had to be deliberate and careful.

Suddenly I realized I was in a single-engine Learjet, and I decided that I really didn't like flying single-engine airplanes any more. The odds of us losing the other engine were probably comparable to the odds of winning the lottery, but it's a morbid lottery that some unlucky bastard occasionally does win. I just wanted to get the airplane on the ground before it was me.

The weather was good in Omaha. I flew a normal visual approach to a long dry runway. It was routine in every way, except that I was holding only one throttle in my hand. After I landed, the parade of fire trucks followed us down the runway and to the FBO.

I shut down the remaining engine and greeted the crowds that were gathering around the airplane. The firemen congratulated me with remarks like "Wow, that looked like a normal landing!" as if it actually required heroic skills to hold one throttle in my hand instead of two. It was a normal landing.

The fire chief and airport operations supervisor each had reports to fill out, so I told them what happened: "One of our engines came apart, so we shut it down and landed." I walked to the back of the airplane to check out the damage. The engine nacelle was streaked with oil. There were twisted, mangled turbine blades, some blades were missing. It didn't look like much, but it was nearly a half-million dollars worth of damage.

News traveled at 80 percent of the speed of sound in my company, which was fast enough in a time before everyone had a cell phone in their pocket. For the next few days people would ask me about my engine," as if giving me ownership of it, or even just give me a congratulatory pat on the back. I experienced a rather silly moment of accidental fame just because the engine decided to come apart while I happened to be operating it. It was like I had now earned an imaginary badge that read, "I proved myself; I'm the real thing." It could've happened to anyone, and anyone would've been able to successfully handle it.

After they hung a new engine on the damaged airplane I had parked in Omaha, the other Kansas City Lear Captain, a young new Captain with a colossal ego, delivered a couple of our instructors to Omaha to ferry the other Lear back to Columbus. He was in the weather, in dark roiling clouds and rain, and he somehow let the airplane get away from him, something that you can absolutely never allow to happen. He recovered from whatever accidental upset he had gotten himself into and didn't wreck the airplane, but now he was in big trouble.

When I showed up for work about an hour or two after the incident, he humbly admitted he was in a lot of trouble. The poor guy was aching with regret, so uncharacteristically humble he almost seemed disembodied from himself as he told me about it. He had called his wife to tell her what had happened, and she immediately vomited. He would have to ride to the chief pilot's office in my jumpseat, which I wasn't happy about. I felt like I was delivering a condemned man to his execution, and I don't revel in anyone's misery.

He was a product of our recent high turnover rate. Of the four Captain vacancies that had recently put me in the left seat, there was a full two years difference in seniority between me and the most junior of the four, the guy who was now in trouble. That's two years of tight deadlines in the angry night sky, maybe two thousand hours of valuable experience.

I had heard he was a little weak in the airplane, with an enormous chip on his shoulder, but I would only expect that from a cocky young guy who didn't have a lot of time in the airplane yet, or a lot of total flight time. It could've been me if I wasn't so busy being scared of what I'd encounter next. He passed a Learjet type rating checkride, so he should've done okay if he respected the airplane and was aware of his own limitations. That was the problem. It's a lot to ask to put a guy in his mid-twenties in command of a high-performance jet and not expect it to go to his head. The feds even have a higher minimum age requirement for Airline Transport Pilots, twenty-three, because they anticipate maturity issues that might go along with command. This guy's ego had been in overdrive, really not unusual at all; we knew we were the gods of the night sky, and he treated the Learjet like it was a savage subordinate that needed to be beaten down and shown who the boss was. With a sudden, accidental roller-coaster ride through angry nighttime clouds, the Learjet taught the young Captain that a respectful partnership with his powerful, slippery steed would have been a more appropriate way to command.

The chief pilot demoted the new Captain back to co-pilot and gave him a few months to find another job, probably the most generous firing I had ever witnessed. I actually had a few chances to fly with the guy before he left. I enjoyed flying with him. He flew the airplane well, because now he flew it with humble hands and mind. If given another chance, he would've done fine.

I was just a kid myself, twenty-eight, but I've always been older than most others my age. This was one of the few times it actually benefitted me.

Our insurance minimums for a Learjet Captain were three-thousand hours of total flight time, with five-hundred hours of jet time and a hundred hours in Learjets, but they had never upgraded anyone even close to those minimums, until now. The insurance adjusters discovered this while kicking tin in the aftermath of the company's two recent Learjet accidents, and they weren't going to let the company get away with pencil-whipped training anymore. Now all the new co-pilots were going to get real initial training in a simulator, and all the future upgrades would go to the simulator for real upgrade training, just like what is now normal throughout the industry. Insurance underwriters have been just as important to improved flight safety, if not more so, than any other single entity. Insurance companies have to keep writing checks for our mistakes long after the dead pilots are feeding the worms.

My co-pilot had a couple of months of administrative leave after a medical review officer mishandled a false positive on a wiz quiz. Or else he ate the wrong brownie at a party. This is my fear with these, drug tests—not brownies, the reason why I'm terrified of poppy seeds, even though I would probably need to sprinkle them on every bite I took to produce a positive test result. I hoped he wouldn't carry the episode through his whole career. One mark, even if accidental, is enough to ruin a flying career.

The weather stayed miserable for most of the spring. I was dealing with thunderstorms, high winds, rain, snow, or fog somewhere along my route nearly every night, the kind of weather in which even the birds were walking, but I had a schedule to keep. I was flying twice as many legs as I was used to flying during my easy life in Charlotte. I was exhausted all the time, but I still wasn't sleeping well, not that it had ever been easy for me to sleep during the day.

While waiting for my co-pilot to navigate his bureaucratic nightmare with the FAA I was breaking in a new co-pilot every few weeks, none of whom had any prior jet time. As much as I enjoyed teaching years ago, on-the-job training was just another burden that was making my job more difficult than it really needed to be. There was a high level of intensity to our flying, the expectation that we would fly every leg at the very edge of the envelope in order to stay on schedule. It was a difficult classroom for both student and teacher, and I was still learning my job as Captain.

One morning as I was about to go to bed, Dawn asked me if I had any dinner ideas that evening. Don't give insomniacs or day-sleepers anything extra to think about before they hit the sack. I slept restlessly, as usual, but I did dream. In my dreams I wondered why Dawn had been stumped for dinner ideas. We'd just go out to one of our favorites, Santoro's or House of Taipei. When I awoke I realized my ideas were from another time and place, a thousand miles out of reach. In my exhausted, groggy state, I suddenly felt like we had made a big mistake; we should never have left Charlotte.

Everyone knew that checks would eventually travel magically through the ether instead of in Learjets. The company was preparing for that day by diversifying into hazardous cargo that no other company was willing to touch. We had always carried some radioactive materials, but these were relatively insignificant and governed by Department of Transportation (DOT) regulations that limited our exposure. The company applied for and received an exemption from these regulations, and now our only limitation was how many boxes of radioactive cargo would fit in the airplane.

This scared the hell out of me, this new invisible hazard. I didn't fear thunderstorms, icy runways, old airplanes, or Garret grenades (my engine that came apart), but I was terrified of the thought of being strapped into my seat for hours while my body was continually being zapped by sub-atomic particles.

Shipping hazardous materials required careful and methodical processes, but there was no indication that any part of our operation had changed. The company was still a check hauling business, which meant the imperative to hurry dictated every aspect of the operation. Our ground personnel were hired for their ability to run at full speed while pushing heavy bins out to airplanes and to toss heavy bags as quickly as possible. Now we were handling materials that were so heavily regulated that even errors on the accompanying paperwork could lead to ten-thousand-dollar fines. To do it right, the company would have to adopt a totally new operational philosophy, and there was no evidence that anyone even recognized this, except the pilots whose careers would be jeopardized by the inevitable violations.

The exemption actually caused some people to no longer regard hazardous materials as hazardous, which needlessly led to a confrontation with the Kansas City station manager. I had already been carrying a half dozen barely radioactive boxes to Saint Louis every night, but suddenly the station manager began loading the boxes in the front of the cabin, instead of in the back, as far away from me as possible.

Exposure is exponential with distance, so halving the distance to the source exposes you to four times as much radiation. Mine was not an exempt flight, but even if it had been, the exemption was not a justification to irradiate someone out of convenience just because the boxes were offloaded at my first stop.

When I went out to the airplane, I would move the boxes to the back of the cabin, understanding that I would have to dig them out when I arrived in Saint Louis. The extra work that I would be doing was worth it to me, reducing my radiation exposure. This really pissed off the station manager, who was another young guy with a new command accompanied by an enormous chip on his shoulder.

The Chief Pilot called me into his office because I had been accused of interfering with the young station manager's job. This was all just a pointless carpet dance for my boss, because he couldn't actually fault me for anything. The company manual stated that the Captain was ultimately responsible for pretty much everything in the universe, and even parallel universes too, specifically including the proper loading of the aircraft. The regulations still required us to minimize our exposure to radioactive shipments, and no DOT exemption could ever exempt us from the laws of physics.

I had not been on an ego trip since upgrading, and confrontation is particularly unnatural for me, something I've always tried very hard to avoid. With clammy hands and a racing heart, I confronted the station manager with the fact that it was my airplane and he had no authority over any part of its operation. I opened my company manual and the Federal Aviation Regulations and asked the station manager to read the couple of passages that I had highlighted. Then I told him that the next time he had a problem with something I was doing, he just needed to ask me.

Although I couldn't be punished for doing something correctly, I was worried that I was now reinforcing my reputation as a rebel by insisting on adherence to the rules.

The rebels were easy to identify, because we flew with our radiation dosimeter badges clipped to the backs of our shirt collars. It was so insignificant that it was really just symbolic, but it was about following the rules. As perverse as it sounds, we were rebels because we followed the rules. Our simplistic company training told us to clip our dosimeters to our shirt pockets, but the regulations stated that the dosimeter had to be worn between our body and the source of radiation; always behind us in the cabin.

We could request a report of our dosimeter readings every month, which I always did, even though my exposure was always minimal, at two or three milirems. One month my report was sixty-four milirems, but my co-pilot's exposure was normal, at three milirems. My dosimeter had obviously been mixed up with the dosimeter of someone who had flown the mother lode, the company's twice weekly flight that exposed the pilots to the equivalent of eight chest x-rays on a single flight. I brought this to the company's attention, because it was obviously wrong, but they wouldn't even investigate it. I wasn't going to reach the annual limit for exposure, so it was advantageous for the company to ignore me, but not for the poor guy who had been irradiated, who could be irradiated that much more before reaching the Occupational Health and Safety Administration limits.

The mother lode operated early on Monday and Tuesday afternoons, so it was pretty easy for the line pilots to avoid. Our flamboyant Director of Operations, the one with whom I traded a bottle of Jack Daniel's whiskey for my Learjet type rating, usually flew the mother lode. He contracted a terminal cancer and died seven years later. We can't know whether his cigarettes, the chemicals in his lawn, the charred burgers from his grill, stress from years on the night shift, radiation from the mother lode, or something else entirely in this toxic environment of our own making caused his cancer. The guy who usually flew the mother lode with him contracted multiple sclerosis.

Personally, I like to avoid things that might endanger my health. I'm not brave enough to trust my future to blind faith that all will turn out okay. It was time to extricate myself from my newly toxic work place.

Selling Myself

With every week that passed, I accrued another eighteen or so hours of jet pilot-in-command time, the most valuable kind of flight time I could put in my logbooks, short of a space shuttle landing. I felt like I was finally qualified to aim for the top. In attempting to generate a list of the airlines I wanted to work for, I could find only twelve. I suddenly felt hopeless, thinking that there were only a dozen jobs in the country that would actually be a step up for me. Any other job would just be a lateral move or even a step back in pay or lifestyle, or both. I knew that each of these companies received thousands of applications, whenever they were accepting applications, often just once a year. I didn't even know anyone at a lot of these companies, and I didn't think a freight dog like me would score well in the beauty contest aspects of the job market.

Nine of the twelve companies on my list required current flight engineer written test results, even though the antique airplanes with flight engineers (third flight crew member in the old jetliners) were slowly being phased out of most airline fleets. My flight engineer test results had expired, so I couldn't apply to those until I could retake the test.

Of the three remaining airlines, one required a thousand hours of turbine (jet or turboprop) pilot-in-command time, which I didn't have yet, but I was getting closer every day. One wasn't currently accepting applications. The other was just about to open an application window for one month only, so my only application would be going to that airline. It would be one application among thousands, for a small airline that wouldn't be hiring very many pilots. I knew my odds weren't good. It was a waste of my time, but I went through the motions anyway.

Two things struck me as I filled out that first job application. If you had read the application, you could have assumed that I had never left Central Ohio, and nearly everything from my past had changed, although I didn't even think of myself as old.

My high school had moved, expanded, and split into two different high schools in the eleven years since I had left. At OSU, the Aviation Department had been absorbed by the school of engineering. Nearly everyone I knew from the flight school had either moved on or been fired. The University's Air Transport Service no longer existed. My old route in Buffalo was gone, although the company still had pilots based there. The company didn't have any pilots in Utica or Columbia, and before I left Charlotte, they had considered moving the route to Florida. Even the company name had changed. Nothing stays the same.

We really needed this application to reach its destination, so we sent it by priority mail. Yes, this pre-dated the online application by a few years; it was actually paper and ink. We would even be able to track its progress, or so we thought. After a week, it was still listed as in transit. How long could it take for an overnight letter to go from Kansas City to Milwaukee? Theoretically, an hour, since it would actually ride there in the belly of one of the airline's DC-9s.

I eventually decided that since the post office had been delivering letters for a lot longer than they had been tracking the delivery of those letters, it had probably reached its destination, a bulging file cabinet from which most applications would never emerge. Dawn felt responsible for our uncertainty since she had taken it to the post office. After another week we received confirmation, in the form of a post card from the airline with a picture of a DC-9 on the front. According to the United States Postal Service, it is still in transit.

My job search was now under way, sort of. It was really a single, blind shot in the dark. I don't ever remember Dawn being inherently optimistic, but for some reason she was sure they would call me. I was just as certain that she was wrong.

Kansas City had a surprisingly diverse array of cultural activities beyond barbecued cow flesh, with the local specialty being the unfortunately named burnt ends, but there had to be, or else why would anyone want to stay in the middle of a big continent? Dawn and I took advantage of the city in a way that only transients really can, but we eventually saw and did most of what there was to see and do.

We knew we were really just passing through, although we didn't know how long we were going to stay. We were far from everyone we knew, and we were planning our wedding from far away as well. Dawn had a miserable job. I was enjoying only working twenty-eight hours per week, but I actually wanted to work more, to put more experience in my logbook and to make more money.

A Learjet Captain position opened up in Columbus, so we took it. We said good-bye to our deer herd that we would watch during our evening walks. Dawn found a new job immediately, before we even had a chance to move. We bought a house. I tried to figure out how to avoid ever having to fly the mother lode, which wasn't too hard since there was so much other flying to be done. The floater pilots (Columbus-based pilots) were absorbing our pilot shortage, which became immediately apparent.

I was holding the worst schedule in Columbus since I was the junior Captain there. I had to go to the airport at six in the evening, preflight all of the airplanes that were in Columbus, and be ready to fly quickly if there was a problem with an airplane at an outstation. If I made it until ten without getting scrambled, I would fly one of the Columbus routes. When I got back to Columbus in the morning, I would usually fly to Charlotte and back to finish off a fourteen-hour work day. I would do three of those in a row, but then they always seemed to give me an easy day on Thursday, which would keep me at forty-eight hours of duty for the week, which was where our overtime started (the Railway Labor Act exempts airlines from having to follow the Fair Labor Standards Act). I would bust my ass all week but end the week with nothing extra to show for it.

At least a couple of times per month, I was still breaking in new co-pilots. All the co-pilots were receiving actual training in a simulator now, which helped tremendously, but they still had to get used to riding a rocket on roller skates.

All of the new co-pilots had spent about a year and a half in the props, and, with about 2500 to 3000 hours of flight time, were flying their first jet. Most had a strong foundation of instrument flying skills—survival in this job required it—but I could immediately tell which ones had depended too much on their autopilots while they were in the props and which ones had really tried to hone their skills. There is no way to fake ability.

The Learjet is an honest airplane in that it will go exactly where you point it. That means you need to know exactly where you need to go, part of what I call air-sense. A ham-fisted hack can get away with not having this air-sense in a slow, stable airplane, because there is more time to react to and correct undesired trends. While this is just sloppy flying in most airplanes, in a Learjet this lack of fundamental air-sense is manifested in an utter inability to control the airplane. This was difficult to teach, and probably even harder to learn, at 80 percent of the speed of sound.

I was worn out, and burnt out, and it seemed there would be no relief. Fatigue, like drunkenness, is especially dangerous because it impairs your ability to recognize how impaired you really are. I was learning how to recognize this, becoming aware of my own limitations. I could tell when my reactions were slower: my short-term memory was unreliable, simple math became difficult, and it was difficult to focus on more than one task at a time. But I was still legal.

At the end of a particularly exhausting week, I was sent out early in the evening on a special mission, followed by one of the Columbus-based routes. After we took off on our eighth leg of the night, my co-pilot, who was flying, called for a checklist. I ran the checklist and then set it down next to my seat. Then I picked it back up and ran it again. I asked my co-pilot if I had just done the checklist twice. He nodded and sarcastically said that I was in good shape to fly to Charlotte. That was next on the agenda for us, legs nine and ten, but first we had to finish leg number eight without making a mistake. We hadn't had a break all night. It was almost five in the morning. We had been abused all week. When we were within range of Columbus, I told dispatch they would need to find a different crew to do the Charlotte turn. I couldn't do it.

I wanted to be home, but it was too exhausting to be abused in Columbus as dispatch attempted to fill the holes in the schedule. I didn't get to see Dawn for more than a few minutes during the week anyway, so I decided to get out of town. Initially that meant going back to Kansas City to fly my old route, since that position still hadn't been filled yet.

I also flew our Dallas route, which allowed me to visit Wilbur. He had left the company to fly passengers in Learjets in Dallas.

Wilbur had always wanted to get away from the night shift, and he thought the airlines might finally consider him if he was flying people instead of boxes. Of course, that meant that Captain Wilbur, with his thirteen-thousand hours of flight time, was at the bottom of a new seniority list as a Learjet co-pilot.

Whenever someone leaves the company, everyone wonders whether that person knows where the grass really is greener, which in aviation is harder to find than the Holy Grail. I asked Wilbur if he thought he had made the right choice. He said he didn't know, but he didn't seem very happy. Maybe it just wasn't in his nature. He said that recently he had received a lucky break for every time the company pissed him off, so he was about even. He said the company still expected you to risk your certificate, and career, to get the job done, so it was just like a daytime version of his old job.

The company started a daytime route in Columbus, and because it was a lot of work, I had the seniority to fly it. I would fly from noon until midnight, with a long break in Louisville in the late afternoon. I was able to hold the route for four months, during which I never flew tired.

I had temporarily escaped from the dark side of the planet, and even from the dark side of the industry. I was spending the winter flying through a bright blue sky, enjoying the play of sunlight on the patterns and textures of the bright carpet of clouds that seemed perpetually underneath me. I found such peace in the beauty around me that I wondered whether resisting our diurnal biology even affected a person's happiness. This wasn't a religious experience; it was more of a Zen-like awareness of what it was to be human again, and not just a chronically fatigued, sleep-deprived creature of the night.

I flew with the same co-pilot most of the time, but I was about to lose him to upgrade training. He asked me to fill out an upgrade recommendation form, which was the first time I had even seen one. I had to rate him in about two dozen categories, the first ten of which had nothing to do with being a Learjet Captain. I was shocked. Upgrading at the company, flying anonymously on the dark side of the planet, was part beauty contest!

I sarcastically wrote that his appearance needed work because he always wore gray. Our uniform shirts were gray, or, as the company once described them, off-gray. How could there be a difference? I answered all the questions at the bottom of the page, the relevant questions about his flying skills, instrument skills, aeronautical, weather, Learjet knowledge, and judgment and decision-making skills. I personally handed the form to the Chief Pilot, telling him I didn't answer the questions that I didn't think were relevant to performing the job.

I had the opportunity to talk to lots of pilots during my afternoon layover in Louisville, a rare chance for a check-hauler to network with day-time pilots.

I talked to a couple of Falcon pilots who flew for a charter company, an odd couple who couldn't have been more different from each other. The Captain was a young guy like myself, except that he still wore the ear-to-ear grin of a kid reveling in the glory of his first real flying job. His co-pilot was older, crusty, and belligerently cynical. This guy I could relate to, although I certainly hadn't been kicked around as much as he probably had, not yet at least; that's for another chapter.

I discovered that the smiling young Captain actually conducted the pilot interviews at his company. The smiling young Captain explained his perverse theory that if a pilot accumulates 2500 hours of flight time, with a good amount of multi-engine time, and hasn't moved on to a commuter or a corporate flying job, there must be something wrong with him. It was obvious that his co-pilot, who seemed like the antithesis of what his Captain described, had been hired prior to when the smiling young Captain became the company's gatekeeper.

I didn't argue with the guy because I had no idea whether he would ever interview me somewhere, someday, but I profoundly disagreed with him, and I figured I could probably fly circles around him too. I guess it wouldn't have mattered anyway, since I didn't fit the mold that he described, a mold that undoubtedly mirrored his own accelerated career progression, moving to another job before he had the chance to master the last one. When I see an inexperienced job hopper who probably wouldn't have the fundamental skills to be able to maintain altitude in straight and level flight without help from the autopilot in a Learjet, he sees a motivated, goal-oriented pilot. When I see a seasoned expert honing his skills ever closer toward perfection, he sees a lazy, overqualified pilot who must have something to hide.

I had a different experience while talking to the pilots of a Jet Star, an old four-engine business jet. They needed another pilot for their unusual fleet, which was like a working museum of antique business jets. The only old business jet they didn't have was an old Learjet, but they respected my experience, calling the Learjet a rocket on roller skates. They all but offered me a job, but I didn't want it. None of the airplanes flew much, which was bad, especially for old airplanes. I would need to move to Dallas, and although I would get some interesting type ratings, none would be very useful for me, and I doubted I would fly any of the airplanes often enough to learn them well.

The world survived into the first day of 2000. In the last days of 1999, several people asked me if I was scared to fly during the Y2K hysteria. I always told them that air traffic control computers crash all the time, so there was no reason to think they wouldn't continue to do so in the year 2000. Airplanes are held aloft by Bernoulli's lift, dead dinosaurs, and lots and lots of money, not by the Gregorian calendar.

I also refused to acknowledge that a new millennium was beginning. When you're counting your fingers, which one do you count as number zero? There wasn't a year number zero either, which meant that the next millennium didn't actually start until 2001. I elected not to join the hysteria; it's not my style to celebrate something so arbitrary anyway.

The greatest challenge of the new year was the weather. The East Coast was getting buried by another winter storm nearly every week. One of them dumped a foot of snow on Charlotte, and I landed in the middle of it. A mixture of rain and snow instantly coated my cold-soaked Learjet with a thick layer of ice. The landing gear was clogged with slush and ice from taxiing through the deep, frozen mess.

As soon as I walked into the FBO (fixed base operator, the general aviation terminal), I asked to get my name in the de-icing queue. Two other of the company's Lear Captains followed me in to do the same thing. We were told that their de-icing truck was broken, which always happens on the rare day in Charlotte that you actually need it. I wondered whether the damn thing even existed. We would have to wait an hour-and-a-half for UPS's de-icing truck.

One of the Captains mumbled, "I have half a mind to leave right now."

He was using the wrong half of his mind. He wasn't a test pilot. An ice-sculpted wing will certainly fly with some contamination, and at some unknown speed, but it wasn't his job to find out how much. As the airfoil anti-ice, in the leading edge of the wing, melts the thick layer of ice, sheets of it are likely to peel off the wing to potentially be ingested by, and possibly even destroy, the engines. If you survive all of that, you still might wreck the airplane if the slush-covered landing gear freezes into the wheel wells, forcing a gear-up landing. By the way, you supposedly know when you've landed a Learjet with the landing gear up because it takes more power to taxi, so the joke goes.

The impatient Captain took half his mind back out to the airplane, with his obedient co-pilot in trail. A thunderous roar of jet blast unstuck their frozen brakes, and they plowed their way toward uncertainty. I stood outside, being pelted by heavy, wet snowflakes, so that I could see what would become of them.

The jet accelerated down the runway and then limped into the air, disappearing into the dark, slushy sky.

The other Captain was watching too, as he ran his bare fingers along the thick, rough ice on his wing. He made his decision, perhaps also with only half of his mind. His co-pilot quietly followed him into the airplane, and they too propelled themselves toward uncertainty.

Others followed, and soon there were only two frozen airplanes left, mine and a Learjet from one of our competitors that was also wisely waiting for the de-ice truck.

It's illegal to launch in an ice-covered airplane, but this is the dark side of aviation, where pilots do anything they want, legal or not. You probably won't get caught unless you wreck an airplane, but we do wreck a lot of airplanes, at least fifteen during my tenure with the company thus far. There is one critical rule that we still must follow, and it's not enforced by pilot-pushing employers or the absent feds, who aren't likely to be out doing surveillance on the stormiest nights: There are old pilots and bold pilots, but there are no old bold pilots. My colleagues who took off in their ice-laden Learjets were lucky pilots, this time.

Before I proceed further with the story, I should say that the absence of the FAA on that miserable night wasn't due to incompetence, negligence, or lack of concern. The FAA just doesn't have enough resources to police a fast-moving industry that can't always be trusted to police itself. While night freight is a competitive business, one of the last vestiges of an earlier, more dangerous era, it is also an anonymous business, where generally only the pilots pay for their own lethal mistakes.

Why do intelligent people do dangerous things when safety is a viable option? It wasn't even Thursday, when everyone was trying to get home, understanding that an airplane broken or otherwise stranded at an out-station could lead to a lost weekend. Maybe it was a sense of duty to stay on schedule and always get the job done. Maybe the second Captain couldn't resist the macho pressure after the first Captain launched. Did their co-pilots trust that the Captains knew what they were doing, or were they just afraid to question these old freight dogs, intimidated by their experience, seniority, or, in this particular case, utterly impressive stick-and-rudder flying skills? Decisions are made quickly. Consequences last forever. The workings in the human mind are murkier than the dark, heavy sky of a winter storm.

The Massachusetts Institute of Technology had recently published a study of thunderstorm penetration by airliners in the Dallas terminal area, which led to some interesting conclusions.

Flights that were more than fifteen minutes late were much more likely to penetrate severe weather near the airport than flights that were on time, a trend which was undoubtedly influenced by a particular airline's proud reputation for on-time performance, as well as by some pilots hurrying to catch their flight home.

After one plane penetrated an area of severe weather, several other planes would normally follow before a nonconformist would refuse. After one pilot cautiously refused a particularly treacherous-looking course, several more would normally refuse too.[3]

These patterns were drawn from monitoring several hundred flights on stormy days. Decision making isn't easy in a congested, fast-moving environment, with rapidly changing conditions and limited information, and external pressures do indeed influence the process. People are definitely influenced by others' decisions, making

123

them sheeple, and they are not a minority. The minority are the ones who chart their own course.

I stuck with my cautious decision to get properly de-iced, which meant deadlines missed and money lost, as well as spending several hundred dollars on de-icing fluid. I had a jumpseater, a company executive, who missed his midnight meeting in Columbus but never questioned my judgment. He also wasn't willing to risk his life to stay on schedule. Even though some of our airplanes had successfully tempted fate, dispatch actually supported my decision; they knew how bad the weather was down there.

As for the guys who launched carrying loads of ice, they were never questioned either. They got the job done, dangerously, illegally, foolishly, but done. If the company was fully committed to safety above all else, these guys would've been reprimanded or even fired, but as long as the freight moves without bending any metal, anything goes.

Two hours late and approaching my duty-time limits, the UPS de-ice truck finally arrived. The thick glaze of ice, and the possibility of being stranded in Charlotte, was washed away by an expensive shower of hot propylene glycol.

We are often forced to make quick decisions, and they tend to be heavily influenced by our prevailing mindset. This is why it is safer to hate the company that you fly for, so that when you are rushed into a decision, you default to "screw the company, screw the schedule." If you default to "stay on schedule, help the company, get the job done," you're more likely to rush into a situation that will compromise safety. This is what killed an American Airlines Chief Pilot in Little Rock on a stormy night in 1999. The strong gusty winds, rain-slickened runway, and long work day didn't necessarily kill him. He died because he was a company man, trying to get the job done, while his First Officer, a line pilot, was calling for a go-around, wise advice that would've saved his life.

One of our Learjet Captains got into trouble when he defaulted to staying on schedule when rushed into a decision in Charlotte. He had a reputation for being very professional, but he was also a company man who wasn't ashamed to say that he wanted to retire there. There was nothing wrong with that, except that tonight his loyalty betrayed him.

The Captain was taxiing to the runway, with a tight schedule and a brand new co-pilot. The new co-pilot was struggling to keep up as they approached the runway intersection. The tower controller told them they would need to make an immediate departure or wait for a long string of arrivals. The Captain had about a second to decide, and he chose to stay on schedule. He was busy helping the co-pilot get caught up, missed a turn, easy to do there in the kind of place now referred to as a "hot spot," and ended up accelerating down the wrong runway, which was closed for maintenance. Only luck prevented him from colliding with the construction vehicles that were hiding in the darkness.

The feds violated the Captain, but they didn't suspend his certificate. He could continue to do his job, but the violation would make it extremely difficult for him to get a new one.

Surprisingly, the company fired the Captain, who had given the company thirteen years of dependably loyal service. His mistake was potentially disastrous, but he didn't even bend any metal. There had only been a few pilots who had been fired for violations or wrecking airplanes, but they were normally repeat offenders or troublemakers. This guy was neither.

It turned out that this Captain happened to be one of the most vocal critics of how carelessly the company was handling our new radioactive shipments. The pilots are really the only filters in an operation that is perpetually in a hurry. We'd all been causing trouble by slowing down, carefully checking the paperwork, reloading airplanes, and bumping shipments if there was a pen mark out of place on the shipping papers, but we were doing all of this quietly. This particular Captain had asked some stinging questions about systemic problems in the operation that angered our brand new DO, who had apparently turned a difference of opinion into a pissing match.

I also heard that he was a target because he may have been one of the pilots organizing the recent union drive. He loyally served the company, but he also understood how naked the pilots were without protection.

One of our co-pilots was fired for failing a checkride, but I suspect his training may have been sabotaged. I had flown with the guy several times. He was smart, he flew well, and I had no doubt that he would go on to be a competent Captain. The company had tried to fire him before when he had refused to fly with a notoriously abusive Captain, but they couldn't find any dirt that would warrant his firing. They apparently gave him a checkride that no pilot could pass, a trick used by nearly every company at some point to purge the seniority list.

If we had union protection, it might have been easier to get these two pilots' jobs back, but the Teamsters' drive had failed by four votes. The vote had been that close, in spite of the fact that more than half the seniority list was composed of naïve young suburbanites who had been brainwashed since birth that labor unions are bad and were undoubtedly still basking in the honeymoon phase of their first real job as a professional pilot. The union supporters hadn't been able to openly campaign, for fear of losing their jobs, but the company did, in violation of National Labor Relations Board rules.

During the union drive, the company bribed us with a new pay scale. This time we all got raises, even the prop pilots, plus real overtime pay, so that we were actually compensated for the exhausting days. We still had no protection, which was what we desperately needed and what I would've gladly given up my pay raise for.

I received an unexpected phone call from the airline, eight months after I submitted my application. They gave me ten days to prepare for the interview.

I was excited to have the opportunity, but I was terrified as well. I didn't know what I was getting into, having no interview experience and limited knowledge of airline operations. Most of all, I was scared of failing at a rare chance for the big leagues.

I could pay a company to prepare me for the interview, but I decided not to do it. I still hated the idea of people trying to profit from my interview, and I was too cheap anyway. The airline didn't charge an application fee, and they even paid for interviewees' hotel rooms. If I got this job, it would be one of the cheapest job searches in modern airline history, really just the cost of the overnight letter that was allegedly still in transit.

I did call two of our former pilots who had been hired by the airline to get an idea of what the interview would be like: apparently the opposite of the strictly technical interview at my current job.

Every minute of my time was consumed by studying for the written test, which would come out of the Airline Transport Pilot test book, and preparing possible answers, rejecting the incriminating stories, and of course, worrying—lots of worrying.

By the day before the interview, I had done all of the studying that I could do. I went into coast mode, which was what I always did before checkrides and college exams. I felt like I did better when I took the time to relax before a big event.

In the afternoon, I coasted off to the airport. I enjoyed first-class comfort and service on one of the airline's DC-9s, where every passenger travels first class. They had been profitably providing this all-first-class service for sixteen years, and I wanted to be a part of it.

I checked into the hotel in Milwaukee. I had stayed there four years prior and I had written a nasty letter to the manager to complain about the poor service. Now I was self-conscious that someone might actually recognize me. Sleep didn't come easy. I was nervous about the interview, and I was even nervous about being able to wake up early. I set three alarms, plus Dawn was going to give me a wake-up call.

I went to the airport in the morning and met the three other pilots who were interviewing that day. An Assistant Chief Pilot took us into a conference room beneath the terminal. He handed each of us a test and collected our logbooks, which produced a stack more than a foot tall. We all had type ratings in at least one kind of jet, and we were all currently flying jets. None of us had our application pulled by someone on the inside. No one bought their way in, although I don't know whether anyone paid for interview preparation. We had all been invited to the interview because of our experience and qualifications.

As I waited for my interview, I looked out the conference room's huge window and admired the massive DC-9 parked at the gate above me. I realized that if I was successful, I would get to fly that big, beautiful airplane. I wanted to fly that airplane. I wanted this job more than ever. I was even more nervous now, seeing exactly what I would lose if they didn't hire me.

I had three one-on-one interviews, one with the Assistant Chief Pilot, one with a line pilot, and one with a recruiter from Human Resources. They each asked different variations of basically the same situational questions. It wasn't hard to think of answers from my own experience, except for the questions about dealing with problem passengers. It was very difficult to give an answer without incriminating myself with questions like: tell me about a time you broke a regulation to help the company, tell me about a time when you broke a company rule, and tell me about a mistake you made that hurt the company. They were too smart to accept that I hadn't broken a rule or made a mistake.

There were easy questions too: tell me about a time when your attention to detail prevented a problem from becoming worse, tell me about an argument you had with a co-worker, tell me about a co-worker who was hard to get along with and how you handled it, tell me about a time when you went above and beyond your normal duties to help the company.

The interview couldn't have been more different than my last interview, which was really just a multi-engine checkride. Everyone was so nice that I had no idea how well I did. Now I could only wait. If they didn't want me, they would send a rejection letter. If I passed the interview, they would call me, and I would have to go back for the next step in the process, the simulator evaluation.

Soon I was sitting in a wide leather seat in another DC-9 for the flight home. We took off and turned east, over Lake Michigan. I heard the JT8D engines spool down as we leveled off a few thousand feet above the cold, gray water. Our climb had been interrupted by crossing traffic, or else we had a problem. I always assume the worst.

I looked back at the right wing and saw the white mist of jet fuel flowing from the wingtip. We had a problem. I assumed we were dumping fuel to reach landing weight. I would eventually learn that the DC-9 can't dump fuel, but you can potentially vent it overboard if all of the tanks are full. Some DC-9 pilots will even momentarily shut off the center tank pumps in this situation to make some room in the wing tanks so there is no chance to fill the vent boxes and vent the fuel overboard. This would be a momentary example of breaking a regulation (airplane limitation) in order to prevent an air turn back caused by a tower controller concerned by the white trail of vaporizing jet fuel spilling out of your wings.

We turned south, paralleling the shore line, and then back to the west. There had been no announcements yet, and I wondered whether any of the other passengers knew what I knew, that we were returning to the airport. I also tried to remember the departure time of my company's first flight out of Milwaukee, because that would be the only way to get home if this flight cancelled.

For the sake of those who hadn't figured it out yet, which was apparently nearly everyone, one of the pilots made an announcement about a little, minor problem and our precautionary return to Milwaukee.

When we reached the gate, an agent announced that the flight was cancelled. The airline's commuter line had one more flight to Columbus in a small turboprop, but it was full. I ran to the nearest pay phone and found out that my company's first flight was leaving in half an hour. I ran through the airport and took a cab to the FBO, arriving just before the Baron left for Chicago.

In Chicago I would have a tight connection for the first Learjet to Columbus. As we were about to land in Chicago, the tower controller cleared an airplane onto our runway, trying to squeeze it out before we landed. He realized it wasn't going to work, so he told us to go around. Now I was thinking that I would miss the Learjet and have to wait for the next one three hours later. Fortunately, they sent us around the pattern quickly and we landed a couple of minutes later.

I finally got home about ten stressful hours after my interview ended. I was fatigued, emotionally drained, and starving, although I really didn't feel like eating. If I did get the job, I hoped the commute would be easier than what I had just experienced.

I thought it would be a relief to have the interview behind me, but the day after turned out to be the worst yet, waiting for an answer. I critiqued the interview, thinking of how I could have answered each question better. I doubted myself. Why would they want to hire a freight dog? There were certainly plenty of more qualified pilots.

The phone rang, sending a torrent of adrenaline through my veins. My pulse instantly doubled. It was a false alarm. The mail lady was on her way up the street. I knew a letter couldn't arrive so soon, but I figured that would be how I would find out. I knew I wouldn't be brave enough to check the mail. Even the thought of walking to the mail box made me nauseous. The phone rang again: another false alarm and near heart attack.

It was getting late on Friday afternoon, and I was beginning to accept the painful reality that there would be no call, that I had failed.

That's when the phone rang. I made it through the interview. Now I would need to wait for them to call me back to schedule the simulator evaluation, the next hoop I would jump through, which might be a few months yet.

I lost my day job when the company shortened the day route, making it more desirable to the senior Captains. We weren't as understaffed as we had been five months prior, when I had last been on the night shift in Columbus. Now, instead of having to fly two more legs after the sun rose, I was getting in bed by six in the morning. This is one of the keys to feeling somewhat normal while on the night shift. If you can get in bed before seeing the sun, and sleep in a very dark room, you can almost trick your body into thinking it hadn't been up all night—almost.

While on my way back from Teterboro at four-thirty in the morning, the dispatcher spoke the dreaded words: "Come see me when you get in." Those words can only mean extra flying, while struggling to stay awake, and wishing I could be in bed. Even though I'd make a little overtime, now that we had a pay scale with real overtime, I really didn't want to make a morning round trip to any of the likely places, like Chicago, Philadelphia, or Charlotte.

I climbed the dreaded steel stairs to the dispatch office and stoically stood in front of the dispatcher with a blank expression, bracing myself for the worst. He told me I needed to leave for Denver and Burbank in a few minutes. I resisted my urge to smile as I acknowledged him and turned toward the door. I was delighted to have to fly my old route again, but I didn't want him to think I was happy about doing a lot of extra work. This wasn't just work; this was an attempt to seize a few fragments of the carefree life I'd had when I was flying this route twice a week, a time that now seemed like a distant memory.

Tired, but too excited to nod off, I watched the continent pass beneath me. I enjoyed racing away from the encroaching morning again, capturing that tranquil moment between night and day and making it last forever, or at least until Denver.

It was a gorgeous morning for sightseeing. I wanted to absorb every beautiful inch of it, mountains, desert, earth, and sky. My co-pilot had never flown over the Rockies or the Southwest, so I pointed out the sights to her along the way. As we approached the San Gabriel

Mountains, I pointed to a repulsive brown cloud obscuring what lay beyond the ridge, like a giant meringue: "That's Los Angeles; we won't be able to see the Pacific Ocean today."

That evening the hotel shuttle drove me to Chevy's for the fresh salsa and salmon fajitas I had been craving since leaving Columbus sixteen hours earlier. They actually lived up to the high expectations of my memory.

I called the hotel to remind them to pick me up, walked down the street, and waited for the shuttle on a perfect Southern California evening, really just a typical Southern California evening. I wasn't worried when the shuttle was ten minutes late, but ten minutes soon turned twenty. I had been reluctant to go to the nearest pay phone to call for fear that the shuttle would show up and leave in my absence. Now, thirty minutes late, and nearing show time for our very important departure, I had no choice. Then I realized I didn't have any more coins. I called dispatch's toll free number and asked them to call the hotel for me.

Ten minutes later a limousine pulled up with an apologetic bellman who had forgotten to pick me up. Arriving at the hotel, my co-pilot was already checked out of her room and waiting outside. I ran to my room, grabbed my luggage, and got back in the limousine for the ride to the airport.

Thanks to Dawn's meticulous preparation, our wedding went as well as it was planned and at a price that we could afford. Most brides get frustrated by the groom's lack of skill and enthusiasm for wedding planning, but it's really probably better that way. The kind of man who can pick out the correct candles and centerpieces isn't normally the marrying kind, unless he lives in the rare state that allows it.

My consolation to Dawn was to plan the honeymoon. That would mean a honeymoon shaped by my biases and neuroses. Could there be a more honest way to begin a marriage? I wanted to avoid the beaten path whenever possible, because wherever there's a path there's an industry to sell the traveler some manufactured aura that I'm not interested in buying. I sought the ocean as I always do, but it had to be a location neither of us had ever been to, and of course, for philosophical reasons, all-inclusive resorts and cruise ships were completely out of the question.

I chose Jekyll Island, Georgia, a secluded nine-mile-long island that had once been a retreat for the wealthiest Americans, who supposedly even devised the Federal Reserve banking system while sipping mint juleps under the island's ancient, moss-draped live oaks. They may have been rich and privileged, but they're all dead now, and Jekyll Island lives on as a State Park in a state of semi-conservation, with a small town in the middle of it.

I cashed in hotel points and frequent flyer miles for tickets to Savannah, where we would stay for a couple of days before heading south to Jekyll Island. I reserved a suite in a beautiful old house in the historic district, turned bed and breakfast, where I promptly got sick. I tried to tough it out, but I ended up struggling from square to square, where I would need to rest in the shade of the magnolias and live oaks before continuing on. If I had been feeling better, I probably would have rushed right past these scattered little parks and missed what would become my favorite part of Savannah.

While resting in one of the squares, groggy with fever, we watched avian romance. A male pigeon strutted in front of the females with a ridiculous swagger and feathers fluffed, exaggerating the size of his shoulders and neck like a teenage boy flexing his muscles. He had his eye on one particular female, and he was completely oblivious to the fact that she was neither impressed nor interested, adolescent avian angst in the garden of good and evil.[4]

This was the moment that I accidentally became a bird watcher, not in the binoculars and life list sense—just an appreciation for how much richer a day is with bird songs and, yes, the antics of the ubiquitous urban pigeon. Although we left the pigeons behind, birds would become the unexpected constant on our trip.

One of the reasons I had chosen Jekyll Island was for its twenty-five miles of bike trails and the very un-American idea that we wouldn't need a car there. The best way to see the island turned out to be by bike. In fact, that was the only way to see some parts of the island, like the deep woods, the salt marshes, and the deserted beaches on the north end of the island. Our rented bikes also allowed us to hear the sounds of the island, the cicadas and birds, the muffled crash of the surf, and the sea breeze whispering through the pines.

We rode on a trail through a dense forest, stopping our bikes at the edge of dark pond. A raccoon scurried into the thick underbrush. A pair of sinister eyes and a black scaly back quietly emerged from the surface film of the still water and slowly swam toward us, stopping about ten feet from shore. If the alligator was truly wild, it would've remained hidden, but this one was obviously accustomed to being fed by people who were probably oblivious to the fact that they were leading the animal to its demise. The state will inevitably have to kill the alligator, because approaching people for food is considered undesirable behavior for large toothy predators.

The island had a few hotels, a few restaurants, houses that were mostly in the island's interior, and of course, a golf course. Otherwise it remains mostly wild, with sixty-five percent of it remaining undeveloped. The island's mascot is the loggerhead sea turtle, a threatened animal that is unintentionally harmed by humans in more ways than can be counted. The dunes are preserved for nesting sea turtles and sea birds. The island contains, and is surrounded by, salt marshes, the nurseries of the seas and the most biologically productive places on Earth.

The island was so alive that you couldn't take a step in the gentle surf without disturbing massive schools of tiny fish, and the fishing birds were always present for the buffet. The most elegant of the avian anglers, egrets and herons of several species, normally outnumbered people on the beach, mainly because we were beating the tourist season by a couple of weeks. The stately and ordinarily shy birds would allow us to sit on the sand and watch from as little as twenty feet away as they gracefully waded through the shallows. An occasional swift lunge with the sharp beak would produce a tiny, wriggling fish, which would, with another twitch, be sent down the bird's slender neck. The fishing was so easy that even some unlikely participants like boat-tailed grackles and fish crows tried their luck in the surf, and succeeded.

There was always an air show above the surf. Loitering flocks of sleek terns would circle high above. An occasional bird would descend to within inches of the water, nonchalantly pluck a silver fish from the water, and climb back to the flock, effortlessly propelled by pure style.

Pelicans would glide gracefully under their huge wings, but their grace would end when their sharp, prehistoric eyes found a school of fish. They would climb slightly and begin a wing-over, fold their wings back slightly, and crash into the water with their huge mouths agape.

Dolphins would often join the feast, just beyond the breakers, probably chasing the bigger fish that were invisibly participating in the feast as well.

A couple of fishermen dragged a seine through the shallow surf and up onto the shore. A few small fish splashed in panic ahead of the net. A tiny gray torpedo sped along the encroaching net, a baby blacktip shark barely a foot-and-a-half long. One of the men grabbed the baby shark across its back and threw it onto the dry sand, where it desperately thrashed in a futile attempt to escape to the ocean. Then, after he put some small fish in his bucket, he angrily stomped the shark to death and left it on the sand.

Dawn and I walked along a deserted beach at low tide, scattered with a couple dozen shells, each trailing tiny rows of divots in the sand, the clumsy footprints from the hermit crabs that lived inside. Later we saw a girl with a bag of shells, along with their unintentionally harvested tenants. The slowly baking hermit crabs would eventually rot, and stink, causing the whole bag to be pitched into the nearest dumpster, another needless waste.

We saw a couple of shrimp boats trawling close to shore. With nets full, one of these collected the shrimp and then purged the nets of the bycatch, all the unwanted creatures that were trapped and suffocated in the nets. Shrimp boats now have turtle excluders, but they still often catch more than five pounds of unwanted creatures for every pound of shrimp they catch, creatures that just get pushed overboard, dead. Soon tens of thousands of tiny, dead silver perch were washing up on shore, more than the seagulls could possibly eat. As the fish rotted in the afternoon sun, the putrid stench of death fouled the air, sea, and sand and lingered at the wrack line even past the next flood tide.

All living things must eventually die, but working on the dark side had already made me question whether there's ever a cause worth dying for. The hermit crabs, silver perch, baby shark, and inevitably the alligator had all just wanted the same thing that we all want, to exist. Their tragedy is that they weren't sacrificed to the health of the food chain, the natural relationship of predator and prey; they were just wasted by man's ignorance.

I really wasn't looking for death on our honeymoon; even I'm not neurotic enough to try to do that. I had just looked for the ocean and an unknown shore, but there was no escaping the drama we found there, and the urge to change what was wrong there. I became uncomfortable with my own place on the food chain. Something didn't always have to die just because I was hungry.

It was especially hard to go back to work after the honeymoon, and a conversation I had with one of our executives in Baltimore one night didn't help. He said the company had a few dozen bank customers that provide them with a couple million dollars of revenue each, but they had four huge customers that provided enough revenue to support the Learjet flying. If those four figured out how to transfer funds with each other electronically, most of the Learjet flying would go away.

Our CEO was trying to diversify the company's business by merging with a freight-forwarding company, instantly doubling the company's revenue. It would give us a non-radioactive foothold to our future, but then our CEO abruptly cancelled the deal because of alleged managerial differences.

There was a lot more to it than that. Our CEO was about to get a divorce, and in the process he was going to lose half of his stock in that new economy he had been so excited about. He was afraid he would lose control of the company since the owner of the freight-forwarding company would suddenly own more stock than him. Ironically the board of directors fired him anyway for sabotaging what would've probably been a good deal, and then the freight-forwarding company sued the company for several million dollars for terminating the merger.

The company's stock had already fallen as investors began figuring out that most of the companies that had gone public recently had no business doing so, the first of many popped bubbles. This childish attempt to stay in control after the divorce made it fall even further. Now the company's assets, mostly airplanes, were worth more than the company's stock. The company could be bought and liquidated for a profit. I really needed to move on.

I showed up for work one day to find the front door locked. Was this the end? Had we shut down that quickly, without any notice? A lineman saw me standing outside and unlocked the door for me.

He told me we'd had another fatal accident and they had locked the doors to keep reporters out, maybe making it harder for them to ask why we crashed so many airplanes, a question that someone really should have to answer.

His name was Guy. I didn't know him, unless this was the innocent-looking guy I had spoken with after his interview. He had just departed Memphis on a sunny afternoon. A couple minutes into the flight he told air traffic control he had an electrical problem. Then he said he was on fire and he was trying to return to the airport. Some fisherman had witnessed the accident. They saw smoke trailing the Baron, and then it started to turn. Guy burned to death before he could get turned around, and the Baron crashed into a lake.

When pilots talk about accidents, they usually point out all of the foolish things the dead pilots did wrong. We can learn a lot from others' mistakes, but this is also a defense mechanism to convince ourselves that we wouldn't be dumb enough to make the same lethal mistakes, to convince ourselves that we control our destinies. No pilot ever goes to work with the intention of crashing, but we all make mistakes. Guy's accident was different, because he happened to be in the wrong airplane at the wrong moment, and there wasn't a damn thing he could do about it. It was a misfortune that could've happened to anyone.

A couple of weeks later there was a letter pinned to the bulletin board, a letter from Guy's parents thanking the company for their help after the tragedy. The company certainly had a lot of experience burying pilots. The letter went on to say that they were glad that Guy was doing what he loved when he died and they were sure that God had a plan for him.

I understand that this was just how his parents were attempting to accept that their son had been tragically taken from their lives. It's another defense mechanism: God has a plan, everything happens for a reason. I just can't accept that a benevolent god could violently take a young man from his family and fiancé because of some divine plan.

Our lives evolve each day, with each decision we make, and with countless random events, of which we have little or no control. Guy had an infinite number of alternate futures, caused by the uncountable number of seemingly insignificant decisions made by him and others around him. Unfortunately, the long chain of events that led him to that Baron on that day turned out to be lethal. He wasn't traveling a course charted in the heavens to fulfill some mysterious good for humanity or the Earth or stars; this was a guy in the wrong place at the wrong time.

I now had the seniority to fly the Columbus routes, except for the day route, or to get out of town when I wanted to make some extra money. We had planned on me being home during a particular week to take care of our new puppy and to get a permanent filling in the hole left from my recent root canal.

Instead the Chief Pilot was sending me to Minneapolis, while leaving a junior Captain in Columbus to fly a route I had requested to fly. I complained to the Chief Pilot, but my protests were futile. The Chief Pilot justified it by saying the junior Captain was an instructor, and instructors stayed in town. He was a prop instructor, and he was taking a three-month break from instructing to fly the line as a Learjet pilot. I argued that if an instructor wants to be a line pilot for a few months, he needs to live by line pilot rules, but he wouldn't budge.

I was partially to blame for the situation. I had known all along that the guy was being awarded flying that he didn't have the seniority for, but I never protested until it actually affected me. If we, the entire pilot group, had collectively protested the first injustice, we would have corrected it immediately, but people tend to be apathetic to things that they think don't affect them.

I left town irritated by my circumstances and by the fact that the advertised meal service on the DC-9 turned out to be eleven peanuts. In Minneapolis, I followed signs down an escalator, up an escalator, and across a street to meet a bus that delivered me to an elevator a thousand feet away, which deposited me in a rental car line that wouldn't move while preferred customers were allowed to walk right up to the counter.

A familiar voice greeted me from the end of the rapidly growing line. I didn't recognize him until I looked closely at his face. I knew him from the flight school, someone I hadn't seen in probably eight or nine years. He had been an all-American boy with a bright future. He was an athlete, an alternate for the Olympic rifle team, Army ROTC, and eventually an Army helicopter pilot. Since I had last seen him, his regulation crew cut had grown into a long pony tail. He wore a baggy bohemian shirt, and he had a cynical look in his eye, which could've been evidence of a drastically changed world view but more likely was just irritation that we were obviously going to grow old while waiting for our rental cars.

We had plenty of time to catch up, although we only exchanged superficial histories. He wasn't flying any more, but I didn't ask him why. He probably had a story to tell. He certainly didn't know how much my own world view had changed. My appearance hadn't, except that now I always looked tired, or so I was told.

Later I heard he had been wronged by his employer, sued them and won, and then just gave up flying, figuring no one would hire a pilot who had taken a previous employer to court.

I flew from Minneapolis to Des Moines and waited for a jet coming from Denver that was running late because it had deviated around thunderstorms en route. My co-pilot was going to fly the next leg, so I reminded him that we weren't going to hurry to make our tight deadline in Columbus. I really didn't want to be there, and although I wasn't going to sabotage the operation, I was also in no mood to do the company any favors.

It was a holiday, or at least close to one. As I passed Dayton at 24,000 feet, I saw tiny glowing puffs flickering near downtown. They were so tiny and dim that it took me a moment to realize they were fireworks. I guess, like Columbus, Dayton was having their annual July gun powder extravaganza a day early, reserving the fourth for each of the individual suburbs to waste their money on their own shows. Just then a bolt of cloud-to-cloud lightning streaked across the sky for ten miles. Now that was truly impressive.

My co-pilot flew a fast approach into Columbus, configuring the airplane late, something I had already told him I don't do. When he asked for the landing gear, I put the gear handle down and only saw two green landing gear position lights. That wasn't good. I flicked the test switch, confirming that the position bulb for the right main was burned out. The landing gear was probably down, but you can never assume anything: To assume makes an ass out of you and me. There were still other ways to determine that the gear was down, but I didn't want to discuss them while rapidly descending below a thousand feet when we still had plenty of fuel in the tanks. Never create an emergency where none exists.

I told my co-pilot, and the tower, that we were going around. Somewhat shamefully, I have to admit some satisfaction as I told dispatch we'd be a couple minutes late in order to ensure I didn't wreck their two million dollar airplane. We slowed everything down, handled the problem correctly, and got back in line for the approach. Dispatch released the other airplanes without us. My freight would miss the hub, which meant missed deadlines and lost revenue.

I finally got the call I had been waiting for, to schedule my simulator evaluation for the airline, the next phase in the interview process. My emotional roller-coaster continued. I prepared for the evaluation by simply doing what I already did every day, hard-core, raw data instrument flying in a slippery, transonic jet. I already hand flew all but the longest legs, unless I was really tired, but most importantly, I had always treated every leg as an opportunity to improve my skills or learn something new.

I flew to Milwaukee in the morning. A lady from Human Resources picked me up at the terminal and drove me to the training center. I was told I would need to score fifteen points to pass the simulator evaluation, but I wasn't told how points were actually scored. Now I was suddenly getting nervous. It didn't matter how well I actually played; I would need to score two touchdowns and a two-point conversion, and I didn't even know where the goal line was or whether that was even the correct game.

I had a chance to talk to a demoralized guy who had just flown the thing. He was an eleven thousand hour 737 Captain at a start-up airline, and he thought the simulator was too hard to fly! He complained that he must've been given the wrong power settings, or maybe there was something wrong with the simulator, because he was chasing speeds the whole time. Now I was really nervous.

It was my turn. I sat in the right seat of the non-motion, desktop contraption that was supposed to simulate an MD-80. In the left seat was a check airman who would be my non-flying pilot. Behind me was the check airman running the evaluation, another check airman learning how to operate this new contraption, a Federal Aviation Administration Inspector, and a line pilot sent by the union. I didn't expect that large of an audience. Actually, I didn't expect any audience, other than the two other people who had to be there. I knew that if any of them saw something they didn't like, I wouldn't get the job.

They gave me a couple of minutes to look over the profile. It looked easy enough. I had to take off, climb, descend, and turn to assigned headings, track to an NDB (Non Directional Beacon, an antique radio station), and then enter a hold at the NDB. Then I would fly an ILS (Instrument Landing System) approach down to minimums.

The simulator wasn't necessarily hard to fly. I nailed the NDB hold. I nailed the approach, and then I was on the ground. The check airman thanked me for coming, and told me that I would get a phone call if I passed; a letter if I didn't. Then I shook lots of hands and left, to go spend the rest of the day with my harshest critic.

I replayed the short flight over and over in my mind, looking for mistakes. I found them. I don't think I reduced to climb power at fifteen-hundred feet like the profile had directed. Would I lose a point for that, or just not get a point that I needed in order to pass? I was making myself sick waiting by the phone. This was worse than the day after my interview.

I had to get out of the house, but I still couldn't get it out of my mind. I had never flown an MD-80, but that thing was easier to fly than the airplane I flew every day. My flight wasn't perfect, but I still flew the hell out of it, and I did it all raw-data. Certainly all those eyes in the room could recognize genuine talent.

I got home to find a message on the answering machine, the Assistant Chief Pilot congratulating me for passing the simulator evaluation. I kept replaying the message, hoping I wasn't just imagining it.

A few years later, I would fly with the line pilot who observed my simulator evaluation, and he filled me in on why I had such a large audience. They had just bought the contraption, and it was proving to be a tough nut to crack. Of the thirty interviewees who flew it, only two of us passed. Since every interviewee was flying as Captain on some jet or turboprop, they decided the machine was probably just too hard to fly, so they invited the other twenty-eight back for another chance, in a real simulator.

When I finally talked to the Assistant Chief Pilot, he said I would need to go back to Milwaukee right away for a company physical, one more hoop to jump through, but at least it wasn't one I was nervous about. He said they would start a DC-9 new-hire class at the end of August and an MD-80 new-hire class two weeks later. He would start calling people with their class dates the following Monday.

Monday passed with no call. That night dispatch sent me to Hartford, Connecticut, and left me there. I knew I would miss my call, since I was one of the last people in the country to buy a cell phone.

I did miss the call. By the time I finally talked to the Assistant Chief Pilot on Wednesday, he said the classes were full, but they would probably have another DC-9 class in January. I was pissed. The first twenty people who answered their phones got class dates. The rest of us were in the pool. After all I had been through to get this job, my future depended on me being one of the first people to answer my phone the next time they had a new-hire class.

Someone needed to go to Burbank the next week to fly the mirror image of my old route from Charlotte (the Burbank-based crew spent Tuesday and Thursday in Charlotte). I volunteered, thinking it would be therapeutic to watch the continent pass beneath me over, and over, and over again, to remind me how insignificant I really was, just an invisible speck between the immensity of Earth and sky.

The Burbank co-pilot was a former Marine helicopter pilot who was now flying the most important route in the company. I hate to admit that I stereotyped the guy before even meeting him, but the only experience I had with Marine pilots was watching the movie *The Great Santini*. I felt especially compelled to share my philosophy with him, that there would be no shame in not getting the job done and that this was no place for hurrying or for heroics.

He was okay with that, and he even gave me an interesting compliment when we got to Charlotte the next morning, that I had a good equilibrium. That was probably the best compliment another pilot had ever given me, because I hadn't always had it; I learned it. He followed that with, "Some people treat this job like they were going to war, but all we're really doing is hauling paper."

He had a good equilibrium too. He had seen enough people do stupid things in his career. He had decided long ago that he wasn't going to die for some Colonel's peacetime war games in Hawaii. He wasn't a loyal ultra-nationalistic type who borrowed his very identity from the Corps. Flying helicopters had just been his day job as he coasted through life in the tropics.

I got an urgent call from the Assistant Chief Pilot at the airline. I called him back that evening from my hotel room in Charlotte. Someone had dropped out of the August DC-9 class because of a family emergency. He said he could tell I was disappointed the last time we had talked, so he wanted me to fill the vacancy. I accepted, although now I wouldn't even be able to give two week's notice. I called Dawn and then I began writing a letter.

I didn't know how I would feel to turn in my resignation letter. I loved and hated the company at the same time. I had grown up there. I had arrived as a novice, but after seven years and six thousand hours of hard-core flying through the dark side, I was leaving as a professional. The company allowed me to see the country and unexpectedly changed how I saw the world. As I passed through Columbus that night, I tried to show no emotion as I stoically handed the Chief Pilot my letter, something that is usually quite natural for me, but I felt my cheeks lift into a smile that was absolutely impossible to repress.

The last time I had flown this route I was trying in vain to relive a moment of my former carefree existence in Charlotte, the blissful time of my life that had resulted from the sole spontaneous decision of my life. This time on the Charlotte-to-Burbank run, quite unexpectedly, I was saying goodbye.

Knowing I was flying a Learjet for the last time was more difficult than I thought it would be. When I set the parking brake and listened to the TFE731 engines unspool into a rapidly fading memory, I realized something amazing was over. It was more than just an airplane. It was like a first love, which I would inevitably compare to all the other airplanes in my future, airplanes that I doubted would quite measure up. The Learjet flew like it owned the sky, and when my hands were on the controls, I felt like I owned the sky too by extension. Ethereal to the touch, it is a truly transcendent airplane that allows a pilot to feel like an artist and occasionally approach perfection. I had already flown the best airplane of my career and I knew it.

Homesick Rick

Soon I was leaving for class, like a leaf caught by a gust of wind. I had only been married for three months, and now I didn't know when I would get home. This career is notorious for failed marriages, for reasons that I was too new to marriage to understand. I hoped I was doing the right thing.

When I met my classmates, and learned their backgrounds, I realized I was exactly average in the class in nearly every conceivable way. We were all married, except for one who was getting a divorce, a detail he hadn't disclosed in his interview. I was the average age at thirty. I had the average amount of flight time, with 7,500 hours. We all had Airline Transport Pilot Licenses with a type rating. We were all Captains on jets or turboprops, except for one who was a DC-9 First Officer at another airline. There was also an Air Force DC-9 (C-9) pilot. There was a corporate Learjet pilot who had flown freight, but most came from the commuters, except they had all done time at the old commuters, without autopilots or automated RJs.

One of the instructors admitted that they liked to hire pilots who'd done hard time, meaning they wanted pilots with lots of experience flying multiple legs every day in all weather. Basically, they wanted strong instrument flying skills—wise since they had a fleet of antique DC-9s. Otherwise, the pattern of similarities suggested they had a mold they wanted to fill, and I got hired because I happened to fit into that mold. I was a lucky beneficiary of an idea I despised, although at least flying experience was part of their mold.

We endured three days of orientation, a company-wide group hug and cookie festival washed down with a syrupy torrent of Kool-Aid. We heard legendary stories about the little airline that could, about how against seemingly insurmountable odds the airline saved itself from certain doom by inventing what would become its trademark, the chocolate chip cookie.

All of the pilots were too cynical to fall for it, an inevitable byproduct of doing hard time in aviation. I knew I had already enjoyed the best schedule of my career, except for staying up all night. I had already flown the best airplane of my career, and now I was taking a twenty-thousand dollar pay cut with six weeks of ground school ahead of me and an uncertain future.

The pilots' patience was wearing thin by diversity training on day three, which was a ridiculous exercise and not necessarily because it wasn't worthwhile. It's just that the people who need it the most are also going to be the most belligerently resistant to it, especially after a three-day pep rally. The naturally tolerant people who don't actually need the training are the ones who don't mind sitting through it, and can you really train a jerk to not be a jerk?

The Chief Pilot, the new Director of Flight Standards and Training, and the ground instructors gave us a more honest assessment of the airline once the pep rally was behind us, except for the projection that we should all upgrade to Captain in thirty-six months. I didn't listen to that anyway. I needed to learn the job before I thought about upgrading. The pilots had their first union contract, and there were continuing differences of interpretation between management and the union, manifested in a large and growing backlog of grievances, contract violations yet to be resolved.

One of the main reasons why the pilots brought in a union, which passed by a very slim margin, four votes I believe, was to have protection from the brutality of the old training department, which ruined countless careers by firing so many pilots in training. Pilots were terrified of training events, some even becoming physically ill from the stress of the absolute jeopardy of each training event, never more than six months away. Even a former Air Force One pilot had washed out of new-hire training, a guy who was surely no slouch. The company only hired professionals, so the high failure rate, actually any failure rate, was just unnecessary harassment.

Now the training department was contractually responsible for training the pilots to standards. I wouldn't say the instructors were spoon-feeding us, but we weren't drinking from one end of a fire hose while being flogged with the other end either. Most importantly, we weren't facing each new day with the threat of being fired.

The content of the training was also an indication that I had entered a new culture. No one tried to explain how to get away with breaking rules by operating in alleged cracks between regulations. No one ever mentioned that if a flight cancels the airline might lose some money. No one mentioned whether maintenance was more expensive at an outstation. The closest anyone ever came to mentioning a schedule was in explaining how long a flight release is valid, and when you need to call and get a new one. No one read the least relevant part of the Federal Aviation Regulations to us in its entirety. The purpose of ground school was to prepare us to do the job safely, correctly, and legally. Completion was never mentioned; if there was any question about safety, the flight would cancel.

The pace of training was relaxed, with a long break every hour. I never felt like I would need to study until late at night in order to keep up. To the contrary, my classmates and I would get together every evening after class at a bar between the airport and the training center, sit out on the patio watching DC-9s roaring into the evening sky, and try to remember why we were torturing ourselves in a classroom for six weeks so far from home.

While we were all sitting in a classroom, having taken pay cuts to begin at the bottom of the airline's pay scale, $38 an hour, basically $38,000 a year, another airline had just accepted a contract with a top end of $355 per hour (about $350,000 per year) for 747-400 Captains and a no-furlough clause. That was $200 an hour more than the top end at my new airline.

Was I selling myself short by thinking I had made it to a career airline? I suddenly regretted not stuffing mailboxes in the other airline's flight department while I was in college, which would've guaranteed me an interview there. There was nothing I could do about now, an opportunity lost.

Eventually the other airline's pilots would lose as well after a couple of trips through bankruptcy court. The exorbitant pay rates would go away completely, as well as their pensions and the company stock that they couldn't touch until retirement. The no-furlough clause didn't prevent thousands of pilots from hitting the street as the airline was slowly dismantled.

I had finally acquired a cell phone, and I usually had a message from Dawn when I turned my phone on during breaks. Because I spent much of my break time listening to voicemails and returning calls, my classmates gave me the nickname Homesick Rick. I didn't mind having a nickname, except that I didn't know about it until four years later when someone said: "I know who you are; you're Homesick Rick."

Anyone who knows me wouldn't be surprised that I was the most reserved member of my new-hire class. I'm not ashamed of who I am, and my classmates didn't make me feel ashamed, but they did have some fun with my persona in a crumbling bar in a bad part of town.

We were there for mini-bowling, and a drunken pregnant lady stumbled into our group. She was so wasted she could barely hold her cigarette and stand up straight at the same time. She was dubbed our "pregnant crack whore," although it was unfair to label her like that; I guess she could have been a meth whore instead. Regardless, she was truly hideous. With drops of slobber flying from her numb lips, she told us that she had gotten knocked up as soon as she got out of prison. Then she repeatedly punched her rounded belly that contained her captive twin boys and said with a drunken slur, "My boys are gonna be mean. They're gonna kick some ass."

It was tremendously unfortunate, especially for these two babies, that this hideous woman was able to reproduce. These babies had been physically beaten and were undoubtedly addicted to nicotine, alcohol, and cocaine or meth, and they hadn't even been born yet. They didn't appear to be from the best genetic stock either. I hope I'm wrong, but I think it will be miraculous for these kids to have happy, healthy, prosperous lives.

As the most reserved and most sober member of the class, I became the subject of a joke. One of my classmates quietly told the pregnant crack whore that I had the biggest dick he had ever seen. This fictitious allegation really impressed the pregnant crack whore, who stumbled toward me with hands aimed at my crotch. As flattering as it was to have a woman fixated on my anatomy, I was relieved when she was soon kicked out of the bar for hurling bowling balls in a drunken tantrum.

After about six weeks of ground school, I had three weeks off before coming back to Milwaukee for three days in the cockpit procedures trainer. Then I would get another week off before going to the simulator.

I finally rode in the jumpseat of one of the airline's old DC-9s. The pilots made me feel welcome, like I belonged there. The cockpit of the DC-9 was much roomier than the Learjet, but being the same thirty-year-old technology, or should I say lack thereof, as my old Learjets, it had a familiar, industrial feel. Worn switches and analog gauges filled the scuffed and cracked aluminum and plastic panels that were even painted the same shade of gray as my Learjets. The cockpit smelled much different than the musty locker room odor of my old Learjets, which had permeated my clothes and hair after flying all night. The DC-9 cockpit was filled with the aroma of fresh coffee brewing and the cookies baking in the galley on the other side of the cockpit door.

I had a lot of confidence going into the simulator. We would get a few sessions in the cockpit procedures trainer, the actual cockpit from an old dismantled Eastern Airlines DC-9, and nine four-hour simulator sessions, which would be a tremendous amount of training and practice compared with what I was used to.

Simulators are always harder to fly than the airplanes they simulate, but even the DC-9 simulator was more stable than the airplane I had been flying every day. Our first three instructors were fantastic and maintained a relaxed, friendly environment. This was how training should be. My simulator partner and I were making a lot of progress, and then we met an instructor from the old regime, who would be our instructor for our last three sessions before our checkride.

Everything about our new instructor oozed nervous energy. We arrived early for our session. He sat down in a briefing room but then jumped up as if he'd sat on a tack, and he kept opening the door to see if the simulator was vacant yet. He looked like he was about to jump out of his skin, and we hadn't even started yet.

His frantic pace continued as we entered the simulator. My partner and I, new to the company and the DC-9, were appropriately slow and deliberate. As I sat down, I placed the takeoff performance card against the instrument panel and set my airspeed bug while my hand was still there. He immediately yelled, "What are you doing? You don't have time for that now!" That was bullshit of course. You always set the airplane up for departure while you're still at the gate, while the passengers are fighting for overhead bin space, not while you're taxiing the airplane at a busy airport on a rainy night, a time when pilots shouldn't be diverting much of their attention inside the cockpit. It's a checklist item, but you're just checking to make sure you set it properly. Besides, this is the airlines; if you're not ready, you don't leave the gate yet. We get points for accuracy, not speed.

As we were getting the airplane ready, the instructor warned me I would need a lot of rudder to keep the airplane on the runway when we lost an engine on takeoff, this being our first day of engine failures. I asked him if it would require full rudder. He looked surprised. In a Learjet, you would jam full rudder and then take out what you don't need, to keep the airplane out of the weeds. The DC-9 was quite docile by comparison; just a little rudder and don't raise the nose quite as high on rotation. You could probably lose an engine after takeoff without the passengers even being aware that anything was wrong, unless they noticed the sluggish climb rate.

A couple of hurried minutes later, I was accelerating past decision speed when we got an engine fire indication. We were at Washington National Airport, so I climbed over the river, maneuvering to follow the engine-out departure procedure. We ran the emergency checklist, but we weren't able to extinguish the fire. We got the airplane ready to return to the airport as quickly as we could. In reality, I would've I would've taken the airplane up to a nice long runway at Dulles Airport, but this was training, so he said that option wasn't available. Everything was going fine, except for the fact that we were still on fire, but the instructor interrupted us. "Do you have all of your radios set up?" I answered yes. "Are you sure?" Yes. "What about the NDB at the missed approach hold?" I explained that I was on fire and I did not intend to miss the approach, and even if I did, I had declared an emergency and there was absolutely no way that I would enter a hold. I had set both ADFs, the radios that receive NDB, to the NDB along the final approach course, which would be much more useful than an arbitrary point that I absolutely would not be orbiting after missing the approach. I had prioritized in an emergency, and now I had to listen to a lecture about something that was completely non-essential to the situation, but he was the instructor, so I had to listen and play the missed approach NDB game.

There's a simple phrase that all pilots know that serves as a framework for prioritizing tasks; aviate, navigate, communicate. Always fly the airplane first. Air traffic controllers can't fly it for you, so they aren't a priority. On the next single-engine approach, I was way ahead of things. We were actually flying for a few miles with nothing to do, a rare moment during an emergency, but once I hit the final approach fix, I would burden my non-flying pilot with three things all at once, one of them being almost trivial, to contact the tower. I decided to have her go ahead and get the least important thing done while we had nothing else to do; I told her to go ahead and check in with the tower before we actually got busy again with important tasks.

The instructor immediately yelled, "You can't do that!" Once again, I was prioritizing during an emergency, this time metering my partner's workload during an emergency. I had already played my trump card: I had declared an emergency, which meant that I could do whatever I needed to, within reason. Any other pilot, instructor, examiner, or controller, would've considered that to be very wise use of a rare slow moment, but right now I apparently couldn't do anything right.

My partner's session didn't go any better than mine; at least there was just as much shouting from the jumpseat. When we went back to the briefing room, we sat down with our notebooks out, expecting a harsh critique based on how much this guy had yelled at us over the past four hours. Our instructor entered the room, and said, "You guys did a nice job. Any questions? Okay, let's get out of here." Without even waiting for us to respond, he turned around and left the room, turning off the lights on his way out, leaving my partner and I stunned, trying to pack up our notebooks in the dark, windowless briefing room.

My partner and I got together the next morning to study. We had each already decided that if today didn't go better than yesterday, we would ask for another instructor. We wouldn't need to. He wasn't exactly patient, but he was certainly tolerable that day. He even gave us a thorough debriefing over dinner.

I ignored the instructor's nervous energy and just tried to get through the end of training. He certainly gave us lots of practice. If flight attendants had brought us a meal service every time we had an engine fire, we undoubtedly would've become conditioned to salivate when the fire bell rang. Every takeoff was from Runway 1 at Washington National, a short runway with a complex engine out departure procedure. Every approach was to an airport with a one-hundred-foot cloud ceiling and minimum visibility and with an engine out or some other emergency.

After one engine failure, the instructor forgot to set the weather, and I saw the airport beside us while we were on our way to fly an approach. I commented that I could dead-stick the airplane in from there. The instructor heard me and immediately reached over to his control panel and killed my other engine. Now I was in a hundred-thousand-pound glider, three thousand feet above Arlington, Virginia. There would be no margin for error, dead-sticking into a short runway surrounded by water on a dark night. I would basically need to thread a needle with the big, heavy glider.

I turned the DC-9 toward the Potomac River, keeping the airplane clean as long as possible (without drag from slats, flaps, and landing gear). Nearing the river, I began configuring for landing and planned my turn to final just like I would if I was dead-sticking a Learjet, aimed at the runway numbers with a steeper glide path and some extra speed. On very short final I called for the last notch of flaps and flattened our glide path, bleeding off our extra speed just before we entered the flare. I set the main wheels down in the touchdown zone, right on speed, and began stopping the big machine, forgetting at first that the DC-9 wouldn't have auto-spoilers or antiskid while on emergency power, a lesson I wouldn't soon forget since I neglected to have my partner start the auxiliary power unit for backup electricity. Even with that considerable handicap to landing distance, I managed to stop the big airplane on the very short runway.

This instructor seemed to get a perverse thrill from crashing the simulator. He wouldn't freeze the simulator when he wanted to stop and explain something. He would just tell us to let go of the airplane and make us watch it crash into the ground, while we were in it, somewhat of a distraction from what he was trying to teach us in the interim. I was certain the instructor thought we would end up in the water at the end of my dead-stick approach, which would doubtlessly have given him much pleasure, and that's exactly where we would've been if I had undershot or overshot the tiny runway built into a river bend by even the smallest margin in either direction. It's where we would've been if I hadn't already had lots of practice in Learjets, amusing myself while honing my skills in the middle of the night, but it's also a skill you need to have an eye for, and not everyone does.

We had the opportunity to have a beer with our examiner the night before our checkride. There could be no better way to get to know someone who had so much control over our fates. Even better, my examiner and I had a common history. He once flew for my old freight airline.

The checkride turned out to be one of the best I had ever had. It went well from the start, but by the time we were doing the last set of required maneuvers, which happened to be a stall series, I realized that the checkride was actually becoming a work of art. I was even getting a little cocky as I briefed my partner for the last stall, having saved the easiest one for last. Brashness was out of character for me, but I was having fun with it. The examiner could hear it in my voice too, let out a slightly irritated sigh, stood up, opened the door, and stepped outside onto the catwalk on the back of the simulator.

After the simulator's hydraulic legs had pitched down slightly, the examiner knew I had finished the stall recovery. He opened the door, stepped back inside the box, and said, "Congratulations. Now do you mind if I fly this thing with our remaining time?"

I had a couple more weeks off, when I got two important calls. One was from the instructor who had abused me for the last three simulator sessions before our checkride. I needed to get three landings in a real DC-9 before I could fly with passengers, and he was calling to schedule a flight with me. He also wanted to apologize for his behavior in the simulator. He said he had been spending a lot of time with his brother who was dying of cancer, and his mind just wasn't on the job. It seemed like a sincere apology. I was looking forward to flying a real airplane with him.

The other call was from another airline, the only other airline I had applied to so far, to schedule an interview. What bad timing. The lazy part of me didn't want to prepare for an interview after finishing new-hire training, just to potentially have to endure new-hire training somewhere else. The cheap part of me didn't want to spend several thousand dollars for a 737 type rating in order to get the job. Training costs are just part of doing business; they shouldn't be passed along to the pilots. The loyal part of me didn't want to dump a company right after they spent tens of thousands of dollars to train me on an airplane I haven't even flown had the chance to fly yet.

Job security didn't seem like an important consideration between the two airlines. They had both always been profitable, even during the early nineties when the rest of the industry was losing money. Both airlines had found their own unique niches, although I didn't realize yet how inexcusably inept my airline's management was at actually exploiting what was a truly unique and superior product. A famous investment sage from Omaha was reputed to have said that no company has ever done so little with so much.[5] Unfortunately I didn't know that yet, that they were actually profitable in spite of their failure to truly exploit their niche. I was expecting to upgrade to Captain in three years, as I had been told to expect. I turned down the interview, which may have turned out to be the biggest mistake in my career, but we'll never know since that story wasn't written. I might not have gotten the job anyway.

I went to Omaha to do my landings, by way of Milwaukee to get my charts. A twenty-minute van ride took me to a hotel that probably had not been approved by the union's hotel committee. I was hungry, I had a terrible headache, and I needed to get to bed. I had to be at the airport at five in the morning.

I knew the squeal coming from the heater in my room would keep me up, especially with my splitting headache. I moved into a new room, with a well-rested heater. I shivered between the icy sheets as the heater slowly warmed up the room. A metallic scraping noise from the heater woke me up around midnight. I tried to fix it the freight dog way by banging on the side of the machine. I tried to ignore it, but nearing one in the morning, I moved into another cold room.

Three hours later I was in a daze, standing ankle deep in cool water from a shower that wouldn't drain, wondering what I was doing there. I hadn't flown an actual airplane in three and a half months, and surprisingly, at that early moment I didn't even miss it that much. I should've been more excited to fly a DC-9, but I was just tired and irritated.

Soon enough I was sitting in the right seat of a DC-9, about to begin my first takeoff in the big jet. I pushed the throttles up about halfway and waited. I watched the needles on all of the gauges grudgingly move as the JT8D engines slowly spooled up. I continued to push the throttles forward until the EPR gauges (engine pressure ratio, a measurement of power) indicated takeoff power. From my new seat, much higher up than my seat in a Learjet, our acceleration seemed sluggish. The rush of wind around the big blunt nose steadily increased, and soon thirty-year-old switches rattled all around me as the old airplane shook. Wind whistled through the gaps around the clear view window, the same gaps that would inevitably drip rainwater and de-icing fluid on my right arm and my charts once I was out flying the line. The instructor called "V1," (takeoff decision speed), meaning we were committed to fly and in the same breath "rotate." With a gentle pull on the control yoke, the nose wheels lifted away from the pavement. The rest of the airplane hesitated and then climbed into the cold morning air.

Take-off in a DC-9 wasn't anything like a take-off in a Learjet, which accelerates smoothly and briskly, without whistles or vibrations, and then eagerly leaps toward the stratosphere. Take-off in a DC-9 was more like how I imagined the big piston engine airliners of an earlier era must've been, except without the growl of radial engines.

My first flight in the big airplane was pretty unremarkable. It was solid, stable, and easy to fly, just what a transport should be. One of my friends had described it as flying a Learjet through syrup. I thought it was like flying a giant jet-powered Navajo, surprisingly responsive for the fact that your control inputs only move small controls tabs on the backs of the control surfaces. From the cockpit I couldn't tell that I now had a hundred-and-twenty feet of airplane behind me. As I nudged the control yoke, I couldn't tell that a hundred-thousand pounds of mass was responding to my commands. The airplane I had loved since I first flew on one in October of 1979 was just another airplane. My left hand controlled a pair of JT8Ds, the engines that propelled all of the jetliners of my youth, but I could barely even hear those distant noisy engines from the cockpit.

The instructor was a different person than he had been in the simulator, more relaxed than I thought he could be. He just sat there and read checklists for me and gave me occasional tips. I would end up flying the line with him several times in the coming years, and it was always a joy.

I can't remember now anything about those first three landings, which means they must've been pretty bad. I had to learn a new picture before I could get a decent landing, since my eyes were so much higher above the runway as the main wheels were already impacting it.

I had passed another hurdle though, and after a single day off, I would move on to the next one, Initial Operating Experience (IOE), flying a real revenue trip under the supervision of a line check airman. I would make my first step into airline operations, but I would still have one foot in training. The training department could still grab my ankle and pull me back to their side of the fence, or worse. There are stories of pilots getting fired on their first day of IOE, but that was under the old training regime. I was still worried that I was about to do a job that I didn't really know enough about yet. I knew how to fly a DC-9, but I only had a vague idea of my preflight and post-flight duties, and I didn't know anything about company paperwork.

Captain Dave eased my fears immediately. He told me I had finished training and now we would just go fly and have fun. He said we would do everything slow and he would let me know when it was time for me to do something. And that is how the day went.

When we reached our cruise altitude, Captain Dave asked me to talk to the passengers. I had never even considered that I would need to do that. I had too much else to think about. I held the phone in my hand, wondering what to say. The only thing I was required to say was that while you're in your seat, to please keep your seat belt fastened, which you really need to listen to, lest you become a projectile if the airplane finds some unexpected turbulence. All the rest is fluff. I wanted minimal fluff and no "ums" to fill the gaps. I composed my thoughts, keyed the handset, and spoke to our captive audience.

One of the flight attendants knocked on the door to tell me that no one could hear my announcement and that I also hadn't hung up the phone. You can't hold the phone like a phone when you're making a PA, because your own feedback will make you talk too quietly. You also have to slam the phone into its mount in order to turn off the

PA. These are things that veteran flight attendants are happy to teach a new pilot.

We soared above a serene sea of clouds that stretched unbroken from Milwaukee to Boston, while sipping coffee and eating eggs Benedict and fresh fruit in a cockpit that was more than twice as big as what I was used to. I was flying again, but now with style. I realized that this was my first enjoyable day at my new job and that I really had been miserable for the past three-and-a-half months as I started down a new and unfamiliar path.

After arriving in Boston, at least a dozen passengers thanked us for the nice flight. While a new load of passengers boarded, I heard a man behind me say, "Say hello to the pilots; these are the guys who are going to fly us home." I turned my head to see a tiny shy girl peeking into the cockpit. I smiled, waved, and said "Hello." I felt like I was finally doing something noble with my skills. I never felt that way about flying money around on the dark side of the planet.

Captain Dave helped me with my preflight duties, and then we flew to Kansas City. After just two legs, five-and-a-half hours of flying, and seven hours of duty, my first day as an airline pilot was over.

Captain Dave and I went to the hotel next door to ours and waited like vultures for the free Tuesday night happy-hour buffet. Airline pilots always know where to find cheap food, and I would eventually find out why.

Four other pilots from the airline walked into the lounge and joined us. With introductions, I told everyone it was my first day on the job. One of the pilots jokingly asked if I was still somewhere back in the contrail. Before I could even respond, Dave came to my defense; "No, he flew Learjets, he's doing fine." Otherwise, they immediately accepted me as one of their own. This was much different than where I came from. I was allowed to have my own identity, even on my first day. I wasn't just Captain Dave's co-pilot; I was First Officer Rick, and it was just assumed that I belonged there among them.

The next morning we left early for New York's La Guardia airport. We flew the Milton Arrival, with all of its turns, crossing radials, and crossing restrictions, with nothing more than the wandering needles of the forty-year-old navigation technology that our DC-9s were equipped with, navigating the same way a pilot would have in 1960.

All of our Learjets had at least been equipped with GPS satellite navigation, but these antique DC-9s didn't even have a groundspeed readout on our Distance Measuring Equipment (DME).

We got into La Guardia without doing any holding but then waited in line for more than an hour to take off. A lot of pilots would rather avoid La Guardia because of common and lengthy delays there. I would learn to love the airport. Flying two holding patterns on the way in and then waiting in line for an hour on the way out meant a couple of extra hours of pay. If the flight was delayed for hours, duty rig would likely give you some extra pay. If the flight cancelled, you'd get paid for something you never even had to do. There really wasn't a down side, unless you ended a trip with a delayed La Guardia turn, which was at times fairly common, but you were almost as likely to have that turn cancel and be able to go home earlier than planned.

If the weather was nice, the flying in New York could be a lot of fun. The expressway visual approach to runway 31 was my second favorite approach in our system, after the river visual to runway 19 at Washington National. The expressway visual allows a pilot to be a pilot, with a descending, sweeping turn from 2500 feet to the runway. To do it smoothly, and to do it well, you're elevating your skills to a level of artistry that separates the novices from the pros.

If you are landing on runway 22 from the Milton Arrival, you start at the enormous Verrazano Narrows Bridge, which actually has a suspended span sixty feet longer than the Golden Gate's, and then fly to the Statue of Liberty and continue up the Hudson River, which is the only true fjord in the Lower 48. You round the top of Manhattan Island and approach from the western tip of Long Island Sound and then land on a short runway built on a pier in Flushing Bay.

If you arrive from the north, you get the Westchester County real estate appreciation tour, and there are some real multi-million-dollar estates, hundreds of them, in the seventh wealthiest county in the country. This is the kind of wealth that most people only get to occasionally glimpse in novels or news coverage of crumbling Ponzi schemes.

I have always been intimidated by the size, the crowds, and the pace of New York, and I still am, but I've learned to appreciate it because it is possibly the most authentic place in the country. It is much too diverse, and busy, to fully develop, perpetuate, and manufacture a marketable identity. New York is the true American melting pot, which actually makes it seem less American than any other place in the country. New Yorkers have a brusque reputation, but they're just people, and they'll go out of their way to help someone in need, which is normally me, something that is always quite obvious to the natives.

We flew from La Guardia to Indianapolis, which had just become the airline's covert new focus city. I say covert, because without a true advertising budget, the company never told anyone they were flying there. I like to think I ignore advertising, the propaganda of consumer nation, but still, if you want to have customers you have to let them know that you're open for business. The company didn't, and the next morning we flew one passenger to Boston. Eighty-four big, business class seats, three flight attendants, a gas guzzling DC-9, and the airline sold one ticket. My cabin announcements were easy. I addressed them directly to Jane, but first I would ask the flight attendants whether or not Jane was sleeping.

The next morning, day four of our four-day trip, we flew from Indianapolis to La Guardia. The flight was booked to five, but another airline sent us about thirty passengers after an RJ (Regional Jet) to La Guardia cancelled. We only had meals for the five passengers that were originally booked on our flight, so all of the other airline's passengers could only drool over the first class, champagne breakfast.

Our extra passengers said that if they would've known about the airline, they would've bought tickets on it. Of course they would have, but they didn't get another chance. The company had to stop the bleeding and ended the Indianapolis disaster just as quietly as it had begun. The company posted its first quarterly loss since about 1985. This would prove to be somewhat of a turning point for the airline, when they truly lost their way, and unluckily for me, it happened to be when I joined it. I didn't know it yet when I turned the other airline down a couple weeks prior.

The next week I was scheduled to finish my IOE on a two-day trip with Captain Bob, who was even more relaxed than Captain Dave had been, in spite of the fact that the weather was horrible. Captain Bob let me fly the first leg to Columbus, which was very foggy. This was my first flight in a DC-9-10, the original un-stretched version. The landing attitude in the—10 is different than all the other models which all have leading edge slats, but I was still too new to the airplane to notice yet. Besides, we only saw the runway for the last few seconds of the flight.

We flew back to Milwaukee, where a couple of inches of snow had fallen in the couple of hours since we left. After a long delay for de-icing, we flew to Omaha and then Newark.

The whole crew met for an early dinner. We were all exhausted, slouched in our chairs as if it was midnight. Everyone complained about how much they would rather be home, including me. I never had a honeymoon period with this job; I knew I had already experienced the best schedule I would ever have.

One of the flight attendants said she wished she could have a normal job and sleep in her own bed every night. This was just an overnight trip. She would be home by noon the next day. She almost could sleep in her own bed every night. I reminded her that there were lots of people with normal jobs who wished that they could have hers, with glamorous overnights in an old Holiday Inn next door to the penitentiary in Newark, New Jersey, within sight of Manhattan but just out of reach. This was just part of the human condition, to want what you don't have.

When we met in the hotel lobby at five the next morning, Captain Bob told me that the Milwaukee airport had been closed much of the prior evening because of the thirteen inches of snow that had fallen yesterday. I mentioned that there might not be an airplane for us to fly. He said, "No, they would've called us."

We rode to the airport in a bus that was crammed way beyond capacity with sleepy pilots and flight attendants from several airlines, none of them smiling. As we walked past the airline's ticket counter, one of our agents asked why we were there. The last flight in last night, the flight that was bringing us an airplane, had cancelled. Crew scheduling forgot to call us.

We had been scheduled to fly to Milwaukee and then to Raleigh and back. Now we were just going to deadhead back to Milwaukee on the next flight out. Bob said he was sorry we wouldn't be able to finish my IOE, and that they wouldn't be able to get me into the IOE schedule again until next month.

I wasn't sorry about that. I wanted to get past this hurdle, but I knew that my inevitable reward for doing so was to sit in Milwaukee on reserve for nineteen days a month, in a crashpad that didn't even have furniture yet. I would much rather have three weeks of paid vacation, including Christmas off, while waiting to get back into the schedule.

Captain Bob started filling out my paperwork from the prior day and then suddenly exclaimed, "You already have twenty-five hours of IOE; I'll sign you off right now." I knew I had enough time, but the check airman also has to be comfortable releasing you to the line. I wasn't going to be pushy, asking him to sign me off without having finished the trip, especially when it would cost me the rest of the month off.

Thirteen years after learning to fly, eighteen months after I applied for this job, nine months after I interviewed, and four months after I started new-hire training, Bob signed off my IOE, and I was officially an airline pilot. From that point on, my life would be controlled by my seniority number. Seniority, or more appropriately a lack thereof, determines everything: what airplane you fly and from which seat (Captain or First Officer), where you're based, the kind of schedule you have (morning, evening, red-eye, stand-up, etc . . .), what days you work, and even when you go on vacation or if you can go on vacation. When you're on the bottom of the seniority list, you get what no one else wants. Conversely, you can't truly choose your course unless you're at the top of the list. That means that only one person truly gets to have seniority while everyone else has juniority.

We bid our schedules monthly within our base, equipment, and seat, in my case a Milwaukee-based DC-9 First Officer, of which there were about a hundred. Your seniority would determine how many of those hundred lines you would have to bid. You might get your first choice, but all you are guaranteed is to get the line no one else in front of you chose. That's the best that you can do until you've moved up the seniority list, and you can have no expectation about how quickly that will happen, or even if it will happen.

All of the DC-9 flying would be broken up into trips that were assembled into eighty or so bid lines. There was normally some continuity within each individual line. A given line might contain the same trip each week, or at least the same kind of trip, and on the same days of the week. If you worked a weekend, you generally worked them all. There were some lines with just out and back trips, where you would return to base the same day, but those weren't very common in the DC-9. Most of the lines had three—and four-day trips, which would normally start on the same day each week. Each line had a different value, based on how much its trips were worth. Each line had a different number of days off as well, from eleven to seventeen or eighteen, depending on how productive the trips were and what the line value was.

If you didn't have the seniority for a hard line, as just described, you could get a coverage line, which would be built from the trips that dropped out of other pilots' lines because of vacation, training, or monthly integration. You wouldn't have any control over your schedule, and you wouldn't even know your next month's schedule until near the end of the month, but it still beat reserve, usually.

The least desirable lines, which also meant the most junior, were the reserve lines. These are the crews who waited by their phones, ready to cover any open trips or to go to work when a line-holder called in sick or if crews were out of position or out of duty time because of irregular operations. A reserve would work more days for less money than anyone else. You may or may not get called on a reserve day, but you had to be in base, so for commuters, reserve meant lots of time away from home. The reserve lines had nineteen reserve days (our contractual maximum per month), assembled into four-and five-day and sometimes six-day blocks. At the time, we had a one-hour call out, which meant you always had to be ready to go to the airport during your reserve shift. Unless the company was badly understaffed, you were just going to make minimum guaranteed pay-at that time, seventy-five hours of pay per month.

Most of the line holders would fly about sixteen days and make about eighty-five hours per month, but that varied by line. If you wanted to work more, you could pick up a trip on a day off or you could trip trade with open time or with another pilot. Ultimately, flight time limitations and trip productivity would limit how many pay hours you could accrue. You could fly thirty hours in a week, a hundred in a month, and a thousand in a year. Some people might look at a thousand hours in a year and think it sounds like a part-time job, but to fly that much; you have to be away from home for most of the year.

Seniority within my new-hire class had been determined by drawing numbered poker chips out of the chief pilot's hat. My number put me in the middle of my class. That meant that until pilots in front of me upgraded, retired, or quit, and subsequently more new-hires came in behind me, all I could do each month was pick which five reserve lines I didn't want. I had to bid every line other than those. I would get what I would get. If there was one particular day I wanted to be off, I would have a fair shot, since I could throw out nearly half of the reserve lines. Two different days I needed off in a month would be tricky; I would have to pick which day was more important.

Having taken a substantial pay cut for this job, we decided to keep Dawn's job, which meant I would be commuting to Milwaukee to sit in a crashpad for nineteen day each month, waiting for the phone to ring.

Being junior usually meant working holidays. On the first day of the new millennium according to the Gregorian calendar, January 1, 2001, I flew from Milwaukee to Ft. Myers, Florida. While flying over Tampa, I could see the stadium where OSU was playing a bowl game, tiny specks on the field. Before taking this job, I would've watched the game and I would've even nervously cared who won. Now I couldn't watch, and I realized I shouldn't care. Victory belongs to the twenty-year-old strangers who play the game, and to the universities that profit from their athletes' success. I don't even remember who they played and who won. Neither do many of the spectators if they did too much drinking, and they even spent small fortunes to go there.

South of Tampa Bay is the wagon wheel-shaped town of Rotonda, which looks vaguely like the green circular center pivot irrigated fields of the high plains. Instead of spraying water from deep within the Oglala aquifer, Rotonda's spigots squirted radials of replicated retirement homes with golf courses and canals up the middle of each spoke.

Even from miles above you can see a distinct change in the salt marsh, which is now fringed with mangrove trees instead of the spartina grass of the marshes to the north. The Pine Island Sound and Matlacha Pass remain relatively wild, due to a disorganized amalgam of preserves and the fact that most of the islands that speckle the area are too small for golf courses or bridges from the mainland.

After landing in Ft. Myers, the Captain and I opened our clear view windows to a refreshing cool breeze that smelled of marsh and sea, the first temperate air I had breathed in a month.

As our sun-seeking passengers left the airplane, we heard lots of compliments about the wonderful flight; something I was learning is common at this airline. The compliments have little to do with the pilots, as long as a ham-fisted hack wasn't clumsily jerking the airplane around the sky and didn't pound the airplane onto the runway at the end of the flight. Just give them an oversized leather seat, a good meal, and free champagne, bake them a cookie, and give them a smile instead of a hassle, and it becomes the best airline experience they've ever had. It was satisfying to know the passengers were actually happy to be on the airplane, even if I had so little to do with the reasons why they're happy.

The next morning I had a four A.M. wakeup call in Boston. One leg back to Milwaukee, and we were done. I had been dreading early wakeups since coming over from the dark side, but I was learning they were actually a lot easier than staying up all night, which I never got used to anyway. I would set two alarms plus a wakeup call for these early mornings, just in case, but I was really just a cup of coffee and a sunrise away from having a normal day.

We were busy as we taxied to runway 27 at Boston. We had to talk to four different controllers on the way out, who issued three different hold short clearances, each one interrupting our pre-departure briefing. Reaching the end of the runway, we actually refused our takeoff clearance so I could give a proper briefing, without interruption.

It was a full flight, and we were at maximum weight for the short runway, a performance limitation, and that assumed our passengers really averaged 175 pounds each, an obsolete number that predated high fructose corn syrup and the 39 cent supersize deals at all of the fast food joints. Runway 27, aimed at the city of Boston, has a special engine-out departure procedure, which I included in my briefing. The left engine's thrust reverser was inoperative and deferred, and although reverse thrust wasn't included in our takeoff performance, we would still be missing a tool in our normal tool box if we needed to abort the takeoff.

Finally ready to go, we accepted our takeoff clearance. I was flying the leg, so I advanced the power levers. The Captain called "power normal," and we were on our way, accelerating down the short, seven-thousand foot long runway. With a last scan of the engine gauges, the Captain said "Look at that," while pointing to an oil quantity gauge, whose needle was rapidly falling toward the bottom of the scale. He then immediately yelled "Abort!" and brought more than a hundred-thousand pounds of metal, jet fuel, cargo, and humanity to a stop on our remaining pavement. The right engine had already lost ten of its twelve quarts of oil, so the Captain shut it down before we lost the rest and destroyed the engine.

If the Captain had flown the leg, and I was tasked with checking the engine gauges between trimming the power levers, and calling out speeds, I'm not sure I would've caught that. The oil quantity gauges were at the very bottom of the right hand stack of engine gauges. I had barely thirty hours in the airplane, plus another thirty-six hours in the simulator, so I still had to look for things. Learjets don't have oil quantity gauges, so I wasn't used to looking for them on the takeoff roll. If I hadn't noticed it, we would have lost the engine, possibly at the worst time imaginable—if not still on the short runway then in the initial climb, clawing for altitude as we executed the departure procedure that would turn us away from downtown Boston.

We took the passengers off the airplane while we waited for a mechanic. The flight attendants served our passengers breakfast and mimosas at the gate.

The mechanic refilled the oil and then asked us to start the engine. Oil gushed from the ruptured oil cooler. The mechanic gave us a technical explanation; "You're oil cooler is fucked." There wasn't a replacement in town, which seemed strange for an engine model that was still somewhat common.

There was another DC-9 on its way to Boston. It would be continuing on to Indianapolis, a market we were pulling out of soon. Someone wisely decided to cancel the Indianapolis flight and give us the other airplane.

Our crew was motivated to turn the airplane quickly; you see that a lot on the last leg of a trip, especially when the flight is delayed. The passengers were already boarding as I went out to do the walk around. Then I saw it. If I hadn't seen it, the large jagged pipe protruding from the bottom of the wing would've hit me in the head as I walked by. It was the telescoping duct that routes hot engine bleed air to the leading edge slats for in flight anti-icing, and it jammed, causing it to shear off and protrude from the bottom of the wing. Now we had two airplanes grounded in Boston.

My black cloud followed me into my next trip. While we were at the gate in Philadelphia, we heard a loud creaking that turned out to be a malfunctioning, sinking jet way bridge that nearly tore the forward entrance door off the airplane. Another airplane grounded. I don't believe in karma, but I did have a bad attitude, and I was having bad luck, maybe just a rookie's bad luck, but in a big way. I had grounded nearly 10 percent of the airline's fleet in just two trips.

There were lots of bad attitudes in the airlines, and I would eventually learn that the grievances were universal, no matter what color your uniform was; the schedules aren't productive enough, pay isn't high enough, you don't get enough time at home, and management is trying to pick apart your contract. So this was the glamorous life of an airline pilot? It was easy to get sucked into the misery, especially when you knew that many of the grievances were legitimate, you were even enduring them, and it could be a long time before it got better.

I never have understood why first year pay is so bad in the airlines. Because it has always been that way is not an acceptable reason. Now I was living it, and it was insulting. I could understand if the company was offering entry-level jobs to low-time pilots, but the company only hired experienced professionals.

I understood why my schedule sucked, but that didn't make sitting in a crashpad for nineteen days each month any easier. I had known all along that I had already had the best schedule of my career, but I don't necessarily think I was spoiled by that—well maybe a little. Part of my despair now came from the fact that there was absolutely nothing I could do about it from the bottom of another seniority list. I just had to wait until my number could hold a better schedule. I could only try to make peace with my new reality and with what I couldn't control.

My classmates were right; I was homesick. My only connection to home was my cell phone, which gave me a terrible headache behind my ear if I talked on it for a half hour. If I develop a brain tumor someday, I'll know exactly where it came from.

I know Dawn didn't know what she was getting into with this, not that I really understood either. When people found out I didn't come from another airline, one of the first questions they would always ask was, "How's your wife handling this?" They understood, more than Dawn or I did yet.

One of the Captains I flew with in my second month told me it was going to take a miracle to hold his marriage together. He also gave me some advice that a Captain had given him many years ago when he was a new-hire at Eastern Airlines; don't ever let your family know you're having a good time at work, because they'll always resent you for it. There was some legitimacy to his advice. We were always out in cities that people pay money to visit, trying to make the best of it while wishing we were home more. Meanwhile, your family may be trapped at home, wishing to get out more; opposite problems.

That seemed like a miserable way to live, leading two separate lives that could never intersect. I didn't know his history, but it was still worrisome to someone who had barely begun his own marriage and his airline career. I didn't want to be depending on a miracle like he was. I wanted to do anything I could to avoid that, and at the time, I took his advice seriously. I think I just let myself be miserable when I was away so I would have nothing anyone would envy, which was easy to do for nineteen days a month in a crashpad.

There was certainly nothing glamorous, exciting, or even remotely enviable about sitting in a crashpad, cheap communal housing for commuting flight crews. There were some young guys who flew for the company's commuter line, who, lacking families or places of their own, seemed to even live in the crashpad. With them came a second chance at the dorm life that I had missed in college, a long bunk room with rows of unkempt beds, cheap posters taped to the walls, a permanently grimy bathroom, a tangle of cords from video game controllers obstructing passage through the living room, a mountain of dirty dishes in the sink, and cheap beer next to moldy leftovers in the fridge. We already had enough camaraderie in the airplane, so as for dorm life, I realized I hadn't missed a thing.

I did enjoy the flying, but that seemed like a minor part of my job. The days I sat waiting for the phone to ring outnumbered the days I flew by at least two, maybe three to one. When we still had a one-hour call out, I had a fairly short leash. I did lots of reading. I watched lots of cooking shows, but otherwise reserve was the beginning of the end of television watching for me. When I was in the crashpad, I felt like I was wasting my most valuable possession, time. I was getting old enough to realize that you never get it back, which only deepened my morose.

I felt very comfortable with my job, operationally at least, by the time I had a hundred hours in the airplane. It was certainly the easiest job I had ever had, and that includes the newspaper route I had when I was fourteen. All of the flight planning was done by a licensed dispatcher. The flight plan, weather, and takeoff performance was handed to you when you went to the gate. The weight and balance was done by a load planner and given to you just before you pushed back from the gate.

The airplanes were old, but they were reliable and well maintained. Actually, the DC-9s were more than just old; they were museum pieces, genuine antiques from early in the jet age. When I learned how to fly, I thought OSU's ten-year-old Cessnas were old, having grown up in a country where automakers change their cars' body styles every couple of years to try to fool you into thinking your car is obsolete. Then I got a job flying freight, and I flew some old, worn-out airplanes. Now I had an airline job, and I was flying dinosaurs. Some of them were five years older than me, including serial numbers two and four, which were actually the two oldest DC-9s in existence.

The DC-9 was stable and easy to fly—I suppose exactly what a transport should be. The rudder was hydraulically boosted, but otherwise you actually controlled the big airplane through un-boosted ailerons and elevators that were positioned by airflow over small control tabs, the only part of the control surfaces that the pilot directly controlled. I was impressed by how well the airplane handled through such an archaic control system, and it was actually satisfying to think that only my muscle was steering a hundred-thousand pounds at transonic speeds, and it really didn't require much muscle at all.

The airplanes were underpowered, which made for some exciting take-offs from short runways in the summer, exciting in a bad way (excitement is what you don't want in airline flying). Our takeoff performance numbers supposedly allowed us to accelerate up to V1 speed (takeoff decision speed) and then stop the airplane, or lose an engine at V1 speed and continue the takeoff, climbing above any obstacles in the clearway on one engine.

To save money on engine wear and fuel, we were told to do a reduced power takeoff at every opportunity. Accountants were essentially taking away margin that we could've had, taking away some of our safety margin during the most dangerous moment of the flight. A computer program calculated how little power we actually needed to get the airplane off the ground, based on our weight, runway length, and temperature.

I experienced a few summer takeoffs from the short runways at La Guardia and Washington National during which I was sure our jet blast had left a wake on the water as the heavily laden airplane struggled aloft. If we had actually tried to abort anywhere near V1, it seemed like we would have ended up going for a swim off the end of the runway. The engines were underpowered, but they were making the correct power for takeoff. The airframes were built like bridges, but they were undoubtedly a little crooked from enduring thirty plus years of hard landings and angry clouds. That left the possibility that we had a plane full of big eaters, and they had all brought big suitcases, which, if they had carried on, also wouldn't even show up in the weight and balance.

I was just starting to notice that while I had essentially dropped out of society during my seven years on the dark side, Americans had been standing in a limitless buffet line. Even worse for my own safety, if someone's butt had grown too big for a standard airline seat, it would likely still fit comfortably in one of my airline's business class seats. Carrying big eaters might have been part of our niche. When we loaded the airplane up to the maximum weight for the runway, which was a specifically calculated performance limitation that our lives could potentially depend on, we may have actually been many thousands of pounds beyond that.

There was a commuter turboprop accident in Charlotte that wasn't caused by being overweight, but the feds did take notice that the seats were filled with passengers who exceeded the FAA standard of 175 pounds. This accident eventually led to a twenty-pound increase in the average passenger weight, but I'm not even sure that was enough. This was strictly an adult average which did not include children, who were already counted as half weights.

Checked baggage, all of which gets weighed, is remarkably just as imprecise. Any bag weighing less than fifty pounds is counted as thirty pounds. Any bag heavier than fifty is counted as sixty pounds. These are accepted averages, but it is certainly possible that you could be carrying a hundred bags that just barely made it under the fifty pound scale at check-in. Carryon bags essentially don't exist, until the overhead bins are full, requiring gate-checks, which suddenly produces thirty pound bags which otherwise wouldn't have appeared on the weight-and-balance at all.

Lap children, babies under the age of two whose parents were too cheap to buy them a ticket, don't weigh anything either. While the munchkins don't really weigh much, everyone knows that they travel heavy, a collection of paraphernalia that rarely gets tallied by the load planners.

On the subject of lap children, the feds allow this dangerous practice, potentially turning babies into unrestrained projectiles, because they assume that if the parents have to buy their baby a seat, they'll just drive to Disney World instead of springing for another ticket, which is statistically much more dangerous than flying. While driving is dangerous, allowing babies to sit on laps is too, and buying another seat costs less than a day's admission to Disney for the whole family.

All of the airplanes were bought used, very well used, including the highest time DC-9 in the world, and all of the cockpits were arranged the way their original owners ordered them. All of the previous owners had bought different takeoff and landing weights for the airplanes as well. The only standardization came from the handful of sister-ships we acquired from KLM and Garuda.

The airplanes had absolutely no extra equipment beyond what was required by the regulations. If it wouldn't help sell tickets, they weren't going to waste the money. The regulations now required weather radar, TCAS (traffic and collision alert system), GPWS (ground proximity warning system), and a reactive wind shear warning system. Each of these systems resulted from airline crashes that could potentially have been prevented by them. The airline industry has its own lobbying group, which always opposes having to spend money on new devices which will improve safety. Some of these devices become required in spite of this political pressure, and sometimes it depends on how big the airplane is and how many people might die in an accident, an idea that a former federal administrator referred to as tombstone economics.[6] Someone has assigned a monetary value to your life, and that is as much as you matter to them.

Every Captain I flew with had a story to tell, most undoubtedly much more interesting than mine. The airline had pilots from nearly every failed airline, Eastern, Pan Am, Braniff, Midway, and others. There were some furloughed pilots who came here and then passed up recall at their other airline. I hope they made the right choice. Lots of pilots came from commuters, the old commuters that flew multiple legs every day in all weather and without an autopilot. These were real pilots, a highly experienced, highly skilled group of pilots who enjoyed flying these antique jetliners and always maintained a relaxed atmosphere in the cockpit. I considered it an honor to fly with them, and to be accepted as one of them.

The pilots demonstrated their skills daily, mostly by what no one noticed; no one felt the subtle control inputs that kept these antique cable and pulley controlled machines pointed continually in the right direction while hurtling through the sky at more than five-hundred miles per hour. Their smoothness was their art, and it required finesse and planning that I personally valued above any air show stunt.

There was one old pilot however, a smoker, who ended every flight with a most incredibly impressive feat of airmanship just to satisfy his nicotine habit. On short final he would position a cigarette between his lips and hold his lighter between the throttles and the palm on his hand. He would precisely and gently set the main wheels down in the touchdown zone of the runway. With his right hand; he would quickly stand the thrust reverser handles up, light his cigarette, and then grasp the control yoke, freeing his left hand to open his clear-view window, all before the nose wheels were even on the runway. Now his right hand could reach beyond the throttles, to depress and spin a large wheel that manually closed the outflow valve, so that the cabin air, as well as the cigarette smoke, was exhausted solely through the open clear-view window. The entire performance allowed him to inhale a couple of extra breaths of noxious smoke before we arrived at the gate, a work of art motivated by a nasty habit. People have asked me about the extra responsibility of keeping a plane load of people safe. I do care deeply about the passengers and also their loved ones anxiously awaiting their safe arrival, but I really don't think of it that way. I have always had a well-developed instinct for self-preservation, and I somehow learned to fly in spite of that. Even as a little kid, I was never brave enough to throw my body toward uncertainty, and this cautiousness was certainly manifested in my late reliance on training wheels and avoidance of contact sports. The pilots are usually the first ones in the airplane to arrive at the scene of an accident. If I keep that from happening, everyone else sitting behind me will be safe too.

Lots of people are scared to fly, often because they are relinquishing control of their lives to a pair of strangers on the other side of a locked door. They are fools to believe they actually have control of their lives when they aren't trapped in a transonic aluminum tube several miles above the Earth. These control freaks always peek into the cockpit and often make fools of themselves while insulting us with questions like, "Did you get enough sleep last night?" or "Are you going to get us there safely?" What would they do if we answered honestly? Would they actually walk off the airplane if we said, "The company puts us in a cheap hotel with crappy beds; they're threatening to replace us with cheap RJ pilots; my furnace at home just broke; and I'm having a long-distance fight with my wife, but I think I'll feel a little more focused after one more cup of coffee." That all may very well be the truth, but most pilots seem to be able to compartmentalize distractions very well. I was flying with professionals, and we were deadly serious about our craft.

There was often drinking on overnights, and there were certainly some very high-functioning alcoholics on the company's roster. People who you know very well had been waiting all day for a drink could also tell you exactly when they would need to stop before they even took their first sip. A Captain even delayed a flight to wait for a breathalyzer after a passenger asked if we drank last night. He didn't want the moron's words to echo through the void without being able to positively refute them.

I flew from Washington, DC, to Kansas City, through a somewhat surprisingly placid dusk sky, while paralleling a continuous wall of thunderstorms that stretched from Pennsylvania to Indiana. It was a gorgeous light show, with bright flashes continually lighting up different parts of the wall of cloud.

A flight attendant came to the cockpit to tell us that a lady was freaking out about the thunderstorms.

The Captain showed the flight attendant the weather on the radar screen, no part of which was closer than about thirty miles from our course. He asked, "Does she actually think we're going to fly through those?"

I answered, "Yes, she does." Then I correctly guessed which lady it was, the control freak in the conservative business suit who had asked the stupid questions as she boarded the plane. I pointed to the turquoise glow of the clear dusk sky ahead of us, above the western horizon, "Tell her we have blue skies ahead."

The flight attendant left and we were at peace again, for about ten minutes. I was expecting to hear about a psycho business-lady terrorizing the cabin, but this time it was a different passenger, an old lady with a heart condition. She also had a window seat on the right side of the airplane and she was undoubtedly uncomfortable with the electric fury off to our north. The other flight attendants found a nurse in the cabin, and the Captain and I began descending to lower the cabin altitude and to get ready to divert to Louisville while getting dispatch and Med Link on the phone. Med Link ultimately decided to have us continue on unless the lady's condition changed.

If we had encountered even a ripple of disturbed air, I was sure passengers would tell stories about the harrowing flight, about how the airplane fell thousands of feet as the oblivious pilots recklessly flew through severe thunderstorms as people were freaking out and having heart attacks. It was just another day at the office for us.

I guess that's not entirely true. My typical day at the office was still just sitting in the crashpad, hoping the phone would ring. It's probably not cool for me to say that I actually wanted to work, but that's why I took the job and it would get me out of the crashpad, unless it was the last day of a reserve shift; that's when you want to be able to just slip out of town.

I was called out to do a Raleigh turn at the end of my reserve shift, just as I was hoping to be able to go home. During our return trip to Milwaukee, thick fog rolled into the airport from the cold water of nearby Lake Michigan. The Captain decided we should do a monitored approach. This meant I would take the airplane and fly a coupled approach to minimums, two hundred feet above the ground. The Captain would be looking for the approach lights, and if he saw them he would say so while pushing my hands off the throttles, disengaging the autopilot, and landing. If I didn't hear anything when we reached decision height, I would disengage the autopilot, push the throttles forward, and initiate a go-around.

As the altimeter unwound, there was no relief from the opaque blackness of nighttime cloud. The Captain remained silent at two hundred feet above the unseen Earth, so I bumped the throttles up to maximum power, pointed the DC-9's big blunt nose fifteen degrees up, and started a left turn (no pun) toward the progressive city of Madison, which was our alternate airport.

One of our passengers was going there anyway. She was happy. The other eighty-three passengers would be getting on charter buses for a two-hour ride to Milwaukee. This kind of fog tends to stay until the wind shifts, and dispatch wasn't going to wait for it.

Six more diverted DC-9s joined us in Madison. Now the crew schedulers were deciding which crews could get on the buses, and which ones would stay behind to bring airplanes back the next day. The Captain and I were sure we would be getting on a bus since we were both on our last day of reserve. They gave us hotel rooms instead.

So this would be my first junior assignment, when they make you work on a day off in exchange for time and a half pay. I would rather have the day off.

Junior assignments are mandatory. If you answer your phone on a day off, or if a scheduler is waiting in the jet way at the end of your trip, you have to go back to work; tag, you're it. There's a story about a pilot who mistakenly answered the phone during the night without first looking to see who was calling. Upon realizing that it might be crew scheduling waking him from his slumber at home, he handed the phone toward his sleeping wife while saying, "Someone's looking for your husband again." It may not have actually happened, because this story circulates through every airline, or then again maybe this trick has been used at least once at every airline. Unfortunately for us, we were captive aboard our diverted jetliner, less than a hundred miles from base.

When I got back to Milwaukee, I looked in my crew time report and saw that the overnight was listed as a reassignment, not a junior assignment. I brought this to an Assistant Chief Pilot's attention. He had an answer for everything, but I knew enough about my contract to go toe to toe with him.

Chief Pilot (CP): "You were reassigned out of domicile, so it wasn't a junior assignment."

Me: "You can't use that, because you could've driven me back by midnight but chose not to."

CP: "I see your point, but you'll still get paid for it."

Me: "No, I won't. I have about thirty hours of credit this month. I had to work a scheduled day off that I won't get paid for. It needs to be a junior assignment or you need to restore a day off."

CP: "We don't need to restore a day off because you didn't go below minimum days off."

Me: "That's because I had vacation this month (four days, my entire vacation allotment my first year). You have to steal a vacation day from me to say that I'm not below minimum days off."

CP: "I see your point. Hang on a second."

He catches the Director of Operations in the hallway. I heard some low pitched grumbling, and then the Assistant Chief Pilot stepped back into his office.

CP: "He says sometimes you're the dog; sometimes you're the fire hydrant. This time you're the fire hydrant."

I think they urinated on me; stealing a vacation day from me and making me work an unscheduled day off for free. We never get to be the dog. We are always the fire hydrants. We can never force them to do anything. We can't walk off the job and shut the airline down when we disagree with management. They tell us what to do, and if it violates our contract, we do it anyway and have to resolve it later. My colleagues fought for a contract so they wouldn't have to be urinated on. It didn't really change that; it just produced a growing backlog of grievances.

I was still on probation, that tenuous first year in which you can be fired for any reason, but I would have to fight for what I valued above all else, time. This time, I was actually brave enough. The day before the grievance hearing, the Assistant Chief Pilot called me to say that they had thought some more about my case and that I was right; I was entitled to either junior assignment pay or a compensatory day off. I chose what I valued, what you can never get back, and it didn't even cost the company an extra dime.

The chairman of the union was pissed when I told him I had settled with management because he said he was going to get me both another day off and junior assignment pay. I didn't deserve both. Contractually, I should get one or the other, so I was quite happy to settle for exactly that and nothing more.

The company's commuter airline was getting RJs, and they were starting to take some of our flying, just little bits at a time, with hints that it would be replaced by bigger and better things for us, which was probably why we didn't protest. First Columbus, then Cleveland, Raleigh, and Hartford, just a small example of what's happening all over the industry, formerly good jobs going to pilots who are willing to work for peanuts.

Nothing seemed to change for me until I was bidding my September schedule. I unexpectedly moved up nineteen numbers, all the way into the hard lines. The line I got wasn't a very good one, but it beat reserve. I had my one-year anniversary. I was off probation. My pay rate went up a lot, but I was also going from minimum guaranteed pay of seventy-five hours to an eighty-nine hour line. That meant I would actually earn 58 percent more that month. I was suddenly making more money than I had at my last job. I even had nine days off in a row before I started my September schedule. I didn't even have that many days off when I took vacation during a reserve line back in May. Plus, I had the satisfaction of knowing that the next time I went to work, I was going as a real airline pilot, not just to sit in a crashpad waiting for the phone to ring.

My life had changed, and not just because of my job. Dawn was pregnant. I wish that I could just say that I was excited, but I had too much anxiety. Fatherhood was a job I knew I didn't know how to do, one that you can't learn until you're actually doing it. I knew my life was about to change drastically and permanently, but through the unknown, I didn't realize it would all be positive. I didn't realize yet that I wouldn't truly find my place in the world until my children were in it with me.

When my co-workers learned that my wife was pregnant, most would ask me if I knew who the father was. An airline joke, I hope?

My first trip as a line holder was an eventful one, more eventful than I would realize at the time. My suitcase handle broke right away, which forced me to trade my suitcase wheels for aching slumped shoulders for the rest of the trip. I got to see the TCAS (traffic collision avoidance system) and the wind shear warning system in action for real on the first day, after a rapidly climbing airplane beneath us violated our aura, and then a couple sharp jolts of turbulence rocked the airplane as we turned final. The turbulence was associated with a stationary front that would be a nuisance for most of the trip.

As we left Kansas City, masses of thunderstorms were developing across the Midwest. I knew they would be worse, and maybe even organized, later, on the way back from Boston. We could actually see the cloud tops boiling upward beside us, toward, and eventually into, the stratosphere.

An American Trans Air jet near us with smoke in the cabin declared an emergency and diverted into Waterloo, Iowa. The Captain said, "Some poor bastard's having a bad day." I felt for those guys. I was almost vicariously feeling sick to my stomach, hoping they wouldn't make the evening news.

As we anxiously listened, the Captain talked about how we're usually only worth five bucks an hour, but on rare occasions we're worth five-hundred bucks an hour. He was right, but I didn't necessarily agree with how he devalued us the easy days. I prefer to think that they don't necessarily pay us for what we do; they pay us for what we can do (in an emergency). And we use our superior aeronautical knowledge in order to avoid using our superior aeronautical skills. Those were philosophies shared by other guys I had flown with.

In Boston, after the passengers left, the number 1 flight attendant (front) left the plane helping a mother with her baby. The other two flight attendants were already cleaning in the back. I was a little startled when I stepped out of the cockpit, and almost ran into a guy who was standing in the galley. The flight attendant was startled too. She never would've stepped off the plane if she knew there were still any other passengers in the cabin. She was polite, but she was trying to hurry the guy along. He handed her his United Arab Emirates (UAE) passport. She handed it back to him, and he finally left.

The flight attendant mentioned the UAE passport as we were about to leave Boston. The Captain remarked that at least it wasn't an Afghan passport, and then he mentioned something about al Qaeda, a name that wasn't part of the nation's daily vocabulary yet, apparently not even in the White House.

We left Boston with a full load of gas, almost thirty-thousand pounds of it. We needed every bit. One of our engine-driven generators was inoperative and deferred. That meant we would have to run the auxiliary power unit, which had another generator, for the whole flight. That alone would cost us nearly a thousand pounds of fuel. We had enough fuel to fly the trip, then to get to our alternate, Springfield, Missouri, with a legal reserve, but we didn't have a lot of extra fuel for deviating en route.

We burned a lot of our extra fuel before we even left the ground as we waited in a long line of airplanes, knowing that the weather was still building. In the air, we asked for every shortcut we could get, even though our antique navigating capabilities didn't allow us to fly direct to the faraway waypoints we asked for. Our first deviation actually helped us, by pointing us toward Kansas City. The Captain mentioned that the trip was going more smoothly than he thought it would. I was going to reserve judgment until we were in the hotel. We still had a long way to go.

The radar began painting a line of weather about two hundred miles away, about our distance to Kansas City. It was getting dark, and we could see the lightning in the distance. As we got closer we could see that the line had already passed through Kansas City. The Captain called dispatch and learned the line stretched from Minnesota to Texas, but there might be a little break, or at the least a softer spot, near St. Joseph. Missouri. I pointed the airplane there to get a better look with the radar. The rain did seem a little lighter, and the controller said a Vanguard Airlines 737 had just gone through there.

The Captain hung up the phone, and told me his plan; "Dispatch said the line is narrow, and there's a gap there. Do you want to try it?"

"What if we get to the other side and can't get into Kansas City?"

They had discussed that on the phone; "The line is already through Omaha. Dispatch already changed our alternate to Omaha."

I reluctantly agreed. I assumed the Captain and the dispatcher knew something I didn't. That part was my mistake. To assume makes an ass out of you and me—and a plane-load of innocent passengers too.

We warned the flight attendants it would be bumpy and then aimed toward the lighter precipitation near St. Joseph. We turned the lights up so we wouldn't get blinded by the lightning, which was nearly continuous. The Captain worked the radar, giving me headings as we picked our way through, trying to find any soft spots.

I was starting to see that this was a sucker hole and there was no way to get through without flying through some nasty-looking stuff, and there was no turning back without taking a beating as well. The Captain and I had to yell to communicate over the deafening torrent of huge raindrops lashing the windshield. I ducked beneath the glare shield not only to keep from being blinded by the frequent lightning but also because I feared the windshield wouldn't be able to hold back the hail that this monster must be making somewhere. It was agonizing to think how much our antique wings were flexing as the airplane violently bucked through the storm, never knowing if the next jolt would be too much. I was more scared than I had been in a long time, not really from what was happening at the moment but more in dread of running into something that the airplane couldn't handle.

We flew out of the back side of the weather, an indescribable relief, and landed in light rain in Kansas City. I was mad I had let the Captain talk me into it. I'm sure he was mad at himself too, although he didn't say anything. And our dispatcher, well, he knew we arrived at our destination.

While waiting for the hotel shuttle, the number 1 flight attendant quietly confided that she had been so scared that she prayed three times during our violent ride through the cumulonimbus. I told her I had actually considered praying, and I'm not religious.

On the bus, one of the other flight attendants said, "You guys did a really good job."

I refused to accept a compliment for a mistake that I had allowed to happen. "Well if we were really good, we'd be in Springfield, Missouri right now," our original alternate airport for the flight. The Captain said nothing.

The next day the Captain asked if I had watched The Weather Channel last night. Of course I had, in an attempt to learn from our mistake. He cheerfully asked, "Did you see how the line started to dissipate around St. Joseph?"

I answered, "Yes, probably because of our wake."

Later, we were waiting in a long departure line at La Guardia Airport, looking at Manhattan silhouetted against a stunning pink sunset. The Captain pulled a camera out of his chart case and snapped a picture. We had no idea how much the skyline would change three days later.

On the way back, we deviated way up into Ontario and then almost to Sault Ste Marie to get around some weather, giving it a much wider berth than was really necessary. The Captain commented that we needed to make up for our bad decision last night, finally admitting that we had screwed up. He also said, "They sure got their money's worth out of us on this trip."

He was right. It was the most difficult trip of my short airline career, but it wasn't over yet. We had to do the early departure out of Boston on Monday morning, and then we were done. The airplane we were supposed to fly back to Milwaukee in the morning broke on the way into Boston Sunday night. They kept us in Boston to ferry the airplane back to Milwaukee later in the day.

Now, stuck in Boston, I was going to miss my baby's ultrasound on Monday afternoon. I was nearly in tears, realizing I was going to miss the first big event of his life. He would never know that I missed it, but I would know. I didn't want to let him down. I finally got home late that night.

Dawn called me from work the next morning to say that an airplane had just crashed into the World Trade Center. My first thought was that some poor bastard was having a bad day. I turned the television on just in time to see the second explosion live, and then I realized it was no accident.

For the next half hour, stunned by grief, I heard a continuous stream of jetliners flying over the house, being diverted into Columbus, and any other pavement in flyover country.

The Federal Aviation Administration imposed several new security measures so airplanes could get back in the air later in the week. There would be no curbside checking of luggage. You couldn't park within three-hundred feet of a terminal. You had to have a boarding pass to go to your gate. The airlines couldn't initially haul mail or freight, which took away even more revenue. The National Guard would walk around in airports, trying to look intimidating with their assault rifles. Not one of these measures would have prevented the attack; they just made some feds feel better about themselves after a job poorly done.

Something that would've worked is an impenetrable cockpit door, like the ones that were on the MD-80s my airline acquired from Scandinavian Airline System. In a region where the police don't carry guns and prisons aren't brutal cages wrapped in barbed wire, someone was smart enough to realize that trouble should be kept out of the cockpit. The airline had to remove the bullet-proof Scandinavian doors and put the flimsy American doors on the airplanes, making them vulnerable to highjacking by terrorists.

As I went through security I could see that nothing had changed, except that one of our flight attendants had a nail file confiscated. She might have needed that nail file to defend herself from terrorists. That made me wonder whether the feds were really that incompetent or whether we were being used as bait to see if there were more terrorists waiting, which caused a lot of anxiety on my next few flights.

My schedule was gutted since my trips flew to all of the places that were still locked down, Boston and Washington, DC. We suddenly weren't hauling any people anyway.

On September 21, I flew to Kansas City and I ran into the flight attendant who had flown with me two weeks prior, when I had really earned my pay. She asked if I remembered the guy who handed her his United Arab Emirates passport. I did, vaguely. She thought he was one of the terrorists who hijacked an airplane from Boston a few days later. She said he had spent the entire flight to Boston flying a flight simulator on his laptop. She said that once she had stopped to watch over his shoulder. He noticed, and he turned the screen so that she could see it better, then he crashed his simulated airplane into a simulated building. She said he was one of three people on the plane who, with subtle nonverbal cues, acted like they knew each other, but none were sitting together. She said it had all seemed strange at the time, but being strange wasn't a crime yet on September 7, 2001.

She was obviously distraught. She had talked to the airline's Director of Security right away but felt like he blew her off. We decided to call the FBI, who we talked to for at least an hour.

They were frequent flyers. They were frequent flyers on every airline as they traveled around the country, observing crew behavior and seeing what they could get away with. If flight crews had been warned that bad guys were about to do bad things on airliners, there would've been plenty of opportunities to catch these guys. The flight crews see it all. We were never warned.

There were actually people who knew what would happen. There was an FBI agent who was blown off when she warned her boss about suspicious people buying heavy jet simulator time.

French intelligence had even sent our government a six-hundred-page report about the al Qaeda threat on airliners earlier in the year. Our sworn protectors didn't listen. Instead, Congress changed the name of the *pommes frites* in a congressional cafeteria to "freedom fries" after the French very wisely tried to warn us about our next gigantic geopolitical blunder a year-and-a-half later in Iraq. They were just the concerned friend trying to take the car keys away from a belligerent drunk, and we were too intoxicated by anger and stupidity to see that they were absolutely correct, both times.

The attack triggered a tribal instinct in people, like bees angered from disturbing their hive. Flags were waving everywhere, nationalism in obnoxious excess. People were too eager to kick some ass to remember that the Soviets couldn't beat the Afghanis, and they even lived in the same hemisphere. I knew very well where the War on Terror would lead: everywhere, without end. You can't bomb people until they quit hating you. Our brutality only helps them to recruit more martyrs as their angry bees look for someone else to sting. You don't have to be too smart to figure that out, but unfortunately smart people never get to run the world; they're smart enough to not want to.

With passengers rightfully scared to fly, airlines were bleeding to death. Ever since deregulation in 1978, the airlines had been in a race to see who would run out of money last, a race to the gutter. That race had just accelerated. Our expenses were increasing almost as fast as our revenue was decreasing. Our insurance costs tripled. Security costs were increasing nearly every week now that we were apparently the nation's first line of defense.

The government decided to give airlines a cash infusion, which justifiably angered lots of people. This wasn't your tax money; this was money from the aviation trust fund, which airlines had been contributing to since 1970. Some of this money had been tapped by Reagan as he attempted to balance his enormous federal budget deficits, but it had never, until now, actually been used for its intended purpose, the support of aviation.

Congress also made some loan guarantees available, with an important caveat: an airline would have to get pay concessions from their employee groups before they could have access to a loan. An act of terrorism was now being used as a union-busting tool, corporate terrorism aided by Congress.

Airlines were pulling back flying, parking their antique gas-guzzlers and furloughing employees by the thousands.

My airline hadn't announced yet whether they were going to furlough. Actually, they never announced anything, and in the absence of information, people tend to make up their own. I heard a dozen rumors. Some mentioned numbers of pilots to be furloughed, some percentages. They were all different. About a third of the rumors were severe enough to result in me being furloughed.

Eventually, the Chief Pilot announced that the number of furloughs had been decided, but he wouldn't tell us the number until tomorrow, and it wouldn't be as bad as the word on the street. I still couldn't sleep that night. I lay awake in my hotel room, worrying. If the real number wasn't as bad as the rumors, I should keep my job, maybe. I wondered whether I would get displaced to the MD-80. If so, we should move to Milwaukee. I'd be back on reserve, and that fleet mostly flew out and backs anyway, with most of the airplanes returning to base every night.

The next morning I was anxious as I dialed the Chief Pilot's hotline. I was shocked. It was worse than nearly every rumor I had heard. The company was furloughing 147 of our 400 pilots. I was number 324. I would soon be unemployed.

A few hours later I was sitting in the cockpit of a DC-9, preparing for my flight to Boston. Pilots are normally pretty good at compartmentalizing their thoughts, but I was definitely distracted, having just learned that I was losing my job, and sleep deprived on top of that. I probably should have just called in sick.

The Captain flew the first leg because he said he'd rather not do the night landing at the end of the return trip that night. Climbing out of Kansas City, he called for flaps up and slats retract. I reached up and moved the flap/slat handle the wrong direction, catching it before the flaps traveled very far in the wrong direction. The Captain, an ultra-standardized guy, meticulous to the point that he was often ridiculed by some of our pilots, just laughed at my mistake. He knew what I was going through, sort of. He was at his third airline, but he'd never actually had to perform his job after learning he was going to lose it. His first two airlines just vanished into airline history without any warning. He never even got a final paycheck from either one. This time he was just going to be displaced back to the right seat, the only person in our crew of five to not be furloughed.

The Captain turned the airplane to the east. The Missouri River meandered across the autumn landscape ahead of us. It was a familiar view, the same memorable view I'd had on my first leg as Learjet Captain, just in a different season, a different time, one of grief instead of hope.

Being the last trip of my one month as a line holder, I wondered if my takeoff from Boston would be my last takeoff in a DC-9. The Captain and I still had to deadhead back to Boston on Sunday to do the early departure to Milwaukee on Monday. I wasn't counting on it though. It had cancelled last week.

I pushed the throttles forward, and watched the engine gauges as the JT8D engines slowly spooled up. On takeoff, the DC-9 is an underpowered, graceless, ground-loving beast, but I knew I would miss it. As we accelerated, the rattles, vibrations, and whistles all steadily increased. I coaxed the nose wheels off the pavement. The rest of the airplane hesitated but then reluctantly decided to fly, almost sighing with relief as the ground fell away. Takeoff in a DC-9 is not a spectacular event, but it was my airplane and I loved it, rattles, leaks, and all. I knew how to bring the big machine to life, and I hated to think I might never get to do it again.

I chased the setting sun, chasing the dragon I guess, trying to make the moment last, a race that a transonic jet can never win in the mid-latitudes. It seemed appropriate, as this was also a futile attempt to soak up the whole fleeting experience, to fulfill my appetite for this activity that I loved, so I wouldn't miss it when it's gone, like a hopeless addict somehow knowing this was truly his last fix.

The edge of night eventually caught us from behind; immersing us in the darkness of the umbra (the Earth's shadow) as the sun slowly fell away from view. The DC-9 carried us inexorably toward Kansas City, toward my imminent furlough. It was time to descend back to Earth, to put away my thoughts, and to accept that all good things must end.

I glided through a sweeping shallow turn toward the runway under the black Missouri sky. The Captain configured the airplane with slats, flaps, and landing gear on my commands while I spooled the engines back up and aimed the airplane at the touchdown zone. As the runway numbers passed beneath our sturdy, swept wings, I eased the yoke back slightly to arrest our descent while pulling the throttles back to idle. We felt a faint vibration of spinning wheels, as the main gear rolled along the pavement. We never actually felt the wheels contact the runway, and I was even able to compress the main gear struts just enough to avoid the secondary thud that often follows a greased landing in a DC-9 as the auto-spoilers deploy, abruptly transferring the airplane's burden from the wings to the wheels. The Captain insisted I take a bow for the passengers as they left the plane.

Airline pilots are technicians. We put our big lumbering transports down in the touchdown zone, slowing a hundred thousand pounds of machinery from a hundred and forty knots to a stop, often in adverse conditions. If you can walk away from it, it was a good landing. If you can use the airplane again, it was a great landing. You can't slide endlessly along through the cushion of ground effect, trying to gently paint the wheels onto the runway. You'll run out of runway and eventually scrape the tail on the pavement as you pitch up further to compensate for decaying airspeed.

Once in a while, you can put everything together just right and elevate our mundane tasks to a form of artistry. With a gently arcing glide through night sky that led to an imperceptively soft kiss with unyielding concrete, I had achieved a moment of greatness, appreciated by only the Captain and me, and now existing only in the recesses of my own mind. If it was my last landing in a DC-9, it was certainly one to remember. I hoped it wouldn't be my last.

The whole crew lingered around the airplane for a few extra minutes, in no hurry to bring the evening to its inevitable end. This was it for the flight attendants. All three were deadheading back to base in the morning, a first class trip to the unemployment office.

Our deadhead to Boston didn't cancel. Early the next morning, we taxied away from the terminal, past a surprising number of empty gates. I had always been amazed by the number of airplanes that parked in Boston for the night and the number of hotel rooms that must be required to accommodate all of the crews. It was hard to believe how quickly it had all changed.

I completed the taxi checklist. The next task was for the flying pilot to give the pre-departure briefing. We normally alternated legs, so it was the Captain's turn to fly. Instead he said, "You really love to fly, and you're going back to reserve. I think you should take it."

I thanked him and then briefed the takeoff. As we turned the corner, we could see that we wouldn't even come to a stop before it was our turn to take the runway. I hadn't seen so little traffic in Boston since I flew Learjets into there at two in the morning.

We climbed over the ocean, passing through thin layers of glowing clouds illuminated by the early morning sun. Departure control turned us back toward the continent, and then the center controller cleared us up to 35,000 feet without interruption. We would get the same efficient treatment for our descent into Milwaukee.

I chose the moment to begin my descent so I could dead-stick it all the way to a thousand feet with the engines at idle. This was raw data, stick-and-rudder flying, using subtle changes of pitch and speed to keep the airplane on an invisible glide path to the airport. To use the spoilers along the way would be sloppy flying, like driving with one foot on the brake and one foot on the gas, as the panels rumbled above the wings. Aesthetics are important, as is the satisfaction of knowing you did it right. I passed through 10,000 feet, which was an intermediate target where I slowed the airplane for the 250 knot speed limit, right on my mental glidepath.

We emerged from the lowest layer of clouds, at about seven thousand feet, to find that the DC-9 was pointed right at the touchdown zone of runway 25 Left. Gliding through about two-thousand feet, I began configuring the airplane to land. I spooled the engines up at about a thousand feet, and our speed settled right at our landing speed. I didn't grease this one on, but it wasn't bad either; I compressed the main gear struts just firmly enough to avoid the secondary thud from the auto-spoilers. If it was my last, it was still one to be happy with. I didn't want it to be my last.

The landing was exactly what was expected from a technician, but it had followed a dead-stick glide from 35,000 feet in a raw data airplane, to a raw data runway, something that is undoubtedly becoming a dying skill among the new automated airplanes. Once again, it was only the Captain and I who appreciated the artistry. Few of the Monday morning business travelers even returned my smile as I took another bow. None realized that they had just witnessed perfection, but the artistry in airline flying is often found in what you don't notice. The passengers don't notice that they're travelling at more than five hundred miles per hour, sometimes encountering winds exceeding those in the most powerful hurricanes, and then plummeting back to Earth at a couple thousand feet per minute. When done right, they notice nothing; no apparent movements to spill their coffee or disturb their sleep.

The company wouldn't care that a precisely flown, efficient descent had saved them fuel. If they noticed any fuel savings, they would correctly attribute them to reduced traffic, which was exactly why I was granted the freedom to descend at my discretion.

I can't say I was actually trying to save them money; this was the company that was about to throw me out into the street. My motivation was to attempt to perfect my craft with every opportunity I was given, even though the opportunities were about to cease. They would be taking away my paycheck and my ID badge, but they couldn't take away my dignity and my desire to do my best.

It would take them until the middle of November to furlough me. I did lots of reserve but not a lot of flying.

I flew an Orlando turn early in October. We cruised through a bumpy sky at 27,000 feet, trying to stay beneath the worst of the turbulence in an angrily contorted jet stream. Passing over Atlanta, I noticed a sleek formation of shapes against the bright sea of cloud several thousand feet beneath us. Once we were above the formation, we could see that it was an Air Force tanker refueling a fighter, with another fighter awaiting its turn.

I couldn't see the missiles under the fighters' wings, but I knew they were there, and I realized that one of the missiles had my name on it. In my youth, I had always been impressed, even enamored, by the performance and technology of these sleek fighting machines, but now I was quite suddenly seeing them in a new and frightening way, the way many people worldwide see them as their leaders quarrel with our leaders over matters that concern so few of us. There was only one reason why these fighters were sharing this angry autumn sky with me: to shoot me down, to kill me, if we should have a disturbance in the cabin that our flimsy cockpit door couldn't contain.

After leaving Orlando, the clouds parted enough for me to see Jekyll Island and think about my honeymoon there and how nice it would be to escape there with a couple of bicycles, a sailboat, and without a care.

The center controller awoke me from my daydreaming by telling us, with a definite sense of urgency, that he wasn't receiving our transponder.

The Captain said, "It's not a good time for that to happen."

That was the truth. The transponder communicates with air traffic control radar. The terrorists had turned their seized airplane's transponders off before aiming off course, so this became a potential first cue that controllers were watching for. We quickly remedied the situation by selecting the other transponder. The controller sounded relieved when all returned to normal. We were nearing Atlanta, so I assumed that the orbiting fighters we had seen earlier were already hurtling toward us with afterburners blazing. Had they already placed the phone call? Was Dick Cheney already standing by, ready to give the order to kill us if we hadn't responded correctly? Maybe it wasn't a bad time to get away from flying for a while.

I got a training notice, alerting me that I would have a checkride the first week of November, a week before they would kick me to the curb. I figured it must be a mistake, the right hand not knowing what the left hand is doing. I called to make sure they really wanted to spend training money on me the week before they kicked me out the door. They were going to keep my training schedule, just in case they recalled me soon. Why even furlough me if you might bring me back soon? They had already reduced the number of furloughs to a hundred, but that was still not enough to save my job.

The check airman thought it was strange too. Upon meeting, he immediately asked whether I was getting furloughed. Then he said, "You passed, now let's go fly the simulator."

I went back to Milwaukee for my last four days of reserve. My phone rang three minutes into my reserve shift, at 4:33 A.M. They had a four-day trip for me. When I showed up at the airport I saw three other DC-9 reserves. Crew scheduling had actually already exhausted our reserves by six in the morning. The company had already furloughed the first seventy or so pilots. Maybe it was too many. There would be more to come, in four days, including me.

Management works very hard to produce efficient staffing models, but the reality for the whole industry is that being correctly staffed is just a fleeting, transient accident as they fluctuate between being over and under-staffed. Hiring and training takes time and will never be able to keep up with marketing changes.

When I met the Captain, he asked right away whether I was getting furloughed. He said I should do most of the flying, but he might take a short leg or two. I ended up flying every leg, and I savored every bittersweet moment, though I didn't achieve any moments of greatness. I was just a distracted technician, soon to be thrown away.

I ran into the Captain in the hotel's breakfast room on the second morning of the trip just as the TV news cameras arrived in Queens to broadcast the smoking wreckage of an Airbus. The world was still hypersensitive to the threat of terrorism. The Captain said, "We'll be stuck here in Omaha for a few days."

The airspace wasn't shut down, our flight to Newark that day wasn't cancelled, and the crash was eventually blamed on overly-aggressive control inputs by the First Officer in response to a wake turbulence encounter with the 747 they were following.

When I ran into someone I knew over the course of the trip, I was saying goodbye as if it was final. I didn't know whether the airline would survive or whether I would ever be back.

A flight attendant tried to console me by saying that everything happens for a reason and I would be better off because of whatever happens. I just respectfully told her that I hoped so, but what I was thinking was that it seemed unlikely that a few thousand people died tragically, a hundred thousand airline employees lost their jobs, and a war started, just so that I could spend more time at home and maybe be forced into an alternate career. It was more likely that I was simply caught in the random events of chaos. Some people can make the best of adversity, but it also doesn't always turn out okay.

The Captains I flew with had all been through furloughs at other airlines, and warned me that applying for unemployment benefits would be the most demeaning thing that I've ever done. That actually wasn't bad. The most demeaning thing I've ever done was to be entrusted with hundreds of lives while flying a jetliner from Newark to Milwaukee, then to Denver and back to Milwaukee, and then a moment later to have to be escorted out of the airport after turning in my ID badge, because without my ID, I was no longer trusted, as if I had suddenly become a different person. I was on the outside that quickly, before my passengers from Denver had even claimed their luggage.

When I was based in Charlotte, it felt like I had dropped out of society, even though I had to make two round trips to the West Coast and back every week. Now I felt like I had been kicked out, complete with the indignity of an official escort to the curb.

I must admit, it was nice to be home without the subtle nagging anxiety of thinking about when I needed to leave for work or having to rush through a week's worth of chores and errands in a couple of days. At first it felt like vacation, but I still lived with the reality that I had been pushed out of the industry. There weren't any flying jobs to be had, and I would no longer be current once there were, which would make it very hard to get a job. The longer I remained out, the harder it would be to get back in, but for now, there was nothing I could do about it.

At five-thirty in the morning, as I would take the dog outside, I watched my old Learjets blasting off toward the stratosphere and wished for a lost time that I couldn't have back. Who could have known? My old colleagues didn't know I was standing outside in the early morning cold, jealously watching them fly the airplanes that used to be mine through an early morning sky that once also belonged to me.

I got the sense that people were uncomfortable with my misfortune, and I'm not sure exactly why. I wasn't ashamed by my furlough; I held a number, and my number had been cut, along with thousands of others industry-wide. Maybe they were afraid my bad luck would be contagious. Maybe it's related to how easy it is for Americans to try to ignore society's problems, like how talking about politics in America is not polite unless you're talking to someone who shares your opinion. It's easier to just move farther out into the crabgrass frontier,[7] try to forget that people are being left behind, and, in doing so, avoid the realization that it can happen to you too.

Fortunately, Dawn and I weren't depending on a safety net, because there wasn't one. We had already built a lifestyle that could be sustained by one income, with our only debt being a conventional mortgage with a low interest rate. I was still jumping through hoops to collect unemployment benefits. If we had been living pay check to pay check, unable to wait for a three hundred dollar check from a slow moving bureaucracy, I would've already been forced into taking a couple of dead-end jobs, if I could find them. It started to look more like a system designed to perpetuate a slave class than a safety net.

We had to worry about medical coverage, because COBRA was prohibitively expensive. We didn't know whether we could even switch to the medical plan offered by Dawn's employer, because her pregnancy was an expensive pre-existing condition. In any other developed nation in the world, this wouldn't be an issue. The rest of the world has somehow figured this out while simultaneously keeping the price tag low. Americans refuse to listen, except to Fox News and the propaganda from the medical insurance and pharmaceutical companies that are profiting from our ignorance. We pay three times more per capita than any other nation, and all of that money only provided access for two-thirds of Americans. We already have all of the problems that we are warned would come with universal coverage: long waits, limited choice, rationing, and compromised quality—much more so than in all of Canada and Europe and even Mexico. But since it's not polite to talk about politics, but it is legal for lobbyists to buy influence, this is a problem that may never be effectively solved.

The union voted on an assessment that would pay the furloughed pilots' COBRA premiums. The proposal failed. Thanks, guys. I would've done it for you if roles were reversed.

I was bitter about a lot of things, few that I could do anything about.

I was bitter that there were people willing to kill innocent people in order to try to please an unseen deity and at our government's inability to protect us from a known threat, but it was much more complicated than that. I was bitter about the policies that bred anti-American anger, such as the CIA's malevolent meddling in Afghanistan, which supported and then abandoned the mujahidin, including Osama bin Laden, and our thirst for foreign resources and willingness to do anything to anyone to maintain our supply. Every American knows the good things we do for the world, but there's a dark side as well.

I was bitter about airline deregulation, which was slowly bankrupting the industry. I was bitter about RJs and rookie pilots' willingness to fly them for poverty wages. If we hadn't outsourced Columbus, Cleveland, Raleigh, and Hartford to our commuter line's new RJs, I wouldn't have been furloughed.

In January I unexpectedly received a recall letter to report back to work on February 15. I actually hadn't even received my first unemployment check yet.

There was a problem with going back to reserve right now. Our baby was due in March, and I would only have a 36 percent chance of being home when Dawn went into labor. Everyone I spoke to told me not to worry, that I'd be home when Dawn went into labor. I always gave the same answer: "No I won't. I'll be in a hotel room in Boston or Austin, with no way to get home."

This would be a common problem, since half of my recall class had pregnant wives, a furlough baby boom. There was no further need to talk about what everyone did during their time off.

The company hadn't found direction during my three months off. Their business plan was to wait until Vanguard Airlines went out of business so that the airline could further expand their Kansas City flying. It didn't seem like much of a business plan, but the executives gave themselves bonuses for it. They claimed the bonuses were deferred compensation from 1998, but still, that kind of a plan deserves pink slips instead of deferred bonuses.

One of the good things about my job is that I can turn it off, like switching off a light, and not think about it again for days until I'm settling back into the cockpit. Now that was suddenly a bad thing. On my way to the simulator, I realized I hadn't actually thought about how to fly a DC-9 in three months, and I guessed my instrument flying skills were probably getting rusty as well. My simulator partner had the same worries.

I was very pleasantly surprised. The DC-9 cockpit was much more familiar than I thought it would be. My arms seemed to instinctually reach for switches and perform flows. Even my instrument scan was fairly sharp. I had unexpectedly performed in a way I wasn't fully conscious of, like a well-trained animal.

It made me think of NASA's second chimp in space, which had been trained for a year to complete some tasks during his space flight. Unfortunately, someone accidentally wired the punishment and reward system backwards in the capsule for his actual flight into space. The loyal chimp performed his tasks correctly and as punishment endured painful shocks for the entire flight—and had to experience extra vibration and g-forces as well. Airline pilots have to endure furloughs, pay cuts, and a perpetual assault on our work rules instead of electric shocks, but we keep performing our tasks correctly in spite of it. I think I'd rather have the electric shocks.

I saw lots of familiar faces when I checked in for my first trip back. Pilots and flight attendants who knew me warmly welcomed me back. Others within earshot welcomed me back, although they never even knew I had been gone.

To my surprise, I flowed from one task to another until I found myself back in the right seat of the DC-9, relaxing for a few minutes before we pushed back from the gate. It began to feel as though I had never been gone.

A half an hour later, cruising to Atlanta through a smooth, blue sky, the Captain asked if I had missed it. "Well, I didn't miss commuting and being away from home." That was assumed, but there really was something I missed but couldn't quite put my finger on. It's kind of like how hard it is to explain how you know you're in love or why you like to go to the beach. I loved to fly, but it was hard to say exactly why. I looked down at the rippled sea of cottony clouds, unbroken for hundreds of miles in every direction, each crest reflecting the morning sky's sublime pastels, accented by the shadow of each trough. Then I said, "I missed the clouds," an easy answer, but there was so much more. I had really missed the art of flying. The clouds were just part of the medium, the landscape on which the artist paints.

I was eating a bowl of clam chowder half a mile from the hotel in Boston when Dawn called.

"I think it's happening."

"Do you think, or do you know?"

"I don't know. I'm waiting for the doctor to call back."

I waited too. When the doctor told Dawn to go to the hospital, I called the Chief Pilot to tell him I was going home, and then I looked through the timetables to figure out how. The next nonstop flight to Columbus was hours away, so I had lots of time to worry. I could connect at a hub but didn't think I'd get home any sooner. I also thought about how I had actually dreamt about a baby last night, which I'm sure was only a coincidence.

Slovenia crossed my mind as I was waiting for my flight also. If we had lived in Slovenia, or one of the other thirty-six countries with health care systems that the World Health Organization rated higher than ours, maybe Dawn would have had a more thorough prenatal exam the day before—yes, one day earlier—instead of the rushed, superficial appointment the HMO mandated. Dawn had actually had some suspicious symptoms, but her doctor shrugged them off and then hurried to the next appointment. With even an extra minute of the doctor's time yesterday, maybe we could've learned that Dawn was already in early labor, and I wouldn't have gone to work.

Part of the problem is that they never believed us when we told them when the little guy was conceived. Dawn and I knew when; we were actually there. They insisted on keeping the wrong date on Dawn's chart, and then they asked me if I knew who the father was.

Nearing departure time, the gate agent printed a boarding pass for me. Then she printed another, and another. She was trying to spare me the indignity of being a security selectee, but she couldn't figure out the super secret code to de-select an off-line jumpseater. You were suspected of being a terrorist if you had a last minute, one-way reservation. That meant airline employees riding standby were virtually guaranteed to become security selectees. These are people who already have ID badges which allow them access to the airplanes. Most people knew this, so a terrorist would certainly buy a round-trip ticket to avoid extra screening, even though they were planning to be dead before the return flight. The round-trip ticket would actually be cheaper too, since no passenger has ever paid the actual cost of flying a seat from here to there when they bought an airline ticket.

I normally like to keep a low profile when I'm begging for a free ride, but this time I intervened. I thanked the agent for her valiant effort to prevent me from being classified as a suspected terrorist, but since it was only five minutes to departure time, I would like to just get it over with before I miss the flight.

The screener unzipped my suitcase, briefly poked at my laundry, found a pocket to unzip, and then used a large wand to vaguely trace an outline of my aura. With that he either granted me passage or bestowed knighthood on me, I couldn't tell which with our language barrier. I grabbed my luggage and ran down the jet way. He didn't pursue me, so I guess I had been cleared.

As I introduced myself to the pilots, I told them my wife was in labor, just in case they needed a reason to burn some extra fuel.

We joined a modest line of airplanes waiting to take the runway. I looked out the window to see a blue DC-9 thundering down the runway. That was the airplane that I was supposed to fly to Kansas City, leaving about an hour late after waiting for a reserve, my replacement, from Milwaukee. After another airliner departed, one of my old Learjets took off, making all the jetliners look fat and sluggish. I had actually flown two of the last three jets that I saw. It's a small world, unless you're really in a hurry to get home to a wife in labor.

Soon it was our turn, and we climbed into the 150 knot headwinds that were keeping me from my baby boy. The flight attendant gave me periodic updates from the pilots, and she moved me to the front row and put my luggage in a front closet. As we were taxiing to the gate, she put my luggage by the forward entrance door so that I could hit the ground running. That's exactly what I did, and my mother was waiting for me outside the terminal.

I stepped into the delivery room less than ten minutes before Jay was born. I was so happy to meet my baby boy that I didn't even think to hand him to Dawn.

I had never been around babies. He was so tiny and helpless, and I really didn't know how to take care of him. Driving Jay home from the hospital was the scariest thing I had ever done in my life, and not just because now he was totally dependent on us. It was the other vehicles. I didn't want them anywhere near our tiny passenger. Worst of all were the cars in adjacent lanes on the freeway. I wanted them to be two lanes away at the least and to warn them about how important of a passenger we had.

Wisconsin's family leave was more liberal than what was required, so I took intermittent leave for the next four months, dropping every other reserve shift. Reserve was great when I only had ten days of it per month, plus now we had a two-hour callout. I would bid the early reserve shift, sleep until seven or eight in the morning, read with a cup of coffee and a bagel, go browse one of the bookstores for an hour, and my reserve shift was already half finished. If my phone rang, I would go fly.

By the time my family leave ran out, I had the seniority to bid coverage lines, and I was averaging about fifteen days off per month. I was truly allowing myself to have a good time at work. Having it all taken away from me adjusted my attitude and made me appreciate how good of a job it really is.

The airline posted a small profit. Vanguard Airlines shut down, which had apparently been the corner stone of our airline's business plan. Did they know something or just get lucky?

Our school district had to renew its operating levy, which wasn't a tax increase, just a simple question that they were required to ask the voters once every sixteen years, whether or not they wanted to continue to operate the schools. The voters said no. Democracy would work so much better if the stupid people weren't allowed to vote. Dawn and I decided to build a house in a different school district on the other side of town. Yes, I'm guilty of doing something I've already criticized, but we were actually moving closer to town, instead of farther out into the sprawl.

We had a good baby, and I was slowly learning how to be a parent. Life was good.

Soon, I started to notice something wrong, and I'm writing about it here because it would affect my career. I'm not necessarily a news junkie, but I started to see a subject come out of nowhere. At first it was just subtle hints, with the feel of barely disguised propaganda, a well-financed advertising campaign, like someone was methodically planting a seed. As soon as it started to grow, I knew exactly where it was going, straight to Babylon. I was also just as certain that it was all a lie. Apparently a president can lie to start a war, but he'll get impeached if he lies about a blowjob. This is not necessarily a political statement, but an observation that Americans seem more comfortable with institutionalized killing than with sexuality. This war was actually marketed to us, like they were trying to sell us a soda, and Americans drank it up. So I started protesting a war a half a year before it even began, back when everyone was still waving their flags and assuring me it would never happen.

I wrote my Senators and my Congressman. I was published in the newspaper, which led to a television interview that apparently ran on two local stations. I get absolutely no satisfaction in saying this, but history has shown that I was right about everything I wrote and said, and that was months before the war even started. But I wasn't able to prevent it from happening, to prevent the needless death and destruction, which is all I had wanted to do.

I don't intend to defend Saddam Hussein. He was a brutal dictator, but he was also one of the most secular leaders in the region, which actually made him an adversary of al Qaeda fundamentalists, Osama bin Laden, and the Taliban. He had no connection to 9/11 or to any of the participants. He also didn't have any weapons of mass destruction.

Saddam was in a bind when we suddenly started picking on him again. The weapons were long gone, which he knew that we knew, but he needed his people to believe he still had them because fear was the only way he would stay in power. Later, with absolutely no weapons to be found, the White House tried to change the subject by saying they were spreading freedom, as if it was simply a benevolent after-effect of a bomb blast, if the concussion and shrapnel didn't kill you and your family first.

Once people started to realize Bush really was going to invade Iraq, the price of oil exploded. I believe the approximate formula for our airline was that a one cent increase in the price of a gallon of jet fuel increased our operating expenses by a million dollars a year. When oil reached forty dollars a barrel at the end of February, our CEO panicked and started parking airplanes again. I got my next furlough notice. My job was a casualty of an unjustified, unnecessary war, and Bush hadn't even dropped the first bomb yet.

The pilot payroll was now just a miniscule percentage of the company's operating expenses, but the union gave the company emergency relief with lower pay rates.

The company was finally replacing their gas-guzzling DC-9s with new Boeing 717s, updated, automated DC-9s with fuel-efficient Rolls Royce engines. They had been thinking about fleet replacement for years, but they still pulled the trigger a few years too late. This was, of course, the airline that spent six months trying to devise a cheaper replacement for our crystal salt and pepper shakers. The disposable plastic replacements were supposed to save us such an enormous amount of money that it made me question not only their math skills but also their general ability to make decisions and run an airline, and this was the work of the Senior Leadership Team (SLUTs?). They were so proud of those plastic salt and pepper shakers that they even rented an auditorium for the official unveiling of the company's salvation, a disposable plastic device so tiny I couldn't even see it from row thirty-six. Mission accomplished.

Our antique airplanes required a lot of TLC to stay in the air, attention the factory-new airplanes shouldn't need for some time. Fleet replacement would take more than two years to accomplish, but the company went ahead and furloughed most of the mechanics anyway. We were seeing a lot more deferred items, things that were broken but wouldn't ground the airplane. The airplanes were still legal to fly, but growing lists of deferred items can be an indication the airline isn't spending as much attention as it should on maintenance.

On the last day of my second to last trip, we had to switch airplanes on our way through Milwaukee in the morning. We would be taking ship 700, serial number two, which at thirty eight-years old was the oldest DC-9 in existence. She was coming from the maintenance hangar and already running late.

Pilots tend to trust the sky more than the maintenance hangar. If it flew in, it can fly out. If it came from the hangar, we can only hope that they put it back together correctly and that they weren't hurrying to stay on schedule. Most of the company's mechanics seemed to work without looking at a clock, as if the schedules didn't exist. This would undoubtedly frustrate a corporate accountant, but that's exactly how I wanted my mechanics to be, unhurried craftsmen.

Our release came off the printer before the airplane showed up at the gate. As the Captain and I looked at the release, we both laughed when we noticed that the auxiliary power unit (APU) was deferred. They had all night to work on it and they still couldn't get it fixed. This happens occasionally, and it wasn't really a problem. The APU is a little jet engine that provides compressed air to turn the engines for starting, and it also turns our third electrical generator, which wasn't required since both engine-driven generators were working. We just wouldn't have a backup generator in an emergency (such as loss of an engine), and it increases our workload at the beginning of the flight. We would need an air cart to start the engines, and we would need to do a crosstie check in the electrical system before the first flight of the day. I would warn the passengers in advance, because the extra check would cause lots of cabin bells and flickering lights as relays opened and closed in our antique jetliner.

During the takeoff roll, I trimmed the right throttle slightly at takeoff EPR (engine pressure ratio, a measurement of power in a jet engine). After takeoff the Captain turned the airplane toward the cold water of Lake Michigan, which was now completely obscured by clouds. I completed the climb checklist, and then I mentioned having to nudge the right throttle on the takeoff roll and asked the Captain whether he thought his hand might have accidentally pulled it back a smidge.

Rick Butcher

Just then the right engine started to roll back to idle. We performed the only memory item during an engine failure, retarding the bad engine throttle to idle. Now the right engine was idling so low that the right generator (engine-driven) was only intermittently able to stay on line.

Every time the generator gave up[8], the crosstie relay snapped shut, which caused the cabin lights to flicker and a cabin bell to chime. Unfortunately, we also use cabin bells to communicate with the flight attendants, and after about eight rapid bells the flight attendants undoubtedly thought we were about to crash (four bells at our airline meant brace for impact). It's not in the manual, but five bells means start praying and six bells means don't waste your time praying because there is no god. By nudging the right throttle slightly, we were able to keep the sick engine idling just fast enough to keep the engine-driven generator on line. We were in real weather, with no APU, so we both wanted to try to keep that right generator as a backup.

I mentioned to the Captain that with all of the bells, the flight attendants would already be on the phone and thinking that we were about to ditch in the lake. I grabbed the phone and found that both were indeed listening, so I gave them a very quick briefing, because we needed to get on with other tasks; "We had an engine failure. We're going back to Milwaukee. We'll be on the ground in ten minutes. No need to brace the passengers. We'll inform the passengers when we have a chance. Any questions?"

I grabbed the emergency checklist, and the Captain declared an emergency and asked to land on runway 19 Right. Since a DC-9 can't dump fuel, we would be landing four-thousand pounds over our maximum landing weight, which seemed a lot smarter than wandering around the clouds until we burned the extra fuel. We completed the emergency checklist, called dispatch, and talked to the passengers, calmly of course. We were ready to land.

Then the approach controller turned us toward the runway 25 Left approach course instead of runway 19 Right, as we had asked. We would have about a thousand feet less pavement, but we still had room to stop. We glanced at each other, then the Captain said, "Screw it, let's just get on the ground."

198

We landed and led a fire truck parade to the terminal. One of the firemen said it looked like we were spilling fuel out of the right engine. We glanced at each other again, this time with wide-eyed expressions, and the Captain quickly reached up and shut off the fuel to the right engine. We both immediately knew we had gotten away with one. We had a ruptured fuel line. We were lucky we didn't have an engine fire or even an explosion. Would the outcome have been different if we had loitered above the airport for a while burning off four-thousand pounds of fuel instead of opting for an immediate overweight landing? Fortunately, we'll never know.

We had only kept that engine running for its generator, electrical redundancy, because we were in the weather without an APU. If we had an operable APU, we would've shut down the right engine, eliminating the possibility of an engine fire as fuel sprayed into the nacelle. And why didn't we have an APU after the mechanics had all night to wrench on it? The company had apparently already furloughed too many mechanics to keep our antiques airworthy. On this particular day, the price of safety may have only been another mechanic's salary.

We had to sit through an event review with a Chief Pilot, a union representative, and management from in-flight (the flight attendant's department) and dispatch, standard procedure after an emergency in order to determine that we used standard procedures during the emergency. After debriefing the event, the whole crew got a pat on the back from management for how we handled the situation. I was singled out for an extra pat on the back by the whole crew for my communication during the emergency. Thanks, but it's not enough to save my job.

I went upstairs to the terminal to catch the next flight home. Arriving in Columbus, I said hello to one of the gate agents. He asked me if I had heard about the Newark flight that morning. It supposedly had an engine out and the other engine on fire over Lake Michigan as it limped back to shore. The story, as recounted by people who weren't there, was still evolving, making the Captain and me to be mythical heroes along the way.

I told the agent, "That was me, and it wasn't that dramatic."

Something statistically noteworthy occurred during the trip. Exactly half of my 8,300 hours of flight time was now in jets, which are supposed to be the most mechanically reliable way to power an airplane, but I'd already lost three jet engines. The other half of my flight time was in reciprocating engine airplanes, which spend their entire lives trying to rattle themselves to pieces. I'd never lost one of those, although I did have to shut down a couple before landing after breaking throttle cables in Barons. Statistical anomalies both ways—which is to say luck, good and bad.

I went back for my last trip, a productive four-day trip with about twenty-seven hours of flying. The Captain told me to fly every leg, and fly I certainly did. I never engaged the autopilot unless the flight attendants brought us food (this was prior to Reduced Vertical Separation requiring the use of the autopilot at high altitudes). The Captain commented on my youthfully fanatic zeal but also complimented my smoothness, the first time saying that he didn't realize that the autopilot wasn't flying. Once again, thanks, but it's not enough to save my job. I knew this was really the last time I would fly DC-9s, since they were really going away. They had already even cut one up into scrap metal outside the maintenance hangar, a sad sight for those of us who loved the old bird.

It was the end of the line for an entire generation of classic airplanes, in which pilots were pilots, their machines were as stout as bridges, and the air crackled as they roared by. These were the legendary jetliners of my youth, that happy time in life when all I did was look up, and I actually grew up to be a part of it, an era that had finally reached its end.

If I did get recalled, I would come back to automated airplanes. If I didn't get recalled, it would be even harder to get back into the industry. All of my experience was with the dinosaurs that began the jet age, and the dinosaurs were finally going extinct.

Living the Dream

Two days after I was furloughed, I wrote a fifty-four thousand dollar check and closed on our new house. We could still afford it because we still based our lifestyle on half our income, with a conventional mortgage, no other debt, and a liquid cushion in our savings account. I'm sure that everyone involved thought of us as quaint rubes for trying to be so responsible in an era of house lust and debt.

I was now a stay-at-home dad and a self-taught cook. My little buddy Jay ate raw vegetables off the cutting board and operated the appliances for me (nothing dangerous). He was probably the only two-year-old in the neighborhood who knew how to make basil pesto or hummus.

I would take my little buddy to story time at the library and to a music class, where I would try to keep a low profile in spite of the fact that I was somewhat of a novelty among the stay-at-home moms. The puzzled looks didn't bother me at all. I've never tried to be normal, and I was doing the most rewarding thing I had done in my life. I had just always hoped that Dawn would have a chance to be the stay-at-home parent.

People always asked me, as if I was too dumb to consider it myself, if I could just go to a different airline. No, I couldn't. In general, either all airlines are hiring or no airlines are hiring. Although there are always exceptions, there is rarely anything in between. Nearly every airline had lots of pilots on furlough, and there would be no hiring until the furloughs are recalled. Most of the regional airlines were hiring as RJs continued to whittle away the domestic market, but I didn't want to resign my seniority for a twenty thousand dollar a year job at a regional.

There was one good airline job, but they required 1,000 hours in airplanes larger than 20,000 pounds. Nearly every company had at least one unique requirement within the standard long list of qualifications. I had 830 hours in DC-9s. I also had about 3,400 hours in Learjets, but the largest Learjet model I had flown was a 19,600-pound airplane, although I wouldn't be surprised if I flew one at more than 20,000 pounds after the last bin of freight *accidentally* failed to make it over the scales. I mentioned the 830 hours to a friend who had just gotten hired by this airline, and he told me to just make sure that my application had at least a thousand hours of DC-9 time. I couldn't bring myself to lie on the application, so I didn't apply.

I got an unexpected call from my scientist step-father Marcus. "I'm doing a stack testing job in Commerce, Texas, and I could use your help. You're a pilot so you don't mind heights."

"Heights? How high is it?" That was a silly question. If it was more than five feet, a fall could lead to injury. Twice that could lead to, well, much worse. If Marcus mentioned heights, it must be dangerously high. I do mind heights. Somehow flying is different; the wind over my wings opposes the pull of gravity. I feel it. I know it. I'm strapped in with a five-point harness.

Except for a little backyard football long ago with people my size; I avoided contact sports because of the fact that when your body collides with something, especially the Earth, it might get hurt. I have a firm grasp of gravity, but I'm not quite sure if I can maintain a firm enough grasp of a ladder to avoid it. As scared as I was, Marcus was trying to help me, and if I'm somehow able to pry my white knuckles off the ladder, maybe I can help him. "Well, I don't like heights, but I'll just work through it."

Marcus is one of the world's experts on dioxins, who, after working for some large companies, is now very happily self-employed. He offers full-service solutions, which means he will climb smokestacks to gather air samples and then engineer solutions for his clients' pollution problems.

He was testing an aluminum plant, pulling three three-hour air samples per day out of a smokestack. It was real work, or at least I think it was, although I haven't actually had a non-flying job since I was seventeen. We didn't have to climb real high, but it was high enough to be uncomfortable. We had to hoist more than a hundred pounds of equipment aloft and set it up. It was loud. It was perpetually dusty, with a gray industrial grit that would somehow even grind its way into your skin. It was cold in the morning. Later we would feel raw, with no escape from the afternoon sun and the relentless, dry Texas wind. And if you weren't careful, it was dangerous.

And Marcus loved it. He loved what he was doing so much that he seemed almost immune to the uncomfortable and challenging environment in which we spent our long days. There were actually parallels to my days as a freight pilot. It was noisy. I hoisted freight into the dusty cabins of old industrial airplanes. It was always cold or hot, and you always had to be careful. And I loved every uncomfortable moment of it.

I climbed the ladder, repeatedly. I had the satisfaction of knowing I had accomplished something I feared, but I didn't reach the point that I was at ease with it, and I don't think you really want to be when a misstep can mean falling to your death.

We all cross thresholds in life which separate adulthood from youth. Maybe it's moving away from home, earning a diploma or professional license, marriage, children, a first job that independently supports a middle-class lifestyle, or even finding the courage to climb a smokestack. For me the most profound threshold wasn't from something accomplished or attained but something lost, specifically a lost time and place.

The first time I went to The Bluffs in Morehead City, North Carolina, in 1977, the condominiums were still under construction. We went for the day and fished from the six-hundred-foot pier that jutted out into the choppy water of the Bogue Sound. I was scared to walk past where the railing ended, not realizing that the dark mysterious water at the pier's edge was actually shallow enough for a seven-year-old to touch the sandy bottom.

During that first visit to The Bluffs, we actually stayed at my Aunt Emily's secluded cottage deep in the forest that bordered the salt marsh in Merrimon, North Carolina. We had arrived in darkness after traveling along a spooky sand road carved from under an impenetrable forest of ancient moss-draped trees. The utter blackness of the unknown realm beyond the beam of the Toyota's headlights, fringed with eerily draped shadows from the Spanish moss, like the dark mysterious water of the Bogue Sound, shrouded what existed, but that I did not yet know, and seemed perpetually just beyond my reach. It inspired a curiosity that will, I hope, never be quenched.

I went to The Bluffs each year afterward, acquiring some of the most important, and fondest, memories from my youth. I spent countless hours out on the pier, mesmerized by the rhythmic lapping of the ceaseless waves under a refreshing breeze, bathed in the damp smell of the sea air, probing the mysterious depths.

The Bluffs and the Bogue Sound were never mine. I was only visiting. I knew that when I could no longer go to them, I would be forever leaving my youth. I crossed the threshold into adulthood while saying my last goodbye to a lost time and place, and so it was with my last trip to The Bluffs.

We were there to work, to pack up ninety-seven years' worth of possessions from my grandmother's condo, to clean, to paint, and prepare the condo for sale. If I'd had the money, I would've bought the unit myself, but I didn't have the money, not to do it comfortably at least. I only wish that I could provide my kids with a similar opportunity to explore unknown realms.

The airline didn't go bankrupt as they had threatened. The new airplanes were still coming every other month, and I had even calculated which airplane would get me back to work, which finally happened in July of 2004, after a sixteen-month furlough, sixteen months that unexpectedly flew by.

No one in my recall class had experience in an automated airplane, probably why we were all still available to be recalled. Actually, there weren't a lot of pilots in the airline who did have experience in modern airplanes, so the company had to develop a transition course to make sure everyone got through, and everyone did.

I went to the airport operations office to get a new airport ID badge. They asked me if I wanted a new photo. I looked at the old picture in their file, and realized I was actually wearing the same shirt. I just had less hair now. That may not be true. I may not have actually lost any hair follicles; they've just migrated to my ears, eyebrows, and shoulders. They noticed the shirt too and commented on it. I said it was appropriate because I felt like I was running in place, starting over there for the third time.

I'm always the last person to adopt any new technology. Dawn had to teach me how to log onto the internet. I didn't get a cell phone until my time away from home forced me to get one. I had just learned what MP3 meant, which, along with travel speakers, allowed me to have my own music in my hotel rooms, a return-to-work gift from Dawn. I didn't send my first text message until the end of 2011. It's not because I'm scared of technology; I'm brave enough to learn. I think it's more that I know I've survived so far without it, so it's not imperative that I have it. Technology only leads to hedonic adaptation, the new feeling that you can't live without the new gadget. Besides, if I wait a few years it'll be improved and usually much cheaper.

Once I do learn some new gadget I'm always amazed by how cool it is. And this was now true for a glass airplane too. (Glass is slang, referring to the television screens that have replaced the analog flight instruments from earlier generations of airplanes). What impressed me right away was how much self-preservation is built into the airplane. The 717 is very smart and doesn't want to let you do anything that might hurt it. The DC-9 will obediently allow its pilots to fly it to its doom, but the 717 will warn you, adamantly protest, and possibly even intervene before allowing you to crash it.

When Boeing acquired McDonnell Douglas, they assigned the airplane a new name, as if it was the genesis of a new jetliner, but the 717 is still just a DC-9. It would've been called the MD-95, or, without another past corporate transaction, the DC-9-95. It was the same reliable, sturdy airplane that was designed with the slide rules of another generation, respectfully updated by the computer generation. The massive, efficient new Rolls-Royce/BMW BR715 engines produced 50 percent more power while burning 35 percent less fuel than the DC-9's old JT8D engines. This was truly a fine machine, but one that Boeing never really wanted. This was an airplane whose lineage had always been a direct competitor to Boeing's prolific baby, the 737.

Technology had eliminated the need for us to do any paperwork on the job, a tremendous improvement. We no longer had to call the company four times per flight to give out, off, on, and in times (OOOI). The airplane did all of that automatically and even eliminated the need for us to have paper trip logs to fill out.

Besides just eliminating a very small duty, this also eliminated the need to occasionally lie about our out times in order to help the gate agents, who were apparently under a tremendous amount of pressure to get flights out on time, pressure the pilots absolutely never felt. In the DC-9, lots of pilots would just call us out of the gate on time if we pushed a couple of minutes late, but that's only masking the real problem, that the company never seemed to have enough quality people to turn flights on time. I care very much about honesty and accuracy, but also, if we always mask a systemic problem, the company will never know they need to fix it. Of course, that assumes the company actually has the desire to fix its problems, but when the solution has a price tag they probably don't. Mediocrity is accepted as good enough.

We would now bid our monthly schedules on line; another huge leap into the late twentieth century. When we bid on paper, I actually had to buy an overnight envelope once when I was going to be home for the entire bidding window. Now I could sit in front of the computer in my underwear (if I wanted to) four hundred miles away while bidding or doing trip trades. You could even ask the computer to sort the bid lines by your own customized criteria so you wouldn't even have to hunt for the lines that you wanted.

While commuting, I was noticing that technology was changing how people interacted at the airport, which is to say it was preventing interaction between strangers. Before cell phones, laptops, and iPods, strangers would have conversations while waiting for their flights, sometimes memorable conversations, with people who they would otherwise never have met. Those days are gone, and it wasn't even very long ago. Now everyone is isolated in their own private electronic cocoons, purposefully oblivious to the world around them, and society is worse off for it.

One of the most interesting conversations I had with a stranger at an airport was with an accountant. Yes, it was truly fascinating. He told me about the euphoric late-nineties when people were making money off of anything and how it was hard to stay ethical while people were getting away with nearly anything. He would advise clients that something they wanted to do with their books wouldn't be legal and they would respond that they could find an accountant who would let them do it.

Besides losing opportunities to meet people with different experiences and different views of the world, people now censor their own news through websites and cable news programs that share their own views and just tell them exactly what they want to hear. This has reduced news broadcasts to a form of entertainment, sensationalized fluff, as networks desperately compete for shrinking shares of ratings and, in turn, advertising dollars. No generation has ever had more access to information, but it hasn't produced a generation that is any better informed, and it is perhaps even less so.

I made it through the simulator training for the 717, and all of the associated emergencies, but I didn't feel like I knew how to get the automated airplane from point to point. That would come with practice, if there was any. After a three-day trip of IOE, I was released to the line, and it was an overstaffed line too. I began to wonder why I had even been recalled. They didn't need me.

We now had a couple of long-call reserve lines with a twelve-hour call out. I was last in the bidding, and for some reason no one else wanted to do long-call. I was able to get it by default, and I did it from home. After I had been home for thirty straight days, a neighbor questioned whether I had actually gone back to work, and I started to wonder whether I had remembered anything from the simulator, which already seemed like it had been long ago.

I was about to call the Chief Pilot and ask him to get me a trip before I forgot everything that I didn't know yet about the new airplane when I finally got called out.

As I met the Captain at the beginning of the trip, I profusely apologized in advance for my imminent incompetence. He was un-phased by my worries, and he turned out to be right. It was still the same job I had already done, but with a Flight Management System (FMS) computer, it was much, much easier than it used to be.

I got long-call reserve lines for three months, during which I flew exactly one trip per month, which was really a nice way to ease back into the working world.

I did three months of real reserve in Milwaukee, and then with new airplanes still showing up, I was suddenly a line holder. The real surprise was that I got one of my first choices in the first month when I barely had the seniority to hold a line. I guess that meant it wasn't a very good line, but it was one I wanted. Sometimes the key to happiness is low expectations. For the next three-and-a-half years

I would get one of my top choices each month, never getting worse than about my tenth choice.

I understood I would be working weekends for a while. I would bid commutable lines, with trips that started late on the first day and ended early on the last day, but those trips tend to be worth less than pure A.M. or pure P.M. trips. These trips required an unproductive day or a short overnight; usually had both. Dawn still had an income, so I was bidding for lifestyle, not pay. I learned that everyone had different priorities, so as long as you had realistic expectations, you were likely to get the schedule you wanted, or at least close to it. If you didn't, you still had the opportunity to swap out your trips with the scraps left in open time while sitting in front of your computer in your underwear four hundred miles from base.

I also understood that without seniority, and without contractual holiday pay, I would be working holidays. I was fine with that. I had learned the history of the holidays, and now they would never be the same to me anyway. In order to not deprive Jay of the experience, we would still celebrate the holidays, but always on a different day, which was actually sometimes the correct day. We even started a new family tradition of celebrating Christmas on the winter solstice, which turns out to be a very old tradition, even older than Christianity itself.

When the Roman emperor Constantine converted to Christianity, and subsequently converted the whole Roman Empire, he also changed the winter solstice festival, Saturnalia, into Christmas. The most popular pagan festival suddenly became Jesus' birthday, a date never actually recorded in the New Testament or any other known source. The holiday is still loaded with pagan symbology, some quite shocking, like the sticky white berries of mistletoe. Otherwise, the holiday has become a commercialized shopping festival.

Another family holiday tradition we would eventually adopt is escaping from our neighborhood for July fourth. I don't really understand celebrating our nation's independence by blowing up small pieces of it. We even celebrate the wrong day. The Declaration of Independence was adopted on July second, and then signed on August sixth. The only relevant event that occurred on July fourth was that a printer made copies of the document, dating his work, so that's the date we remember with pyrotechnics, the printer's holiday.

Actually there is one important event that occurred on July fourth, although it was in the year 2001: Jay's conception—probably more than he wants to know.

We can watch our community's firework display from our yard, and that's really quite enough to satisfy my explosive urges, but then we have to endure the neighborhood's arms race, which grows larger every year. These aren't firecrackers and bottle rockets; these are professional in magnitude, and destructive potential, but handled by amateurs. This is no exaggeration; a couple of people in my neighborhood annually handle enough gunpowder to level a house. I don't want it to be mine. Besides being dangerous and illegal, it's irritating to have your windows rattled until one or two in the morning when your small children just want to sleep.

My neighborhood is not necessarily unique. I flew into Los Angeles at about ten in the evening of the fourth. As we descended into the valley, flashes were coming from every neighborhood, and they never stopped as millions of people disposed of their incomes in a dangerously parched landscape that gets no rain in the summer. When we checked in with the tower, the controller cleared us to land, then told us to use caution for fireworks on final. I'm not sure how he expected us to avoid them. As we descended through three hundred feet, the world briefly disappeared as we flew through a cloud of gun powder smoke. I couldn't even escape by going to work.

I may have become cynical, but I was very happy. I was living my life on my days off, celebrating each day as if it was a holiday, and on my work days I was enjoying my job more than I ever had. Having it all taken away, twice, helps you to appreciate what you have. It also helped that I was holding a line and getting one of my top three choices every month. No sarcasm here; I was living the dream.

The flying was easy. In an analog airplane, you're eyes have to continually scan six flight instruments with a miniature horizon in the middle, plus engine gauges. In a glass airplane like the 717, all of the flight instruments are combined into a very large miniature horizon with a full-time flight director on a nine-inch screen. Flying that used to require a sharp instrument scan now just requires a good stare at the full-time flight director in the middle of the primary flight display, and the auto throttles manage the power for you.

Next to the primary flight display is the navigation display, an identical nine-inch screen, but this one is a map that displays your course, airports, navigation fixes, nearby airplanes, and either weather or terrain.

The separate, dual inertial reference systems are updated by dual global positioning systems (GPS) and actually calibrate themselves as you fly. The airplane automatically tunes navigation radios as you fly, and then it automatically tunes the appropriate localizer frequency at your destination, setting itself up for the approach. The airplane will even land itself if you choose not to disengage the autopilot. If you have to fly a non-precision approach, the airplane will generate a glide path to the runway, which is much easier, safer, and aesthetically pleasing than the old dive-and-drive technique of descending quickly to minimum descent altitude, leveling off there, and then looking for the runway.

The airplane tells you when something is wrong with it, and it sends an e-mail home to maintenance too. It's still just a DC-9 airframe, so it's reliable and built like a bridge. The airplane also has more power than a DC-9 pilot could even dream of.

My only worry about the airplane was that it would be able to fly itself better than I could fly it, that I would just be along for the ride, my skills rendered useless. Although you certainly can just go along for the ride if you have no self-respect, my worry turned out to be unfounded. No offense to software engineers, but software engineers taught the airplane how to fly, so the airplane had an oversimplified understanding of pitch, power, and airspeed. In climb, the airplane would clumsily pitch up and down, chasing the target airspeed rather than just pointing the airplane where it needs to go and allowing slight deviations in airspeed. I actually could fly the airplane better than it could fly itself, but I have to admit that it'll fly a very nice approach to minimums, and of course, the autopilot had an infinite attention span that no pilot could ever match. I always hand-flew the airplane up to altitude before letting the autopilot handle the monotony of cruise. I hand flew every visual approach and never gave the autopilot a landing, except when I was required to in the simulator. This was an automated airplane that still allowed a pilot to be a pilot.

In general, our entire pilot group was new to automation, and there were some situations in which the pilot who knew the automation the best was essentially in command. I learned it quickly. After a couple hundred hours in the new airplane, I didn't have much use for that all too common phrase in the modern automated cockpit: "What's it doing now?"

I eventually learned a new way of thinking that wasn't taught in our glass class but certainly will be some day. In order to fly an automated airplane as safely and as efficiently as possible, you need to maintain two streams of thought simultaneously. One is what you would do with the airplane if you were flying it, assuming you knew how to fly it well. The other is what you know the flight management system (FMS) is going to do with the airplane. You have to occasionally nudge the airplane in order to keep those two tracks in parallel with each other. To do this, and get the most out of the airplane, to elevate the craft to an art form, you must have a foundation of raw data flying skills as well as a solid understanding of how the FMS flies the airplane; without both, you're inevitably just along for the ride.

Some people will certainly defend the computers' efficiency and say the flight management system can save more fuel than I can. They're right, to a point. The computer can calculate an efficient profile, but then it inevitably loses some of that efficiency by being a little sloppy in executing what it plans. I can help it avoid that sloppiness. The computer also only plans a linear descent, and I've figured out a more parabolic descent profile, which is much more efficient, but really isn't taught anywhere.

Glass has a serious downside in how it's failing to develop basic flying skills in a new generation of pilots, the pilots just getting their feet in the door today. Around 2005 and 2006, the regional airlines were hiring every pilot with a commercial license, some with as little as 250 hours of flight time. These pilots didn't have the experience to know how and where to point the airplane at all times, and they were getting into the right seat of an automated regional jet. A friend called them the children of magenta, because all they know is how to follow the flight director command bars and the magenta line the FMS generates on their navigation displays. It will take an exceptional level of situational awareness and discipline for an inexperienced pilot to learn the requisite pure stick-and-rudder flying skills while watching the FMS fly the airplane. Besides being less efficient and a little sloppy, there will inevitably be accidents. Even a magic airplane can't protect its pilots from everything.

Worse still is that now there is a fly-by-wire regional jet, an airplane that has computers to interpret your control inputs as if they were simply autopilot commands, an airplane that makes you think you're the ace of the base, keeping the airplane rock-solid straight and level, but in reality the airplane's computers are doing all the hard work to keep it steady for you. This is safer for the occupants, but in an entry-level jet, it's not a good airplane for helping a novice pilot learn how to fly. Technically, you're not flying, because even when you're hand-flying, the autopilot is actually still flying.

When the automation receives bad inputs, the airplane can become thoroughly confused, to the point that Boeing's engineers couldn't even figure out the flight recorder's data after I flew a thoroughly confused airplane that gave us a false stall indication, with a continuous stick-shaker, while climbing at nearly three hundred knots. There was no procedure yet to help us filter the contradictory information that we had to interpret. All we had left was that learned sixth sense, air sense, raw flying sense, that knows that a certain pitch attitude and power setting will yield a certain acceptable speed, regardless of all the erroneous warnings with which our magic airplane was bombarding us.

The outcome was much different for a thoroughly confused Air France Airbus and its 228 occupants in June 2009. The airplane was airworthy and would've been perfectly flyable with total reversion to raw pitch, power, and airspeed flying, the old art of flying from a lost era. They ended up in the ocean off the coast of Brazil.

An airbus nearly collided with me once while it was flying an automated visual approach into Denver. The company was one that, by policy, even required automated visual approaches, those fun moments when pilots ordinarily get to be pilots, on their own to maneuver the airplane to the runway.

The visibility would've measured in the hundreds of miles if a landlocked weather observer had been able to measure that far. I was already on final for a south runway, descending toward an easy arrival on a sixteen-thousand-foot long runway with the airbus converging from the east to line up with a parallel south runway. Our airplane's Traffic Collision Avoidance System (TCAS) shouted "traffic," to let us know that another airplane was nearby. We looked to our left to visually find the offender. Then our TCAS became more serious, commanding us to climb. This was a resolution advisory, an evasive maneuver to prevent an imminent collision. I followed the command, reversing our descent, and then looked back to the east to see the massive airplane pass right under us, having failed to turn final for its assigned runway for whatever reason. If one of the pilots had been hand-flying the visual approach, instead of having been along for the ride by company mandate, we wouldn't have had this near collision, and if our airplane wasn't equipped with TCAS, there would've actually been a collision.

As a line holder, time seemed to be passing much too quickly. I would go to work four times, and then another month was history. I would have done nearly anything to make time slow down. A fed who rode in our jumpseat suggested that I join the FAA. He said the job can make one year seem like ten. I knew that it would be too difficult to sit in a jumpseat, as he was doing, jealously watching someone else fly. I couldn't do that yet; I was having too much fun. I was living the dream.

Now when I checked in for a trip, it was likely I already knew the crew, or most of it. I would usually know from looking at the crew list whether there would be any personality conflicts in the crew, but there really wasn't a lot of that; the ones who couldn't play nicely together usually trip-traded to avoid each other. I even knew who would want to go out on the overnights and who would likely just slam-click. I'm not much fun, but any time someone in the crew wanted to go out, I would go too. I was never the life of the party, and never will be, but we always had a good time. I was making some great friends, even if we would only fly together a couple of times per year.

I enjoyed the camaraderie on the job, and I got along well with everyone I flew with. It was just assumed that everyone who was there belonged there, that we were all professionals. During the course of a four-day trip, separated from society by a bullet-proof door and countless miles of deep blue sky, we could solve the world's problems. It seemed that way at least—maybe just a little hypoxia contributing to our delusions of grandeur. I occasionally even learned things about my colleagues that I suspected their spouses may not even know, and then at the end of the trip we would go back to our homes, hundreds of miles apart. Trust and respect were part of the environment.

I no longer heeded the advice from the old Eastern Airlines Skipper with the resentful family that had been handed down to me from a Captain when I was a new-hire. I was having fun on the job, and I told Dawn everything. She knew I would rather be home, but I was doing what I loved and I was happy, and she was totally supportive.

I even told Dawn about the flight attendants who flirted with me, rare as it was. Where were these girls when I was single? It was all just innocent, for me at least. There were some guys who got themselves into trouble, and their marriages probably suffered from it, regardless of whether their wives ever knew. At the end of the day I always walked alone to my solitary hotel room, but for a few fleeting moments, I was a legend in my own mind.

The airline hired a new vice president of marketing, the former CEO from the Kansas City-based airline that we had been waiting to go out of business. With him on the payroll the airline saw better utilization of the airplanes and they filled all the seats. It started to look like they could send an airplane virtually anywhere and fill it up.

This was in spite of the fact that the airline had eliminated most of what used to make their product special, what separated them from the rest of the industry. The airline was cheapening their product to the point that it was just commodity seats, like what every other airline offered, but was still somehow winning awards, maybe with help from the legacy that some didn't realize was already gone forever. All they had left were the cookies, and they weren't even very good. I thought they should change their slogan from "Best care in the air" to "We suck less than everyone else."

I heard that the new VP of marketing said if he had only known how poorly managed the airline really was, he would've kept his old airline operating for longer than he did.

The company made two more enormous blunders, one being that they didn't take their options for another twenty-five 717s. Since the airplane was a bastard stepchild inherited from a merger, Boeing permanently ceased production upon delivery of our last airplane, actually dismantling the old McDonnell Douglas assembly plant after the last airplane rolled through the production line. Once again the airline had a dead-end fleet, something they truly excelled at acquiring.

The airline decided they could save money by firing the airline's ground handlers (bag smashers), some of whom had been with the company since the beginning. Their replacements would be employed by the airline's commuter subsidiary at a fraction of the pay.

Finding minimum wage workers who were able to pass the federally mandated drug screening became quite a challenge, and they would generally lose more than half the class by the second day. In fact, it looked like they wouldn't even be able to hire and train enough people, but the date for the changeover was apparently already written in stone.

It turned out to be a memorably bleak day. There were enough people to park us at the gate on our way into Milwaukee, but they promptly disappeared. I ended up having to go down below to the forward cargo hold to retrieve the gate checked strollers, which happens occasionally and I'm more than happy to do.

We knew there would be delays, but an hour past our departure time, we asked operations when we could expect to leave. At the very least, we needed to tell the passengers something, and we were not going to lie. We told our passengers that the company had just outsourced our experienced ground handlers, this was the first day for an all replacement force, and we had no idea when we would be ready to leave. The operations tower was already in triage mode, trying to get flights out one at a time. They had closed half the gates for lack of personnel, and inbound airplanes were stacking up on the taxi-way, some waiting for more than three hours before they could even park.

I left the cockpit to assess our progress. The Captain followed me down the jet way stairs to find that we hadn't even been unloaded yet. We decided to do it ourselves, and then we loaded the airplane as our outbound luggage arrived. That was the only way we would be able to leave.

A commuting flight attendant was in the airplane, taking pictures of us loading the plane, photographic proof of management's blunder. She would eventually get fired, and I wouldn't doubt if her pictures were what first put her on their shit-list.

I wondered if the airline would have to shut down for a few days; that and begging the fired workers to come back seemed like the only remedy after fourteen hundred hours of flight delays in a single weekend. You can't run an airline without people to push back and park the airplanes, sort, load, and unload the bags and freight, and service the water and lavs.

There were still significant problems once they hired enough people. Everyone, except for the MBAs who dreamed up this stupid plan, expected accidents as the inexperienced help drove belt loaders and long trains of baggage carts near multi-million dollar airplanes, perpetually in a hurry. Accidents happened, and every time metal was bent, it cost them much more than what they were expecting to save with a smaller payroll. Two airplanes were even pushed into each other on one notorious occasion.

It is also very hard to keep employees when you pay them fast-food wages, so inexperience became a systemic problem. Twice while doing my walk around, I had to actually show people how to connect the air conditioning ducts to the airplane. The airline also wasn't able to keep the number of mishandled bags low either, and the airline would pay for that with delivery fees and the lost trust of inconvenienced customers. There were even thefts of and from luggage.

During a walk around I found a tow bar hooked to the airplane's nose wheels without having the airplane's steering bypassed. This was a very serious omission, because if the airplane had any hydraulic pressure and we moved a rudder pedal or the tiller, anyone within the arc of the tow bar would get their legs broken, or worse.

During an especially clumsy push back, the tug driver got the airplane jacked around at an odd angle and then jumped out of the tug and left, apparently walking off his challenging job in the middle of a push back. We were stuck there, attached to an empty tug, halfway out of the gate, with the engines running, waiting for the supervisor to come out and finish the job.

After another push back, the marshaller walked out in front of the airplane to guide us out, but as he turned toward us he didn't cross his wands to keep us stopped, like he was supposed to do. His wands were at his side, because that's where his arms have been for most of his life until taking this job. Unfortunately, that was the signal to the Captain that we can move, but the tug was still under the nose of the airplane, on my side, where the Captain couldn't see it. I realized this when I heard him release the parking brake. I stopped him before the airplane moved, before we crushed the nose of the airplane on the roof of the tug, saving the company a few million dollars, if the airplane would've even been salvageable.

I have to say that everyone tried very hard, but sometimes—most of the time—you get what you pay for, except with exorbitant executive salaries. In spite of the resultant damages, inefficiencies, and lost productivity, the company's thirst for outsourcing would not be quenched, but that's for another chapter.

All of our furloughed pilots were back at work, and the airline was actually hiring new pilots. I was moving up the seniority list. The company was evaluating replacements for the MD-80s, and the eventual order was alleged to allow expansion. I figured out how many additional airplanes would be required to get me in the left seat, and it wasn't very many.

There were even dates circulating for when we were supposed to hear the big announcement for the fleet replacement. All the dates came and went and still there was nothing, even though there were only two viable choices, literally A or B: Airbus A-320 or Boeing 737. This was still the same management team that took six months to decide on new salt and pepper shakers, the same management team that didn't take options on more 717s before Boeing permanently shut down the old McDonnell Douglas assembly line, the same management team that outsourced the Milwaukee ramp and took away everything that made us the best domestic airline, except the cookies.

Fortunately, I wasn't depending on the company for my happiness. Pilots are good at compartmentalizing things, loving the job while hating the name painted on the side of the airplane and the symbolic cookies served in its cabin. When you finish a trip you leave the job at the gate where you park the airplane, and you don't think about it again until it's time to start the next trip. I've certainly complained, but I've had good reason to, and I still loved my job as much as I ever had.

Jay was four years old when he surprised me by saying, "Daddy, I'm not going to fly airplanes when I grow up." It surprised me because I didn't think I ever talked about work while I was at home. I didn't even know that he knew I flew airplanes. That was my other life, the one my family never saw. I told him he would spend a lot of his life working, so he needed to enjoy what he did, but I asked him why my career was already so definitively disqualified. His answer was, "Four-day trips." He was my little buddy while I was furloughed, and he missed me when I was away.

In a different conversation during the same year, Jay asked why I had to do four-day trips. I told him I needed to make money so we could pay for the house, utilities, and food. Jay said, "You could fly one-day trips and we could live in a smaller house." Smart little guy, certainly smarter than his old man.

I was making more money than Dawn was for the first time in my career, but we had seen such wild swings in income every year that we didn't even know how much money we really needed to live. My accountant must dread her annual appointment with us. The interest rate on our mortgage was low, and that was our only debt. We needed another car, so we wrote a check for it. The other two cars were great airport cars, and they had been paid off for years. We opened the windows and turned off the air conditioning whenever the weather permitted. It saved money, but we also liked the fresh air. We cancelled our cable once we realized we rarely ever turned the television on. I had discovered the library, so I didn't buy as many books as I used to. I didn't get rid of clothes until they rotted, so I was still wearing some clothes that I wore when I was sixteen. If you're never in style, you don't have to worry about going out of style. If we needed to buy something, we bought it. If we wanted to do something, we did it. Otherwise, the surplus went into the savings account, and we had a substantial surplus.

All around us, we saw consumption fueled by ever increasing debt. Few people bothered to save money because they thought their houses would continue to appreciate forever, allowing them to amass wealth that only existed in theory. We wanted no part of it, and we never imagined that the irresponsibility of others would affect us, but that's for another chapter.

We didn't want to leave Jay all alone in the world once we were gone from it, so we were going to try to give him a sibling. Dawn had recently been asked during a checkup whether we were going to have any more children. Her doctor prescribed pre-natal vitamins, even though Dawn wasn't even pregnant yet.

Three weeks later Dawn had a thyroid storm, along with some other symptoms that we would eventually learn were indicative of a mineral overdose, which even effected her menstrual cycle. We already ate an extremely healthy diet, plus the fortification of some processed foods has replaced old health problems with some new ones. People no longer die from anemia, but now people die from hemochromatosis, iron poisoning. Dawn's prenatal vitamins contained enough iron to swing a compass. She stopped taking them, and her symptoms started clearing up, very slowly.

Five months after fighting for preapproval we were finally able to see an endocrinologist, a wait that far exceeds the wait that Canadians and Europeans expect from their national health care systems. We did a tremendous amount of research during our months of waiting, and the young endocrinologist got very defensive when she realized we might actually know as much about the thyroid gland as she did. So there's another threshold into adulthood: when you're several years older than and maybe even just as knowledgeable as the specialists you just paid hundreds of dollars to talk to for five minutes.

This was also an anecdotal indication of how broken our health care system really was. The doctor was actually becoming hostile as she said that the only possible treatment would be to destroy Dawn's thyroid gland and to put her on a synthetic thyroid hormone for the rest of her life. One pharmaceutical causes a serious medical condition, which is treated by a lifelong regimen of other pharmaceuticals— pharmaceuticals with their own marketing budgets that fund free dinners and trips for cooperative doctors.

We ran out of there and never looked back. After oscillating between hyper—and hypo-thyroid as her body tried to return to its former equilibrium, Dawn finally had a normal thyroid test a couple of months later, something two drug-pushing doctors assured us would be impossible. We looked at a calendar to estimate when she would be ovulating. I did some trip trades so I could have some extra days off in a row at the right time. Then Dawn was pregnant. Three weeks into the pregnancy, KC, our dog was the first to know, just like when Dawn was pregnant with Jay. Three weeks into her pregnancy with Jay, the dog became inexplicably destructive, something she had never done. This time the dog suddenly began sleeping on the bed in the guest room, a previously forbidden act but one I could live with.

We had actually been hoping Dawn would be laid off because of the amount of severance for which she was now eligible. It never happened. Neal was on his way into the world, and we considered Dawn going to part time or even quitting after he was born.

Since I was a line holder, I had a much better chance of being home for Neal's birth. I arranged my schedule so I would have ten days off in a row near the due date.

We had a false alarm that I left a trip early for. Dawn wasn't as close as we thought, so I reluctantly went back to work. If I took more time off now, I would have less time to spend with him after he was born.

In Tampa I made the softest landing I had ever made in a hundred-thousand-pound jetliner. I didn't even feel the subtle vibration as the wheels spun up, probably thanks to some extra grease in the wheel bearings after one of our factory new airplanes had a wheel bearing fire that pre-empted CNN's prime time schedule on a slow news day. The Captain followed my landing with an incredibly smooth stop at the gate, the airplane exhausting its last ounce of kinetic energy, easing to a stop just as our marshaller crossed his wands. We ran the parking checklist, and then I turned toward the Captain and asked, "Are we on the ground yet?"

I expected a smart remark tossed right back at me from the quick-witted Captain, but instead he just said with an uncustomarily straight face, "That was the smoothest landing I've ever seen in this airplane." That meant a lot to me, because he had taught most of the company how to fly the airplane, being one of the first instructors to get checked out in it.

Then I realized he had mentioned that he'd never flown this particular airframe, ship number 917. Mine was technically the only landing he'd seen in that airplane, and yes, he was making a joke. It was still worthy of a bow to the passengers.

I got up and opened the cockpit door. A lady stopped to give me a hug as she was leaving the airplane, squeezing me much tighter than what would be considered polite from a stranger. That was the only hug I ever got after a landing, but the landing was memorable for another reason; it was my last one for a month and a half.

That night Dawn called me at two-thirty in the morning. I was in Kansas City in a hotel room that was so dark I had trouble finding my phone. There were no nonstop flights home. None of the connections looked very good, and I couldn't even get out of town until six. Dawn had a fairly quick and easy labor with Jay, and I had just barely made it home in time. I knew I was going to miss this one.

A couple hours later, as I was going through security at the airport, my mother called me. I could hear my new baby crying in the background.

I burned all of my sick time on family leave, again. Dawn took her limit of family leave, and then she took a week of vacation (my grandmother's one hundredth birthday party had been on the schedule for a while—well, for a hundred years).

Dawn went back to work as a part-timer, Tuesday through Thursday. I would fly a commutable three-or four-day trip on the weekend, so we were getting by without any day care. We just didn't have a very good lifestyle, and we still had a newborn to take care of. After three months of this, Dawn quit her job. She was finally able to do what she had always wanted with Jay but that my unstable career had prevented.

The airline was still hiring, and I was steadily moving up the seniority list. I finally had the seniority to bid summer vacations. I could have weekends off if I wanted them, but I was still getting more productive trips on the weekends. I even broke with tradition and took all of the holidays off one year. When I got my December schedule, Dawn and I sat down with a calendar to figure out when we would celebrate Christmas, an annual ritual for us. We looked at all of the possibilities but then realized we should probably just celebrate on Christmas for once.

I eventually got rid of the crashpad after realizing I would usually only need to stay in Milwaukee once or twice a month, and I once went three months without staying there at all. When I needed to, I would get a cheap hotel room with thin walls, but it was still better than the crashpad, usually.

It's really not very often that your neighbor's headboard is rhythmically banging into the thin wall, but it always seems to happen when you have just a few short hours to sleep before catching the first flight home in the morning. I was irritated, hoping they would just get it over with quickly, but so exhausted that I fell asleep anyway. Then I woke up to my bed shaking. "Please, not again!" I was still irritated and groggy with sleep inertia when I realized it was actually my bed that was shaking, and I was the only person in it. It was an earthquake, which would've been a more welcome novelty except that I really needed to sleep.

I had the flexibility to get junior assigned whenever I wanted. Crew scheduling would leave a message on my cell phone. If I wanted to go in to work on a day off, usually just a day earlier than my next trip, I'd call them back. They needed me, so they'd give me a positive space pass to Milwaukee, eliminating any potential commuting headaches. They even held a flight out of Columbus for me once. Then they'd pay me 50 percent more to do my job. I could either just stay on the trip they junior assigned me to, or if I really wanted to make a lot of money I could have them work me back to my scheduled trip once it started. The airline was now perpetually short of pilots, so there were plenty of opportunities for them to pay me Captain's wages for being a First Officer. A few times, I flew right up to the legal limit of thirty hours during a modified five-day trip, and a considerable number of those hours would be at time-and-a-half pay.

The immediate goals of an airline pilot, besides the obvious imperatives of not getting killed or violated, are time off and money. When I bid my schedule each month, I looked at the maximum amount of pay I could earn for the fewest number of work days. We all did this, and it in no way reflected our work ethic or how much we enjoyed the job.

I thoroughly enjoyed my job. It was never boring to me to be flying to the same twenty-five or so airports trip after trip after trip. The airplanes, the airports, and the hotels were familiar, comfortable, and predictable. We had enough dynamic variables already, so it was nice that some things always stayed the same. Adventure was something I would rather avoid. I had my favorite restaurants and favorite walks in each city, and I always had plenty to read. This was the job from which I hoped to retire.

Commuting was the most stressful part of the job, but I felt I had one of the easier commutes. I had a one-leg, on-line commute to Milwaukee with little competition for the jump-seat. When our agents saw I was listed for a flight, they would just check me in and give me a seat. A couple of times when I was listed on the evening flight they even called me to tell me the flight was running late so I could spend a little extra time at home.

The worst part of my commute was that Americans were getting too fat. The thirty-two-seat jets I rode to work on—another dead-end airplane, of course—were originally designed to carry exactly thirty-two passengers, plus maybe a jumpseater. When the airlines had to increase passenger weight by twenty pounds per person, it effectively took three seats away from these airplanes. There were only a few airplanes that could absorb the difference, so I had to look on line to see which airplane was coming to Columbus when the flight was going to be full. If the wrong airplane was coming, I would have to take an earlier flight or make a two-leg commute on a different airline, and it was because of the consequences of super-sized meals and the all-you-can-eat buffet, things I never thought would affect me.

The problem is much more complex than big portions and buffets and the cheap subsidized commodity crops that make them possible. No society has ever been so disconnected from its natural environment and the basic elements of survival, such as the pastoral production of healthy food. We know about gigabytes, but we often don't even know what are the healthiest bites on our plates—usually the kale leaf or the parsley sprig that appears solely for garnish and generally ends up in the garbage.

Part of the problem is that no HMO (Health Maintenance Organization, in case future readers are lucky enough to not know what they are) wants to truly invest in prevention when a competing HMO is likely to be the fiscal beneficiary of their efforts because of rampant job hopping and layoffs. If they knew they would likely be paying for your self-destructive sins twenty years from now, they would give real incentives to doctors and nurses who could nag their patients to change unhealthy behaviors.

France has even figured out that regulating clothing sizes keeps people healthy. When someone realizes they can barely fit into their old size eight, they're usually motivated to do something about it by the nagging snugness in the waist. American clothiers (who sell garments stitched in Malaysia and Bangladesh) keep making their size eights bigger and bigger, knowing that it will lead to more consumption of not only high fructose corn syrup but also overpriced clothing that would actually last twenty years if only you could still fit into it.

We had an unusual exercise in recurrent ground school, our annual reprogramming, and it was evidence of a financially motivated cultural change in the company. We broke up into groups of about four pilots each and were presented with brief narratives of emergency situations, some of which were vaguely familiar because they were all emergencies that had occurred at the airline during the past year.

After discussing each emergency within our group, we would reach a consensus for the proper course of action, which we would in turn share with the entire class. The class was largely unanimous with each situation, which also happened to mirror the way that the real emergencies played out, a degree of consistency that should've made the training department proud. Then the Director of Training, who really didn't teach any more since ascending to the director level, told us how our solutions were wrong, all of them, including the actions of the crews who had actually experienced the emergencies in flight.

It's worth noting that no one died, and in fact no one was even injured, and no airplanes were wrecked, or even damaged, but the Director wanted us to handle the emergencies in cheaper ways and in ways that didn't disrupt the generation of revenue.

The room was filled with looks of disbelief, at least from those of us who had been pushed to continue on by prior employers, mainly the ones who had done hard time on the dark side of the industry. Our job during an emergency was to keep everyone alive, not to preserve schedule integrity and save money. That's what we did when we weren't handling an emergency, which was the other 99.99 percent of the time. We had to be able to define our immediate objective, and our pilots were an experienced group who were exceptionally good at doing that.

One of the many things I loved about airline flying was that, until that bizarre exercise, we were immune to any discussion of how much it cost to find the safest possible course of action, which was all that mattered operationally. Suddenly it seemed like I had gone back to night freight, where safety was theoretically important, but only if it didn't cost too much or delay the freight.

We also learned that First Officers would only go to the simulator once a year instead of twice as it had always been. The Director of Training's reason was that a couple of other airlines had decided to only send First Officers to the simulator once a year, so our airline lowered the bar to match them, in both training costs and proficiency.

As much as I didn't like going to the simulator, it was a vital exercise. Recurrent flight training events were especially important because they were packed full of unique and extremely challenging situations that we always learned from, and now the First Officers would miss every other one.

Years later I flew with a pilot whose airline (a regional airline) had a training program that only required demonstrated proficiency for certain maneuvers during initial training. It had been years since he had performed a stall recovery. It showed, and we were even training, so he knew about it in advance, in a controlled environment and at a safe altitude. His clumsy stall recovery was a wild gyration between secondary stalls and excessive altitude loss, not good enough for when a pilot would actually need to recover, without warning and at low altitude.

I actually put this training to use once while departing Boston when the Captain accidentally retracted the slats when he was only supposed to retract the flaps, which suddenly increased our stall speed by about forty knots. The hundred passengers never knew they rode through a stall recovery. This wasn't supposed to happen because of a gate that prevented inadvertent movement of the flap handle all the way to the slat retract position, but the gate wouldn't always stop the handle after a flaps-five (five-degree flaps) takeoff, the lowest flap setting we could use, which wasn't often encountered. I learned to watch for it, so I caught the handle the next time someone inadvertently did that to me.

Fuel in the tanks means more options operationally, and more options increases safety, but it costs money to carry extra contingencies in your fuel tanks. The less fuel you have left, the more likely you are to reach a point of no return, a point where you're committed, when you no longer have enough fuel to resort to plan B as plan A begins to unravel—a situation you never want to find yourself in. As the airlines got leaner with fuel in their effort to save a few bucks, we would find ourselves in these situations more often. We would land with the low-fuel light glaring at us so often it had become almost normal.

It was actually sometimes a blessing when the weather was marginal at our destination because we would be carrying enough fuel to fly from our destination to an alternate airport. We used to be able to list alternate airports when the weather didn't require it, or to just order additional fuel for the unknown, but now it seemed like we had to justify every additional pound of fuel we tried to upload. If the weather was good, we might be dispatched with just enough fuel to fly to our destination with a legal reserve (which doesn't belong to us except by emergency authority), plus maybe fifteen minutes of holding fuel, which we could burn through quickly if we were flying faster than holding speed or, even worse, if we had to slow down enough to have to throw the slats and flaps out.

We always knew how much it would cost to carry extra fuel, since a reminder was now printed on our flight release, but we never knew when we would actually need it. On a beautiful but chilly morning in Pittsburgh, we knew we would burn a little of our holding fuel before we even got off the ground. Our dispatcher didn't consider that we would have a heavy frost, or maybe didn't know that in Pittsburgh we would need to taxi the airplane to the de-ice pad in order to get that frost removed.

We discussed how we were using extra fuel before we even left the ground, but the weather was supposed to be beautiful in Kansas City. It was indeed a beautiful morning. The sky glowed in the early morning light without a cloud in sight and without even the slightest ripple to disturb the air. The cockpit air was filled with the aroma of each new pot of coffee the flight attendants brewed, of special importance after a scheduled reduced rest overnight.

A lone, renegade towering cumulus cloud pierced the placid morning sky. "Where did that thing come from, and more importantly, how close is it to the airport?" It was an unforecasted anomaly, rapidly building in ferocity and racing us to the Kansas City airport. Especially with enough opportunities, and we certainly had a lot of opportunities, things don't always turn out how they are supposed to. Unfortunately, on this particular flight, we didn't have enough fuel for a safe remedy. It appeared we would beat this developing monster to the airport, but not by much. We didn't have enough fuel for a diversion, and besides, St. Joseph, Missouri, was likely still obscured by some early morning river-valley fog. More fuel would have given us more diversionary airports. We just had to beat this thing, and we were essentially already committed to do just that.

I flew a high-speed arrival, trading even more fuel for speed, but then we had to slow down to follow one of our gas-guzzling MD-80s coming in from San Francisco, who was undoubtedly even more desperate to land than we were. We landed on the East runway, trying to put an extra mile between us and the rapidly approaching storm. The outflow gust had just reached the airport, triggering the wind shear alert system. Ordinarily, this would've triggered a go-around, but now the airline was too cheap to give us enough fuel for a go-around. I landed with a forty knot direct crosswind.

The full fury of the storm arrived while we were taxiing to the gate, with marble-sized hail and raindrops that spread to the size of half-dollars upon impact with the windshield. We saw our bag-smashers retreat from the hailstones and then the lightning kept them inside. We could only stop just short of the gate and wait as the storm raged. "Who cares if we run out of fuel now; they can tow us the last hundred feet." Our passengers were now captives, growing impatient. They would never know how lucky they really were, trapped but at least safely on the ground.

During my tenure in the airline industry, it seemed as though the bar was being lowered industry wide. Customer service, pay, benefits, retirement, work rules, hiring requirements, and, most importantly, safety were being inexorably eroded in a great race for the gutter, the inevitable culmination of deregulation, the sacrifices imposed upon us to help fund your hundred dollar airfares. The industry was hiding behind respectable accident statistics from a couple of lucky years, aided by the self-preservation built into the newer automated airplanes. Luck always runs out eventually, and the aftermath of every accident inevitably shows how it was a preventable tragedy.

With only thirty-six airplanes but established markets with loyal customers, I figured that the company would eventually be bought by another airline. There was a secret takeover attempt, but our CEO refused to sell. The buyer increased its offer and then campaigned through the media, which eventually led to the election of a couple of new board members, handpicked by the buyer.

Our CEO still refused to sell, waging his own media campaign. He claimed he was trying to save the hometown airline and its superior product. To believe him, you had to overlook the fact that he had already degraded a once-exceptional product to the point that the only thing that now separated the company from every other airline was a cookie I had grown to despise. He was literally trying to save the cookie, which was even the name of the website that was part of his campaign.

It's worth mentioning that the CEO's wife owned the company that made the cookies and that a very large number of the CEO's stock options would have been under water if he had sold the company at the offered price, but I'm sure he was only concerned with what was best for his community, his customers, and the employees who generated the revenue and kept his customers the happiest customers in the industry.

The CEO decided to solicit help from the CEO of his largest local competitor, which seemed like an odd move, and together, these strange bed-fellows found a private equity firm willing to offer a higher bid, with other people's money.

A bidding war ensued between our two suitors, with the private equity firm offering a sum that the other airline couldn't quite match, $452 million. The board of directors, even the members nominated by the other airline bidding for us, unanimously decided to sell to the private equity firm. Their responsibility wasn't to the future of the business, the community, the customers, or the employees; it was to that moment's stock price and nothing else.

Our CEO somehow kept his job along with a $10 million payout from his stock options, but he wasn't necessarily still running the company. The new owners hired an expensive firm full of hypercompetitive thirty-year-old MBAs to come in and restructure the airline to the satisfaction of whatever incestuous relationship they were servicing. These were some ruthless bastards, on steroids, the kind of people who graduated at the tops of their business classes, had good haircuts and good golf games, and who would remorselessly sell their first-born to a brothel in Thailand in order to make partner in the firm.

Meanwhile on Wall Street, an extremely powerful investment bank that had a suspicious track record of profiting from every market bubble in the past hundred years successfully pleaded to the Commodity Futures Trading Commission for the reversal of a Depression era regulation that helped protect farmers from market manipulation. This reversal created, well, of course, market manipulation, manifested in a sudden speculative frenzy in commodities markets that sent the price of oil soaring to $147 per barrel, in total defiance of normal market pressures.

The price of jet fuel, now a typical airline's largest expense, tripled. The price of a ticket didn't. In fact, ticket prices were still as low as they had ever been, because passengers will search the internet for days just to find a ticket that's ten dollars cheaper.

The airline announced that they were eventually going to be parking the MD-80 fleet. The MD-80s burned a lot more fuel than the 717s, a convenient excuse, but they actually had lower seat-mile costs (the actual operating cost to fly each seat). They had a lot more seats than the 717s, and the airline actually owned five of the airplanes, with tiny lease payments on the other ones. Even with the slowing economy, there were still markets that they couldn't seem to throw enough seats at because the industry had already begun reducing capacity, desperately trying to drive yield up.

The loss of the MD-80s would mean furloughs, again, but the cuts wouldn't be deep enough to get me this time. I was scared enough that I decided to update my resume, which was a long process. I hadn't kept my logbooks up to date since I'd logged my ten-thousandth hour of flight time. Now I was already two years behind.

We would soon learn how the thirty-year-old MBAs intended to negotiate with the airline's stakeholders, all of them—what the union called "shock and awe." It would prove to be just as functionally ineffective as Donald Rumsfeld's version of "shock and awe" in Iraq.

All it did was piss off everyone. In retrospect, that may have been exactly what they were trying to do, as they packaged the airline neatly for yet another sale. Unlike the airline's management, these bad-asses had a plan.

The thirty-year-old MBAs asked the pilots to work for less than half of our current pay rates, and they also asked to take away vacation and work rules. They said their demands were immediate and not open to negotiation and the airline would shut down if we didn't give them everything.

The union asked them to open their books to justify such drastic demands, information that was promised but never came. The union refused their demands. Deadlines passed. The airline didn't shut down.

The company quit making payments to Boeing and Rolls-Royce for the 717s. Then the thirty-year-old MBAs went to Boeing and said, "This is what we're willing to pay for the airplanes." Boeing actually agreed. The airline was going to keep the airplanes for $165,000 per airplane per month, which was really a bargain. They became dead-end airplanes when Boeing shut down the assembly line, so what else would Boeing do with them? Park them in the desert at a total loss? Then a really smart guy said, "Let's come back tomorrow and talk about $160,000."

Boeing was sufficiently pissed off by the next day, so they asked for the airplanes back. Now the airline really had a problem. You can't operate an airline without airplanes, and it had become apparent that management's threat to shut us down was only a bluff; they weren't going to walk away from $452,000,000. They had to find some airplanes quickly.

Meanwhile on Wall Street, the speculative frenzy in the oil markets ran out of momentum and prices tumbled all the way back down to where supply and demand would have held them. The financial industry complained that it was suddenly out of money, blaming the crisis on their bad mortgages, which was a steadily growing problem, not necessarily a sudden crisis. The timing of their cash crunch looked a lot like they got caught with their hands in the oil barrel. It wasn't illegal, but it wouldn't have been popular for them to say, "Our greed made you pay four dollars a gallon for gas; now hurry up and bail us out or the whole economy will collapse."

The economy had already been receding before the soaring energy prices; the financial panic made it much worse. This only deepened the mortgage crisis, because people who were living paycheck to paycheck couldn't stay in their houses as the paychecks ran out. I was worried that the country would slide into a depression like what my grandparents had lived through, except for the fact that people were still camping out for three days to be the first to buy the latest video game and spending a billion dollars a year on ringtones for their cell phones. Was that evidence that the economy wasn't totally collapsing, or proof that our species has hopelessly lost its way?

The company announced that they were pulling back to a twenty-one airplane schedule, but they hadn't told us yet that they had gotten a little too full of themselves and had their airplanes repossessed. I tried to figure out whether twenty-one airplanes would be enough to keep me on the payroll. It would be close.

It also didn't help that the FAA had changed the retirement age from sixty to sixty-five at the end of the prior year, delaying retirements until 2013. A very large pilot group had campaigned for the change after their pension plan was eliminated during one of their airline's trips through bankruptcy court. Whether a pilot supported raising the retirement age usually seemed to depend a lot on how many ex-wives they were still paying for and whether or not they had a life outside of the cockpit, or conversely whether that life included extremely expensive toys.

Then the CEO dropped the bomb on us on September third, our day of infamy. The first line of the memo read: "I'm pleased to announce." A few paragraphs later he mentioned that he would be furloughing three-quarters of his flight crews while he outsourced our flying to twelve 76-seat RJs crewed by pilots who were making a mere fraction of the money we made. Soon to be parked by another airline, those were the only airplanes that could be found on short notice. Boeing would let the airline keep nine 717s on short-term leases in order to fly their twenty-one airplane schedule.

Our contract (the pilots' collective bargaining agreement) was now amendable, and the company opened by saying that we might eventually be able to fly the outsourced airplanes if we were willing to work for the wages they had demanded of us back in June. Their First Officer wages would make a pilot eligible for food stamps. We were professionals. That was not acceptable, but they were pointing a gun at our heads.

As regional jets (RJs) had grown larger, pushing the boundary between regional airline pay and work rules well into mainline sized airplanes, I had known all along that a pilot group was going to have to stick its neck out in order to reverse, or even just stop, the trend. I just never thought it would be mine.

I was ready to walk off the job if the union said so, but they were never going to order an illegal job action, which a strike would've been. We could've called it a safety stand down since we were all probably too distracted and disgusted to safely fly swept-wing, flush-riveted, transonic jetliners. A lot of guys were already doing that, just calling in sick for all of their trips.

We had mainline pay rates, pay rates developed when we were still flying sixty-seat DC-9-10s. Now they were making us buy our jobs back to fly a seventy-six-seat airplane, which is still a pretty big airplane, for a fraction of the pay.

Our contract had weak scope, but we had protection specifically for this situation. They could subcontract out our flying for up to 180 days, but they couldn't furlough because of it. The union grieved this immediately and sent it to expedited arbitration so we could resolve it within months instead of years. We needed to do something before our replacements were in our seats.

The union held a rally a week after the day of infamy, on September eleventh. After the rally a couple hundred pilots and flight attendants, in uniform and carrying signs, walked from the union office to the airport and back. We blocked traffic a few times, but it was all for show. Television cameras filmed our march, but it undoubtedly got less local news coverage than the *American Idol* semi-finals.

The union scheduled a guerrilla picket to coincide with the next contract negotiation. Before we left for picketing, we lined up on both sides of the sidewalk to the union office, a gauntlet of pissed-off, soon to be unemployed pilots. I had carried the aluminum poles to our big union banner down to the bus, but when the VP of flight operations and two of the thirty-year-old MBAs arrived, I held the poles under the crook of my arm as if I was aiming a machine gun at them. They faced some angry stares and profanities, and I wouldn't have been too surprised if someone had snapped and it escalated into an ass kicking. It wouldn't have accomplished anything though. Maybe a few pilots would've gone to jail. The young MBAs probably would've proudly displayed their cuts and bruises like badges of honor, board room brutality taken to a new level.

The CEO now had bodyguards, but surprisingly, he flew on his own airline a couple of times. The bag smashers lost his luggage both times. Thank you for the support, guys. If he had shown up on my airplane, I would've grabbed my suitcase and left. On my way out of the airport, I would've called crew scheduling to tell them I had the shits, and it probably would've even been true. Anger was tearing at my insides already; I couldn't imagine actually having to face the asshole.

Our pissed-off pilot group was more unified than ever, bound by a visceral hatred of the individuals who were perpetrating the injustice about to be done. Attempting to calm the blazing emotions, a few were even saying, "This is just business; it's not personal."

They were stealing my contractually agreed rights and my livelihood, and they would get away with it unless the union could figure out how to stop them. I tried to hide my anger and worries, but my kids could still sense it. Jay and Neal weren't fully aware that some corporate thugs were stealing their future, but they were worried enough that they weren't sleeping well at night. With my kids feeling my anguish, this wasn't just business, it was very personal.

The anger only got worse after our replacements started showing up in Milwaukee. Every time one of our replacements would make a radio call, one of our pilots would say "scab" over the radio or just key their microphone so that any transmission was just a loud unreadable squeal.

I followed one of the replacement airplanes to the airport on a breezy, rainy day, really just another day at the office. The replacement pilot complained about the bumpy ride on the approach to the runway twice, with a sense of urgency in his voice. Their ride through rain and wind should've been effortless, their fly-by-wire airplane absorbing and correcting the atmospheric tumult we were correcting manually, and instinctively. The Captain and I glanced at each other, both shaking our heads. A dreary day on the cusp of winter, but not extraordinarily so, the day contained mundane challenges to which at least two of our replacements, the pilots flying the airplane in front of us, had not yet grown accustomed. They landed and gave the tower a braking action report with the same sense of urgency, which obviously meant they were sliding around on the wet pavement, mistaking their limited abilities for impaired braking. There is a difference, and it's an enormous difference when seventy-six unsuspecting passengers are sliding around with them on what is essentially a training flight. I asked the Captain, "It's raining; how are these kids going to survive a Milwaukee winter?" They were carrying our passengers on our routes, and because of this, I still felt responsible for their safety, even though the company had illegally given our flying to the lowest bidder.

I would actually talk to the replacement pilots, because most were Columbus based and they would often deadhead to and from Milwaukee on the same flights that I commuted on. I gave them brochures from our union and explained that they were taking our jobs. Some had been oblivious. Some knew, were sorry, and didn't want any part of our flying, but they were still taking it from us, doing what had perversely become an entry-level job.

If we had been on strike, our replacements had a contractual right to refuse the flying. Unfortunately, the Railway Labor Act is very specific about when pilots can strike, which is almost never. Management also wasn't allowed to lock us out, but that's exactly what they were about to do.

Some of our pilots were campaigning during their cabin announcements, and a few were even getting into trouble over it, even though the company manual actually tells us to be honest with our passengers.

I flew a four-day trip with a bitter Captain who assured me that I could say whatever I wanted to say over the PA (passenger address). We flew a northern route into New York. As all of the palatial estates of Westchester County came into view, I grew angry at the greed that led to successive bubbles of legitimized corruption for which we, the rest of us, always have to pay. The perpetrators have figured out how to privatize their profits and socialize their losses. As I kissed the passengers goodbye, I said that New York had sunny skies, with a slight chance of falling bodies on Wall Street. At the gate, a lady said my remark wasn't funny. It wasn't meant to be. I had no sympathy for the greedy speculators, throwing themselves out of windows, chasing their falling fortunes and their plummeting oil futures.

A couple of days later, we were leaving Seattle a little late and we both had flights home that would be tight to make. We flew very fast to make up time. I showed the Captain a trick to fool the auto-throttles that one of our instructors had showed me once when dispatch wanted us to get an airplane from New York to Los Angeles as quickly as possible. It worked great, but there was a price to pay, for our new owners to pay. We burned an extra eighteen hundred pounds of fuel from Seattle to Kansas City and then an extra five hundred pounds to Milwaukee.

All of the pilots had been saving fuel to help the company, but since the CEO had dropped the bomb on us, many bitter pilots had been trying to burn extra fuel. I had heard some were even cruising with the spoilers out, effectively crossing the country with one foot on the gas and one foot on the brake. Yes, it was unprofessional, but we were still human too, and pissed, and it was the only thing we could do to hurt the company that was illegally throwing us away.

It probably didn't even hurt the company because they probably knew it was coming, just part of the closing costs in their deal with the devil. We got memos warning us not to say anything too controversial to our passengers and asking us not to call in sick, but we never heard about the sudden surge in fuel burns.

I got in the airplane to fly a Vegas out-and-back. Right away, another bitter Captain brought up the subject of PAs, saying, "My mother told me that if I don't have something nice to say, I shouldn't say anything at all. So I don't talk to the passengers anymore at all."

I had devised a PA that I thought would deliver the message that our passengers' safety had been outsourced to the lowest bidder without getting me into trouble. "Do you mind if I give all of the PAs tonight?"

As we started descending into Las Vegas, I grabbed the phone, and asked the Captain how long he had been flying and how much flight time he had. Then I pushed the PA button:

"We'll be landing in Las Vegas in twenty minutes. The airport is reporting clear skies, light winds, and a temperature of ninety-five degrees. I would like to take this opportunity to say that it has been my pleasure to fly you around the country for the past eight years. This is one of my last flights with the airline. Your flight crew tonight has fifty-two years of combined flying experience, and thirty-two thousand hours of combined flight time, but we're about to be replaced by inexperienced, low-paid flight crews whose combined ages may not be fifty-two."

We opened the cockpit door as soon we parked. Neither of us was prepared for the response from the passengers. Not only had all the passengers actually listened to me, they all had something to say, every one of them. Passengers even lined up outside the cockpit to shake both of our hands and thank us before going off to shake hands with one-armed bandits. Passengers asked if they could write letters, so I gave them the CEO's e-mail address, not that it would change my fate.

I took a brief stroll through the terminal to avoid having to use the nasty lavs in the airplane after the long flight to Vegas. I passed rows of obnoxiously conspicuous slot machines and called Dawn to sarcastically tell her that we were just about to get our lucky break. I was kidding, but actually tempted by desperation. I couldn't do it though, knowing that a dollar stolen by a machine was a dollar I couldn't feed my family with.

I gave the same passenger address and got the same response after the return flight to Milwaukee. We even got a couple of hugs, and a few people who lingered to talk with us. One man wouldn't even make eye contact with us as he fled, probably a boss who had outsourced some of his loyal, hard-working employees in pursuit of shareholder value. Otherwise I had reached 197 people that evening, but still, that wouldn't save my job.

This was about much more than my own selfish anger at having my job outsourced. Your safety deserves a degree of maturity that is hard to find in young hot-shots eager to conquer the world. I've been there. As a young freight pilot, I got the job done quickly and cheaply, even in situations where my pilot-pushing employer would've agreed that the most prudent action would've been none at all. Only my own life had been endangered.

Not every regional pilot is an inexperienced kid, but during times of rapid expansion and quick upgrades, there will be plenty of flights crewed by a couple of young punks with very shallow pools of experience and maturity to draw from in a challenging and dynamic world.

On a dreary winter day, just another day at the office although a little more work than most, I taxied to the de-ice pad in Kansas City with a good friend who had once been the airline's Chief Pilot. Freezing drizzle glazed every open surface, but we could tell with a glance at the damp frigid sky that conditions were deteriorating, and deteriorating faster than the weather could be updated. This was the kind of day that required a full de-icing program, a hot shower of Type I fluid to remove the ice we already had, plus an expensive additional shower of cold Type IV fluid to more effectively prevent new ice from forming.

We configured the airplane for de-icing and waited behind one of our replacements, a regional jet that would get sprayed before us. My friend and I glanced at each other with our mouths agape as we overheard the other crew, the young punk replacement pilots, ask for only Type I on their wings and tail. We had been continually monitoring the weather broadcast, so we knew that the precipitation had just increased from freezing drizzle to freezing rain, the temperature had fallen another degree, and the closest runway was now closed for ice removal, three extremely significant changes. The holdover time for Type I fluid, the time that you can expect the fluid to delay the formation of new ice, was now only three minutes according to our holdover charts. They had the same charts in their manuals. Our manuals were in our laps; theirs were obviously not.

It would take them more than just three minutes to get sprayed, which meant that parts of the plane could already have fluid-failure and new ice accumulation while other parts are still being sprayed, and now they would have a long drive on slick taxiways to a distant runway, the farthest one at the airport. This was potentially an accident about to happen, but why? Were these guys in a hurry? Did they not have much experience in weather and didn't realize this gray day was the real thing, that abstractly hypothetical day they had read about in a weather textbook? There were plenty of cues that pointed to the worsening conditions: the darkening gray sky, the intensifying precipitation on their windshield, or if they really weren't paying attention, periodic statements by the air traffic controllers that a new special weather observation was available, an important cue that something significant has changed. Had they been told by someone in their company that de-icing fluid was expensive, making these loyal guys feel compelled to save their employer some money? In reality, most airline Chief Pilots, theirs included, would probably fire pilots for not properly de-icing under those conditions.

I turned to the Captain and asked, "What do we do? We can't let these guys kill our customers."

His first response was, "I don't know how we handle this one."

I suggested we go ahead and tell the de-icers what our request will be, casually adding that we'd be happy to buy the other guys some Type IV as well, like we were offering to buy them a beer at the hotel bar. Our employer was probably buying their de-icing fluid anyway. My colleague still wasn't sure what to do. They taxied away before we could agree on a remedy.

They would be taking off with some ice on their airplane, but they would survive it, if both engines kept running after possibly ingesting sheets of ice that would inevitably peel off the airplane, and if a ham-fisted hack didn't try to abruptly yank the airplane aloft, stalling the ice-laden wings. There were too many ifs, which meant they weren't properly, or maturely, managing risks, but they were just young punks, the best pilots a poverty-level wage could buy. I wasn't just stereotyping them; we could hear the youth in their voices, and their employer was growing so rapidly that they were hiring every pilot they could get their hands on. Weather is a subject learned by immersing yourself in its soggy, gray, mysterious abyss, but under no circumstance should an airline pilot intentionally decide to be a test pilot with a planeload of passengers.

My friend was now a line pilot, and a damned good one, but he had also been a management pilot, a job that manages politics as well as risks. If I could have that one back, I would've just keyed my microphone and given the replacement pilots a lesson rather than waiting for my friend to think about it. It would've been a chance for those of us who know these things to mentor the guys who occupy the cockpits that we were being locked out of, because soon we won't be there to babysit them as they learn their way in the world, with our passengers strapped into the seats behind them.

To line pilots, risk management isn't an abstract exercise measured in dollars on a balance sheet; it is life and limb, mangled metal, smoking craters, and the stench of death. Mitigating real physical danger is what we do every day, and there is no way to measure it until you have to pay for the aftermath of a mistake. If we do the job right there are no statistics, no newspaper headlines, no costly litigation, and no untimely funerals. Danger lurks anywhere, from mundane details to complex situations that don't always conform to our emergency checklists. You need to bring a big toolbox to the cockpit every time you come to work, but if you're lucky, and if you do everything right, you'll rarely ever need to open it. My value is incalculable, and I'm only junior within a highly competent, very experienced pilot group.

I had wanted to retire from the 717, but with as few of them as there were, I knew for certain I was really flying it for the last time. Was I even flying for the last time? That seemed like a minor worry to me then. I was more concerned about my family's survival in a country that seemed to be crumbling all around me.

Prior to this tragic episode, my dreams had normally been much worse than reality, maybe an indication that life was very good. It had always been a relief to wake up from them, reality being the refuge from the anxieties terrifyingly manifested in my dreams. Maybe it had all just been too good to last, too remote from the inescapable misery of the human condition, but now, when I could sleep at all, I was waking up to a reality as bleak as my worst nightmares. There was no escape, no moment of relief upon awakening. I was living the dream, but not as I had hoped.

Prison Sex

I was busy trying to make as much money as I could before I was furloughed again, while Dawn was busy at home organizing my job search. All of the good jobs were overseas, and Dawn knew which airlines were hiring and which ones would hire American pilots. We got books and videos from the library, trying to learn more about the countries we were applying to, which was really anywhere except for some African nations with smoldering conflicts and drug-resistant malaria, although I would inevitably end up sending some resumes there too.

Although I sent a couple of resumes there, the European Union was pretty much off limits, requiring a different kind of license.

It would be a lot of trouble, probably a lot more than we realized at the time, but we were actually a little excited by the possibility of escaping from a crumbling empire. We were treating it as the ultimate family adventure, an experience that would truly prepare Jay and Neal for anything that the world has to offer them.

There were still three airlines in this country that were accepting resumes, airlines I probably wouldn't have considered otherwise. One of them called me immediately to schedule an interview. The airline had about a dozen Airbuses that stayed busiest during the winter, shuttling tourists to Mexico and the Caribbean. The airline usually furloughed pilots during the summer, and traditionally many of their pilots wouldn't return once they were recalled, having already found other jobs. That's why they were going to interview me. This time, all of their pilots came back from furlough, an indication that there was really no other place to go. And now there wasn't a place there for me.

Many of my friends went to work for government contractors who were busy profiting from our partially outsourced wars. When they were asked in their interviews how well they played in the sandbox, they weren't just being asked how well they would get along with their co-workers; they were being asked how they would handle flying in a Middle Eastern war zone. I would personally rather go pound nails, not that there were any construction jobs to be had either.

There were several job boards on the internet that posted pilot jobs, and I paid to subscribe to three of them. At first I thought it was great to be able to send out fifty resumes in an afternoon, a level of productivity that wouldn't be possible without the internet.

Then I figured out the dark side of the internet job search. The companies whose jobs appear know that thousands of pilots see their post. A few among the thousands will inevitably have the correct type rating and even be current in the airplane, basically turn-key pilots. While this is good if you're lucky enough to have the right type rating, companies knew they no longer had to pay to train pilots. That means that unless you are extraordinarily lucky or well connected, the type ratings you have are the only type ratings you'll ever have.

I was very qualified on paper. I had about 11,700 hours of flight time. I had a college degree. I've gotten along well with every pilot with whom I've ever flown. I've never failed a checkride, which would soon become a question asked by every employer after it was noticed that several regional jets had been crashed by pilots with histories of checkride failures. I've never had a speeding ticket or accident, which most employers look at now as an indicator for your respect for safety rules. Even more importantly, I had a clean flying record. I had thousands of hours in glass jets and thousands of hours in analog jets, thousands of hours in big jets and thousands of hours in small jets. I had thousands of hours of pilot-in-command experience, and I had thousands of hours under Part 135, the charter regulations, and thousands of hours under Part 121, airline flying. I even had some gray hairs now, a superficial trait that potentially indicates you've been flying for a long time, which I had been. I had experience, and I could fly any jet someone would be willing to train me in, if only they were willing to spend the money to train me.

I was one of many with these qualifications.

A further complication was the way airplanes were insured, favoring time-in-type over other qualifications, which I considered a potentially misguided actuarial mistake. This meant a young punk with merely a couple thousand hours of flight time, a hundred of which was recent experience in a particular type, would be more insurable than a seasoned veteran who just checked out in a new type, nothing more than a variation on a theme, but who otherwise has seen it all and has developed the awareness, maturity, discipline, and savvy to avoid the mistakes that cause most accidents.

Accidents avoided are statistically unquantifiable by underwriters, but there is still plenty of evidence to support my position. I combed the NTSB accident reports of a particular type of business jet, and very few of the more than one hundred accidents could be regarded as even remotely type-specific. Most of the accidents followed attempts to salvage bad situations that resulted from poor planning, execution, or other mental mistakes, what I refer to as heroics, which are likely to result in the airplane going off the end of an otherwise sufficiently long runway. These bad decisions that follow what appear to be rookie mistakes can lead to an accident no matter what type of airplane the pilot is flying, so the underwriters would be much wiser to value a pilot's total experience.

Unfortunately, my experience was in antique DC-9s, plus a new and unfortunately rare derivative, and antique Learjets that I hadn't flown in eight years. Besides training costs, anyone who hired me to fly a different type of airplane would bear the burden of convincing an insurance underwriter that I would somehow continue to fly safely in a different airplane. A lot of companies also don't want to touch airline pilots, correctly assuming that they'll leave as soon as they can get back into the airlines. My prospects were not good, especially since there were so few jobs to be had.

I got an interview with an infamous charter company based at Willow Run Airport near Detroit, a company I absolutely never would've even considered in better circumstances. This was a place Dawn had very specifically not wanted me to apply to after two of their 747s crashed within six weeks' time earlier in the year. In a normal job market, if such a thing exists in aviation, this was the place you have to resort to if you have a criminal record—at least that's its reputation, but not true. They needed Learjet Captains, and they told me I would make sixty to eighty thousand dollars per year. I needed a job, and this was one that would pay the bills. I knew enough to not let them pressure me into getting myself in trouble. How bad could it really be?

I took a purposefully tricky written test, which I knew I passed. Then I interviewed with the Chief Pilot and the Director of Training. I had to describe nearly every system in the 717, and I answered lots of DC-9 questions too, as well as some Learjet questions, although I hadn't flown one in years.

The Director of Training became fixated on the 717 fuel system because he didn't believe me that it was actually simpler than the Learjet's fuel system. This was a man whom I would learn had very little flight experience and the Learjet was the only Transport Category aircraft he'd flown. It was actually getting irritating. I bit my tongue, but I wanted to tell the guy to walk down the hall and find someone who knew the DC-9's fuel system to confirm my explanation. The company owned an antique DC-9 and it was even parked right outside the hangar.

The Chief Pilot was fixated on the two weeks on, one week off schedule, which I must admit, did suck. I explained to him that it was the same ratio of days as a ten-day off reserve line at an airline, but the days came in different-sized chunks. He obviously didn't believe me either.

What had started out as a decent interview had degenerated into a death spiral of alternating questions about the DC-9's fuel system and work schedules, without any progress on either subject. Then as if an imaginary timer went off, or maybe just my spiraling interview finally crashing into the ground, it was over. They told me they would call me in a week to let me know if I gotten the job, but with the bizarre way the interview ended, I already knew I didn't.

I was mad during the long drive home to Columbus. I wasn't going to get this job, one of the only jobs to be had, because a guy who knew nothing about DC-9s didn't believe me about how to pump fuel into the engines and another guy didn't believe I would do anything to feed my family, including two weeks on and one week off.

I talked to a friend from my airline who was going to be interviewing at the same charter company later in the week, even though he also didn't have a criminal record, yet. He came up with a different approach to the schedule question, an answer that probably helped me as well since we were coming from the same airline, if I was still on the fence. We both got hired, in spite of the fact that we apparently didn't understand the fuel system in the airplanes we had been flying for the past eight-plus years.

I was furloughed at midnight (CST) on November 30. Seven hours later I started indoctrination with the charter company in a windowless classroom in a cold, drab, corner of an ancient hangar at Willow Run Airport in Ypsilanti, Michigan.

One of the first things the Director of Training, Max (not his real name), said was also our first red flag; "Good, everyone showed up." There were six of us—my friend from the airline, Phil; Bob, a furloughed pilot from another airline; Bud, a retired 747 Captain from the charter company's sister company; Jack, a furloughed Lear pilot from another charter company; George, a five hundred hour pilot who paid $27,000 to have the opportunity to log some jet time (not their real names); and me, and unless you skipped ahead because of perverse curiosity about the chapter name, you know my story. We had all been hired as Captains except for the inexperienced guy who bought his job as a pay-to-play co-pilot, another warning flag.

Max promptly told us his rules for the class, the way a warden would give the rules for a prison work-release program. If we were a minute late, we were fired. We would get an hour for lunch. If we were a minute late coming back from lunch, we were fired. We would have a test nearly every day for six weeks. If we scored less than a 90 percent on any test, we were fired. There would be no flying stories, but that was because Max hadn't flown enough to have any himself. The rest of us had, and did, and everyone can learn from a story in which someone admits they'll never do something again.

Next, Max informed us that the company had just laid off a number of people that day and all the rest would be taking 20 percent pay cuts. Business was slow, but they somehow thought they still needed us. What a way to get started. No one wants to actually board a sinking ship, which is what we apparently had just done.

The barrage of bad news continued until after six, without a lunch break. We did take short breaks at least, so Max could make another cup of decaf and go out into the bitter cold to smoke a nicotine-free cigarette.

That evening my friend Phil and I went to Bob's room to share in the misery and open a bottle of wine, one of among the two cases

Bob had brought with him from the wine stores that he owned. We had all wondered how bad it could really be. Based on our first day of class, it would be worse than any of us had imagined.

Everyone showed up for day two, due more to inertia than eagerness. That's when we found out that what the company considered two weeks of work was actually fifteen days, and what they considered to be a week off was really only six days off. It was like they were stealing two days from us each rotation, giving them an extra work day and giving up an extremely precious day off. Then Max told us we didn't get any vacation time, ever, because they already give us a week off after each rotation—that is, if you're willing to say that six days is actually a week. I never even considered that there might not be vacation.

The next surprise was that we would have our annual recurrent ground school during a week off, and for some reason recurrent was six days long. That means everyone had to work five weeks straight without a day off, with no extra pay in exchange for losing six days off, not that any amount of money would make it right.

Not long after getting back to the hotel that evening, Phil called: "Get over here to Bob's room. We figured something out."

I walked down the hall to Bob's room. There was already an empty wine bottle on the desk. Phil and Bob looked at me like they had cracked a secret code, and then they shared their revelation with me; "Here's the deal. This is like prison sex. We're not going to avoid it, so we need to try to make the best of it. We're all going to get through this."

I carefully glanced back at the door to determine whether I could run for it, just in case prison sex was more than just a terrifying metaphor.

"Prison sex" became our motto during ground school, until it was replaced a month later by "Are you fucking kidding me?" The answer was always no; they weren't fucking kidding, ever, about anything. We would learn that this was truly a strange place.

There was a pilots' meeting the next week that Max made us attend. All of the company's pilots who weren't on the road filed into a cramped conference room. The pilots who were out on the road had to join us by conference call. These events are usually like reunions, with pilots smiling and shaking hands as they caught up on news with friends they haven't seen in a few months, or at least that's what we were expecting. There was none of that, and none of the pilots even remotely seemed as though they might know each other.

Morale on the line was apparently very low. Perhaps the pilots were expecting news of furloughs or pay cuts since the company was steadily sending employees out the door and cutting the pay of those that remained, even though they were actually hiring pilots. The pilots had already had a pay cut, since so much of our pay would be determined by how much we flew and business was slow. As new guys, our presence was unwelcome for two reasons: because we would cut into their already dwindling flight pay, and because the company was hiring street Captains instead of upgrading their co-pilots.

It was apparent that management knew everything that happened in the company, and they were even more certain that they were always right. The tone was condescending, and the pilots who were actually brave enough to question anything were quickly snubbed with canned responses.

It was a toxic environment for many reasons; a lot more than the apparent low morale witnessed at the pilot meeting. There were two roads to the hangar, both crumbling from neglect, which actually seemed to be normal in the motor city. One road passed a sewage-treatment plant; the other passed a landfill, the expansion of which was the only nearby activity to be seen in a city that had arguably already slipped into an economic depression. Between the two ancient roads, looking out of place among the decay and the waste, was a beautiful wooded ravine carved from the snow-covered plain by the creek that gave the airport its name.

Willow Run Airport had been busy a few times in its history, mass producing bombers during World War II and, most recently supporting just-in-time inventories at the auto plants. Now, with the automakers sliding into bankruptcy and much of their production now in foreign lands, it was just a crumbling ruin. Even the rats had left long ago. Old abandoned airplanes, partially cannibalized, lined the periphery, some still painted with the names of long bankrupt freight airlines, slowly fading into oblivion. It was costing a lot more to support the airport than the revenue it was generating. As soon as funding ran out, it wouldn't take long for the airport to disappear beneath the encroaching landfill in our disposable world.

After a couple of weeks, Phil remarked, "We haven't yet seen an airplane move under its own power." We couldn't figure out why they had hired us. None of us really understood the convoluted pay system yet, but it was becoming clear from the utter lack of activity that we would not make the money we had been told we would make.

Phil and I got bad news from the union at our airline, while checking e-mail during a break in the cold, dreary hangar. The arbitrator, who finally made it back from his long Tuscan vacation that delayed his ruling well beyond the reasonable timeline for expedited arbitration, decided to allow the company to violate our contract and the Railway Labor Act by locking us out. I had been certain we would win—hope that had been sustaining me, certain that my job would eventually be restored, rescuing me from the prospect of prison sex; it was spelled out clearly in our contract with the company, a legal document that was apparently now worth no more than an Indian treaty. Even worse, with an expedited arbitration, there is no appeal, even though our expedited arbitration hadn't been expedited. I wouldn't be surprised if the airline's CEO paid for the arbitrator's vacation.[9]

I was apparently too naïve to realize that in the highly controlled process of labor dispute resolution, the company always wins. This injustice, one of too many, was particularly discouraging for Dawn and me. We had both virtually dedicated our lives to loyally working hard, following the rules, and always doing the right thing. It seemed to be getting us nowhere. What was our sense of morality teaching Jay and Neal? Unless you're willing to lie, cheat, and steal, people will walk all over you, repeatedly? How could we honestly teach them to live virtuous lives when we knew it won't bring success in our culture of legitimized corruption and greed where no good deed shall go unpunished by the ignoble?

Max was continually disparaging co-pilots, which was strange since that's all he had ever been before the loss of his medical certificate took him out of the cockpit. George endured a tremendous amount of abuse, always being the first person that Max picked on.

Max made us memorize endless lists, phone numbers, addresses, and other barely relevant minutiae, which only prevented us from devoting brain power to more important material. None of us were going to study until two in the morning like Max said he had done when going through indoc, a feat he only accomplished because of his hyperactive thyroid glands, complications from which had also caused him to eventually lose his medical certificate.

Max had a doctor's appointment that led to hospitalization. The Chief Pilot, John (not his real name), filled in for Max for the rest of the week. John handed us a test that had a blank flight plan form. We had to fill in what each square was for. This was ridiculous, even more so than all of the memorized phone numbers, which we made a point to complain to John about, frequently.

Bob looked at John and sarcastically asked, "Really?" John shrugged his shoulders. Bob asked again, this time more forcefully, "Really?" Then Bob opened his Airman's Information Manual to the page with the flight plan form, copying his test straight from the book. John didn't say anything, so I opened my book too. There were nifty computer programs now that would file flight plans for you. If you really had to pick up a phone and call in a flight plan, the briefer would prompt you for any entry that you forgot, if they answered the phone at all, which wasn't guaranteed now that the government had outsourced the once excellent network of Flight Service Stations to the lowest bidder.

All of us scored less than 90 percent occasionally on tests, but none of us were asked to leave as we had been warned at the beginning of the first day. One person in class didn't already know Part 135 regulations and didn't already have a Learjet type rating had the most sub-ninety test scores, probably every one of them in fact. He had also paid $27,000 to be there. The company would never fire a source of revenue.

Max was back the next week, but looking ashen and weak. He asked what it meant if you were tingling all over. Phil immediately drove him to the hospital in Ann Arbor and then we all left town for a week, scattering like a herd of cats. Phil probably saved his life. Max had a blood clot in his lung.

Bob never came back. He got a job offer from a regional airline, and then Phil did a couple weeks later. They both decided that making

$20,000 per year as RJ First Officers would be better than prison sex. It felt like they had left me all alone in a hostile cell block, and they even took the soap on a rope.

How bad can it be? When I saw the checklists, I realized the company truly had its own culture, an inbred, mutant culture unlike anything I had yet seen or even imagined in my worst nightmares, much different than the way we did things at my safe, insulated, and comfortable airline job. While there are always several ways to do something, one way is generally safer than all others and is never a secret; it is written with the blood of all those pilots who've gone west for good.

Checklist philosophy here was like a tedious ping-pong game, with the non-flying pilot only reading the extraordinarily long checklists, not actually performing any actions, unnecessarily distracting the flying pilot from what is truly important, the safe operation of the airplane. The reason for this unorthodox philosophy is the assumption that the Captain can't trust the co-pilot to flip switches correctly, which wouldn't be an issue if they actually hired professionals for both seats, but why hire professionals when novice pilots will pay to do the job?

All of the checklists were ridiculously long, loaded with items that could be completed before even starting the engines and items that experienced pilots just know to do without consulting a checklist. Hidden within and diluted by all of the irrelevant items are the killer items, the real purpose behind a checklist, which would be easier to miss among all the fluff. Learjets are not very complicated airplanes, but these checklists seem to try really hard to make them so.

I understood the reason for the bizarre checklists, a lame attempt to idiot proof an airplane that was never meant to be flown by idiots. I thought this reinvention of flying to accommodate the weakest pilots in the company would actually make the operation less safe, for numerous reasons. And if it wasn't as safe as it could be, that meant that it was more dangerous than it should be. I wasn't happy about that, but I needed a paycheck. I had to play along; professional pilots are obligated to conform to their employer's standard operating procedures (SOPs), no matter how strange they may be.

I had spent the previous eight years flying into the same twenty-five airports week after week. While those are the busiest airports in the country, they are airports I know well. Now I would be going to unfamiliar airports on dark, rainy nights, with low-time co-pilots who had paid a small fortune to shortcut their way into high performance jets, trying to move the airplane without any wrong turns or runway incursions, and the last thing I want to do is to be looking for switches in an antique homebuilt Lear 25 with both pilots diverting too much attention inside the airplane for a dangerous game of checklist ping-pong. Every airline understands the need to always keep one pilot outside the airplane, without distracting them with tasks that the other pilot should be doing for them and tasks that should've been done earlier. This place was apparently different than every other place in the industry.

Max taught us how to preflight a Learjet, which for this class, was a little like a kindergartner teaching a published author how to read. He knew he was way out of his element, and he responded by being meaner than usual. He got under the airplane and drained fuel from each fuel drain valve and there are lots of them. Aside from being a totally pointless exercise to do every day in a jet, now I understood why the airplanes leaked jet fuel all over the hangar floor. Pilots were opening these valves before every flight and the valves were wearing out.

When Max finished his exterior preflight, I told him that he forgot to look in the hell hole. This was obviously an uncomfortable task for him already, and now he had a knot on the side of his head and jet fuel-soaked clothes from falling on the fuel-slickened hangar floor. His face was suddenly flushed with anger as he barked, "You can go look in the hell hole now, if you really want to." They apparently don't do that here, even though this inconvenient compartment in the Learjet's belly is where all the important things are, including the current limiters, the hydraulic reservoir and accumulator, and the fire bottles.

When we did the interior preflight, Max made a point of saying that there were eleven ways to disengage the autopilot in a Lear 25. He demonstrated by engaging the autopilot eleven times and subsequently counting eleven beeps as he pushed different buttons, then moving on to the next item. I interrupted by asking him whether the autopilot worked. He didn't understand my question. "You know that you can disengage it, but you didn't do an operational check."

Then I showed him how he can actually check the servos, which makes the autopilot do what it's supposed to do.

Max was a decent guy, inherently loyal, very knowledgeable for his experience level, and an extremely hard worker, and he truly believed in what he was doing, but sometimes he seemed to be slightly missing the point. Max seemed to be sometimes incapable of separating what was truly important from the noise. What I didn't know yet was how much of this could be attributed to his lack of experience or if he was a window into an entire isolated, inbred culture that didn't understand what was truly important, like a lost tribe of head hunters who stubbornly insisted on disregarding ideas that the industry has collectively come to understand are safer.

Every company claims that safety is their priority, but a company's true purpose, to make money, is perpetually in conflict with this priority, probably more so in an on-demand charter outfit than anywhere else in the industry. I understood this eternal tension, and I understood I was the only person I could truly depend on. I just wondered how alone I would truly be.

At this point I knew I was wasting my time and wanted to be done with it. I'm sure Max knew there was nothing he could teach us, which only kept him uncomfortable and irritated. Jack asked John if we could just leave, to give us a few extra days off before we went to Wichita for our simulator training.

On the way to Wichita, John told me that he was going to pair me up with George in the simulator for the whole week. I was going to essentially be flying single pilot in an airplane I hadn't flown in more than eight years. Actually, it would probably be worse than that. I would have to carry George, who would probably be a liability for me because of his inevitable mistakes. He was in way over his head, and he was my co-pilot. This was a guy they hired for his check-writing ability, not his checkride ability.

I already had enough anxiety about going to the simulator, knowing that having flown an automated airplane I hadn't needed an instrument scan, or even needed to touch the throttles, in about six years. I knew I would be rusty, especially since simulators are always harder to fly than the airplanes they simulate, and classic Learjets were already hard enough to fly.

My first hour was even uglier than I had expected. I was glad that a simulator evaluation wasn't a part of the interview. I wouldn't have gotten the job. This was another dark side of automation: without practice, your skills do deteriorate. You might still need those skills when the automation goes dark. The next hour was better. I would need to sharpen my skills quickly, because they were expecting me to perform as a Captain.

Then I had emergencies, just one at a time at first and strictly single pilot. At this company the Captain had to fly the airplane and run the emergency checklist, not even trusting the other guy's ability to read, which was unlike anything I'd ever seen. Worse still, since there was so much variation within the bastard fleet of old Learjets, the company chose not to use a quick reference handbook (QRH) to compile the emergency checklists, so I had to fly the airplane while digging the emergency checklists out of the yellowed pages of the antique airplane's cumbersome flight manual. The Learjet requires two pilots, but when I needed him the most, I wouldn't be allowed to use the resource to my right. Someone had decided that instead of making sure the co-pilot was qualified, they would make him sit on his hands.

George meant well and tried hard, but he wasn't much of a resource anyway. It was too much airplane, too many emergencies, and everything was moving entirely too fast for his level of experience. You can buy some hours to pencil into your log book, but you can't actually buy the ability to tame a slippery, high-performance jet. Like any skill, mastery required practice, meaningful repetition—experience well beyond what any training course has the time to provide.

By the last day, day five in the box, John gave me three simultaneous emergencies. As soon as I was managing one, he gave me another, and another. I got the airplane safely onto the ground through unmercifully thick fog, essentially single pilot, set the parking brake right on the middle of the runway, pulled my phone out of its holster, and said, "I'm going to dial one of those phone numbers I had to memorize and tell those people to come get their damn airplane."

John knew very well that I was making fun of Max's class, but he laughed anyway. John was a decent guy, as was Max. The problem here was the culture, and that emanated from another source.

I had my Part 135 checkride in the airplane, a tired looking Lear 25 that was a year older than me. An FAA inspector, the company's Principal Operations Inspector (POI), wanted to observe the checkride. John was reading the before landing checklist to me as I intercepted the glide slope on my first approach. This was the unnecessarily long checklist that required me to hunt for switches in an antique Lear 25, switches that were in different places in each airplane, and this was the first approach I had made in this one.

As John was halfway through reading the checklist, the fed started yelling at him, "You're making this guy look all over the airplane. He needs to be flying the airplane. You need to fix these checklists."

The fed was right. I had already aimed the antique rocket-sled downhill toward an unyielding planet that I wouldn't be able to see until I was within a stone's throw of it. Company policy was to hand-fly approaches without help from the 1960s vintage autopilot, so I needed to make sure I accurately flew to the right spot. My co-pilot should be the one looking for the hydraulic pressure gauge and the anti-skid lights and then start looking for the approach lights.

When we got back to the airport, the fed turned to me and said, "Excuse me, we need to debrief." John and the fed stepped into the pilot's lounge, the fed slamming the door behind him. I heard shouting for about ten minutes. The fed stepped out of the room, shook my hand, and left.

I asked John about the exchange that had virtually rattled the closed door. He said, "He hates our checklists and never misses an opportunity to tell us."

He wasn't really there to observe my checkride. In fact we had to cut it short after one of our generators broke. He wasn't interested in finishing it after they pulled another museum piece out of the hangar for us to fly. He was there to yell at John, even though John didn't have the authority to change anything.

When the feds are yelling at you, you need to change what you're doing. Right or wrong, this is a fundamental truth when the guy who's yelling has the power to shut down the operation on the spot.

The feds can consider you guilty, and don't even need to give you a fair chance to prove them wrong. This guy even knew what he was talking about; he was exactly right. I was thrilled, knowing that the screwed up game of marathon checklist ping-pong would need to be changed, an operational change that would make us safer.

Unfortunately, another fundamental truth is that political influence trumps everything, including safety. The company's General Manager complained to the supervisor at the local Flight Standards District Office (the local Federal Aviation Administration office), and our Principal Operations Inspector was reassigned.

The company had two lucrative contracts, one for an air ambulance service, the other a government contract to fly bodies back home from the wars. The pilots assigned to these contracts, which were supposed to be assigned equitably, made decent money, the money that I was told I could expect, nearly five times more than our pathetic guarantee. Unfortunately, when you flew, it was because of someone else's misery, a boy returning from an unnecessary war in a box or someone slowly, painfully nearing the end.

Otherwise the company flew any kind of charter that they could get: freight, passengers, air ambulance, or organ harvest, chasing money around the sky at 80 percent of the speed of sound. Business was slow, and if you weren't out doing the contract flying, you were likely to make minimum guarantee, which was an insulting fifty-seven dollars per day for a Learjet Captain, based on trip mileage. You would have to break a whole week's guaranteed mileage in order to make more than that. I was not seeing the sixty to eighty grand that I had been told to expect. In fact, I would've been eligible for food stamps if I hadn't already had so much money in the bank.

My first trip was an all-nighter, foreshadowing what was to come. It was an IOE (Initial Operating Experience) trip with another Captain, an experienced, hard working, blue-collar pilot who had been serving the company in some form for decades, once as a 747 Captain, now as a 727 Captain, and on his days off from that, a part-time Learjet Captain. This guy dependably got the job done, but his can-do attitude was appropriately balanced by his street smarts, survival skills I'm quite sure he had often learned the hard way.

It was an air ambulance trip, ordinarily an easy trip, except that we loaded a 350-pound man with a broken leg into the Learjet, a feat I wouldn't have thought I could do before I had to do it.

We flew through an inky black sky for hours, delivering our patient home to Valdosta, Georgia. In the FBO, I sat down at a computer to file a flight plan back to base. The wallpaper picture on the computer was of a handsome blue 717 from my airline climbing into a bright blue sky, one of my old airplanes, a ghost from my recent past, haunting me in the middle of the night.

The job was demanding even when I wasn't flying; especially when I wasn't flying. I was on call twenty-four hours a day for fifteen days straight. I wasn't sure this was even legal, although the Part 135 regulations were written just vaguely enough that companies get away with being continually on call, depending on interpretation from the local Flight Standards District Office (FAA). I never even considered this when I took this job, with eternal reserve being so far from what I considered to be reasonably safe. I would quickly learn to hate the startling, piercing, frantic beeps of a pager that I could never turn off. Worse than a cringe from fingernails on a chalk board; it was the cruel sound of my career being gambled with little preparation, on a moment's notice.

Part 135 flying, charter flying, is statistically ten times more dangerous than Part 121 flying, airline flying, and for many reasons. On-demand charter is a cut-throat business, especially since internet brokerages can allow every charter company to bid for every trip. There is no escaping the financial reality that profit depends on completing the mission. The airplane must keep moving and costs must be controlled, creating perpetual tension from two competing pulls. A company that spends too much money on safety won't be able to give competitive quotes as brokers troll for the lowest bid on every flight they sell. This was my new daily reality, and it required a braver man than I.

I never knew what kind of trip I would get paged for, and I only had a fifteen-minute response time for freight and organ-harvest trips. My crash pad was twelve minutes from the airport, and I don't break the speed limit. So I really only had about three minutes to brush my teeth, zip my suitcase, and hit the door. I had an hour response time for other trips, in which I would need to be in uniform. Even still, I always had to be ready to go. On one rotation I was number one to go out for thirteen straight days, 312 straight hours in which I was supposed to be continually ready with three minute's notice. The only downtime I would ever get during a fifteen day rotation was the ten hours of legally required rest upon completion of a trip.

It's not possible to always be ready. The airlines were thankfully no longer allowed to have twenty-four hour reserve shifts. The vague language in Part 135 won't change until a Senator dies in the care of a patently fatigued crew. Until then, I constantly lived with the possibility that I might have to fly all night after being up all day, which actually happened twelve times during my first six months on the job, too many to just be an unlucky anomaly.

My commitment to this job would amount to more than six thousand hours in a year, literally the equivalent of three full-time jobs. My reward would be determined by the luck of the draw: whether I would get any lucrative trips when my number was up.

Only a handful of the co-pilots had bought their jobs, the ones who had absolutely no experience. Most of the rest of them still had much less experience than any of my prior Lear co-pilots had, guys who had a solid foundation of hard-core line experience. Few of these pilots had any real single-pilot instrument experience to help them develop their skills. They weren't very well trained because training costs money, and now they weren't flying nearly enough to stay current. They all tried really hard, but a Learjet is just no place for an inexperienced pilot still learning the fundamentals.

Some were slow to recognize trends, and when I pointed out a trend that needed immediate correction, they often didn't have the confidence and finesse to make a positive correction, and that was if they even knew how to react. Sometimes it seemed as though some truly didn't know whether they needed pitch or power and just remained frozen, unable to react, like a deer in headlights, in a slick airplane that wasn't going to wait for them or forgive mistakes as it hurtled through another mile of sky every eight seconds. It wasn't enough for me to give professional advice, like that they were being set up for a slam dunk and they weren't going to be able to slow down enough to configure the airplane. I learned I had to give very specific commands instead, like "You need to be at idle right now."

Some of the co-pilots could control the airplane well enough when there was a horizon, but some would fall apart after dark or in the clouds. Their instrument flying skills weren't sharp enough for the nimble Learjet, and no one was really flying enough to stay sharp, an undesirable side effect of the slow economy. If they had to fly an instrument approach, some would become totally unglued once they tried to perform the extraordinarily long list of ping-pong items on the before landing checklist while flying the airplane.

These lessons all came together during an NDB (Non-directional Beacon) approach in an unforecasted snow shower in London, Ontario. My co-pilot was behind the airplane, flying the worst possible kind of instrument approach imaginable, our only option with a howling northwest wind and GPS that was so old that we couldn't fly an instrument approach with it, while both of us were unnecessarily busy with that ridiculously long and intrusive ping-pong checklist. I told him that he needed to get the thing down, but it was already too late.

When I saw the runway, there was going to be no way we could get down to it. I told him to go around. He jammed the throttles forward, but without pointing the nose up into a climb, a whiplashing blast of raw turbojet power propelled us toward the frozen ground.

We didn't have the fuel for this since the weather was supposed to have been good. We had to get in on the next try because there wouldn't be enough fuel for a third try. I told him that I was sorry, but I was going to fly the next approach. By the time we made it around the pattern, flew another approach, and landed, we only had seven hundred pounds of fuel left in the thirsty Lear 25, maybe twenty or thirty minutes' worth of low-altitude flying, not nearly enough to be comfortable or legal.

After watching another approach begin to unravel for a different co-pilot, I decided that if the co-pilot was flying and we were in instrument conditions (in clouds or reduced visibility), I would just run the before landing checklist so that he could fly the airplane without distraction. That was how it should've been; the flying pilot's job was to fly, not throw switches. This broke with the company's strange procedures, but I was using Captain's authority to retain a higher degree of safety. I applied the rule to myself as well. If I flew an approach to near minimums, I would brief my co-pilot that he would be running the before landing checklist himself. I would just be flying the airplane, as it should be. I would glance at the landing gear position indicator to make sure we had three green lights, but otherwise I trusted him to make it through the tedious checklist as I listened. The fed who had observed my checkride would've approved.

This was truly an environment unlike any that I had been in. I was used to being the least experienced pilot in a professional crew. Every professional pilot was once a novice and made their share of rookie mistakes. I made plenty too, all alone in the middle of the night when only I would have to potentially pay for the consequences. That's just part of learning, and these guys all worked hard and wanted to learn. Maybe I was expecting too much from them; I probably was, but I knew that my life and my certificate were on the line every time my pager beeped. I expect perfection from myself in an activity that absolutely demands it. It's not acceptable to make the runway less than 100 percent of the time. Inexperienced pilots have to devote so much attention to the basics that they really don't have the excess mental capacity to sufficiently expand their awareness. That comes with time and experience. Mother Nature and old, worn-out Learjets won't sympathetically wait for a new guy to catch up. I knew I would essentially be flying single-pilot some of the time, and it really didn't need to be that way.

This was now a systemic problem in aviation that was exacerbated by the RJ boom. For the first time in my career, I was actually seeing the level of talent and experience that was also getting hired into RJs, which were getting bigger and more prolific every time a major airline went to bankruptcy court. The right seat of a large transonic jet had suddenly become an entry-level job. It had happened before, but always as the exception. Now it was the rule. These were big, high-performance airplanes, flown by inexperienced pilots making poverty wages, and they now accounted for half of all airline departures.

I purposefully specified departures because I knew that each departure would not lead to a successful arrival. Accidents are inevitable, and that's why nothing can be left to chance. Even having an experienced Captain in the left seat would make every flight safer, but the regional airlines don't want to pay for that experience. There are lots of very experienced RJ Captains out there, and some stagnating regional airlines, but a rapidly expanding airline with quick upgrades will have to get by with a couple of cheap novices, a lot of luck, some inevitable close calls, and an occasional accident.

Unbelievably, 1500 hours of flight time, Airline Transport Pilot License minimums, were all that the FAA actually required of a jet Captain. More experience is required by insurance companies, maybe 2500, 3000, or even 4500 hours of flight time. When I had 4500 hours, I was a fairly new Lear co-pilot, and I knew for sure that I wasn't ready to upgrade. Even then I considered that to be low time.

Requiring considerably more experience to serve as Captain in an airline jet, say 10,000 hours, raising the bar considerably, would be one of the best things to ever happen to the industry. Each flight would be inherently safer, and the co-pilots, tomorrow's Captains, would learn from today's experienced mentors. It would be a genuine commitment to safety that would also inevitably bring living wages to the regional airline industry. The experience is out there, but it is not cheap. If ticket prices actually covered operating costs, which they don't, it might require a price increase of a dollar or two on certain flights. I know I'd be willing to pay.

There happened to be a recent pair of contrasting accidents. A highly experienced crew successfully ditched an Airbus in the Hudson River, saving all aboard, after losing both engines to a flock of geese. Then an inexperienced, undisciplined crew stalled a perfectly flyable airplane, breaking one of the first and most fundamental aerodynamic rules learned in flight school, actively holding the airplane into the stall that the airplane would've flown itself out of if they had just let go of the controls, tragically killing a plane load of innocent people as well as a man allegedly in the safety of his own house.

This was not solely the fault of the crew, although the Captain didn't disclose all of his prior checkride failures when he was hired and he self-selected his way into the industry through a pay-to-play program. They were inexperienced, and when you don't know, you don't even know what you don't know, so you willingly leap into situations that are over your head, somewhat oblivious to all of the potential situations you don't know how to handle. They were flying a big airplane. Their airline was expanding, but the pay and working conditions there are so bad that they're never able to put experienced pilots in the left seats so the novices can learn from professionals. This is so systemic there that novice pilots willingly sign on just for the quick upgrade, but don't you deserve more when you buy an airline ticket? If you had a brain tumor, would you try to search out the cheapest brain surgeon, or the one who had bought his way past the expected vetting process?

The flying at my company, especially the contract flying, was supposed to be divided equitably among the pilots since we had no control over what we were assigned. I didn't see that happening. I was being left out of the money.

I couldn't even get decent trips in base. There were two lucrative trips on the schedule. I was next in the rotation. I was actually going to make some money. Instead, I was paged in the middle of the night to fly to Washington Dulles to pick up a couple of mechanics and some airplane parts and fly them to Pittsburgh. I had to stay up all night for fifteen bucks worth of per-diem and mileage that wasn't enough to break guarantee when I could've actually made some real money on the other trips.

They made us stay in Pittsburgh for a few hours, hoping they could sell us again from there to avoid having to pay for the empty leg back, which was already built into the price of the charter anyway, a strategy to try to double-dip that rarely pays off. The only price is to the decaying faculties of the fatigued pilots who are being kept from their beds.

My attitude indicator, the artificial horizon, the centerpiece of an instrument scan, failed on the flight back to base, so now I had a bad attitude in more than one way.

Already full daylight, I fell into bed and pleaded with the sandman for a couple of frustrating hours. I eventually gave up and made myself a cup of tea, accidentally pouring boiling water on my hand in the process. I was definitely impaired, but how much? How could I quantify it? I would be legal in a few hours, legal for another all-nighter, and unfortunately I was next to go fly again since the other Lear Captains went out on the two lucrative trips.

My trip was bad luck, but the next week I had a lucrative ambulance trip unexpectedly stolen from me for someone else's training when I was next in the crew rotation, premium pay that was supposed to have been mine to earn. I was so sure that it was mine that, with just under two hours to departure, I called dispatch to tell them that I didn't get my page. That's when they broke the news that a pilot who was behind me in the crew rotation had decided to leap over me and call it training, awarding himself premium air ambulance pay as well.

My new reality suddenly hit me like a violent jolt of severe turbulence; I was a $20,000-a-year Learjet Captain. With more than twenty-one years of experience, and almost twelve thousand hours of flight time, I couldn't even support my family, doing something that I did well, a professional skill even, and there was nothing I could do about it and nowhere else to go.

Five months after being furloughed, which was also five months into a job that was worse than I expected and was bringing in less than a third of the money I had been told to expect, I finally reached rock bottom.

When a late night freight trip suddenly popped up near the end of my rotation, a one-way down to the border, I took it. I had been the next Captain to go out for more than a week, sitting in base, not making money. The dispatcher expected me to pass it up. A reasonable person, a person who hadn't just reached rock bottom, would've passed it up for numerous reasons. I was going to make some money, not a lot, maybe a few extra dollars of mileage plus forty bucks in per-diem, but that was money I was feeding my family with. The company wasn't going to pay me what I was worth, so I had to take whatever I could get, even if it would cost them an expensive airline ticket the next day. If they were sharing the wealth, or even just sharing somewhere near what they'd told me to expect, I'd be willing to save them some money by passing on a one-way trip at the end of my rotation, but if they wanted to pay me fifty-seven dollars a day to be a Learjet Captain, it was only fair for them to get fifty-seven dollars worth of reasonableness from me. My threshold for caring was way beyond that.

I hadn't flown many trips yet at this job, having been stuck in base while other pilots were on the road making money, but it was already apparent that every trip was a unique adventure, and usually in the middle of the night, dangerously challenging our fatigued minds. I really didn't want adventure; I just wanted to feed my family.

The first problem occurred as I leveled the antique airplane off in cruise. The right throttle wouldn't budge. I told my co-pilot that the throttle was probably frozen. The antique Lear 25, the oldest one in the fleet and the oldest Learjet I had ever flown at serial number five, had been parked outside, out in the weather for a couple of weeks since it had last flown, through a few soggy days with temperatures hovering just above freezing. It was warmer in Memphis; it would likely thaw in the descent.

This would be hard to win in a company that demands that the job gets done. If I brought the airplane back to base and the frozen throttle thawed before I landed, I would have lost them a lucrative charter on an airplane that wasn't broken. If I continued on to Memphis and the plane actually had a jammed throttle or broken fuel control, I would have lost them a lucrative charter and made them spend the money to fix the airplane at an outstation. I would probably get an earful from management either way.

I started the descent very early because I was going to have to descend with one engine still generating climb power. As I briefed the approach, I stated, "You do understand that if it's really jammed, we'll have to shut the engine down with the firewall shut-off before we can land?" There was no way we could land the airplane with one engine still making climb power. The surprised look on his face told me that in fact he had not realized this, nor had he ever been in a situation that would require such a drastic act.

The throttle did break free, above the freezing level even, around 20,000 feet. The turbojet's heat had thawed whatever was frozen, and I figured it had dried it out too. It was warm in Lubbock, Texas, and San Diego, so I continued on.

I let my co-pilot fly to Lubbock through the dark night sky. He tried real hard, but I could tell he didn't have a confident sense of where he needed to point the airplane. The Learjet was taking him for a ride, and it became most obvious approaching the runway in Lubbock. There was a little wind, with a few gusts. Without steady, positive control, the airplane bucked along aimlessly through the mildly disturbed air. We entered the landing flare aimlessly crooked.

I knew he was not going to get this airplane on the runway without colliding with it, sideways.

Entering the landing flare, I grabbed the controls. With a quick jab of rudder, balanced with a pull of aileron, I slipped the airplane, straightening it out with the runway centerline, and then I eased the main wheels onto the pavement, the second time I had to take the airplane from a co-pilot in fifty hours of flying. I realize I expect a lot from my crew, but an absolute minimum level of competency should include the ability to get the airplane back on the ground in good weather without crashing it.

I flew the leg to Brown Field in San Diego, a little airport on the border near mountainous terrain. The runway parallels the runway in Tijuana, so if you land on the wrong runway, you're in the wrong country too.

As soon as we stepped out of the airplane, the lineman told us that the airplane was leaking. It was more than a leak; we literally had a curtain of hydraulic fluid spilling out of the hell hole, that critically important place where our pilots supposedly didn't need to look during a preflight inspection. This was already my second hydraulic problem during my short time at this place, in an airplane with only one hydraulic system.

Learjets were certified as Transport Category Aircraft in the mid-1960s, but without any hydraulic redundancy, I doubt the airplanes could get the equivalent certification today. Once you lose your hydraulics, you might have access to four-tenths of a gallon of fluid through an auxiliary pump so that maybe you can get a few degrees of flap extension to lower your landing speed a little, just maybe, and just a little. Otherwise you have pressurized nitrogen to blow the landing gear down, and for emergency braking, but you won't have antiskid. Many of the airplanes in the fleet have thrust reversers, but they were intentionally pinned shut to avoid having to buy an expensive new hydraulic accumulator. That means a no-flap landing at high speed, eating up pavement, possibly with some blown tires. Most Learjets, except for the one we happened to be flying that night, have a drag chute, which I know from experience is very effective when deployed at high speed. This is not exactly what I would call redundancy, but it's still preferable to prison sex, as long as you have a couple miles of runway, which we didn't.

My other hydraulic failure had been during taxi while I was in my Initial Operating Experience, so I was flying with another Captain, who was also a furloughed airline pilot who would not allow himself to be pushed around.

We were in Louisville, somewhat between the two maintenance bases, and the General Manager actually asked if we could get the airplane to one of them. No, the General Manager wasn't an accountant or an MBA, although it wouldn't surprise me if he had an MBA; he certainly thought like one. He was a pilot, a designated examiner in Learjets even, which meant that he was authorized to issue Learjet type ratings and knew their limitations well.

My first thought was the class motto, no, not prison sex, but "Are you fucking kidding me?" Even if flying a Learjet without hydraulics was acceptable, which it most certainly is not, our choices were a very short runway in Morristown, Tennessee, and a slightly longer, but still not real long, runway in Detroit, which was still covered in snow. The obvious answer was simply "No," but given the absurdity of the request, we would've been justified in using the advice that Wilbur had given me when I had upgraded ten years earlier and escalating our answer to "Fuck no."

I was starting to see that the reason why they had piled on so many simultaneous emergencies in the simulator was because they were expecting us to frequently use those skills in these antique airplanes. Malfunctions weren't just an abstract possibility; they were a daily reality, and there was an obvious imperative to always get the airplane back to a maintenance base.

Now we were stuck in San Diego, but dispatch was still asking me whether I'd stay with the broken airplane into my days off, making no money while it was getting fixed. Not a tough decision. I had formulated my answer, "When John comes in this morning, tell him I'll stay with the airplane for a few days if I can start my next rotation that much later."

This was it. I was pretending to be a team player, knowing I wouldn't need to be. My offer was reasonable, and I would have done it without a complaint—well with some complaints. When someone micromanages with an iron fist, people become afraid to stray from the trolley tracks. It's easier to just do nothing and let the scheduled crew change occur. John is a good guy, but I knew they would never even ask him, and if they did ask him, he would work something out. Instead they would have to spend money on cab fares and airline tickets.

This trip also solved another problem for me. I really had not wanted to go to the pilot meeting that morning, and I didn't even want to listen over the phone as the General Manager relished his opportunity to condescendingly treat a group of professionals, and our ambitious sidekicks, like a bunch of children. Sorry, I was in rest, having gone to bed at four A.M. Pacific Time. If you want me to know what transpired in the meeting, send me an e-mail that I can forget to read.

I spent seventy-five dollars on a cab ride across town. I traveled first class on American Airlines, apparently the last seat left out of San Diego that day. The seats were nice but no better than what we had throughout the cabin at my old airline. The service was surprisingly attentive, and the passengers were happy. The food was classy. The merlot was surprisingly good (I wasn't in uniform). The chicken wasn't painted (a joke from my airline where most lunches in our otherwise excellent menu featured a rather unappetizing fillet of chicken breast painted with the illusion of grill marks and seasonings). And there were cookies, chocolate chip cookies. Normally I'm disgusted by the thought of them, a bias poisoned by my bitterness toward the airline that locked me out and all that the airline could have been. These were actually quite good, still warm, with a delicately crisp crust surrounding a soft interior.

My experience was better than first class used to be, and it was everything my airline had once been and still could be if it hadn't been squandered through mismanagement and missed opportunities. The thought of it made me even angrier for what I'd had but lost. Now I had truly reached rock bottom.

When I went back to work, I sent the Chief Pilot an e-mail. The subject was just a dollar sign. The e-mail asked if we could talk. We scheduled a meeting in which I begged him to get me out of town so that I could make some money.

When I showed up to start my next rotation, a co-pilot and I had airline tickets to Amarillo, Texas, to replace a crew that had been sitting in Texas for a week, waiting in vain for another freight trip. We had to find the car they left us in the long-term parking lot, which turned out to be an airport crew car with a key hidden under a floor mat. We had to drive through the darkness and thick fog to a small town in the stark, rugged West Texas prairie called Borger, where the airplane was parked.

A small town in the middle of nowhere is an idea that I like, once I get past the possibility of inbreeding. This one, though, was downright depressing. The sign at the edge of town said the population was 14,302, but from the number of houses with broken and boarded-up windows and rotten, collapsing roofs, that's probably overstating a number that varies widely based on the price of a barrel of oil.

My co-pilot wanted to photograph the squalor, the refineries, the rusty refuse from an industry that has flowed and ebbed a few too many times, and the shiny polished and painted statues of oil derricks and pump jacks that unwittingly mocked the town's very existence, photographs that could never truly capture the aura, completed by the sulfur stench wafting from the two big refineries, carried through the town by the unrelenting prairie wind. A former Soviet fighter pilot from Ukraine who had been stationed in Mongolia for three years, my co-pilot was actually appalled by the decay. From between massive oil tanks and forests of steel smoke stacks, there were glimpses of the rugged prairie, once the virtually impenetrable heart of Comancheria, which would have had a pastoral beauty if not for this town, which is like a scar that is never given a chance to heal.

At the airport we found a heartbreaking graveyard of dismembered Mig-23 fighters, one of the types my co-pilot flew in the Soviet Air Force, apparently bought for their engines to power oil and gas pipelines and now decaying on the ground.

John got me out of base, but this wasn't what I had meant. I wasn't making the money that went with the contract flying; I had still been left out of that. I was staying at a hotel with a free breakfast. I would skip lunch. If I ate a cheap dinner, I could keep the rest of my per diem. It wasn't much, but even at a buck-fifty per hour, it was actually like getting a 50 percent raise. That's how bad this job was.

I was glad to finally put this place behind me, although my escape was actually fueled by the very subterranean fluid that perpetually shackles the place, an inescapable cycle of boom and bust determined by transactions in a far away mercantile exchange. It was another all-night trip, of course, and although I flew a couple thousand miles that night, it wasn't far enough to offset the days of sitting. I still wouldn't break my pathetic guarantee. I was working for per diem—that is, if I didn't eat.

I ended up in Birmingham by way of Phoenix. It was nice to be back in vaguely familiar surroundings, but it wasn't enough to pull me out of my funk. One of the girls from the FBO, a gorgeous brunette who appeared not to have aged a day, even remembered me from when I had regularly flown from there thirteen years prior, one of many long lost but familiar faces I would see whenever I would get out of town.

After a couple more futile days of waiting in Birmingham, I ended up having to take the airplane to Morristown, Tennessee, where the company had an office and a maintenance hangar for reasons no intelligent business man could ever justify. They needed the airplane for an extremely lucrative FBI trip, which I would not get to fly since I would suddenly go to the back of the rotation as soon as I landed in Morristown.

Now I was really pissed. I sent the Chief Pilot an e-mail explaining exactly how the crew rotation was rigged against me, an outsider, to the benefit of the Captains who had grown up there. Then I explained to him that my wife was a compensation analyst who knew whether compensation plans were legal. Yes, I handled this like a man, resorting to the ultimate threat, telling my boss that my wife would beat him up if he didn't include me in the lucrative contract flying.

He never even responded to me, but he got me out on the air ambulance contract on my next rotation. I sent him an e-mail thanking him. He responded by saying that he didn't do anything; it was just my turn. That was bullshit. It was not my turn, since the system was rigged so that it was my turn once every fifteen weeks. He had to throw some money my way to shut me up in an absurd pay system that probably wasn't legal, not even under the protection offered to them by the Railway Labor Act.

Being out on the contract flying was almost like having a real job, except for the fifteen straight days on the road. The money was good, although because of our convoluted pay scale, we actually got paid more for sleeping than for flying. My ten hours of paid rest each day was worth more than if I flew 1,154 miles that day. We always had an hour response time to the airport, but the medics often knew about trips a day in advance. They avoided night flying, knowing there was less support for airborne medical emergencies in the middle of the night. There tended to be much less adventure, and adventure was something I really wanted to avoid.

The hardest part of air ambulance tours was that there was really no way to pack for a fifteen-day trip that would likely take you throughout the hemisphere and possibly even further. After each flight I would wash all of my dirty laundry in the hotel sink, knowing that my clothes would have at least ten hours to dry before I would fly again. My hands were raw, but the collars of my uniform shirts were never whiter than when I was scrubbing them by hand with a bar of hotel soap.

The medics even got released from duty every evening, so you could actually drink a beer if you wanted to, although I couldn't spend four dollars or more on a hotel beer knowing I needed to feed my family with that money. My money was not disposable.

I arrived in Rochester, Minnesota, late on Monday evening. My co-pilot wanted to get a burger at the deserted bar next to the hotel. I tagged along for the company, but I didn't eat. Trail mix got me through the evening, and now at ten o'clock, I would survive just fine until I could devour the hotel's free breakfast in the morning.

Two men appeared at the bar. Their slow, unsteady movements and obnoxiously loud and subtly slurred speech indicated that their evening had started much earlier. One of them pointed to my co-pilot and I while obnoxiously announcing, "Those two guys are pilots or gay. Maybe they're gay pilots." It usually is quite easy to identify us, in pairs, in the vicinity of hotels—pilots that is.

They sat next to us and asked us who we flew for. When I answered, one said, with the most sincerity possible from such an inebriated person, "I'm really sorry." We would hear that a lot. He noticed I wasn't eating, or drinking, so he asked me what I had eaten that day. It says something profoundly bad about the industry that he knew exactly what I was doing, sacrificing so I could bank my per diem. He ordered an appetizer for me and insisted that I eat. It turned out that he was actually a friend of a friend, which is quite common. With enough talking, nearly any two professional pilots can come up with at least one mutual acquaintance. A wise pilot makes no enemies.

They were corporate pilots, a segment of the industry that certainly has some good jobs but not always good job security. A company jet is a large and obvious target for belt-tightening corporate accountants. Suddenly that doesn't seem quite as risky, relatively speaking, now that an airline was able to somehow get away with locking out its entire pilot group.

I found I had a double-elite status among many of my peers. Most pilots would take pity on me already because of my current employer, but even more so when I told them which airline I had worked for, how I had lived the good life, which had illegally been snatched away. When I would airline to and from airplanes, a brief conversation with the pilots would often lead to a first-class upgrade if it was possible.

The air ambulance airplanes stayed wherever they were parked after the last trip, so you're normally hundreds of miles away from the office, which is a very good thing in a micromanaged company where everyone seemed to know everything.

Going into Toronto, my co-pilot put our flight plan, which was printed on innocuous twenty-weight office paper, in the gap between the glare shield and the windshield of our forty-two year-old Learjet. I joked that if we weren't going into another country, we'd get yelled at for potentially scratching the antique windshield. That was the kind of company we worked for. They treated us like children.

My co-pilot had a friend from Toronto who showed us the town. It appeared to be truly prospering, in stark contrast with the struggling rustbelt cities on the American side of the Great Lakes. The Canadians regulated their banking system sufficiently to avoid the near collapse we had just endured. Canada also wasn't having a mortgage foreclosure problem, even though home ownership rates in Canada were the same as in the United States. Canadians also weren't going bankrupt because of illnesses, and they don't have to wait five months to see an incompetent endocrinologist. They even live longer too.

Some nationalists might tell me to go live in Canada since I so admire our under-appreciated neighbor. Well, I tried. I sent plenty of resumes north of the border, without any response.

It was a beautiful day, and all of Toronto was outside enjoying it. My co-pilot's friend asked me if I noticed any differences between Toronto and the United States. I said, "Yes, the people aren't all fat." Then he asked me what kind of food I wanted for dinner. I said, "Canadian food." They seemed to think it didn't exist. Does that also mean American food does not exist?

My co-pilot mentioned that all of the fat Canadians were inside, sitting in front of their TVs. He's probably right. We seem to be exporting obesity to the rest of the world as we export our dysfunctional lifestyle.

Jay has always wanted to live in Canada. Latitude aside, maybe he's on to something.

I got an e-mail from the Chief Pilot a week later. It read, "Explain this to me." There was a picture of a Learjet about to land in Toronto, my Learjet. A folded sheet of paper was visible on the glare shield, breaking one of the thousand peculiar company rules, this one attempting to protect a non-recyclable windshield in a forty-two-year-old airplane that was mere hours from being transformed into beer cans.

I didn't know what was more absurd, that someone took the picture and posted it on the internet, that someone in the company found the picture through the ether, or that there was actually a rule about placing paper on the glare shield of an antique airplane that was so close to retirement. Or that my career had taken such a tragic turn that I was actually in the middle of this.

It was a very nice picture, framed by a bright blue sky, with the sun actually sparkling off the otherwise drab paint job. It was undoubtedly the best that airplane has looked since 1967, but are you fucking kidding me? No, he wasn't, really. The Chief Pilot was a decent guy. He just grew up in this bizarre culture, so he really didn't know any better.

Before I even responded to the e-mail, which was so ridiculous I had already forwarded it to many friends, my co-pilot called the

Chief Pilot and accepted full blame for the offense. This was a noble act in a company where the pilots fear the iron fist of management.

I told the Chief Pilot that it was a very nice picture, and it was funny to me because we actually talked about the paper on the glare shield right before the photographer recorded the incriminating proof. He would've really been pissed if he found out I had sent his e-mail throughout the airline industry.

A couple of weeks later I ran into the co-pilot again in the pilot's lounge. He was doing chart revisions for one of the airplanes. The Chief Pilot came in and sat down. He was now management, but he was still really a line pilot at heart, just one of the guys. The co-pilot was getting frustrated by how many charts were missing from the binder. I told him I would go into the hangar and check the glare shield for them. The Chief Pilot laughed, even though I was making fun of him and this absurd place, which I had found myself doing around my boss entirely too often.

I had applied to more than two hundred jobs on six continents (I didn't know of any airlines in Antarctica), which had resulted in four phone calls, a handful of e-mails, and one miserable job that wasn't anything like what I had been told to expect.

In a moment of utter despair, I briefly searched for compensation jobs for Dawn, only the second time I had done that, and immediately found a job that was ten miles from the house. Dawn applied for it over the weekend and got an invitation to interview at the beginning of the week. She got the job, with a salary of what I had been told to expect but that had never materialized.

We were suddenly cash positive again, especially since I finally got out on some contract flying.

Everyone hated my schedule. Neal, at three, actually thanked me for coming home, bringing me to tears. It was difficult for everyone, including the dog, who acted out once by eating Jay's homework. Really, it wasn't just a clichéd excuse. I was sacrificing too much for little return. Moving had never been an option; this wasn't a job worth moving for with the only lucrative flying being fifteen-day tours that I wouldn't be home for anyway. I hoped this schedule would just be temporary.

When I had started making the three-plus-hour drive to Detroit, I stumbled onto an idea while eating an apple. This was not a new idea. The apple encased five seeds, each one so genetically diverse that the fruit of the progeny were unlikely to look anything like their parents. I had recently read about a biologist who was traveling across England cataloging new roadside varieties of apples, each propagated by the simple act of tossing a nibbled apple core out of a car's window.

Microbes continue to evolve, but our food supply doesn't. John Chapman, known to history as Johnny Appleseed, had crossed this very path, spreading genetic diversity and cider across the frontier. I would attempt to continue his work.

We had picked eighty pounds of apples the prior autumn, from two new varieties. I would eat an apple during my commute across the Ohio countryside, on back roads that the author William Least Heat Moon would have dubbed Blue Highways in his classic journey.[10]

I would choose spots within throwing distance of the road. They would need to fall into places where a sapling wouldn't get mowed down and where they weren't close enough to farm fields that they would be sprayed by toxic chemicals that kill everything except for the bioengineered corn that covers much of the landscape, identical rows of identical plants stretching beyond the horizon.

There is nothing remotely pastoral about this modern corn, a commodity crop so greedy and energy intensive that its production is better described as soil mining than farming. This is not the corn you nibble from the cob on a lazy summer evening barbecue. Much of it will feed cows, which are not meant to eat it. It fattens them quickly while simultaneously giving them a fatal case of heartburn. Much of it will become high fructose corn syrup, which, now ubiquitous in cheap processed food, quickly fattens humans while simultaneously giving them a fatal case of diabetes. Most absurd of all is that some will now become ethanol for our oversized family attack vehicles, an inefficient scam to move a subsidized commodity crop disguised as environmentalism.

Industrial corn was also helping to turn small towns that were once nearly self-sufficient into meth-filled slums. Maybe these towns can have true farming again someday, maybe even with varieties of apples found nowhere else, a transformation that will require much more than a thoughtfully placed apple core and a one-man boycott of industrial agriculture.

I was trying to make the best of what I had by writing the book I had wanted to write, accompanied by a minimalist writer's lifestyle, which I really hadn't wanted. With Dawn earning a good salary, I no longer had to starve myself at work, but I created a favorite crashpad recipe—rice, beans, and collard greens—in which five dollars' worth of ingredients and one large pot could feed me for five nights.

I found something to like about Detroit, which was critical to allowing me to face the prospect of fifteen days trapped in solitary confinement. Detroit actually has probably the best public radio station in the country, with an eclectic repertoire unlike any that I've ever heard, and I've heard most of them. The station still has live DJs, a welcome personal touch that is missing from the canned programs steadily taking over most of the frequency band.

The daytime DJs have a particular affinity for the French romantics, especially my favorite composers, Claude Debussy, Erik Satie, and Maurice Ravel. They regularly pulled some unusual and unexpected transcriptions of some of my favorite pieces out of the ether, such as Debussy's Reverie for flute and harp and Images for Orchestra and Cimbalom (sounds like a dulcimer, but with a wider range), Ravel's Bolero for harmonica and piano (really), and Satie's Gymnopedie for guitar, or for harmonica and jazz ensemble.

Americans seem to think classical music is pretentious and boring, which is truly unfortunate because it's an art form that is still an art, not bound by marketability and a tidily packaged radio format, and it belongs to all of us. Detroit's public radio truly has something for everyone. I've heard Frank Zappa compositions, a haunting orchestral arrangement of a Jim Morrison tune, and even a piece for orchestra and bagpipes! Then for some more variety, they play jazz in the evenings.

If you're near Detroit and curious, I highly recommend listening to 90.9 megahertz, no matter what music you like to listen to. You'll hear something you've never heard before, and, inevitably, you'll hear something that you'll like. I liked it so much I would often listen to the streaming feed over the internet while in a hotel room far away.

And that was how I spent my workdays, writing, listening to music, missing my family immensely, and, on rare occasion, flying an antique Learjet on a moment's notice. Financial worries were no longer keeping me awake at night, but my pager still was.

After what constituted a brief nap, my pager unexpectedly woke me up and I threw some clothes on, brushed my teeth, and drove to the airport through the dense fog of sleep inertia. Had I dreamed the pager's annoying beep and the subsequent conversation? Was I really supposed to be going to the airport?

When I got there I asked them if I was supposed to come in, as I only vaguely remembered talking to them a few minutes prior. I was indeed supposed to be there, doing what I dreaded most, a fifteen-minute callout after an hour of sleep, after being up all day.

Sleep inertia is real. Your mental impairment can remain equivalent to the impairment from a couple of drinks as much as forty-five minutes after waking, which was when we needed to be departing at five hundred miles per hour into a dark night in an antique jet.

I was never prepared for all-nighters. I wake up early in the morning, and as hard as I try, I just can't turn myself off during the day so I can take a nap. And you never know when you'll need to stay up all night.

I flew to Lynchburg, Virginia, where I didn't get lynched, then to Palm Beach, Florida, where I didn't go to the beach.[11] They kept us in Palm Beach until our duty time was about to expire and then had us fly to Morristown, Tennessee, where I fully expected us to rot until the following Monday.

I actually never intend to rot. I can't remember what boredom is like, although for some reason I fear it, probably more a fear of losing curiosity and purpose in my life. With enough books in my suitcase, as well as the one I was still writing, I don't just waste away in my hotel room, although after only one hour of sleep in the previous thirty-six hours, I felt pretty wasted.

Exhausted, I fell into my bed at about eight P.M. The bed spun uncomfortably as if I'd had too much to drink, something I don't enjoy in the very least. I was physically and mentally impaired from sleep deprivation alone. I had done difficult years on the night shift at my freight job, but I'd never had bed-spins induced by fatigue. I was almost legal to fly again, but I decided I would refuse to if my pager woke me during the night.

I felt surprisingly well rested the next morning, and it was a good thing too. In the middle of the day we actually got paged. It was a long one, all night, of course.

We flew to Fort Lauderdale to clear customs outbound and then to Santo Domingo, Dominican Republic, my first trip across the Caribbean.

The shallow sea below, literally baja mar, the Bahamas, was speckled with hundreds of islands of every imaginable size and shape, each rimmed by cream-colored beaches and transparent, sparkling green water, becoming turquoise with depth and always mottled by the texture beneath, the eel grass beds, rippled sand flats, coral reefs, and, ultimately, the unfathomably cerulean water of the open ocean.

That was over the Bahamas, which were spectacular, but I only had brief glimpses of the Dominican Republic through the rain and thick, heavy clouds. I knew there was a ten-thousand-foot-tall mountain hidden in the mist, a lethal obstruction that the enhanced ground proximity warning system in the 717 would have displayed for me in vivid colors on a moving map. I desperately wanted my old job back.

In Santo Domingo we picked up two thousand wiring harnesses destined for cars, allegedly American cars, some of which may eventually sport nationalistic "Buy American" stickers on bumpers that were possibly built in far-away lands.

The air traffic controllers spoke better English than our last president, our handler seemed genuinely happy to see us, and the customs agents didn't have a care in the world. They didn't care whether we even had passports; they just quickly stamped forms that they didn't care to read while joking with our handler.

Three corroding, derelict airliners, each one representing a different era in air travel, had been haphazardly dragged into the dense, lush grass behind an ancient hangar, hidden from the tourists arriving in the shiny new jetliners parked at a modern terminal a half mile away.

On the way back to the continent, after dark, we flew for two hours through infinite blackness, a black sea below and black sky above, interrupted only by occasional flashes of lightning.

We cleared customs inbound in Miami, which was a strangely unpleasant experience but supposedly less tedious than in Fort

Lauderdale (so I had heard, but turned out not to be true). We waited inside the stuffy cabin, hoping for customs agents to come outside so we could open the door for some fresh air (rules are different at each port of entry; in Fort Lauderdale you can just walk into the building). When they finally did, they stopped thirty feet from the airplane with feet spread in a fighting stance, silhouetted by the blinding flood lights behind them, their hands placed nervously close to their holstered pistols, just in case an antique Learjet was the first wave of a hostile invasion. Their manners matched their body language. They questioned everything we said. These people were apparently trained by the Gestapo, and unfortunately for all of us, they are our ambassadors, being the gatekeepers for a country that takes itself a little too seriously most of the time.

Then we had to reposition twice to buy fuel from two different vendors, because of cheap stupidity, a frustrating combination of ailments for which there is no cure, only escape, which I longed for. Then we flew to Traverse City, Michigan, with a stop for cheap fuel in Morristown, Tennessee.

Flying up Western Michigan, I noticed fuzzy lights across the dark countryside. Thick fog was forming in the wake of the rain that had passed through earlier in the night, something you never want to see in a straight-pipe Lear 25, a thirsty airplane in which you're always thinking about where you can put the airplane down before the fuel tanks are empty. After flying an approach to minimums, I decided I'd had enough adventure for the night.

The company thought otherwise. They wanted me to reposition the empty airplane back to Detroit, even though I'd already flown the legal limit of ten hours, in a work day that, due to customs and fueling delays, had now exceeded the legal limit of fourteen hours. They seemed to think it was legal to continue since there was no revenue on board. Does that mean I don't have to count the empty flight to the Dominican Republic either? I didn't think so.

I'd been awake for twenty-one hours, flown for ten, hadn't eaten since breakfast, and they wanted me to fly a circling approach to minimums to a short, wet, marginally lit runway at five in the morning. I told them they could find some hotel rooms in Traverse City instead. I think the dispatcher was pissed, even though the hotel rooms wouldn't come out of his paycheck. Oh well. My threshold for caring was way beyond what they paid me, not that I'm willing to perform heroics for any price, and getting back to base definitely involved heroics. I never heard anything from the Chief Pilot after digging my heels in at Traverse City, which is a credit to him. If I'd explained the situation, I'm sure he would've backed me up.

They don't realize it, but I actually saved them money because I still had enough fuel to get the airplane back if the weather was good. If they had wanted me to bring the airplane back early in the morning when the weather sucked, I would have had to buy expensive fuel in Traverse City, because I would've needed fuel to go to an alternate airport, plus some contingency fuel. By five in the morning, our anticipated arrival time, Willow Run Airport fell below circling minimums just like I thought it would, so I would've inevitably parked the old bitch at Detroit Metro Airport anyway, incurring other expenses as well. I should have been an accountant, although judgment is difficult to put on a balance sheet. Or better yet, I should've been born rich—but if I had been, I doubt I could've written as interesting of a story.

Before I knew it I had missed the summer, and with Dawn working, the rest of the family had too.

I took Jay and Neal to visit my father on Norris Lake in East Tennessee, a huge, deep, mountain reservoir built by my maternal grandfather, which flooded the land of my paternal grandfather, an unusual family dichotomy, but one that inextricably ties me to the place.

My father had bought his first house on this lake twenty-five years prior. The previous owner needed to get out from under the lake house after being victimized by a huge bank fraud that was perpetrated by two of my distant cousins whom I had never met, one of whom had even once been a gubernatorial candidate in Tennessee who went from worrying about polling numbers to worrying about prison sex.

Where had the twenty-five years gone? Surrounded by mountains and forests, Norris Lake was the other watery realm from my youth, where I would spend much of the summer in my teen years, summers that seemed as if they would never end. I would race the first rays of sun to the lake, and sometimes I would still be out after dusk, and it was all mine. Back then I never once considered that the deep green water, the mountains and trees, and even time itself didn't belong to me.

A few years ago my father had built a new lake house, much farther down the lake in a village called Sharp's Chapel, which is actually where Barney Butcher, a Pennsylvania Deutsch ancestor, had settled after fighting in the Revolutionary War. No, they weren't Dutch, they were Deutsch, but no one remembers that now, or cares. Barney was even born in Germany, immigrating to Pennsylvania in Colonial times and then to the Tennessee frontier after the war. Our roots sank deeper into the Clinch River Valley than we had ever known.

My maternal ancestors were concurrently settling only twenty miles to the north and thirty to the south. My family was truly part of the landscape in deep time, yet I knew virtually no one.

We took a long boat ride, up the lake, past the old lake house, which had changed enough that I recognized it only by its location. We rode into Dodson Creek, a beautiful nearby creek arm nestled between extremely steep wooded slopes, a place so topographically challenging that I was certain it would remain forever wild. It didn't, and the endless summers of my youth also did end. The wilderness of my youth was now suddenly filled with weekend mansions that many of their owners could just as suddenly no longer afford to keep. Every precariously perched house had steep stairs that led to obnoxiously luxurious docks that smothered the once secluded and placid water, each equipped with a private navy of wave runners, which had become as numerous and much more annoying than mosquitoes.

This was no longer the lake I had known. My ancestry was part of its history, and I even had some of my own fishing stories to tell, having once pulled a fish out of Dodson Creek that was half as long as I was tall, but in seeing a few year's worth of change, I felt I no longer belonged there as I once had, and not by choice. Another part of my youth had quite unexpectedly disappeared at summer's end.

I suddenly understood why my grandfather, the Butcher who had been dispossessed of our family farm in the old Clinch River Valley, had never seemed very excited about us regaining a piece of shore that stood over his drowned land and his lost youth. It was not the same place as when it all, the Clinch River, the valley, the mountains, the forest, and even his future, still belonged to him.

Escape

A friend from my new-hire class at my old airline was flying Beechjets for an air ambulance service that paid him a respectable salary, with more days off than I had. It was such a good job that he actually took an early furlough for it the prior year.

My friend's company acquired a Lear 36, just a Lear 35 with a larger fuselage fuel tank and longer range, in Honolulu for patient transfers back to the continent. He told his Chief Pilot that one of his friends had thousands of hours in Learjets and was currently flying air ambulance in them. His chief pilot was very interested and asked him to get my resume and send it to him.

That meant more grown-up decisions for us, maybe. Hawaii seemed like an interesting diversion for the family, although expensive and a lot of trouble to move to. We would have to give up the potential for an extremely valuable benefit from Dawn's new job, half-price tuition for Jay and Neal at OSU, assuming she stays there for another nineteen years, which may be more of a curse than a benefit.

A week later, my friend learned that his company was losing a contract in Cleveland and that he was getting furloughed because of it. They were still planning to hire for their new Learjet though. I wanted to escape from my job, but going to a company that would furlough my friend, a highly experienced jet Captain, just to avoid having to pay for a Learjet type rating didn't seem like much of a reward.

In solidarity, I didn't want to take a job that should belong to my friend, an irrelevant protest, because someone else would. There is always someone else. As Wilbur says, "All we are is a bunch of rats fighting over the cheese."[12]

I also knew exactly what would happen to me if they ever decided to replace their Lear in Hawaii with one of their Hawker jets, which are probably better suited to the mission anyway, after going through the trouble of moving my family there. I really didn't want to work for a company that would so easily throw away a dedicated, experienced employee rather than spending a little money on a type rating. I actually hoped they wouldn't call me so that I wouldn't have to turn them down.

I still desperately wanted out of where I was, if only there was somewhere else to go.

My friend Wilbur lost his job flying for a charter company. Since he didn't have a family, he would stay out as long as they asked him too, which was a Chief Pilot's dream. He also brought a tremendous amount of experience, and I know he did an excellent job. I've flown with him enough to know that his was a safe airplane. Unfortunately, Wilbur wasn't afraid to voice his opinion to his boss, sometimes necessary when you're being operated by a shoestring but a trait that apparently also marked him for furlough as business slowed down. They gave him no warning, and even shut off his company credit card the day before giving him the ax, leaving him stranded in Canada.

Being completely cooperative and compliant doesn't necessarily protect your job either. Two other pilots at Wilbur's company were picked to be fired because they were the next pilots due for recurrent training, and training costs money.

My airline, along with another national airline, merged with a regional airline that apparently wanted to break free from feeder contracts and operate a national airline. It suddenly appeared I might have a place to go back to—that is, if the pay and work rules were worth going back to. I wasn't sure yet whether I could consider it hope; that would depend on seniority integration, which would likely be very ugly with four separate pilot groups with vastly different experience levels, lifestyles, and career expectations. Anything was better than what I had now, except junior First Officer pay at a regional airline, which was a real possibility if my pilot group got screwed during the seniority integration, still to come.

My pathetic guarantee barely paid for day care for Jay and Neal and for a place to stay while I was in Detroit. I would actually have to get assigned to some of the contract flying to make this financially worthwhile. That meant the only thing the job was really giving me was currency, which only mattered if I didn't have an airline to go back to.

I got some more of the lucrative ambulance flying, but it didn't last. Before I met one of our medics, I saw the tag on her suitcase that read "It's all about me." I pointed it out to my co-pilot, and asked, "Do we have one of those?"

The high-maintenance medic, who was employed by the company that chartered my company's airplanes, found out that our airplane was the airplane that was involved in a near tragedy a year prior. The crew hadn't turned on the cabin air, a killer item buried within, and dangerously diluted by, the irrelevant items in the company's unnecessarily long checklists. They were saved by a sharp air traffic controller's suspicion that they were getting hypoxic and by the fact that the pilots were still barely coherent enough to execute the controller's descent commands, saving them from repeating the accident that killed pro golfer Payne Stewart in a Lear 35. The incident had nothing to do with the airplane, but she was obviously scared of it. She was constantly asking what our cabin altitude was, something they normally only record once during the live legs.

We flew a short trip, from Providence, Rhode Island, to Waterville, Maine, then to Boston. The next day we were going to fly to JFK (New York City) and then Cleveland. Before we left, the nurse asked me to stay low on the leg to Cleveland because of how our cabin altitude had exacerbated her toothache during our trip to Maine. I told her that it couldn't have because we actually kept a sea-level cabin during the short, low-altitude legs we had just flown. The airplane holds a sea-level cabin altitude all the way up to 24,000 feet, and it was working perfectly.

I thought her malady was a shoulder ache; not a tooth ache, but I guess that was because we were about to load the luggage into the airplane. She was becoming a pain in the ass for me, because she talked her company into switching our airplane after flying to Cleveland. That was going to cost me a lot of money since I would make almost nothing in base, and if the airplane didn't move by noon on Monday, I would be taken off the contract, replaced by a Captain who had a fresh fifteen days to give.

When the medics returned from dropping the patient off at the Cleveland Clinic, I told them that the ceiling at Willow Run was right at circling minimums and that I wasn't going to risk their lives by flying a circling approach on a stormy night in a fast-wing Lear

25, which had takeoff and landing speeds a good twenty knots faster than other Learjets. Circling approaches weren't even legal in airline flying, and for good reason: they're dangerous. The last fatal accident in the charter company had even been during a circling approach at night.

The high-maintenance medic was actually angry I wasn't going to needlessly risk her life, immediately saying that it was probably too late to cancel her hotel room in Detroit. That was really not my problem. Her company might have to pay for two hotel rooms that night, but that was nothing compared with the money she was making her company spend to needlessly fly back to base to switch airplanes.

My co-pilot mentioned that she might also be trying to get to Detroit because she was screwing one of our pilots. I was skeptical, and then even more so when I learned about the difficult reputation she had earned with the pilots and the other medics.

I was going to get one more day of pay at a decent wage, but I cancelled the flight for a legitimate reason, the same reason I had stayed in Traverse City a month prior. Ironically, I was standing my ground at Cleveland's Lakefront Airport, that tricky place where I had flown so many late-night circling approaches in snowstorms as a twenty-three-year-old novice freight pilot. What had I learned from the experience? Just because something is possible and legal doesn't make it a good idea. I had once been brave enough. Now I knew better. We would be much less likely to die that night if we were safely resting at the Hilton Garden Inn in Downtown Cleveland (I do locate the nearest fire escapes in hotels, just like I count the number of seatbacks between my seat and the nearest exit when riding in an airliner; I've done practice evacuations with smoke, during which you are completely deprived of your eyesight).

The next day we flew the airplane back to Detroit. I made a point of telling the nurse that this little diversion through base would cost me a couple thousand dollars in lost pay, because I would get replaced, something she knew but didn't care about.

The weather was much better, sufficient to allow a visual approach, but the sky was still filled with bumpy-looking little cumulus clouds. I asked my co-pilot to take her for a ride, so he plowed through every angry looking cloud he could find and then punctuated the rough ride with a bone-jarring landing in a strong, gusty crosswind. He's a good man.

My co-pilot and I did get replaced, but then they gave me an airline ticket to Montgomery, Alabama, to meet up with a Lear 25 with a freight floor that was parked there. I would be working for per-diem, waiting for them to sell a freight trip that probably wouldn't be worth the hassle.

I stayed in a new hotel near the Hyundai assembly plant. I bet you thought they made foreign cars. Except for the hotel's free breakfast, the only nearby food was from Waffle House, Burger King, and Subway. In spite of the bleak dinner prospects, I decided I just wanted to stay there until they gave me an airline ticket back a week later. I didn't want to work. My heart wasn't in it. I wanted out of my job, but the next best option immediately available was to just stay in the hotel, writing and earning per-diem at a buck-fifty an hour. I was fine with that, just as long as I didn't have to work.

My bed was comfortable, and I was probably even the first person to ever lay in it, but sleep didn't come easily and allowed no escape from my discontent. The frantic piercing beep from my pager woke me from an odd restlessness state at three in the morning. I don't believe in karma, but my pager does seem to know exactly when I don't want to hear its painfully annoying beep.

I had no motivation, I hadn't slept well, and I had one of the hardest workdays of my career ahead of me. It would certainly be the longest. I flew to Laredo, Texas, to clear customs outbound and to refuel, then on to Guadalajara, Mexico, to pick up the freight. We were flying a load of auto parts to Windsor, Ontario, for General Motors. I bet you thought they made American cars.

We flew halfway down Mexico, but we rarely caught a glimpse of it through the monsoon clouds that cheated me from seeing an unfamiliar land. In the antique Learjet, I trusted the cartographers and my navigation skills to keep me away from the hidden mountains near the airport. When we finally caught a glimpse of Guadalajara it was much greener than I expected, probably from Pacific moisture brought in on the seasonal winds. New homes spread out into the countryside, except these were handsome townhouses, not like American suburbs with huge yards that their owners rarely set foot in.

We had to wait in Guadalajara for hours. I would have liked to have waited there for days, but the delay would cause our duty time to exceed what we could be legally scheduled for. The broker probably knew this, but by withholding that information from my company, they would be able to legally schedule us for it by saying we had encountered unforeseen delays.

We cleared customs again in Laredo, since our gas-guzzling Lear 25 didn't have the range to go from Mexico to Canada. They were pleasant people, nothing like the militantly hostile creatures I had dealt with in Miami after returning from the Dominican Republic; it just took a while. The whole day was taking a while. I had never thought of Shreveport as a northern city, but we were flying a long way to the north to get there.

Before leaving Laredo, I called our dispatcher to ask if they could have some food delivered to the airport in Shreveport since we hadn't eaten all day and wouldn't have the opportunity to. She said, "I'll have a pizza delivered, but the company's not paying for it because that's the way it is." We were flying a $25,000 charter, but the company wouldn't even buy a $21 pizza.

In Shreveport my dispatcher put me through to Canadian customs while listening in and recording the call. The customs officer figured out that there was someone else on the line besides me, and then the process stopped once the eavesdropping dispatcher mentioned that they record the calls. The customs agent didn't like that.

Our General Manager, the one who micromanages everything, from his ridiculously tedious ping-pong checklists to our shitty pay and schedules, was in the dispatch office, and he took the phone. He actually yelled at this poor Canadian customs agent, repeatedly. The patient customs officer gave him several chances to finish the call by saying, whenever he could actually get a word in, "If you just tell me you aren't recording this, we can continue." The General Manager was so eager to fight that he couldn't hear the hints, and they were more than hints; the officer was practically telling him to just lie so that we could just get the call over with. That's apparently how he is, always looking for a fight, and so sure that he's right that he won't listen to a Canadian customs agent who was actually trying to not fight. Simple questions from pilots often degenerate into condescending name calling. The customs agent was much more patient than he needed to be but eventually reached his limit for absorbing abuse and hung up.

I realized that this job would never get better until the General Manager left, and he wouldn't leave until he dropped dead of a heart attack. There was no remedy for the kind of madness that permeates people who think they run the world; there was only escape.

The incident was working its way up the Canadian chain of command, but instead of escalating into a true international incident, the Canadians graciously gave us another chance to get the job done.

As I got in the airplane with our over-priced pizza, I told my co-pilot that there was a small chance we could end up in jail when we got to Canada. Not really though; all of the Canadian customs agents were very nice and generally not paranoid that their country was perpetually on the verge of invasion.

My co-pilot made a remark that at least we'd already had the worst. I told him not to say something like that until we were done with the trip. He was just relieved to be out of Mexico. I'm never relieved until I set the parking brake at the end of the trip, and then I only feel like I just got away with another one. You can never let your guard down.

My co-pilot taxied out at Shreveport, and he either didn't understand our taxi instructions, which I had just reviewed with him, or lost track of where we were. I was head-down, running our General Manager's ridiculously long god-damned checklist when I saw the runway hold signs in my peripheral vision. I yelled "Stop!" while lifting my feet up to the brake pedals, and we brought the airplane to a shuddering halt just short of the runway as an airplane was about to land. This was just one of the many lethal hazards that I worried about the moment I first saw these fucked-up checklists, and I barely saved us from a runway incursion and possibly a collision, this time.

Visually clearing a runway before crossing it is so basic of a fundamental that your parents first teach it to you as a toddler: looking both ways before crossing the street. This was about to become our mistake, but this simple rule had already saved my ass twice after air traffic controller's mistakes, once at La Guardia Airport with a hundred passengers on our airplane and possibly as many in the landing airplane that we didn't pull in front of.

In Windsor I asked the customs officers if either of them had been the recipient of that embarrassing tongue lashing from my boss. One of them had been, smiling as he admitted it. I apologized for my boss's behavior, and we all laughed about how much of a jerk I had to work for, only it really wasn't funny; I still worked for him, they didn't, and all I could think about was escaping.

I had just enough fuel for the short flight to Willow Run, but I wanted a bigger margin in my tanks, especially because of how tired I was getting. I wasn't going to let myself be rushed by anything, not even by the Lear 25's insatiably thirsty turbojets. My dispatcher was going to have me taxi to a different FBO for cheaper gas, but then she decided to let me stay where I was because it would only cost twenty-one dollars more there, the exact price of the pizza that they wouldn't buy for us in the middle of an exhausting work day with no breaks.

I took off and pointed the airplane toward the setting sun. Just across the river, Detroit was pleasantly silhouetted against the orange sky, the only time I had ever been so glad to see it. I'd made a little extra money, maybe twenty or thirty bucks above my guarantee after subtracting the price of the pizza, but I earned a lot more than they would ever pay me. I wasn't going to think about that. All I could think about now was a hot shower and then escaping into a deep sleep. As expected, the trip wasn't worth the hassle.

I didn't even open my pay stubs any more, not that I was able to figure them out anyway. If the purpose behind this bizarre pay scale was to encourage productivity, I found it to have the opposite effect, incentive to not work unless you were lucky enough to be able to actually see a return on your efforts.

I had a day to rest, sort of. The Director of Operations reportedly once said, "It's nice to wake up in the morning and realize that yesterday was a day off." I'm pretty sure he was being serious, although I wasn't there to hear him say it. It's really not a day off unless you already know in advance that it's a day off, the very antithesis to a fifteen-minute leash imposed by a pager that happened to not ring on a given day. I do have to admit that when you are next up in the crew rotation and you wake up in the morning and realize that your pager didn't ring in the middle of the night, it feels like you dodged a bullet, but it doesn't feel like a day off. The relief is often temporary, because if it doesn't ring that day, you'll go into another night of nervous sleep, afraid the thing will ring at the worst time.

The next day, when it did ring again, I had fifteen minutes to get to the airport for a freight trip and the Chief Pilot was going with me to give me a checkride. I knew this was coming up at some point, and being an outsider in this strange place, I was dreading it. I hadn't been able to bring myself to study for it at all, and how can you really prepare yourself for something when you have fifteen minutes' warning? I really didn't want to be there, so it was also really hard to care.

It was an easy trip to Buffalo and Cincinnati on a beautiful day after a surprisingly decent night of sleep. It happened to be in the same airplane I had just flown to Guadalajara, and maintenance actually fixed everything I wrote up, which wouldn't happen at a lot of companies, and I was pleasantly surprised that it happened there. I knew I hadn't been flying enough to be as proficient as I would like to be, but I pulled off a solid performance. After the flight John even only asked me questions that I actually knew the answers to. How did he know? Or maybe I had been doing this for so long now that I knew most of the answers.

The next day, after another decent night of sleep, I got a trip from Worchester, Massachusetts, to Queretaro, Mexico. It happened to be the twenty-second anniversary of my first flight lesson, an event that now just served to remind me that I was getting old in a stagnant career, especially since I happened to be accompanied on the trip by a twenty-two-year-old co-pilot. I must've just seemed like a bitter old man to him. He'll certainly have the chance to learn the hard way too, unless his luck is better than mine.

We were in a Lear 36, so we only had to make one fuel stop. Mexico was still smothered by monsoon moisture, but the clouds parted just enough for me to fly a visual approach between the mountains under a gorgeous sunset. I wanted badly to stay, to briefly escape to an exotic land, but they had us fly the airplane up to Laredo, Texas, until they could sell us again.

Most of my Mexican trips would end with a flight to Laredo, America's largest inland port, and now that the Little Professor at the mall across the street from my hotel closed its doors, America's largest city without a bookstore. The city has belonged to five different countries, if only briefly, during the past two centuries, but it retains an undeniably Mexican ethnicity. Laredo was acquired by treaty at the end of the Mexican-American War, after which the citizens voted to remain Mexican, a referendum that was promptly rejected by the US Army overseeing the newly acquired lands. So maybe I was having Mexican overnights, just on the wrong side of an irrelevant border a mile away.

The job was tolerable on a day like this, except for the fact that I had been gone for thirteen days and I still had two more to go. How much had I missed during that time, time that is now gone and I'll never get back? I wasn't just grieving for myself; it was what I was taking away from my family that hurt the most. Jay and Neal didn't want an absent father. Jay had always hated the four-day trips from my airline job, but what we faced now was so much worse, with no end in sight. Neal didn't understand this at all, now actually thanking me for coming to his house during my brief trips home. I told him it was still my house too. Jay asked if we were divorced, having heard the term without knowing what it meant. They weren't old enough to understand the sacrifice we were all making. Dawn did understand, but the reality of it just seemed to be getting more difficult. I didn't want to be just passing through my children's or my wife's lives, something that the seventeen-year-old kid who started me down this path couldn't have known.

Dawn and I were expecting the fifteen-day rotations to get easier, but they actually seemed to be getting worse. I thought I had been handling it all pretty well until I saw how much pain my absence was truly causing my family. I had taken this job thinking it was temporary, thinking I could do anything for a year. It had now been ten months, and there was no end in sight. In fact, if I stayed much longer, it would only get much worse, with my recurrent simulator training and recurrent ground school occurring during my days off, which would mean eight straight weeks on the road without a single day off. This was already a job that didn't have vacation time, ever. My family was more important than my career; this job didn't allow the time for both.

Back at the airline, the last of the hundred-seat 717s were going away, to be totally replaced by hundred-seat jets that management was trying to call RJs. The last of our pilot group, experienced professionals all, were being furloughed and replaced by kids willing to whore their way into the industry, oblivious to the fact that their willingness was degrading the profession to the point that it would no longer be worth the effort to get into.

No one cares about what I've worked so hard to attain and tried to improve with each flight: judgment, skill, knowledge, discipline, and experience. Well, no one cares unless they're in the back of my plane, helplessly gripping their armrests on a dark and stormy night. Airlines have placed a dollar value on your life, and they've decided that paying poverty wages to young punks is cheaper than ensuring your safety under the watch of seasoned professionals.

You may have even helped enable your potential demise by searching the internet for hours, or even days, just to find a ticket that's ten dollars cheaper, without realizing that you might eventually get what you pay for, selling off your own safety one mouse click at a time. The internet was probably actually worse for the deregulated airline industry than the terrorist's attacks on September 11, 2001.

Our replacements came within ten feet of killing two plane loads of passengers when they mistakenly crossed a runway hold line in Los Angeles just as a 757 was taking off. The newspaper article identified my old airline in the near disaster but failed to mention that replacement pilots had made the nearly lethal mistake. Vindication is the last thing I want, but it's perpetually just a heartbeat away.

The union took our scope grievance back to the arbitrator who had previously denied us our contractual rights. They were sure that now they could prove that the company had lied to him before, but he refused to even hear our case; we had no right of appeal. Our contract, which had allegedly been a legally binding agreement, had been blatantly violated and now thrown away for good.

I had been afraid of going back to the same arbitrator, thinking he was likely an arrogant guy who wouldn't be able to admit he had been wrong before, his ego standing in the way of justice and four hundred pilots' careers. I had wanted to pursue a criminal collusion case since we could probably prove that our former CEO and the CEO of the airline we merged with had conspired as early as June of 2008 to violate the Railway Labor Act, defrauding us of our livelihoods by illegally locking us out. I wrote to everyone in the union's leadership but never even got a response. The union fights fairly; unfortunately, corporate America does not.

Even our dignity was now gone. We, an entire experienced, professional pilot group, were now facing the prospect of getting stapled to the bottom of a regional airline's seniority list, beneath the very kids who replaced us and who were indirectly helping to destroy the very profession that they won't retire from until the year 2048. If my airline's pilots have any future there, it'll be because our new employer is taking more and more flying from the major airlines they contract for, which is exactly what they are positioned to do, an unstoppable juggernaut that destroys pilot contracts, turning the only remaining good jobs into shitty ones, potentially with me as an unwilling participant.

Was it time to get out for good, or would I whore myself out with the slim hope that someday I might be able to do something, anything to try to restore dignity to the profession that I loved? It felt more like time to escape. Without the ability to simply strike, the airline industry would never get better until the government reregulates it, which the country just wouldn't have the resolve to do as long as they could continue to buy cheap tickets from an industry hopelessly racing to the gutter.

At some point in every trip, I tried to remember to apologize to my co-pilot for my bad attitude. Always bitching, I had become the kind of chronic bellyacher I had despised when I was young, naïve, and willing to endure any imaginable deprivation to fly an airplane. I understood that happiness was a choice, but it seemed unobtainable, for now, without making another choice: to just walk away from something I still loved.

In fairness to the job, I would have had an entirely different experience there if only I had been at an entirely different place in my life. If I wasn't married, if I didn't have children, if I was still young enough to abuse my body with unscheduled all-nighters that I wasn't prepared for, and if I hadn't already experienced the good life at a good airline, the safest job in flying, I would've been more willing to just accept the job for what it was, and for what it was not. But if this was the best I could do, it wasn't worth the sacrifice.

I would like for my eventual resignation to be an act of protest, but unfortunately, there are always unemployed pilots knocking on the door, hoping to replace me. I do believe the owner of the company is a decent individual. He knows people eagerly subject themselves to this, some even paying him lots of money for the opportunity to fly shiny jets, so there can't be anything wrong. The blame is shared by many.

If I was going to just get out of a profession that was plummeting toward infamy, what was the point of me hanging onto my crappy job? I was out on the air ambulance contract again, riding a wave of good luck that carried me through several tours, so I was at least making money, but my heart truly was not in it. I felt like I already had one foot out the door, without the strength to pull it back in.

Unfortunately, we had a lot of flying to do. My co-pilot had apparently been chosen as a candidate to upgrade, an uncommon distinction in a place where learning occurs only through some mystery of faith, and I found the resolve to work by trying to teach him, trying to impart twelve thousand hours' worth of street smarts, and generations' worth of airline wisdom, wisdom I've learned from all those who've gone before me, on my eager successor. I wanted to teach him things he would never learn inside this isolated, inbred culture, things that might help keep him alive once they awarded him with his fourth stripe. If I truly was on the way out of the industry, maybe some of what I had learned could live on, some part of me, along with a part of all of those from whom I've learned.

We were accompanied by a train wreck of a med-crew, a nurse who seemed to be a raging alcoholic and an insomniac respiratory therapist (RT), somehow appropriately neurotic sidekicks for our fifteen-day journey through absurdity, an adventure unlike any I had yet experienced.

We had to airline out to our airplane, which this time meant a trip through Chicago O'Hare, a place overflowing with reasons why air travel has become a chore. The pilots of our RJ made an unbelievably hard stop on landing, uncomfortably so, especially since we still had more than a mile of dry pavement left when we exited the runway (probably a land-and-hold-short operation, but still uncomfortable). I dryly told my co-pilot that airlines pay landing fees based on how much runway they use, and I actually had him for a moment, a very brief moment.

We started in Rochester, Minnesota, a nice enough place to wait in autumn, except for the fact that it is always so hard to get, and keep a room at the Hilton Garden Inn, with the never-ending stream of traffic through the Mayo Clinic. My co-pilot was hoping for a trip to Reno so he could see the air races, which was a bit too specific for a job that was only likely to keep us in the same hemisphere. I didn't want to go anywhere, but it was not up to me. Right when it was apparent we would have to change hotels, we got a trip to Denver and Ft. Lauderdale.

Landing in Ft. Lauderdale, I made a left turn off the runway toward the FBO instead of the familiar right turn toward the old gate at the airline terminal, a depressing turn to make after such a depressing turn of events.

The FBO was unlike any that I had seen, with a family theme instead of the expected South Florida tropical theme. Pictures of children filled a wall, children of the employees, I presume. A pedal-powered toy airplane was parked in the lobby, waiting for the rare child who might pass through there. Two slushy machines whirled next to the standard coffee urns, mango and watermelon. The pilot's lounge had video games, which were actually on the wrong side of the runway since the kids were taking the airline jobs from the older, experienced pilots.

I liked the FBO, very much in fact, but it was also disturbingly incongruous to display a family theme in an industry that is so incompatible with families. My kids, who I wouldn't get to see for nearly two more long weeks, would love the place, but they would never have a chance to go there.

We stayed in a hotel where a certain airline puts its crews, an airline that negotiates liquor prices at its crew hotels, spiked Kool-Aid to help keep the peasants happy. Our medics got the special discounted crew prices from the bar but still managed to run up a hefty tab. Then they sat out by the pool, where they claimed to see some sinister-looking long-legged raccoons prowling the landscaping. There are some exotic critters in South Florida, but this was my first indication that we weren't going to have the A team in the back of the plane.

We actually got another trip in the morning, all the way to Reno even, but we couldn't stay. We flew a patient to Cleveland, which was much too close to base, but fortunately they didn't reel us back in. My paycheck depended on avoiding that.

I called my friend in Cleveland, the Beechjet pilot from my old airline, to find out that it was actually his last day of work before getting furloughed from his air ambulance company, reason enough for me to buy him a beer. I owed him one anyway from a La Guardia overnight almost three years prior, when he realized that I had only allowed myself one beer because I was too cheap to buy a second one. The nurse tagged along, although she didn't need an excuse to drink, nor did she have the intent to stop.

My friend went back home to Michigan, unemployed again, the fourth time in eight years. The nurse retreated to her room with a twelve pack of beer and wasn't seen again for a couple of days. We stayed in Cleveland for nearly a week, close enough to base that I couldn't escape the nagging fear that they could easily reel us back in any time.

As I would walk to restaurants, an occasional homeless person would beg me for money. I was uncomfortable ignoring them, but shamefully, that's just what I did, even the one wearing a United Airlines First Officer's jacket (really), still in survival mode myself in a country where people are disposable.

I later learned that Cleveland is among the growing list of cities to prohibit panhandling, so now after society has thrown someone away, we've also taken away their constitutional right to say that they're hungry.

Or thirsty, some people might say. On a different trip, with the same co-pilot, I walked past a row of make-shift wishing wells in Santa Barbara, California, bowls and signs placed on blankets next to the pier by the otherwise silenced panhandlers. The only one that seemed to be attracting any significant pocket change from passerby was the one with the sign that read *Won't lie, need beer.* He was apparently being well rewarded for his honesty, and for his alcoholism.

Thankfully getting away from base, we flew to Dayton, to fly a patient, his wife, and daughter to Burbank, California. Upon meeting them, the patient's wife, an obviously nervous flyer, asked me how long I had been flying. The medics simultaneously said that it was my first day, although I didn't consider the question to be a joking matter. "Twenty-two years; I'm older than I look."

It wasn't a joking matter to the patient either, who apparently spent much of the flight west bound talking about how a certain infamous Captain who had recently crashed a perfectly flyable plane in Buffalo didn't belong in the cockpit. A strange coincidence, the RT actually grew up with the dead pilot, knew him pretty well in fact, and she didn't appreciate her patient pissing on her dead friend's grave.

With his numerous checkride failures making news headlines, I think we already knew he wasn't part of the A team either, but I blame the industry more for putting inexperienced, mediocre pilots in the left seat of a big airplane. This guy whored himself out by learning to fly at a zero-to-hero pilot factory and then by buying his way into the right seat at a pay-to-play airline. It sure doesn't help the situation when people are willing to do that.

Aside from his less than spectacular training record, and the fact that he paid to play at one dirt-bag outfit in order to gain enough experience to get into one of the most notoriously awful regional airlines, an airline most people have never heard of, hiding under a deceptive paint job of the trunk line they feed, I don't necessarily think the guy shouldn't have been in the cockpit; he just shouldn't have been in the Captain's seat yet. There are no shortcuts to competency; it must be earned. There isn't any time for that when you work for the lowest bidder in the airline industry, a company aspiring pilots specifically go to for a rapid upgrade to Captain, possibly before they're ready.

The National Transportation Safety Board used the flight data recorder, radar, and air traffic control tapes to produce a heartbreaking video of how the accident occurred. The sad reality was that if the guy had just let go of the controls, the airplane wouldn't have stalled. Rarely can an accident be so easily traced back to such a simple, fundamental error. And if only there had been an experienced pilot in the airplane . . . never mind, the passengers would never have paid a buck more per person for the airline to pay for experience; we're all to blame.

After more than nine years since I had flown there, I remembered the arrival into Burbank by sight, and I had a beautiful day for it, with uncharacteristically clear, smog-less skies in the valley.

In the FBO, a slender, highly polished, and possibly even surgically enhanced girl in stilettos was crammed into a shockingly tiny red flight attendant uniform, her skimpy, tight skirt barely covering her rump and tight blouse squeezing her ample cleavage out the top. It was so shockingly revealing that it was actually a little uncomfortable to look, although eye candy was the very point of it. She meant for us to look, or more likely her pimp intended for us to look. She worked for an exotic aircraft brokerage that would charter an airplane for a client and send a girl along as in-flight entertainment, giving a new meaning to whoring yourself out to fly.

We took a detour on the way to the hotel so that the RT could buy cigarettes and the nurse could buy a bottle of vodka, a bottle which apparently didn't survive the night, even though we had to fly again early in the morning.

Before six the next morning, I shared the elevator with an attractive lady in a short, tight sequined dress and dark sunglasses to shield her from a sun that had not yet risen, who made a bee-line for a waiting taxi, without a piece of luggage, undoubtedly a high priced companion for a fellow traveler the night before.

The nurse soon arrived in the lobby, looking like a clown, trying to disguise her hangover under a thick barrier of makeup that fooled no one.

The incredibly clear skies followed us all the way to Durango, Mexico, along the rugged Sierra Madre Occidental, the mysterious rumpled spine of Mexico's Golden Triangle, the producing region in Mexico's drug war.

We were greeted by a typically cheerful Mexican welcoming committee, except for el Commandante, who claimed our Mexican permit was expired. The company's permit wasn't expired, but my Spanish was rusty enough that I didn't know that with certainty. I had actually tried to read it during the flight down.

Our handler said that el Commandante would make us buy a temporary permit to leave, which I was beginning to realize was really just a bribe, semi-legitimized, something I wasn't prepared for and was honestly indifferent to. I wasn't going to argue with the man.

He didn't intend to give me the opportunity anyway; he pretended to not know a word of English, even though he would become the highest ranking official I would meet during all of my Mexican travels. If the company wanted their airplane back, they'd figure out how to get us out of there. I certainly wasn't going to worry about it; there were hotels in Durango, and we still had a few days left in our trip. Our handler said he would take care of it and just pass the charges along to my company.

A Mexican Army helicopter landed nearby, pouring out about twenty heavily armed infantry soldiers. We had left the San Fernando Valley and, two hours later, landed in a war zone, Mexico's drug war, a war that wouldn't have been happening without so many buyers in Mexico's northern neighbor.

Soon our ambulance was driving through the gate, and it was a low rider with polished chrome, custom detailed, right out of the barrio, with tiny, wide wheels. The nurse totally missed the cliché and only noticed that it had more paramedic equipment than would normally be found on an ambulance doing basic patient transports. I guess that should be expected in a war zone—the first-class medical equipment, that is.

El Commandante got what he wanted, and we got our passports and pilot licenses back, as well as an extra permit we didn't really need.

On the ground in Phoenix on a scorching 105 degree afternoon, with a cardiac patient in a rapidly heating aluminum tube, time mattered. The ambulance was at the FBO, but the crew walked so slowly through the stifling air that they almost appeared to be swimming through it. After an unnecessarily long drive around the parking lot, through the gate, and across the scorching ramp, the crew swam to the back of the ambulance, still in slow motion. On the way to the hospital, the ambulance driver asked our medics if they'd brought any good weed back from Mexico. I guess that explains why they seemed to be in a totally different plane of existence while we were in the plane roasting; they were consumers in Mexico's drug war.

My co-pilot and I were eating breakfast the next morning when the RT burst into the hotel's restaurant in a panic. After rolling out of bed, she had intended to take her thyroid pill, noticed it didn't taste right, and then realized, too late, that she had taken a sleeping pill. She tried to make herself vomit but couldn't. I made an inappropriate joke about her ability to suppress her gag-reflex that fortunately sailed way over her head and off into oblivion. She had actually slept all night, which was apparently rare for her, but now she had screwed that up with her accidental sedation.

This left me in an awkward position, since I was really just in command of an airplane that was chartered by the med-crew's employer. I wasn't really in command of the med-crew. Her chemical impairment wasn't actually a safety-of-flight issue, although there was a chance it could affect a patient's safety during a medical emergency. I suggested that she should probably make sure we didn't fly any patients that day. She chose to ignore me and hoped for the best. What else could I do? I warned her that if the stoner ambulance crew picked them up again, they were all likely to be found in a ditch a couple blocks from the hospital, with her and the ambulance crew giggling to themselves and the nurse passed out, trying to sleep off another hangover.

I didn't see the crew again until the hotel's free happy hour that evening, where the nurse downed four generous glasses of cheap wine before retreating to her room with another twelve pack of beer. They had an organ harvest trip pop up for us early the next morning, but we couldn't fly it because the nurse wouldn't, or couldn't, answer her phone.

Later the medics actually surprised me by freeing themselves from their typical medicated stupors in their dark, smoke-filled hotel rooms, even though their ambitions were questionable, to gamble.

The RT admitted that she overdoes it, so she only allows herself to gamble once or twice a year. She was up a thousand bucks at one point, but she just couldn't cash out and ended up losing six hundred bucks worth of her winnings before finally pulling herself away from the machine.

The nurse bragged that she at least knew when to quit, an ironic statement from which I could not hold back a spontaneous laugh. She was being serious. After being up three hundred dollars, she finally quit when she was forty in the hole. She mistook the fact that she lost a smaller dollar amount of peak winnings for superior restraint, this coming from someone who didn't know how to take a last sip until she collapsed on the floor, unable to respond to an ambulance trip ringing into her phone.

On my last day of the rotation, day fifteen, I got my long-awaited call from dispatch, but they weren't calling me to tell me about my airline ticket home; they were calling me to ask me if I would stay another day. They had a trip from Phoenix to Prince Edward Isle, Canada. We could have a fuel stop and crew change in Detroit. That would mean sixteen days on and only five days off, and that was only if the nurse was sober enough to drag herself out of bed the next morning, if the patient remained stable enough for transport, and if there was an empty hospital bed at the destination, depending on the highly undependable. I could easily see that turning into seventeen days on and four days off.

I could ask to start my next rotation two days later, but there was a big catch. I would forfeit another chance to get sent out on contract flying and I would go to the back of the rotation, on my one chance to lead the pack for the next fifteen weeks, which meant I could only rely on making my pathetic fifty-seven dollar per day guarantee, which was really not worth it. My days off were too precious, and there was really no way to ever get them back. I told them they could buy me an airline ticket back.

I arrived at Detroit Metro Airport at midnight of day fifteen. I never got back any earlier than that. I called dispatch to see if someone could pick me up and drive me to Willow Run Airport. They normally would already have someone en route, but understaffed that night, they couldn't send someone until two or three in the morning. I couldn't get a cab because the company that provided all cab service from Detroit Metro, the sole permit holder for some bizarrely corrupt reason, had just gone bankrupt. A limo driver who was standing close enough to me to hear the conversation offered me a ride.

I drove away from Willow Run Airport on the new road that had just opened, a road to nowhere. The potholes and fractures from the old crumbling road were gone, but so was much of the lovely ravine where Willow Run Creek had meandered for millennia, and half the trees that sheltered it, and now, so was I.

I was finally going home, escaping my toxic, dysfunctional environment for six short days. I didn't ever want to come back. If I had already flown a Learjet for the last time, I was at peace with that, for the moment at least. I still loved the activity itself, but it just didn't seem worth it any more, at least not in the present conditions.

I did come back, but I told the Chief Pilot that I would only fly until my recurrent training was due. I wouldn't be staying for that, working eight weeks straight without any real time off. Business had picked up considerably, and I wanted to try to put some money into savings before I quit. I guess that still made me a whore, but at least I had drawn a line in the immediate future that I would not cross.

They fired Jack but wouldn't tell him why. It may have been because a couple of trips had cancelled when he decided not to fly broken airplanes, decisions that had already caused him to endure unnecessary tongue lashings. Or it may have been because he had cracked a secret code and figured out that they were paying us wrong for the contract flying, usually resulting in underpayment. Or maybe it was because he was circulating ideas through the pilot group that would simplify and bring equity to our convoluted pay scale, ideas that provoked an especially angry, rambling, and, as always, condescending letter from the General Manager. Jack wasn't starting a union drive, but I guess subordinates sharing ideas was threatening enough. A brave voice of reason got his throat cut in a cut-throat business.

I made it past my first anniversary, so I was just two years away from my first pathetic pay raise, a penny per mile, something I always knew I wouldn't stay for. The owner of the company surprised me with a very generous Christmas bonus, the only Christmas bonus of my career, ironic since he was the only person I had ever worked for who didn't self-righteously claim superior status as a devout Christian. He seemed like a decent guy, as did everyone else here. They were all hard workers too. One person with unchecked power is enough to ruin everything, in this case the Napoleonic General Manager, who won't meet his Waterloo as long as pilots kept eagerly signing up to fly his shiny jets and as long as feds who had safety concerns were reassigned.

The airline industry won't realign its priorities—mainly, safety undisputedly above all else, even, dare I say, profits—until we, all of us, decide the industry is actually a vital link in the nation's transportation infrastructure and not just a ruthless competition to sell commoditized seats for unsustainably low prices. Costs and safety are sloping lines on a secret boardroom graph, so while desperately cutting costs, we're also hopelessly retreating down the wrong line with our fingers crossed while industry apologists try to say that a lack of accidents today is proof that we've arrived at a mythical destination of absolute safety. Flying is very safe, but settling for less safety than is possible is the same as allowing it to be more dangerous than it should be. The next tragedy is perpetually just a heartbeat away and is always preventable.

When my resignation letter read that I was quitting so that I could pursue other interest and spend more time with my family, it was actually going to be the truth. I wouldn't change anything by quitting, but I also wouldn't change anything by staying, protesting, and inevitably becoming a martyr like Jake. Maybe I can be a writer and expose your corrupted safety. As a new career, that's a path that probably has an even lower chance of success, but I think I'm brave enough to try, maybe. Whatever happens, I know my family will be happier with me at home.

I did a lot of flying toward the end, and it all seemed easier, even the last-minute all-nighters, of which there were plenty. I certainly wasn't getting used to those; I just couldn't escape from the realization that I would soon be free.

My co-pilot during my recent trip through absurdity was given a chance to upgrade, and he actually passed his checkride on his first try, a feat so incredibly rare that the examiner, the General Manager, didn't even bother to bring along a blank temporary airman certificate with which to reward my friend's exceptional performance. Prior to this successful upgrade, I assumed it was just the General Manager's policy to fail every co-pilot on their first attempt at the type-rating, a cruel rite of passage that traps pilots there by permanently staining the pilot's training records, which are now portable, public, and in the spotlight because of the history of checkride failures that preceded the recent Buffalo crash. Congratulations and fly safely, Captain Thomas.

At the same time that I was reveling in my imminent freedom, I was still getting much satisfaction from successfully meeting the challenges of the job, from crosswinds at the airplane's limit to flying approaches to minimums, seemingly everywhere, from Ontario, Canada, to Mexico and the Central Valley of California, where I had to fly the same approach twice because I had forgotten to ask my co-pilot to turn on the pilot-controlled approach lights on an extremely foggy morning at a non-towered airport. It was too foggy to see anything but the lights burning through the fog. I finally got the Mexican overnight I had been wanting, and I witnessed the most spectacular stretch of the Rockies I had yet seen, the Canadian Rockies, on a flight from Edmonton, Alberta, to Spokane, Washington, on an incredibly frigid but clear day. I was good at something and even still enjoying something I was about to walk away from. I knew very well that when I closed the door behind me, it would be very difficult to get back in.

On the last day of what had turned into a seventeen-thousand-mile sixteen-day trip, I flew a man to Denver who had suddenly been stricken with a debilitating illness, but from our almost ceremonious send-off, I felt like I was delivering him to the great beyond. I probably was. His parents were saying good-bye to him as if it was final. It reminded me that I had a lot of catching up to do with my own family. What I've missed, I won't get back.

I was probably already a little on edge from a recent fatal Learjet crash at another Detroit-based charter company. Details had been sparse in the couple days since the crash, and this one seemed to be a head-scratcher so far; the Lear 35 was turning final in Chicago on a pleasant late winter day when it inexplicably plunged into the ground. This was a disturbing kind of accident in which there are no obvious reasons, and our dead colleagues can't tell us what happened.

From Denver I had an airline ticket back to base. While waiting for the airplane, I had a long conversation with the Captain who would be taking me there. He had flown with my uncle Bob years ago, before he retired, and now this Captain was also retiring soon too, although more than six years early, something he obviously hadn't quite made peace with yet. I certainly sympathized with his conflicted retirement, rapidly approaching my own voluntary unemployment.

The Captain asked the flight attendants to take good care of me, and he apparently shared some of my story with his crew as well. As we were descending into Detroit, a flight attendant discreetly handed me a bottle of wine and said, "Here's a toast to whatever the future brings you." It was a gesture that nearly brought a tear to my eye on an already emotional day. I was in the company of strangers, but they were acknowledging that I was still part of their community; I was still an airline pilot, even as I was heading into the unknown somewhere beyond the cockpit door.

I took the bottle home to Dawn and told her we would be opening it the bittersweet day after I turned in my ID badge and my goddamn pager and headed home for good. Would it taste like uncertainty, regret, freedom, or hope? Maybe it would just taste like a cheap airline merlot.

Joining the Flying Circus

With a little more than a month left on the job, and maybe even in my flying career, Dawn found a job post for a Learjet captain for a single trip from Columbus to Gunnison, Colorado, that weekend. I was out of town on an air ambulance tour, so I couldn't fly the trip, but I needed to respond to the job post to offer seat support for any trips in the future, maybe a last chance to stay in the cockpit in a job market that was still deteriorating and likely wouldn't improve for years.

The post was on a job board I hadn't paid for, but the guy's phone number was listed by mistake, the poster's mistake. He actually answered his phone, and after hearing the brief version of my story, considerably shorter than the one you're reading, he asked me to send him a resume.

By the time I got home from my air ambulance tour, he already knew more about me than I realized. He had a part-time pilot named Mark, whom I had flown with eighteen years prior when I was a flight instructor and who had just happened to see my resume come off the printer, and he put in a good word for me. It's a small world. I had essentially interviewed for the job, if it could be called a job, years ago without realizing it.

My interview with the self-appointed Chief Pilot, a white haired, evangelistic, wise looking old man whom I had briefly spoken to on the phone, was more of a pep-rally, a burst of sunshine, a sales pitch with after-burners from a man I'll call Chris Columbus after the explorer whose legacy it was to be either loved or hated by so many for his attempt to spread Christianity throughout the world—and to make money exploiting it. He had access to a small but immaculate fleet of otherwise idled business jets, and I was apparently getting in on the ground floor, if there was a floor. Chris was trying to dry lease the underutilized airplanes to jet-less rich people, and he gushed with a salesman's excessive forced charm.

He was going to give me some flying, but I didn't actually get hired; I became a contract pilot, an ambiguous state of self-employment that was part chauffer, part mercenary, and, of course, part whore. Chris said that he would get me type ratings in all of the airplanes, an extremely rare find in an industry where no one wanted to spend a dime to train someone. I had been prepared to drop out of the industry, so I thought I had found something good. Even better, as policy, they didn't do circling approaches, because, like me, they were no longer brave enough.

I only got paid when I flew, but my day-rate, at four hundred bucks, was an entire week's guarantee at the charter job I was quitting. Chris charged the clients five hundred for my services and said that the difference paid for my training, which I was happy with until I figured out that there wouldn't actually be any training. He somehow managed to get me a Citation type-rating without spending a dime (and eventually a type rating in the newer CitationJet as well); he figured out how to get other people to pay for just a little extra airplane time and some extra jet fuel without them realizing it. I didn't realize yet that he funded what he needed by theft. You might say his thievery was resourceful, but by him taking his cut every time I flew, it also made Chris my pimp, which I guess also made me his bitch, and whether this was good or bad changed, sometimes drastically, from one day to the next. There was no sense of stasis, no comfort to be gleaned from the predictability of a steady job. In spite of that, I admit that I took a sip of the Kool-aid, really the first taste of my career. I wanted to believe I had found something good.

As I met more pilots in the local corporate flying scene, I learned that many had been promised type ratings by Chris, but he rarely delivered; he just stopped calling them when he couldn't deliver. My timing was lucky because he just happened to have an owner-operator paying him for some training at the time. I hadn't caught on to that yet. I had only noticed that there seemed to be a lot of people who owed Chris favors. He seemed to be able to produce a contact for anything he needed.

Dawn was exhausted from holding everything together during my absence for most of the preceding fifteen months. Now that I had quit, I flew contract trips on six of my first eight days of freedom. Our lifestyle wasn't improving. I had quit my job because I was always gone, and now I was still gone. This, and a couple of other triggers, including possibly another thyroid storm, caused her to totally break down while I was unreachable in the Bahamas. I hadn't discovered Skype yet, not that it would've prevented anything.

After a week of not being able to leave the house, Dawn was able to go back to work. We needed the steady paycheck and the medical benefits, but we knew she wouldn't be able to fully recover until she could leave her job at the Medical Center. Dawn and I are both wimps around medicine, and a doctor's office was another one of the triggers that helped to topple her.

I needed to find steadier work, but to do that I needed to just keep doing what I was doing. I was staying current, flying, networking, and hoping to break into the local corporate flying scene, possibly one of the hardest things for an unconnected former airline pilot to do in aviation.

Since I was an independent contractor, Chris correctly assumed I would eventually find some other flying outside of his control, so he even planned ahead by asking me to bill those trips through him so he could take his cut, even though his alleged training investment in me was minimal, if anything. Now that's truly pimpin'. Chris periodically reminded me of this with his hand out, but since his memory wasn't dependable, it wouldn't take him long to forget I had flown a trip for someone else and it wouldn't come up again until the next trip.

The irony of self-employment was that I was expected to be available to fly whenever Chris called me to ensure my phone would keep ringing in the future, so I actually seemed to have less ownership of my life than ever in my career. Chris also expected everyone to help with ancillary duties, a form of sweat equity, compensated by the hope of assignment to the next trip.

At the same time that Chris wanted us to do his work for him for free, tasks the aircraft owners were undoubtedly paying him for anyway, he didn't trust us to do our own work correctly. He also didn't trust us to be ready on time, so he would lie to us about the departure time, forget he had already done that, and change the departure time yet again, sometimes confusing the schedule to the point that even the client wasn't sure when they were supposed to be leaving-and they had scheduled the trip. The day before a trip, he'd call me to ask every detail about the trip.

"Did you make the flight plans?"

"They were somehow already generated Chris; I'm not sure how."

"Did you file them?"

"Yes, Chris."

"What about the customs manifest?"

"It's submitted and approved, Chris."

"Do you have your passport?"

"Yes, Chris."

"Do you have maps?"

"Yes, Chris."

"Caribbean charts?"

"They're already in the plane, Chris."

"Did you make a trip kit?" He would always print a set of enlarged charts for his sixty-eight year-old eyes, and he expected everyone else to need to do the same thing. He expected us to do everything exactly the same way he did; there was no variance allowed from his unwritten and sometimes unusual procedures. I have to admit that a few were actually good ideas, well, very few.

"It's done, Chris."

"Remember to take the life raft."

"It's already in the plane, Chris."

"Are you fueled?"

"Yes, remember we fueled before we put it away a few days ago?"

"Did you schedule a pullout time?"

"I called line service to put it on the schedule, but they somehow already knew about it." Chris had already called them but had forgotten that, again.

"Are you going to get some doughnuts?"

"On my way to the airport, Chris." This was not my first rodeo. I even knew that the little doughnut holes were more popular than doughnuts because a passenger could grab one or two without any guilt. The larger doughnuts would always go uneaten.

Chris would inevitably show up at departure time to see us off, no matter how early, to make sure everything was really done as well as to make an appearance, a reminder to everyone that he was the ring leader, the self-appointed Chief Pilot of the flying circus. The pimp.

He would always bring his own box of doughnuts, even though I had already told him that I would be doing that. He would try as hard as he could to stay in control of the trip, even attempting to be the relay between me and the client during the course of a trip, almost pretending he was an extra crew member, which was just an extra, unnecessary hindrance that significantly increased the chances of a miscommunication. Indeed, this extra layer did cause many needless miscommunications.

There was a reason why Chris had to keep his mitts on everything, besides the fact that he was a control freak who assumed he was the only one who knew what he was doing; if he wasn't flying the trip, he wasn't necessary. We were independent contractors operating airplanes on behalf of a client who had operational control. Technically, Chris was just an irrelevant pimp. It was easy to steal a client, and Chris knew it. Hell, it wasn't even stealing because he didn't own them anyway. Maybe my sense of ethics was just too naïve, but I didn't want to steal anything; I just wanted to fly my trips.

Chris would call us in, the clown posse, for a pilot meeting every other week or so, and each meeting was exactly the same: forty different topics barely grazed by the same sound bites and skillfully dodged questions in an hour-long whirlwind, punctuated by the eternal refrain: "I know three people who want to lease that airplane. This will be the best year of our careers, and we're all going to make a hundred thousand dollars." It was all bullshit, but he could put on a good show.

Dawn didn't trust him, and why should she? She had only known me to work for scoundrels. Why would my pimp Chris be any different? Chris was certainly eccentric, and a bit controlling, and I was getting a little tired of him constantly saying that this would be the best year of our careers and that I would make a hundred thousand dollars a year, but I really believed he had good intentions. At my day-rate, I really didn't want to be away for enough days to make that much money, but I didn't need to worry about that yet; we weren't that busy. I was just glad to be staying current, making decent money, and still working in a business that I had just recently, and reluctantly, tried to drop out of.

The closest I got to receiving any training was a brief opportunity to do some stall recoveries and a steep turn in the Citation while on a maintenance positioning flight, and then Chris sent me to an examiner for a type-rating checkride, with a dishonest endorsement claiming that I had ten hours of training in the airplane. This wouldn't normally be a good idea, but the Citation is the generic jet, docile, very easy to fly, and with underwhelming performance. It is the only jet I've flown that won't blow right through the speed limit while climbing (250 knots below 10,000 feet). Every jet checkride has the same boxes to check, which I had done dozens of times in much more demanding jets than the "Slow-tation", so now I just had to look for switches in different places in a very stable airplane, and that quickly, and cheaply, I was qualified in another airplane, a prolific airplane that was actually still in production, although just barely.

But the reason I was there was to fly a Lear 31, the last of the classic Learjets, basically a Lear 35 without tip-tanks and with fifteen years of product improvement beyond any other Learjet I had ever flown. Except for its limited fuel capacity, it was an awesome machine, the best handling Lear I had ever flown. It went high quickly and seemed to really want to be at 45,000 feet, where, even up in the thin air, it retained the Learjet's famously nimble handling. This was a glass cockpit Learjet, with a FMS (Flight Management System) computer and nearly every modern convenience except for auto throttles, and even that was okay, because in this fun little rocket, I wanted those throttles in my hands.

I had a neighbor, Frank, who was recently furloughed from a very large local charter and fractional ownership company. I didn't know him well, but I assumed he was probably a pro. He and I were at the same freight company years ago, but I didn't know him from there. I knew he had been flying business jets ever since, so I sent him an e-mail asking him which airplanes he was qualified and current in.

I needed a co-pilot for a Learjet trip that my old college friend wasn't available for, and I suggested Frank to Chris, who immediately turned me down, saying he didn't want any new faces around there yet. Chris had other plans; he always did, so it was strange that he ever even asked me what we should do. He said he knew a guy, didn't have any experience but he was a natural-and a friend of the Learjet's owner. Politics trumps everything, especially in my strange new realm. I figured it would only be for the one trip.

Frank didn't know I had found something locally, but he had been watching airplanes come and go and figuring out which ones lived in the area. He somehow found Chris, which was truly impressive detective work, and Chris had already invited him in for an interview on the same day that Chris told me that he didn't want to use my neighbor because he didn't want anyone new.

Chris and Frank talked for about an hour, and then Chris had an epiphany that caused him to ask Frank if he was my neighbor. Frank was initially taken aback by the question, but as soon as he managed a "yes," the interview was over; Frank was part of the clown posse.

Frank was a find; a true professional with a lot of experience. He's quiet and reserved like me, only smarter and not as lazy, and he is so squeaky-clean that he makes me feel like a sinner on the verge of hell. He's standardized, so disciplined that he almost doesn't seem human, meticulous with every detail, and he's another hard-core purist like me; when we fly a trip together the autopilot and flight director get some time off, and the passengers will still get the smoothest ride they've ever experienced in a moving vehicle. I would eventually end up flying a lot with him, and he's as good as it gets. Frank is so hardcore that, fifteen years prior, when he finished indoc at our freight airline, the only pilot to graduate in his class of eight, he was given five choices of bases, and he actually chose Utica, New York, so he would have to do a lot of flying, often in miserable weather.

Unfortunately, I still had to get Chris's low-time boy legal, bare-minimum FAA legal, Chris's idea of a qualified co-pilot, three take-offs and landings, which without any training are more like partially controlled collisions with the Earth. And ground school? Well, I made a list of the most critical things we absolutely needed to discuss before we got in the airplane; the rest we would have to do on the fly, pun intended. I was flying single-pilot until he had a chance to learn some things.

When queried, Chris had told me that the guy had 250 hours of jet time; in truth it was 16, really just 16 hours of watching Chris watch the autopilot fly from here to there in the underwhelming Citation, jet experience of the lowest quality except that, in just those 16 short hours, he and Chris somehow managed to line up with the wrong runway at Port Columbus on a nice day and also had accidentally strayed off a taxiway in St. Louis and got the plane stuck in the soft ground, also on a nice day. Chris was completely to blame for these serious blunders, but I didn't know about them until many months later. By then the duo had added an altitude bust to their frequent misadventures while departing Teterboro (they didn't cause a loss of separation, so they only got a tongue-lashing from the controller and not a violation). At this point I hadn't even seen Chris fly yet, to be able to question his competence, and I hadn't caught him in enough lies yet to question his honesty; the time would come for both. The Kool-Aid was already beginning to sour.

And was his boy a natural? There are many inherent mental and physical attributes that help to make a good pilot: good spatial orientation, ability to concentrate on a task with several facets for long periods of time, ability to plan ahead in time and space, fine motor finesse, and the discipline to study and learn. These are just part of the foundation that you build a good pilot on, but no seven-hundred-hour pilot is ever going to even begin to look like they know what they're doing in a Learjet, especially without any training and without lots and lots of practice.

Part of Chris's charade was to put four stripes on the young pup's shoulders, Captain's bars, to try to pass him off as qualified, in appearance at least; just three bounces and four bars, and he was a qualified jet pilot. Dawn had to pick us up at the airport once after repositioning the Lear, and she was pissed when she saw Captain's epaulets on Chris's seven-hundred-hour pilot, knowing how far away he was from being able to actually earn those stripes.

This was much worse than the pay-to-play co-pilots from my charter job, considering that the pay-to-play pilots at least received some real training. They also only wore three stripes, co-pilot's bars. If I were to lose consciousness now, I had serious doubts about our flight ending properly, on a runway, with all pieces still attached, none mangled and charred. On a more practical level than my incapacitation, I make mistakes, and I want someone who knows enough about the job that they'll point them out to me. I could overlook those nagging thoughts for one trip; I used to fly single-pilot every night, but all grown up now, with my family depending on me, that was no longer in my comfort level.

Chris quit calling my college friend after he wasn't available for another trip, and after a couple of arguments with Chris. My old friend was always on the right side of the argument, but accuracy meant little to Chris. Arguing with the old man only got you fired. Chris wanted to have his hands in everything, and he usually had some unconventional ideas.

Some of Chris's ideas were so alarmingly unconventional that Frank and I couldn't figure out how a sane, seemingly intelligent person who had been in the industry for a very long time could reach such bizarre conclusions. Frank eventually cracked the code, and it was so simple that I had looked right past it; when given multiple options, Chris always chose the option that put an extra hundred bucks in his pocket. That even partially explained why he fired my old college friend, to whom Chris was paying the full billed co-pilot wage of $350 per day for all of his sweat equity, with nothing left over for the pimp. Chris was only paying his new guy $200 per day, so when his new guy and I flew, our pimp made a $250 profit. Sometimes he would even charge the client for two Captains, pimping $400 for himself and cheating everyone, especially the client who expected to be flown by two fully qualified co-Captains.

His profit was immediate while the checks he wrote me were coming later and later, until he was about four months, and more than $17,000, late in paying me.

I obviously no longer had motivation for any sweat equity, but since Chris thought Frank was smarter than me, Frank was always asked to do chores now instead of me anyway, which didn't really make sense because omniscient Chris would still ultimately veto all of Frank's ideas and efforts, ideas that were always firmly rooted in safety, logic, and accepted industry practices.

We were slowly learning that Chris had an interesting history, in business and with the feds. Chris genuinely wanted us to be busy enough that we would each make a hundred grand, as long as he got his cut too, but otherwise he was the worst scoundrel we had encountered yet, unless he has chosen you to be a beneficiary of his good will, a rare and precariously fleeting distinction which required you to overlook many serious flaws, including having a pimp. This was his second attempt at a dry lease or pseudo-fractional operation. The first was a few years earlier, with a wealthy partner who had two jets on order. The partner had enough of Chris, and ended the venture without any warning, then not long after died in a plane crash.

We were in the least regulated segment of the industry, Part 91, but we strangely seemed to be getting more than our share of ramp checks from the feds, mainly because they were looking for illegal charter operations and they were very suspicious of Chris in particular, and for good reason. I had to educate myself quickly about dry lease agreements and how to make sure they were legal. I started doubting the accuracy of Chris's legal interpretations when he shared his philosophy that you only need to be 80 percent correct when dealing with the feds. He was only correct about the passing grade for the written test required for a new certificate or rating; otherwise the neglected 20 percent is enough to get you violated, which will then make you 100 percent unemployable for six years, waiting for the violation to be purged from your records.

The job market was still horrible, but I actually got an interview with a hip new upstart airline after passing a somewhat grueling online intelligence assessment, giving me a fleeting moment of hope for unambiguous employment, that is, if the young airline is able to establish its footing before bleeding to death, a risk I was surprisingly happy with, given my circumstances.

Nine pilots were to interview on my big day, but only four of us even showed up, my first warning flag after investing several hundred dollars in airfare and hotel for this rare chance, an airline interview in the worst airline job market of my lifetime. The interview panel was an hour late and then spent well over another hour congratulating themselves for being such a cool airline and great place to work, the next warning flag. They didn't need to convince me to go to work there; I needed, desperately, to convince them I was the right pilot for the job.

Their tardiness allowed the four of us to become instant friends. It was an amazing thing; we were competing for about the only airline job out there, but we were only supportive of each other. We were all qualified, we'd flown big airplanes, we'd been kicked around, and we would've liked nothing more than to all be sitting next to each other in the next indoc class.

The eventual interview wasn't the least bit technical; nothing at all about flying airplanes. The Chief Pilot asked to see my logbook. I produced a stack of them, five-and-a-half pounds of not just paper and ink but lessons learned, mistakes, triumphs, places seen, weather intimately felt, and memories; all that made me who I am. He quickly flipped through a couple of pages of the most recent logbook, closed it, and then looked down at his list of pre-scripted questions. I felt like I just had a few brief chances to prove that I was hip enough, in a Silicon Valley, metro-sexual kind of way, to fly for their ultra-hip new airline. I was screwed. I've never, not even as an adolescent awkwardly trying to find my way through the world, tried to be hip. I have, since I was an adolescent, obsessively tried to become the most knowledgeable, most highly skilled professional that I can be, but without a single technical question I didn't have the opportunity to show them that.

It took weeks for the rejection to reach me, odd since it was just a short thoughtless e-mail that unexpectedly stung me from the ether. Only one pilot of the four who interviewed that day got the job, a guy who had a personal recommendation letter from one of the pilots on the interview panel. He deserved the job, but the rest of us did too. This was the first unsuccessful interview of my career, and it was hard to just let it go and accept that I was still stuck in the flying circus.

The flying circus certainly was an adventure, even enviable to some of my unemployed friends who weren't enduring the many frustrations of Chris's unorthodox ideas.

I was flying to places where I would undoubtedly never go otherwise. I flew into remote northern resorts, where we had to chase deer and sandhill cranes away from the uncomfortably short runway before taking off because we couldn't risk a collision and abort with such slim margins. I flew to the Rocky Mountains and to the High Desert beyond. I flew to the Bahamas often enough that considerable parts of this book were actually written there, but I still took the time to see all of Grand Bahama Island, parts no tourists ever see. I ate raw conch salad from a waterfront shack in a conch fishing town that isn't on the map and somehow didn't get sick; my immune system was apparently stronger than the crusty funk glued to the cutting board on which the conch was prepared.

I stretched an incredible number of miles out of the Lear 31's small fuel tanks, but I had to go nearly to the edge of space a few times to do it, 51,000 feet above the Earth, an incredible height to which very few jets can actually go, where the air is only about a tenth as dense as at sea level, the sky is a noticeably deeper blue, and from where I could allegedly see for an astonishing 942 miles to the distant horizon (if air was truly transparent and if my math was correct). I've been asked if I was able to see the curvature of the Earth from that height. I didn't look for it, but it was obvious that the Earth was very distant, a subtly textured map impossibly distant, almost as far away as my easy, comfortable life at my old airline job.

I even simultaneously juggled three trips at once, airlining across the country from one airplane to another, one of the more exhausting five-day trips of my career but also the most lucrative, if I ever get paid for it.

I had a couple of long Las Vegas layovers and I went home a winner, and I didn't even gamble. The hotel gave me a five dollar coupon for their slot machines, which, since it was free, I decided to spend at a quarter slot machine. To my amazement, and to that of the other pilot, who was busy burning through his own coupon at the machine next to mine, I actually won. The coupon required that I exhaust my entire five dollars before I cash out, which I did, without even considering an extra pull. Stoic, but proud, I presented the voucher containing my winnings to the cashier, but then accidentally cracked a smile as she read the amount, which caused her to laugh at me, undoubtedly also by accident. She then handed me my anti-climactic trophy, two wrinkled, grimy singles which looked like they had trickled down from a g-string at one of the men's clubs up the street, and a somewhat tarnished-looking quarter. I was initially disappointed that my coin wasn't shinier, that my dollar bills weren't crisper, but then it struck me that slot machines had become the most productive investment, by percentage, in my lifetime portfolio. I had trusted my 401k and IRA to money managers who were supposed to know what they were doing, but what I have to show for it so far (eighteen years) is no better than if I had put it all in a slot machine and pulled the handle.

I know, I had really only turned five bucks into two and a quarter, but the five dollars was never mine. I was, in fact, going home with the casino's money, although a good accountant would be able to call my winnings losses, maybe even reducing my tax burden if only I was a corporation.

It may surprise some people to know that I had actually gambled one other time in my life, years ago, during an Omaha overnight, back when my airline used to put us up at a hotel with a casino across the Missouri River in Council Bluffs, Iowa. Earlier in the day it had come up in conversation that I had never gambled, and the rest of the crew seemed to want to try hard to change that.

I reluctantly agreed to feed a hard-earned dollar into a slot machine, and to my amazement, I won. I had doubled my money. I said, "Okay, let's cash-out," which prompted fervent protests from my crew. This was democratic gambling I guess, undoubtedly just like what happens in mahogany trimmed corporate boardrooms. Unanimously outvoted, the button was pushed again and we lost it all—but for the record, I had won. Don't ever trust flight attendants with money. You probably shouldn't trust the Board of Directors either. In spite of my success, I still insist that slot machines are rigged, but then again, maybe everything else is rigged too.

I prepared for a gamble of a very different, inconceivably complex sort, when Chris asked me to go to Angola with a week's notice to pick up a Lear 35 of unknown airworthiness that a broker had supposedly just acquired in a horse trade. Frank had crossed the Atlantic in a Learjet many years prior, and he wanted to give it a try with me. I swallowed the anxiety that rightfully accompanied jumping into dark, turbid, crocodile filled waters way over my head, and I actually became excited about the trip, an adventure of a lifetime, but then Chris ended up doing it himself with an African pilot. It was probably for the best, since only Chris can jump into a seemingly impossible challenge without charts or even visas, just his street smarts, which I was just beginning to question, a pocketful of cash, a scattering of sunshine, and just enough good luck and make it happen.

As usual, there was much more to the story than anyone could ever know, not even the CIA, who allegedly supported the insurgents who had allegedly used the airplane in a civil war. The airplane had been in the center of an international scandal, had allegedly been used to violate United Nations sanctions, and was possibly even involved in a coup attempt, as well as having been modified with an inconspicuous camera port in its belly, a true spy plane.

After he brought the airplane back, I asked Chris if he knew the airplane's history, and he said, "Yeah, I knew it flew for the CIA, and it smuggled diamonds too," smiling a little too knowingly as he added the smuggling comment, which made me wonder why someone spent fifty grand to get the airplane back over here from Africa when they didn't even know if they were going to scrap the old bird or refurbish it. It reminded me of an earlier era, when cocaine was supposed to have been chic, when expensive illicit cargo was smuggled north from Central America, and the airplanes were considered expendable because they were worth so much less than their cargo.

Chris was current in Learjets now, but that was just because of bumbling through a 61.58 checkride with an extremely generous examiner (I know because I was there). He actually hadn't had any Learjet training in decades, probably not since he flew 20-series antiques in the early '70s. He had an experienced pilot with him on the African trip, but after he flew the Lear 31 with a co-pilot who had never had any training in Learjets, he admitted to me that he wasn't comfortable in the airplane. The admission caught me by surprise, coming from such a big talker who'll never back down from any challenge. Weak pilots never understand how weak they really are, because when you don't know, you don't know how much you really don't know. That's why I don't fault inexperienced pilots for their inexperience; I just don't want them to be in command of high performance jets. Chris actually did recognize his weakness, but unfortunately it didn't keep him from occasionally flying the airplane with untrained co-pilots, and for that I consider him criminally negligent. The Kool-Aid had now soured so completely that it was stinking up the entire community. I was seeing more and more that it had always been sour; I just hadn't noticed yet.

Chris frequently bragged about his 23,000 accident—and incident-free hours of flying over his forty-seven-year career, but if that was actually true, which I was beginning to doubt, along with everything else he ever said, it was only because of exceptionally good luck. There seemed to be no end to the shenanigans, most being stories from credible sources, but many that we actually witnessed as well. He had me fooled from day one by his prohibition against circling approaches, but I could only guess that this rare example of restraint was due to a near disaster that scared him so bad it turned his hair white. His old charter company had a fatal crash in a Lear 23 during a circling approach at Pellston, Michigan in 1970, maybe when he was employed there. The dead pilots might have been a couple of friends. Otherwise, there seemed to be nothing he wouldn't do to get the job done.

He flew a Citation without any brakes, after giving Frank an unnecessarily hard time for refusing to do it (pressurized nitrogen is strictly an emergency back-up, which by-passes the anti-skid and greatly increases stopping distance, making an aborted takeoff from all but the very longest runways virtually impossible). He flew through the day into evening, rented a car, and drove all night, just so he could be in position to fly another airplane the next morning, after no sleep. He even flew an airplane after drinking some wine with dinner—not because he's an alcoholic; he's not. There was just a job that needed to be done, and he only has a go switch. Good judgment means also having a stop switch and knowing when you need to use it.

Chris couldn't have been this reckless throughout his long career; no one can summon enough luck or divine benevolence to survive that. He was an inherently loyal man on his last gig, a very important gig, trying entirely too hard to please very important people, highly successful people who would be much more pleased by their pilot being extra careful when they are entrusting him with their lives, really the only times that they ever feel they aren't totally in control of their own destinies. Some people self-destruct with drugs and alcohol, or maybe gambling or marital infidelity. Chris seemed to be on the verge of self-destructing because he was unwilling to accept that no one knows all there is to know, no one has been around for long enough that they don't need training, and sometimes you just can't get the job done, loyalty and heroics gone dangerously wrong.

Frank and I were sharing our many frustrations, grievances, and, as always, new stories about Chris's bizarre big-top antics over a beer on an overnight when Frank wondered aloud about how much happier he would probably be if he had never sent Chris a resume and had never gotten caught up in our present circus. I reminded him that it wouldn't have mattered; he still would've been there, sitting next to me in the lounge of a faraway hotel, because I was about to suck him into this circus at a point when I didn't yet understand what I had gotten myself into.

Then I opened a stale fortune cookie and read "You will become an accomplished writer," a peculiar accident, an odd choice for the evening snack at the manager's reception at the Embassy Suites, and just what I needed to hear.

With OSU Airport's short, five-thousand-foot runway, we had balanced field length issues on hot summer days, which means having enough runway to accelerate to decision speed and either abort (at one knot prior decision speed) or continue the takeoff after an engine fails, something we plan for before each takeoff in a multi-engine airplane. But not Chris; he would rather load the airplane too heavy with gas and take his chances that both motors will keep running. He actually told me, "There are more pilots who run out of gas than lose an engine on takeoff; no one ever loses an engine on takeoff."

That was ridiculous. That was the most dangerous moment of the flight, when you have no airspeed or altitude, a finite amount of pavement ahead, and you just suddenly commanded your previously idling engines to endure the highest temperatures and pressures they would ever endure.

Disputing his grossly flawed logic, which risked getting me fired, I told him I had lost two engines on takeoff during my career, one while at maximum weight for the short runway I was taking off from. Surprised, he asked what happened to my engines. When I told him about blowing an oil cooler on a JT8D and pumping all of our oil overboard in a mere heartbeat, he thought for a moment and then barked, "That engine would've run for fifteen hours without oil." Unlikely; with old metal bearings rubbing without lubrication at 12,000 RPM, my guess is closer to fifteen seconds, maybe, which would've left us struggling to climb at maximum weight, aimed at downtown Boston.

Chris had even tried to re-enact my blown oil cooler by having us unknowingly fly an airplane for months with a cracked oil cooler. Only Chris and one mechanic knew about it, a mechanic who didn't consider the airplane to be airworthy and who made Chris sign a letter absolving him of any liability for the eventual emergency caused by Chris's willfully negligent mismanagement (quite possibly on OSU's short runway).

So Chris made it 23,000 hours without losing an engine on takeoff. That doesn't mean he won't lose an engine on his very next takeoff, and I've watched him takeoff 1,000 pounds over maximum takeoff weight from a short runway in an under-powered Citation. He's taking a chance, one that doesn't need to be taken. He doesn't even need to choose between the risk of eventual fuel starvation or a high-speed aborted takeoff. With proper planning, both risks are mitigated, as well as many others. That's why we get paid the big bucks, because anyone can steer an airplane through the air; a professional gets the airplane to the destination safely every time, without taking chances.

Chris was not unique in his thinking; there are plenty of people who take chances. Risk taking is even rewarded in our society. It is the entrepreneurial foundation of a free-market, but it has no place in a safety-critical activity, especially with transonic hurtling machinery and tons of explosive jet fuel. Maybe you just break an unseen pedestrian's leg with your car while rolling through a red light during a right-hand turn, your eyes turned only toward the oncoming traffic, or maybe you spill 200 million gallons of oil into the Gulf of Mexico while trying to hurry an unstable well into production, or maybe you melt down four nuclear reactors because you didn't install sufficient backup cooling systems in an earthquake prone land, or maybe, just maybe, you kill a planeload of innocent passengers after an engine quits on takeoff, and damn it, you loaded the airplane too heavy to get her stopped or get her flying before she collides with an unyielding object off the end of the runway, and now all of that extra fuel just intensifies the post-crash fire. Me? I'm not going to take off without balanced field length, because I'm not brave enough!

There are still plenty of dangerous guys out there like Chris and there always will be, as long as airplanes are operated on the cheap instead of being operated properly.

And then it happened. No, not an engine failure on takeoff; Chris and a pilot with no formal Learjet training smacked a wingtip on the runway while landing a Learjet. They got very lucky; with so much weight out in the tip-tanks there are plenty of accident reports of Learjets cartwheeling from this, which is nearly always fatal. (A couple months later in Mexico there was a fatal Learjet cartwheel during a training flight, a fiery accident that wouldn't have occurred at all if the training was conducted in a flight simulator.) Chris and his co-pilot were lucky to have not cartwheeled, but they still wrecked the airplane. Accidents have a monetary threshold (as well as injury), and although I didn't hear how big of a check had to be written to pay for a new wing skin, it would at the least be disingenuous, if not a blatant lie, for Chris to continue to brag about his accident—and incident-free career. He had practically dared himself to crash the airplane, continuing to fly it with untrained pilots after telling me that he wasn't comfortable in that little rocket.

A bigger check needed to be written a few months later after Chris destroyed an engine in a Citation from foreign object damage (FOD). Whatever went through the engine, probably lots of ice, damaged every fan blade, with part of many blades missing. Incredibly, the mutilated engine kept running, though damaged, vibrating, and no longer giving Chris an inter-stage turbine temperature indication, but it very nearly became Chris's first engine failure on takeoff. It would've been, if not for how robustly the engine was engineered and built. The airplane had been parked outside in the snow and ice in Northern Michigan all weekend, and Chris is not the kind of pilot who would let accumulated snow and ice or over-priced propylene glycol de-icing fluid keep him from getting the job done (he said he had the wings and tail sprayed; that's a good start, but not enough if there is still ice clinging to the top of the fuselage). Yes, he got the job done, overflying dozens of perfectly good diversionary airports while flying all the way back home with a badly damaged engine, a certain violation if the feds had investigated.

Obviously, disagreements over safety and legality issues were inevitable, and the disagreements would only get you fired. Possessing the knowledge of how to do things correctly created a perpetual tension that was only relieved temporarily through Chris's absence. The dead bodies (firings) in the flying circus were mounting. Even my neighbor Frank, a true professional, had already been fired through no fault of his own, leaving me the sole remaining qualified, current, competent, sane pilot in the flying circus. Chris was bringing in replacements, but these were not of the same caliber as Frank or my old college friend; these were desperate people whom he had conned into paying him for a chance to fly under the empty promise that he would actually train them. The flying circus had taken a dire turn, while further lining Chris's pockets.

The arbitrator finally published the airline's new seniority list on a Saturday evening of a holiday weekend, giving him enough time to skip town and escape the ire of some potentially rogue pilots with nothing left to lose. I had hoped for better, but I've become too cynical to be too surprised by his chickenshit award; there is no true justice in a land where everything is for sale. He hid behind a hollow argument that we didn't bring anything to the table because we didn't have any airplanes, but that was highly disingenuous, since we eventually learned that the company actually paid a huge penalty to return the airplanes to Boeing early. His introductory comments acknowledged that my pilot group was more experienced and farther along in our careers, but then the award seemed to be designed to make sure the company didn't have to pay for any excess training events. He had the authority to restore us to our old flying, which was still being flown by our replacements, or, even better, to simply write the new list by date-of-hire, recognizing experience level, but those options would've required the company to spend a lot of money on training to correct the mess they created for themselves, a costly inconvenience which would've also made it much more difficult for Mr. Arbitrator to get hired for a future arbitration. Except for slotting a small number of our pilots in half-way down the list beneath the most junior Captain at the regional airline, my pilot group got mostly stapled to the bottom of the new seniority list, beneath the entry level pilots who replaced us as we were illegally locked out. I could go back to my old job eventually, but I would have to wait for a couple hundred vacancies, and then I'd go back at just a fraction of my old pay, just to swing the gear for a Captain who was born the year I started flying (there were at least two of those now senior to me). It seemed more like continued punishment than a prize, an opportunity of last resort.

The seniority integration insult was followed two days later by another swift kick in the groin when an eight-hundred-hour pilot was picked over me for a salaried corporate pilot job, to be Frank's co-pilot, a job for which I had already been given a verbal offer.

The good thing about being at rock bottom is that the only way left to go is up, or at least that's what I had thought, but it was hard to consider myself doing anything more than barely bumping along the nadir since reaching rock bottom two years prior when I realized that I had been suckered into becoming a $20,000 per year Learjet Captain. Adding to my dejection was the persistent, nagging worry that Chris and his new clown posse of indentured servants would hurt someone, a fear that was literally keeping me awake at night.

Fortunately, I was doing some other flying by then too, with a couple of good guys who flew well and made good decisions, professionals who had even done some hard time in the Regional Airlines. Trips with them were a welcome escape from the flying circus, usually to New Orleans for a few days in the French Quarter, but it still wasn't steady full-time work. They both already knew how much of a knucklehead Chris was; they had both known him for years.

After hearing me bitch, probably obsessively, about my worries and frustrations, one of these guys, Bryan, told me about one of his similar experiences from many years prior. He watched three people get in an airplane with someone he knew to be a weak pilot. They crashed a couple days later, on their return trip. They're all dead now.

I didn't want to live with the remorse of not warning people of the danger they were in. I've always wanted to avoid confrontation, but being in Chris's flying circus, existing under constant tension, as a rubber band permanently stretched to the point of breaking, a confrontation with Chris was now virtually inevitable. I knew it would get me fired, but sacrificing some contract flying for a client's safety was something I had to do.

I had a three-day trip to Florida and back for the client who leased the Learjet, who I'll call Tom, to be followed by a trip to the Bahamas. At departure time for Florida, Chris told Tom and me that I wouldn't be flying him to Freeport, Bahamas, afterward; Chris would be taking the trip. Chris was taking the trip in an airplane he was admittedly uncomfortable in, with a student who was paying an obscene sum for his first jet time, a training flight, with my friend and client, Tom, unaware of the potential danger he was in. Tom had operational control, and only he, not Chris or any other clown, made these decisions. Walking out to the airplane, Tom asked me why Chris was taking the Freeport trip. Just as surprised, I told him that if I talked too much, I'd get fired, but then I climbed into the cockpit and started the engines, the whole time wondering whether there was any way to rectify this diplomatically.

We blasted off like a rocket into a fine spring day. Seconds into the flight I pulled the throttles back, settling into 250 knots at 3,000 feet, where departure control made us momentarily level off before clearing us up into the high thin air that very few jets could reach. The right throttle had the slightest binding as I moved it. Cleared to climb again, I advanced the throttles, still with slight binding in the right throttle. This was barely noticeable, but it had my attention because that was the only warning I had before that same throttle cable had broken the year prior. Broken throttle cables are extremely rare in Learjets, but the right engine's throttle cable in this particular bird had already broken twice in the same spot. I assumed there must be some hidden chafing occurring in one spot, and I assumed it would just be a matter of time before it happened again. When the cable breaks, you lose control of the engine, the fuel controller just rolls it back to idle and shuts the engine down, but until then, it was running fine. I would have the mechanic take a look at it, even though I knew they would find nothing; they couldn't find the point of chafing when they threaded the new cable the year prior.

My co-pilot, the next new recipient of Chris's benevolence, had less than a thousand hours of flight time, maybe ten hours of jet time, absolutely no training in jets beyond the obligatory three takeoffs and landings in type, and he was obscenely drunk on the Kool-Aid that Chris was serving him, which admittedly, must taste pretty good to such an inexperienced pilot trying to get a foothold in the industry. This wouldn't be anyone's first choice for who they wanted helping them during an emergency; nothing personal, just one of those unpredictable moments that you need a well stocked toolbox for, and the only way to stock your tool box is through training and experience. My co-pilot had neither. En route to Florida, I went ahead and got out the QRH (quick reference handbook, the emergency checklists), and briefed him on all of the checklists that we would need to run and what my thinking would be if the cable snapped as

I retarded the throttles to descend, a little training in the moments before we would face the real emergency.

Engine failures seemed fairly mundane to me anymore; it certainly seemed routine as I was explaining the procedures for an emergency that seemed inevitable. I don't know why Chris considered them to be so rare that he doesn't need to plan for them on every takeoff. Maybe his luck had just been better than mine. Maybe he's that sure that God will take care of him. Maybe he's certifiably crazy.

The cable didn't snap, we landed with both of our motors, Tom went to stalk turkeys in the dense Central Florida brush, and I went to the hotel where my worries ate holes through my innards.

Frank and I, the A-team, were flying the airplane into Kansas City the last time the cable snapped. After landing, I matter-of-factly told Tom that we had just lost an engine. He didn't even believe me at first, since he hadn't felt so much as a twitch in the airplane, we had calmly handled the emergency, and I wasn't showing any emotion, other than being sorry that we couldn't continue on to Billings, Montana.

Chris had decided to take the Freeport trip because of another new pilot who was actually paying him an obscene sum to get qualified in the airplanes. Tom was expecting his trip to the Bahamas to be crewed by qualified professionals, not by a dangerous old scoundrel who knew no limits with an untrained student on a pseudo-training flight. Chris admitted he wasn't comfortable in the Learjet, had now even wrecked it, and would be flying with a guy who had a whole two hours of jet time, and of course, no training other than the obligatory three takeoffs and landings. If they were to lose an engine, which was a distinct possibility with the suspect throttle cable, I wasn't confident of a safe outcome. Actually, if they didn't lose an engine, I wasn't confident of a safe outcome.

I took some long walks in Florida, thinking about what I should do. This would be easy at an airline, where I would take my concerns to the union's professional standards committee; now I was in an unorganized realm with little oversight, where dangerous knuckleheads occasionally appoint themselves Captain or even Chief Pilot simply because they have a client with an airplane who they've been able to fool, not necessarily because they're ready to command a transonic jet.

There was never any reasoning with Chris about anything; he was always too certain that he knew everything. Maybe I could talk some sense into the new pilot, well, maybe; I had already tried unsuccessfully to warn him about Chris, warn him not to give the old man a small fortune in exchange for pencil-whipped training. I stopped in the shade of an enormous, sprawling, moss-draped live oak and called him. An osprey gracefully swooped into the clearing and plucked a tilapia from the dark, tannin-stained pond, the unsuspecting fish thrashing futilely within the vice-like grip of sharp talons. It's a dangerous world; you have to be ready for loitering raptors, and other in-flight hazards, at all times. I warned Chris's student that Chris didn't know enough about the Learjet, wasn't comfortable in it, had wrecked it last fall, and there was a pretty good chance that a throttle cable would break on them. Learjets are slick, high-performance machines that are not to be taken lightly, a whole different kind of animal from the slow propeller-driven airplanes that this guy had flown. I talked to the guy for an hour, but there was no getting past the Kool-Aid and the fact that he was paying Chris to be able to fly the airplanes, and to get type-ratings in them, paper type-ratings without any real training, in a dangerous world where circling raptors perpetually pursued the unsuspecting.

I know some of you are wondering how these kinds of shenanigans were even insured. Chris was a charmer, a salesman, had a wise, distinguished appearance, and used important words like safety and training at the right times in conversation, even though the numerous acts that I had witnessed made it increasingly clear that the words meant nothing to him. He conned an insurance company into giving him check airman status in an in-house training program that didn't exist (except on paper, a curriculum written by Frank but then completely ignored by Chris), so he could sign anyone off as insured who he wanted to, regardless of training or experience, enabling him to create his own slave class of untrained laborers. It was undoubtedly the biggest con to ever happen in a conservative business that now universally makes every pilot go to real training in a flight simulator once a year.

I had sent myself to recurrent training, real training in a Learjet simulator, with my own money, since Chris wasn't going to, even though he'd been skimming money off of me all along, allegedly for training. As perverse as it sounds, my recurrent training even pissed him off, because he wasn't controlling it, wasn't directly profiting from it, and probably more importantly because he correctly assumed that I would begin charging him the full five hundred bucks per day that he charged the client for my services. With my training expense coming out of my own pocket, I was going to be firing my pimp, who promised training but never delivered and didn't have to because of the insurance con. I was technically an independent contractor and never worked for him anyway; he just tried to make everyone think they worked for him so that he could stay in control and keep lining his own pockets. In a dry lease arrangement, the leasee has full operational control and the pilots work directly for the leasee.

After a couple of sleepless nights in Florida, I told Tom everything: how he wasn't getting the two Captain qualified pilots on each flight like Chris had promised, how potentially dangerous Chris was and how much aircraft damage he had recently caused, and most importantly, how this was not a charter operation or a flight school and that Tom had full operational control; he could decide who flew him and how it was done.

It didn't surprise Tom too much; he was way too smart to be fooled by any of this. He had already figured out that the guys I was flying with didn't seem to know anything about the airplane and that I never let the other guys fly; I wasn't going to give Tom, or anyone else, a rollercoaster ride training flight. I'm not a stick-hog, but I know what this nimble little rocket is waiting to do to a novice. Tom had recently run into a furious aircraft owner who had just fired Chris for the flagrant mismanagement of his airplane. He had already given Tom an unexpected earful of Chris's shenanigans, as well as plenty of angry obscenities directed at Chris.

As much as I dislike confrontation, I had passed a point from which there was no escaping it. Chris yelled at me with fury that I would only expect from a desperate man, desperate to keep me from knocking down his house of cards, or circus tent. I was brave enough to take it with a smile, relieved that the most stressful era of my career was finally over.

Chris tried to pull the I'm-the-chief-pilot bullshit with Tom as well, but Tom set him straight with some yelling of his own. Tom told Chris that he wouldn't get in an airplane unless I was flying it, and it still really could've worked, but then he ultimately decided he wouldn't come back as long as Chris was involved in any way. He couldn't trust that Chris wouldn't do something to sabotage something, and I agreed.

When Tom walked away from the Lear 31, I lost about half of my contract flying. He asked me for help in arranging transportation, so I became a consultant, an unpaid consultant. I even turned down an offer for a commission from the charter company that I put some of his flights in. As much as I needed a steady stream of income, I didn't want anyone to think that I had tried to steal a client or had less than noble intentions.

Chris is a master at covering his own tracks, a pathological liar, and I knew he would lie about me and the entire episode to try to trash my reputation and to pretend he was a saint. That's what he did to all the other dead bodies he had thrown out of the flying circus. I also knew he wouldn't pay me the money he owed me, just like all the other people he fired. I decided to strike first, and hard, with an e-mail explaining the episode to everyone involved, including the airplane's owner. It was angry, maybe even over the top. Okay, definitely over the top—way over the top. I called him a knucklehead, an insult I reserve for only the most breathtakingly incompetent pilots.

Chris was still flying the airplanes in his private little kingdom and even put a Learjet trip in the schedule, from Cleveland to Miami. This bothered me in many ways, most importantly that I had sacrificed myself and nothing had changed. Chris was still dangerous, still negligently risking people's lives, and was still the self-appointed Chief Pilot. I'll admit to being a little jealous that the trip was going to fly without me when I needed the work, but this looked like one of those trips with ambiguous legitimacy that I wouldn't have touched anyway, what I'm assuming was an illegal charter.

During another restless night, I dreamt of having a contract trip in an ancient Lear 23. I met the other pilot planeside, discovering just then that he didn't know anything about Learjets. The airplane was a ratty-looking beast with grimy white-washed paint, sitting crooked on a partially deflated main landing gear strut. I climbed into a tattered seat and didn't recognize anything, not even one dusty switch. It was serial number 13, much older than any Learjet I'd ever flown, and I flew a short, very uncomfortable positioning flight in Southern California before being rescued by the alarm clock and by the relief that it had only been a dream.

Since I actually knew its serial number, I searched the internet for the airplane I had just dreamed of. It was easy to find, a headline maker. It was destroyed in a fatal crash in Guatemala in 1987 as it limped back to the airport after an engine failure. The Lear 23 had an undeniable impact on the industry in many ways, with a quarter of the fleet producing charred impact craters in the Earth, an atrocious statistic that undoubtedly drove many prospective aircraft buyers to the underwhelmingly slow, straight-winged, blunt-nosed, benign-looking Citation. 20-series Learjets may have been a handful, rockets on roller skates, but you never had to worry about having enough power to drag them around the pattern after losing an engine. Piling one up in a smoking crater after an engine quit seemed more likely from someone who hadn't practiced it recently in training, if ever. That's the kind of thing that could happen in the flying circus after a routine emergency, which is not an oxymoron at all; professional pilots train for emergencies until they seem routine, just one of the reasons why flying, when done correctly by professional pilots, is statistically so safe. The era with pencil-whipped qualifications, on-the-job training, and alarmingly frequent Learjet crashes is now a distant, dangerous memory, except in the flying circus.

The dream bothered me enough that I decided to warn the owner how dangerous Chris was in the Learjet, with a half dozen very specific examples. The owner is an attorney, a pilot, and a smart man, so he must've understood, even more than I did then, that I effectively dropped an enormous legal liability in his lap. If he allows Chris to hurt someone in that airplane after being formally warned by a professional type-specific expert, it is at his own financial peril. My beloved Learjet would be growing dust again in the back corner of the hangar, but unfortunately Chris was still flying Citations, still endangering unsuspecting passengers, about whom I was still deeply concerned, with his utter lack of judgment. It seemed there was no way to fully close my chapter in the flying circus. Like a ghost, Chris would haunt me until he retired, if he ever retired; his career would more likely end in a big ball of flames.

I could tell the feds to watch Chris, but they supposedly already were watching. They would have to catch him violating a regulation before they could suspend his pilot license, and even then it wouldn't matter; losing his license isn't going to stop a guy like Chris. He had apparently already been flying for hire with an expired medical certificate. The regulation that was written specifically for dangerous pilots like Chris, FAR 91.13, careless or reckless operation, was easier to enforce in an accident investigation than a ramp check.

Chris did slander me by saying that I was drinking too much and going through a divorce; none of it true. He was in damage control mode, and there really weren't enough people left who believed him for those lies to spread.

I got paid, and I got Frank paid too, money he had been trying to collect for several months.

I finally went to the bank to deposit a long awaited, very much belated paycheck. The beautiful young teller surprised me by asking whether I was a pilot, which she gathered from the pilot services remark on the check. Then she asked me one of those dreaded questions with no simple answer: "What's that like?" I would've loved this attention from a pretty young girl twenty years ago, back when I still considered this strange enterprise of flying airplanes to be glamorous, not that I had ever chased glamour, but now it was hard to honestly contemplate her question immediately after handing her a check I had waited so long for, money I didn't think I would ever see. I had once had my dream job, but the more than two years since being locked out of it had been a continuous struggle, most recently a moral struggle in which I chose to give up my place in the flying circus by warning my passengers of the danger they were in. Now my unsteady footing as a contract pilot would be even less steady. So that she wouldn't think I had ignored her, I broke the silence by telling her that I was thinking of a short answer to her question. Then she answered it for me: "Interesting?"

"Yes, it's interesting," I replied with a smile. I couldn't have picked a better word. I achieved a dream I'd had since I was a little boy, and with dignity, earning everything I had achieved. I had done and seen so many things that I'm thankful for, and I still loved it as deeply as I ever had. I still had to work at getting past some bitterness, but my grievances were really just trivial; adversity is part of the human condition, the inevitable fate of even the most sheltered. The only thing we can always control is our contentment with the events that unfold before us, fair or not, but otherwise we're all really just along for the ride, an interesting ride, and now that I truly understand that, I think I'm brave enough.

June 2011

Well, I couldn't end this book with a trip to the bank; I stayed in this circus of a flying career for the love of flying, not because of any thoughts that I would get rich. I also couldn't end with Chris's shenanigans in the flying circus. That would be like letting that bastard knucklehead beat me. And then there was June 2011.

I couldn't go to sleep. I never did on Dawn's bad nights, although she was now having a lot more good nights than bad ones, still recovering from the events that unfolded in the last few chapters. She still had little bouts of anxiety, mini-panic attacks, and some insomnia, and she was still peripherally involved with the medical field, which she felt was one of the many triggers for her breakdown. I had been looking for steadier work all along, but it seemed more important now than ever. Dawn needed a break, but it just hadn't been possible yet.

The job market was still terrible, but I still checked the internet job boards religiously, several times per day, as discouraging as it was.

Back to insomnia; a vague feeling that I'd forgotten something important was nagging at me as I lay in bed, staring at the dark ceiling. About midnight, I realized I hadn't checked the job boards since early morning. Maybe that's what was nagging at me? Well, one of many things.

I got up to take a look, and there it was; a corporate pilot position in Western Pennsylvania. I didn't have the type-rating, but they didn't require it. They required five thousand hours of flight time, a relatively high minimum, so I figured they were actually seeking the right person, with experience, not just cheap labor. Even with the deluge of resumes the company received, I knew I'd be a contender for the job because I had one more very important asset for them as well: a good wife. A good Chief Pilot knows that a career of endless travel is hard on marriages, and an important part of keeping a pilot happy is keeping his wife happy too.

By one in the morning I had written the best cover letter of my career, maybe one of the best ever written by anyone, emphasizing not just my experience and qualifications, which were way above average in the corporate world, but also that Dawn is from near there with lots of family nearby. I even mentioned that we got married near there. I went back to bed, but sleep still wouldn't come easily, now because of adrenaline, and a rare moment of hope. After nearly three years of tossing darts into the ether, one had finally hit the bull's eye. I was more certain of it than ever before.

It would be a month of restless nights and more darts into the ether, a month so tumultuous that it deserves its own chapter in my book.

Three local companies had recently hired corporate pilots, the job I wanted, the job I needed, but all three purposefully hired low-time pilots, wanting to crew their airplanes on the cheap, rather than with the best pilots available to fly their executives; people who would undoubtedly much rather have the most experienced and best qualified pilots they could get, a desire often forgotten by the time another rookie is hired for cheap.

Frank's job, the job I had been promised, lasted only two months. I guess the retracted verbal offer wasn't the kick in the groin I thought it was at the time.

A local multi-billion-dollar corporation leased the Lear 31. They had several pilots who were qualified and current in Lears, so they were unlikely to need any contract help. I was able to get a meeting with their director anyway to try to beg him for some contract work. One of the first questions he asked me was whether I was associated with Chris, and it was fairly clear that any association was an immediate disqualifier.

The other Lear 31 in Western Pennsylvania that I had been hoping to fly some was no longer airworthy because the owner didn't plan on using it enough to justify the expense of an inspection that was due. Suddenly it seemed that the six grand I had spent on my Learjet recurrent training course would've been better spent on slot machines in Vegas, my typical bad investment.

I got a rejection letter from an airline in Hawaii that flew 717s. Then I got another letter from them telling me to disregard the rejection letter, which had been sent in error, but then I still never heard another peep from them.

I had a phone interview with the head-hunting firm the western Pennsylvania company had hired to filter through the thousands of resumes for the corporate pilot job. I was indeed a contender, as I expected to be after finishing the midnight cover letter, and my resume made it to the Chief Pilot's desk, even though they had apparently now decided they may not actually fill the position until the end of the year, if they filled it at all.

Then I got another call, from a dart I had thrown into the void a month or so prior but then promptly forgotten about. This was a charter start-up that had just bought two MD-80s from my former airline. They were going to move quickly. It was Friday, and they wanted me to interview in Winston Salem on Monday or Tuesday.

Within an hour of getting the call from the MD-80 job, I got a most unexpected call from a company that had two old 737s on contract with the Forest Service for hauling firefighters. I had never even applied there. In fact, I had never even heard of them. A good friend with whom I had flown extensively back at the airline was about to go to work there, for the second time in his turbulent career, and he recommended me for the job too. They were just calling me to get my resume.

My interview in Winston Salem couldn't have gone any better. The Chief Pilot and a recruiter placed my resume on the table and asked me to tell them about my career, from the earliest line on my resume. They actually let me talk about my favorite subject, me, for a virtually uninterrupted half hour. Then they asked me questions specifically related to carrying an airplane on your back for two weeks, exactly what I did at my charter job, except this would be an MD-80 instead of a Learjet. They asked me if I would be willing to move to Guam, which I never quite answered. I'd certainly be willing to rotate in and out of Guam, but moving there was a lot to ask with what they were offering, which was not a lot.

While driving home from the interview, I got a call from the Forest Service contractor that had just called asking for my resume. I had a phone interview while driving north on Interstate 77, and they went ahead and offered me the job, needing to put someone in training that week. Unfortunately it was only contract work, two weeks each month until the end of fire season. I could make good money during the two weeks, but only if there was a lot of flying to be done. I felt that there were too many uncertainties and it suddenly seemed like I had opportunities. I turned it down.

The owner of the Lear 31 and a Citation that I had, until recently, flown, wanted a meeting with me. He had been paying attention, having printed every angry e-mail I had sent to Chris. I had copied him in the e-mails, wanting him to know what kind of a knucklehead was managing his airplanes, and there they were, stapled into a stack, with the particularly incriminating passages highlighted. Chris had already left for Brazil and wouldn't be back for months. The owner wanted to try to keep me around, so he offered to try to keep me busy in his airplanes. I would fly with him when he needed to go somewhere and I could try to pick up other contract work when he didn't need me.

I wanted no part of the flying circus any more, but I was beginning to believe that Chris was on the lam, maybe permanently. There were rumors circulating that the Justice Department was after him for some shenanigans that he was specifically told he could go to jail for and that the feds were after him for another altitude bust, one he apparently even tried to run from. Whatever the reason for his long exile, he was bent on leaving his mark on Brazil as well, getting involved in a bio-fuel venture with a missionary organization that was simultaneously exploiting the natives, bilking investors, and clear-cutting the rain forest—so wrong, on so many levels. God told him to do it.

I discovered that I already knew half of the pilots at the MD-80 charter operator, pilots from my old airline. I contacted several of them and they told me to run away as fast as I could.

Meanwhile, a recruiter from there contacted me to tell me they were going to be giving me an offer, for contract employment, but my contract wasn't ready yet. It probably wasn't even legal, just their way of keeping a pilot in slavery without having to pay any benefits. I was expecting the contract to say I needed to move to Guam, and I was going to counter by saying that I would rotate in and out of Guam. It was okay with me if they said no; I could say no too. According to my friends, a bunch of dangerous bottom-feeding slave-drivers like Chris were running the place, so it wasn't really that great of an opportunity. More of what I'd been through before, but I needed the money.

A charter company in Western Pennsylvania offered me a job to fly their Lear 35, a gorgeous, well-equipped, high serial number airplane. The owner was a decent guy whom I had spoken with a few times over the prior two years and even met with twice, but it was hard to move for a charter job, with few scheduled days off and plenty of all-night organ harvest flights. I knew it would be very hard to sell my house, so I could only move for a really good job and I wasn't sure that charter quite qualified.

A local charter owner, one of my former students from twenty years prior, a good guy who was already throwing me a little contract work, offered me a job, but he could only offer me a day-rate, even though he wanted me to be available exclusively for him full-time. It was obviously not a very good deal, but it was the best that he could offer. Charter was still slow, as cut-throat as always, not much more than trading money, and this particular airplane was even for sale.

So I now had four offers, none great. The best one was the Lear 35 charter job that I would have to move for, but I worried I wouldn't be able to sell my house, and it was just a charter job, in a business perpetually hanging by a thread, with the inescapable pressure to keep the airplane moving, to always get the job done.

The feds shut down the MD-80 operator before they could offer me a class date.

The next best offer would be to stay a contract pilot, but more than just maintaining the status quo—attempting to support my family with contract work. We were losing our summer babysitter to her high school band practice, and Jay and Neal weren't going back to day care. This was when we had planned for Dawn to quit her job, so that's what we did. We were brave enough.

I had so much on my mind that I left the house one evening to pick up pizzas and somehow made it all the way back home without stopping at the pizza place. That one worried me. I had always thought I could compartmentalize distractions enough to stay on task. Driving a mile to pick up pizzas was an easy task.

To this point my contract flying had just been extra money in the bank since we could pay all of our bills on Dawn's salary with money to spare. Now my livelihood depended on my phone ringing and a full schedule, and a day off suddenly became like an unwanted encumbrance, a wasted day I wasn't using to support my family. How strange it was to be sulking on my days off, those precious days that were my most cherished commodity through my sixteen years of scheduled flying and then especially during my recent charter schedule of fifteen days on, six days off. Far from being a chore, my days spent flying were a relief to me as a contract pilot. When I was out flying, out making money, I usually seemed to feel I would make this unpredictable revenue stream work, as close to peace as I could get in the circumstances. I didn't feel that way while at home, waiting for my phone to ring again, needing it to ring, with a persistent, aching fear that it wouldn't. Needless to say, I couldn't turn down trips unless they conflicted with other trips already on my schedule. I would go through several stretches in which I flew for more than two weeks straight, making more money than I ever had in my career. The worst situation was when I had to turn down trips because of trips already on my schedule and then the original trip canceled. It happened once; all of my clients needed to be flown, and at the last minute, I ended up with nothing.

I was still getting calls for possible jobs, many from the flurry of resumes that I had sent out in that strange month, June 2011.

One was an e-mail from a charter company that needed a couple more Learjet Captains for their contract with the very same air ambulance company I had already flown with at my last job. I had known that I would get a response from them, although I hadn't thought about it since applying. My cover letter didn't need to include much more than my 12,500 hours of flight time, my nearly 4,000 in Learjets, a perfect record, and the fact that I had already worked with all of the medics at the air ambulance company, having travelled with them for fifteen days at a time during my charter job.

That e-mail was addressed to six other pilots as well. I looked at the other e-mail address, and saw that Frank was one of the fellow contenders. I talked to their Chief Pilot and to Frank and discovered we were the only two recipients of the e-mail to actually respond, even though neither of us took the job. The pay was bad, with a suggestion that it might be restored back up to what it had been years ago, still not very good, and the schedule was the same fifteen days on and six days off I had worked at the last charter job.

The successor to my old airline called me to offer a spot in an upcoming training class. I did have a seniority number there still, a painfully low one, but they were only willing to offer first-year pay, first-year RJ pay that is, about twenty thousand dollars a year, just a fraction of what I had once made. I told them I wouldn't come back until they recognized my longevity.

More than a couple of times during this period, I heard a Chief Pilot say "It is what it is," which I've come to realize is code for "I understand that what I'm offering is total bullshit, under conditions that probably aren't even legal under the loosest interpretation of the Fair Labor Standards Act, and I even have enough sense to be ashamed to offer it, but I'm not ashamed enough to change anything."

I interviewed for an instructor position with a local business jet training facility. I'm a line pilot at heart; I never tire of the view of the Earth and clouds stretching to the distant horizon and I love the art of flying, the accomplishment of a well-flown arrival, gently settling onto a runway in a faraway place, but this would be a good job, with a good salary, and I would remain current on whatever jet they assigned me to teach in, even if my flying would just be inside a box on the other side of town. This would be a grown-up job, and I was okay with growing up to support my family. I would do a damn good job at it too.

I had less than a week to prepare a fifteen minute lecture on a subject of my choice. I chose catastrophic hydraulic failure in a Learjet. I created a PowerPoint presentation that integrated the emergency checklist, systems review, and practical considerations to help ensure that the emergency procedure is executed correctly. I rehearsed my lecture over and over, but my very best performance by far was the one that counted, with a roomful of instructors and managers during my interview.

After my lecture, my first interview question was one I was expecting: Why do you want to teach here?" I never considered flight instructing to be just a time-building job while I was doing it. I gave it everything I had, I loved it, and my performance was formally recognized by my superiors, students, and peers. Every job I've held since then gave me some new and different experience to make me a more complete pilot, and teaching business jets to professional pilots, sharing all that I've learned, was the culmination of that.

I'm too battered and bruised to get cocky, but I almost was during the short drive home from my interview. I had given a perfect lecture, they didn't ask any interview questions that I wasn't expecting, and I was extremely qualified for this. I would miss plenty of things, but I would have a real job, unambiguous grown-up employment, I would get a new type-rating, and through hours of studying and teaching, I would come to know the new airplane as well as anyone else on the planet.

I was utterly stunned when they called to reject me two weeks later. Their attorney-approved statement was that they were pursuing more-qualified applicants. Even in the current job market that was bullshit. None of the three instructors I knew there had any jet time at all. One was a program manager for a jet, even though his complete lack of jet time necessitated a restriction on his type-rating that he couldn't fly it unsupervised.

I called a friend who I flew with occasionally and who had formerly taught there, and he was just as stunned. "How could anyone be more qualified than you?" He thought for a moment and then added that I was too perfect. "They're afraid that you'll leave as soon as the job market picks up. They want someone who'll be stuck there." If I had left half of my logbooks at home, or maybe fabricated a fake reason why I would be trapped there, some blemish on my record, I probably would've had a better chance at a job offer.

That was absurd, but I'm afraid it was my new reality. This is a job where life and limb and multi-million-dollar machines are on the line every minute you're on duty, and there are a lot of companies that aren't that interested in obtaining the best talent they can get. In my twenty-four years and twelve thousand five hundred hours of flying, I have seen so much that can never make it into a textbook, knowledge and experience that should be passed on, but business jets are sometimes being taught by pilots who don't even have any jet time.

As if mocking my incessant failure, most recently my exceptional interview presentation on catastrophic hydraulic failure, the Lear 31 developed a mysterious hydraulic leak that defied efforts to find it and made everyone involved seem amateurish.

I would park the airplane after a flight with red hydraulic fluid painting the airplane's belly and still dripping from the nose wheel well. The mechanics would put the airplane on jacks, hook up a mule to keep fifteen hundred pounds of pressure in the system, and swing the gear, repeatedly. They could never get it to leak. Not a drop of fluid.

This happened over and over, continuing to tease us with an un-diagnosable leak for more than a month. The baffled shop owner, a man with an unmatched knowledge of Learjet systems, asked me if I had any ideas. I told him that he could chill his hangar to minus sixty, retract the gear. and let it sit for a couple of hours. I was only half joking; the airplane seemed to leak after spending a couple of hours up in the cold thin air of the stratosphere.

The shop owner had a tremendously experienced crew of mechanics and one had already had a similar idea. Instead of hitting the nose gear actuator with fifteen hundred pounds of force, he turned the pressure down on the mule, swung the gear, and then increased the pressure while the wheels were in transit. Like any other technical skill, maintenance done right is an art, and the gush of red fluid past the bad o-rings in the nose gear actuator after this epiphany was pure artistry.

I got a much coveted interview with a profitable New York based airline with a reputation for customer service and also a reputation for taking a high percentage of pilots who are lucky enough to get the invitation.

Two books had been published about the airline, both books being a combination of new-age business theory and propaganda, neither a genre I like to read, but I immediately read them cover to cover.

Eight years of flying for *the* customer service airline gave me plenty of good stories for the completely non-technical interview, but my best stories were from contract flying. I had helped a client move furniture at his house in the Bahamas. I drove to a client's lake house in rural Wisconsin to pick up his luggage before the flight home to prevent him from having to make two trips to the airport. I compiled a client's travel expenses for a year, but first Dawn had to teach me how to make a spreadsheet. During the eventual interview, one of my interviewers asked whether all of this was part of my job description. "Yes, anything the client needs is part of the job." There was a lot more to the job than just flying the airplane.

My pilot services invoices had three words typed at the bottom, "Safety, Service, Integrity," important ideals that guided every client interaction and that I believe had helped make me become a universal client favorite in an incredibly short amount of time. These words were very similar to the airline's core values, something the airline supposedly wants to hear you regurgitate in the interview. It wasn't just rote regurgitation for me; they were already my foundation as a contract pilot.

I had a chance to talk to other interviewees before the big day. One pilot I talked to was a young, low-time RJ Captain who actually asked me if there was anything important in the two books about the company. "Only the company's history and the entire corporate and operational philosophy." They were vitally important to understanding the company's vision, and success, and we all had a couple of weeks to prepare for the interview. This was the kid's chance to make it to the big leagues, and he didn't seem to be taking it very seriously.

I drove to Pittsburgh so I could fly to New York on the airline, which I had never ridden on. Waiting for the flight to leave, I introduced myself to two other interviewees, whom I had correctly recognized by their conservative suits, short haircuts, and nervous demeanor. I also introduced myself to three of the airline's pilots, who were all jump-seating to work.

The interview started in a big room with a couple of Chief Pilots talking about the airline in front of a couple dozen anxious-looking interviewees. Everyone had a scheduled arrival time, really for the wiz-quiz, but then you could stay as long as you wanted for Q & A with the Chief Pilots. After a thorough review of your logbooks, you would be summoned to another room for the interview with a line pilot and a young representative from human resources.

No part of the process was technical, which was perversely becoming normal in the airline industry. In fact an uninformed observer would doubtlessly have trouble determining that these were pilot interviews at all. Even in an automated fly-by-wire airplane, flying is still a skill performed in complex machinery travelling at 80 percent of the speed of sound many miles above the Earth, and it always will be. A low-time Air France pilot just put one in the ocean off Brazil after a little pitot ice confused his airplane's automation and the automation handed the airplane back over to a pilot who hadn't done any raw-data, attitude instrument flying since he was a young flight student, and then only briefly. The result was disastrous. The accident investigation revealed that this scenario, confused computers letting go of the airplane like it was a hot potato, had occurred a number of times in Airbuses, but never made the headlines when more qualified pilots were at the controls.

I stayed for a good part of the day, introducing myself to everyone who sat anywhere near. These pilots weren't really competitors; a few of us had figured that out but a surprising number hadn't. They were future classmates in indoc, friends who would be with you for the rest of your career. It was a relaxed atmosphere, but they were still watching everything we did. It didn't bother me at all. I was in my element among a roomful of peers, certainly the environment in which I'm most at ease. I actually wasn't anxious at all, about the interview at least. My only worry was about a biopsy that I'd just had on a scab that wouldn't go away on the top of my hand. As if I needed to be reminded that I might have skin cancer, every hand I shook mashed my bandage deeper into the oozing wound on the top of my hand. The interview was going to be easy as long as I could get through the next handshake.

My interviewers told me they were only going to ask me four questions, but first they wanted to know why I was there. I'm not a math genius, but technically that made five questions. I gave them a dissertation about how I used to be part of something great, that I knew a satisfaction few airline pilots knew anymore—knowing my passengers were truly happy to be on my airplane. It wasn't the chocolate chip cookies; it was the genuine dedication of everyone who interacted with the customers. That was gone now, and I wanted to once again work for an airline that still had the vision to try to provide a superior travel experience and not just mass movement of commodity seats.

The line pilot responded with, "You, know, they still sell those cookies (airline branded) in Milwaukee grocery stores."

Before I could even think of how to respond to such a clueless statement, the young human resources rep asked me, "Did you try the blue potato chips? They're so good!"

My old airline had the chocolate chip cookie. This airline has the blue potato chip and the individual seat-back television. These were all just marketing gimmicks; they weren't the real product, but the airline sent two people to interview me who very clearly didn't understand that. Then the human resources rep warned me not give any technical answers because she didn't know anything about flying. This was a pilot interview, right?

The airline had interviewed over fifty pilots that day, and at some point I realized that I was among the oldest. I was only forty-one; how had that happened so quickly? Passengers want wise, experienced, gray-haired pilots flying their airplanes, but something in this airline's filtering process made me think they wanted youth rather than experience. I guess I used to be one of them myself, when I was thirty-years-old and average in my old indoc class. I had previously fit into an airline's hiring mold, but that was now a long time ago.

I waited for a week, hoping to get a call from the airline but not from the dermatologist.

First the dermatologist called to tell me that the lesion was a precancerous actinic keratosis and needed further treatment. That was the call I didn't want. Twenty-four years of flying, my hands always in the sun with just plexiglass and thin air to protect my skin. Since my hands were always in the sun, they never got burned, and since they never got burned, I never thought to put sunscreen on them. They were getting more damaged every time I went way up into the stratosphere, well above where the jetliners fly—every time I flew the Lear 31. Applying sunscreen would become a vital preflight ritual.

A couple of days later, I was taking Jay home from the hospital after eye muscle surgery, already one of the most awful things I had ever done, when Dawn read the ill-timed e-mail from the airline informing me that I wasn't selected. Dawn was so mad that she kicked the couch and dislocated her big toe. I was mad at myself for not eating a god-damned blue potato chip during the flight to New York since I had answered the interviewer's apparently very important potato chip question honestly. I have too much integrity to have just lied and said that I had partaken of the crispy blue communion. Dishonesty probably would've been rewarded with a bonus point, even though I would still have been too old.

The airline hired the young, low-time pilot who had asked me if there was anything important in the two books he neglected to read, and they hired most of the other young guys too. They probably ate the potato chips. Dawn and I felt like we just couldn't get a break. I'm not old yet. I could've given them twenty-three good years, and they could count on me to not put one in the ocean after the computers get confused by some pitot ice.

So I was still a contract pilot, which was fine as long I stayed busy and the checks kept coming. For three straight months, I went into each bleak new month with very few trips on the schedule, thinking about how I would have to tap savings to pay my bills, and somehow each month ended up becoming the most lucrative month of my career. I was flying Tom again in his leased Learjet. I flew with my friends Marc and Bryan as often as I could, and Bryan recommended me to another company's Chief Pilot, who gave me some really good trips, some Knoxville overnights that allowed me to see my father and some Mexico trips, including a five-day trip to Cabo San Lucas, probably the coolest layover of my career, where I could watch whales from my hotel balcony.

I flew that airplane in and out of Mexico so often, always clearing customs inbound in Laredo, that we were apparently targeted by customs as possible drug smugglers and given an extremely thorough inspection.

Pellston, Michigan, near the northern tip of the Lower Peninsula, was a place I didn't particularly like to fly to, haunted, not by a ghost but just some bad juju. There was plenty of lake-effect snow, no hangar space, no Type IV de-icing fluid to give a reasonable holdover time in the snow, no air traffic control tower, limited cell phone service, and no Hilton Hotel. But there was more; it seemed like an unlucky place to me. It was where Chris had destroyed an engine in a Citation a year prior, even though he had been asking for trouble everywhere he went with his systemic recklessness. It was also the site of the fatal Lear 23 crash during a circling approach by a former employer of his, an accident I suspect might have rightfully scared Chris away from circling approaches.

It was actually a lovely winter day in Pellston. I took off and pointed the airplane toward the low January sun. My co-pilot—a remaining member of the clown posse, lingering only because Chris was still, amazingly, the absent gatekeeper for the owner's insurance policy and because he really wasn't qualified to go anywhere else— had just screwed up the before takeoff checklist a moment prior. I waited for him to complete the climb checklist and for us to get out of the sterile environment below ten thousand feet, and then I was going to talk to him about checklist discipline, one of many things that Chris would never teach him.

The poor guy didn't have any experience and wasn't trained, so every trip with him is another flight lesson. It was now a year after Chris had me first fly the guy, a year in which he had accrued very little experience to help make up for his lack of training. I'm not even sure how the guy ended up on the trip. The client, really about the only client left that Chris could even pretend was his, had recently called me to help him; he had figured out that his trips were being flown by amateurs. This job is hard to fake; it takes a lot more than a crazy old man putting false Captain's bars on your shoulders. It seemed everyone was calling me for help with their problems. I was establishing a reputation for competency and, just as important in the intimate realm of corporate flying, integrity. Now if only one of these people who needed my help also needed a full-time pilot, I would be set. I educated the client about how he had operational control of his trips and that he could decide who flew him. I gave him the names of some competent, qualified, trained, and trustworthy pilots to ask for, but somehow, someone had made a crewing decision for him, contrary to what I told him he could do. I was still scratching my head over that, and now I was only in Pellston by accident, to finish the trip for another pilot who couldn't, even after the client had told whoever that his sister, an extremely nervous flyer, wouldn't even get on an airplane unless I was flying it. Since somehow another crew had started out, she didn't make the trip.

I was angry about a lot of things, but not necessarily at my co-pilot; he didn't know how much he didn't know. He would just be the recipient of my lecture on checklist discipline. I was mad at Chris, furious really, for failing to give these guys any real training, never ensuring that they knew basic concepts of jet performance, or even the most basic fundamentals, and then sending them out into the world, endangering themselves and others.

My sunglasses were fogging up, which seemed a little strange in the dry air of a pressurized business jet. I was certainly steamed. I took them off, only to realize that it wasn't my sunglasses. Then I smelled it. It wasn't fog. I looked back to see that the cabin had already filled with smoke. Deep in my thoughts about training and experience and how Chris's god-damned ghost just wouldn't seem to go away, I was apparently the last one to notice the smoke. Even my co-pilot seemed to notice, but he hadn't said anything to me about it yet, a lack of assertiveness that could be remedied by some Crew Resource Management training, just more required training that Chris never gave him.

This was the same guy who was with me a year prior when I thought the Lear was about to break another throttle cable on the way to Florida. On that flight I had an hour and a half to explain the emergency checklists we would be running and what we needed to think about. There was no time for that now. I had once heard that no one has ever survived an in-flight fire of more than sixteen minutes. I was getting us back on the ground as soon as I possibly could, and I already knew I wouldn't be getting any help.

I turned the airplane back toward the airport, informing air traffic control during the turn. I told my co-pilot to get out the emergency checklist, but, knowing his lack of familiarity with it, I went ahead and completed the items I already knew were on it. I really couldn't wait for him to find it.

It seemed to be taking the airplane forever to get back to the airport, one of the greatest disadvantages of flying the underwhelming Citation, its big blunt nose and long straight wings plowing the air, laboriously keeping us from zooming back to our salvation. If I was in a Learjet, I would've flown the downwind leg a hundred knots faster. I would already be on the ground.

Trying as hard as he could to be of some help, my co-pilot offered to run the approach checklist. We were way past that; we were back to the airport. It was time to extend the landing gear and run the before landing checklist. We would be on the ground in a minute.

Someone I flew with at my airline, I'm sorry I can't remember now who, once said, "We don't get paid for what we do; we get paid for what we can do." This was one of those extraordinarily rare days, thankfully, when I had to reach deep into the toolbox and do all that I could do, be more than just an airplane driver, more than a human autopilot, while staying centered appropriately between the opposing undesirable pulls of panic and inaction. Luckily, the idea of willingly steering into the unknown was once too abstract for me, which certainly contributed to the long journey I had travelled to become that person on that day: a contract pilot, with only a promise of a day's pay, flying an airplane that might be burning. My knees were certainly weak that evening once I'd had some time to contemplate the event, but I'm still doing what I love to do, and I know now that I'm brave enough. I was even thankful, at least a little, that when I started down the path I've travelled so far, I didn't know the way.

A Day in the Life of a Contract Pilot

I was having a career year, flying as an independent contractor, part time for six or seven clients, making more money than I would have if one client had me salaried. I was even making more money than when I was an airline pilot. I was enjoying the flying, the travel, the variety, and knowing that my clients were very well cared for. It was also wearing me down, serving so many masters and not being able to turn down a trip unless I had a schedule conflict.

I was on a trip with Bryan, in New Orleans, starting to think my trip to Freeport, Bahamas, for Tom in a couple of days would not be going. It was okay if it didn't; Bryan's trip had just been extended for a few of those same days, with a couple of easy days of sitting in Louisville. I would still be making money, and I would be done by the weekend so that I could go to Knoxville to see my father receive an award.

But then Tom decided he was going to Freeport on Friday. I needed to be on two trips at once, one of the complications from serving so many masters. I hated to leave the trip with Bryan, but he could crew his Citation much easier than I could crew the Learjet. It was giving me a splitting, stress-induced headache thinking about it. Pilots really didn't grow on trees, especially not qualified, current, available, Learjet pilots. I felt obligated to fly Tom. He wasn't my highest producing client, but he was really my first client, he's a friend, and there weren't many guys who could fly him in the Lear.

And that was the next problem; who could I get to fly with me? All of my potential co-pilots were already on other trips. I even called Wilbur, who was newly unemployed again, and he couldn't do it either. I had already told Tom that this might be a problem, and he asked what the co-pilot even did, the implication being that I could just take someone from the clown posse for just one trip. I had done it before, learned, and left it behind. No one in the clown posse was even 61.55 bare minimum co-pilot current in the Lear (three takeoffs and landings in the airplane in the past twelve months). I didn't really want to reopen the trick bag of getting the clown posse involved; it had taken too long to climb out of Chris's mess before.

I explained to Tom what a co-pilot really did. "He reads the checklists and runs the radios, if he understands how to talk on the radio; he swings the gear and throws other switches, if he knows where the switches are and what they do; he runs the FMS, probably one of the most difficult part of getting into a new airplane; in an emergency he runs emergency checklists, a potential weakness in the clown posse since they haven't actually practiced emergencies in a simulator in any kind of jet; and most important of all, if he sees me making a mistake he needs to be able to say, 'Hey, dumb ass, what are you doing?'" Tom was right when he said I could do it all myself 98 percent of the time. It's the other 2 percent that I worry about.

I continued to shake the trees and found a guy I'd flown a Lear 24 with in Kentucky, except he was actually on a layover in Florida in the middle of a trip. I would have to airline him up to Columbus, but that was fine since I was going to leave the airplane in Florida and airline home that evening. I would rent him a car, and he could drive back to his layover.

I got home in the evening, but for me, there was a lot of work to be done, still suffering from my stress-induced headache. I had to generate flight plans and customs manifests; I had to collect a bunch of information on the other pilot, use it to buy his airline ticket, and add him to the customs manifest. I had to buy my own airline ticket too, since I was leaving the airplane in Ft. Lauderdale. Somewhere in there, I forced myself away from the computer to take a bike ride with my family. For the first time in my career, I'm bringing work home, with all of the planning, preparation, and afterward, accounting.

The next morning I had to get the airplane ready a little earlier than I would've normally because then I had to go pick up the other pilot, Robert (not his real name), at Port Columbus Airport on the other side of town.

My client was actually going to beat me to the airport, which is normally not good, but then he had to return home for a forgotten item. When it's your airplane, you aren't late, or early, for your flight. We need to be ready for them when they're ready, so we mostly wait. It's just part of the job, and it doesn't bother me at all;

it's actually relaxing to just wait without trying to fill each moment with productivity.

Today was a good day to be running late, with Freeport being drenched by heavy rain for the past forty or so hours. It could only get better, unless the meteorologists decided to assign a name to the tropical system that was obviously forming there.

I had been making this trip once or twice a month for some time, and it was one I loved for many reasons. I had crisscrossed the country countless hundreds of times, flying to an ever-expanding list of towns, but there was something special, the novelty I guess, of leaving the homogenized sprawl of suburban Ohio and landing in a distinctly different land of soft white sand, translucent green and blue water, the rhythmic clacking of palm fronds in a damp salty breeze, and life lived in slow motion.

Flying to Freeport is a rare opportunity to fly back in time, before air traffic control radar coverage. You have to follow airways in and out, making position reports to the Freeport air traffic controllers so they can keep us separated without the help of radar. I always review the radials of the airways in and out of Freeport, because more than a couple of times a last minute reroute has prompted me to go to green needles, the old fashioned way, while my co-pilot rebuilds the route in the FMS (Flight Management System).

From Columbus, you approach Freeport perpendicularly to the runway. On cloudy, rainy days, you try to get low enough so you can see the airport before having to join the twelve DME (distance measuring equipment) arc and fly the arc all the way around to the final approach course for either runway. Or worse, if there is already an airplane on the approach, you have to fly to the airport and hold, a thousand feet above the airplane on the approach or the airplane holding beneath you. When the airplane in front of you lands, you have to fly the full approach, including the procedure turn to reverse course, an inconvenience most pilots never again experience after earning an instrument rating.

Hurricane Irene had knocked out the Instrument Landing System to runway six the year prior, and with no indication that it would soon be repaired, non-precision approaches were the only way in on foul weather days. After passing a few cranes in the port, there were no obstacles higher than the pine trees, but still, you only had non-precision approaches to work with.

The transmitter for the weather broadcast had also blown away in Hurricane Irene, so Freeport Approach Control read the weather to you at initial contact, a mere thirty or forty miles out, instead of the more typical hundred-plus miles.

Jacksonville Center cleared us directly to Freeport from near Savannah, a gift that Miami Center would eventually take away as they put us back on the trolley-tracks into Freeport's non-radar environment. I simply accepted the clearance with a "Thank you," knowing we would eventually need to deviate well away from any planned course because of the distant, ominously tall tropical storm clouds that were sprouting from the warm, shallow Bahamian seas.

Thunderstorms are a problem when they're over the airport. They are usually a simple obstacle when you're en route; you just deviate around them. In the Lear 31, normally cruising at 45,000 feet, I often don't even need to do that; I'm above most of them, all but the very highest tops. What goes up must come down, and I was inevitably going to need to descend into the weather ahead. It was going to be bumpy, but these weren't the violent looking thunderheads of the mid-latitudes that you never want to penetrate. There were scarier looking areas that I was deviating around, but otherwise these were just dense, tropical-looking clouds, and even though my radar was being partially attenuated by the heavy rain within, I could see that the weather extended all the way past Freeport. If I wanted to go to Freeport, there was no way to completely avoid it.

Super-cooled water droplets can supposedly exist down to minus forty degrees Celsius and then freeze on contact when a cold-soaked airplane runs into them, at least according to contemporary weather textbooks. It was still minus forty-five as I was nearing the cloud tops, a little warm for that altitude, and the clouds just looked especially wet. I turned on all of the anti-ice systems, not just the usual precautionary dose of engine inlet heat I would normally use before penetrating such cold, high clouds.

The clouds proved to be just as wet as they looked, instantly glazing every unheated surface as soon I hit the clouds, the biggest load of ice I had seen since flying into Boston in a winter storm three years prior. The ride was rough, but not violently so. The rain was heavy enough to produce static interference in our radios, but we could still communicate, barely. If it had been night, we would've seen dancing blue sparks of St. Elmo's fire on the windshield.

As we were nearing the point where Miami Center hands us off to Freeport Approach Control, they advised us that there were five airplanes stacked above Freeport in holding patterns, and the last airplane to try the approach couldn't see the runway, had to miss the approach, and was already on its way to Florida. I saw no point in being sixth in line to fly the approach, holding at ten thousand feet above Freeport, with no guarantee that we would even see the runway at the end of our approach, an approach we wouldn't even get to fly for another half hour.

I decided to go ahead and divert to our alternate airport, Ft. Lauderdale, really the only thing we could do and a very easy decision to make with our limited fuel capacity. Miami Center turned us, gave us a reroute, then another, and another as they tried to squeeze us through the bottleneck off the Florida coast between a few nasty areas of weather through which no one was willing to fly.

My insistence on having a qualified co-pilot for the trip was paying off in a big way now, with this day turning into one of those 2 percent days that Tom mentioned when he was asking me what a co-pilot does. You just never know when they'll occur. We had only flown together once, Robert and I, a short repositioning flight in an antique Lear 24, but now we were complementing each other perfectly as we divided our duties without even having to talk about them. One of us would see the other working on a task, so the other would just go on to the next one. We both knew what needed to be done and how to do it correctly. This is what happens when you put two professionals in the airplane; we were part of an efficient, well-oiled machine, even though we were mere acquaintances.

We had even more work to do once we got the airplane on the ground in Florida. We took on three hundred gallons of fuel, more than enough for a holding pattern from hell, as well as a return trip to Florida, and for two-dollars-per-gallon cheaper than what we would've bought in the Bahamas. I filed a new flight plan, submitted a new manifest to customs, and paid our bill. Tom even jumped right into the planning, finding the phone number for the Freeport Air Traffic Control Tower without me even asking for his help. The

Bahamian controller said most airplanes were getting in now and there currently weren't any airplanes in holding patterns.

It was still raining heavily in Freeport, with a fierce wind from the north, but if we were going to get in, there was no waiting for the rain to stop. New showers kept developing just upwind of the island in the southwest corner of the mythical Bermuda Triangle, a continuous soaker that had now been officially named Tropical Storm Beryl.

Moments later we were once again hurtling through Beryl's churning clouds and heavy rain, number one for the airport on the instrument approach. We flew out of the side of a cloud at fifteen hundred feet, catching a brief glimpse of a frothy, wave-ripped sea just a couple of miles off shore from Freeport. We didn't know it yet, but Tom's daughter, a dive master at a local resort, was lost in that very water with several tourists after the dive boat blew away from its mooring. She and her subjects had already been rescued by the time we found out about it later, fortunately none of them panicking while briefly lost at sea.

We flew back into the clouds before reaching the final approach fix, descending through a dark gray void toward where the runway should be. Beryl's wild ride had thoroughly tricked my inner ear, forcing me to totally disregard all visceral cues as I cross-checked the flight instruments. This was what instrument flying was all about; this was as tough as it gets.

The approach brought us down to a little over four hundred feet above the ground, right in front of the runway, but we were still immersed in the thick clouds, without even a glimpse of ground contact to make me think we might be near the ragged edges. This was nuts; it was raining and blowing like hell down there, and we couldn't even make it out of the clouds that close to the ground. I was just about to shove the throttles forward and point the airplane toward Florida again when we flew out the side of a cloud, seeing the blurry runway ahead through the pouring rain. I pointed the airplane toward the touchdown zone and asked Robert to flip a switch to blast the outside of the windshield with bleed air, the closest the Learjet had to a windshield wiper, but still not very helpful in the torrential rain.

My height above the drowned pavement was especially hard to judge through the rain-splattered windshield as Beryl's wind tried to blow me off the centerline. I had eleven thousand feet of runway, more than twice what I needed, so all I could do was slow my descent, prevent the lateral drift, and fly it on. The runway edges were submerged in puddles that seemed to run the entire length. I slowed the airplane to crawl while taxiing in, trying to avoid spraying water everywhere from the deepest puddles.

A lineman dressed for a gale at sea parked us on a high spot and then parked a vehicle at the forward entrance door to drive us through the ankle-deep water between the airplane and the stairs to the customs office. Some of the airplanes parked in the tie-downs had water over the tops of their wheels. Tom's wife, waiting for us in Freeport, had told him water was ankle deep. She hadn't exaggerated. The Learjet is limited to three-quarters of an inch of standing water for takeoff and landing. Fortunately the runway had better drainage than the rest of the airport, at least as long as you stay on the runway centerline.

Finally ready to reposition the airplane back to Ft Lauderdale, we taxied out like mice in a maze, trying to avoid the deepest puddles on the acres of pavement by the international terminal. There was already a wrack line in places, with soggy debris blown into piles, like clumps of seaweed washed up on the beach. I wouldn't have been surprised to see a bonefish swim by. Arriving at the end of the runway, we could see that it still wasn't flooded yet and was still more than twice as long as we needed. Then the Tower told us that the airport was closed but didn't say why, visibility or flooding or what. They asked us if we wanted to taxi back or wait. I said we'd wait and I asked how long it would be closed. We wanted to get out of there. I didn't think I would be able to make my flight home from Ft. Lauderdale, but I wasn't going to let myself think about that. I always carried an overnight bag anyway, and I actually didn't have a trip for another the client the next day. The controller didn't answer my question but then abruptly granted us our freedom, clearing us for takeoff.

We flew through the same angry clouds that rocked us on our way in to Freeport. They weren't any less violent now, probably even worse. Without passengers, comfort wasn't an issue now, and although not pleasant, the only really scary weather nearby was some tornados in Nassau.

Soon enough we emerged from Beryl's clouds and turbulence and flew over a placid, late afternoon, silvery sea. Now this was fun flying. Dealing with Beryl had been fun too, but in a different way— satisfaction in a job well done in spite of many challenges. There was no doubt I had earned my pay.

We cleared customs quickly, repositioned the airplane to the opposite corner of the airport, and put the airplane to bed. With a half-hour until my flight left, the last flight out that I could use, I tried to decide whether I would give it a look or just go to a hotel. I was exhausted, sweaty, and hungry, but I got a ride over to the airline terminal and made my flight with minutes to spare, undoubtedly disappointing my seat-mates as I claimed my middle seat between them.

The kid sitting to my right was a banner-tow pilot, his first time-building job as he embarked on his own journey. Like me at that age, it was evident that he didn't fully understand what he was getting into. It's probably better that way. I can't speak for him, but I wouldn't have been brave enough. I would've missed out on so much, most importantly a trade that I still love. I didn't even try to offer any advice; there was no roadmap to lead me to where I was other than to just always do my best, stay out of trouble, and be honest with everyone I met. I'm not even sure that's working for me; it was for that day and for the day that I went back to Florida to get the airplane. I had no guarantees beyond that, but so far, whenever I have a few empty days on my schedule, someone seems to call me to fill them. Inevitably, a new airplane may show up in town, and I had established enough of a reputation that I should have a chance at a job to fly it, at least a fighting chance anyway. I was brave enough to keep trying. Maybe, just maybe, this flying thing might continue to work for me.

Glossary and Abbreviations

ADF (Automatic Direction Finder) An antique navigation radio that uses a simple arrow to point to a radio station.

ADI (Attitude-Director Indicator) A miniature horizon (attitude indicator) with flight director command bars, the center-point of a pilot's instrument scan.

Anti-ice Equipment Intended to prevent the formation of structural icing on the airplane.

APU (Auxiliary Power Unit) A small turbine engine that provides electricity and air to the airplane when the airplane's engines aren't running or if ground power isn't available. It also indirectly provides water pressure in some airplanes, which makes it the world's most expensive coffee maker as a sleepy crew prepares the airplane for the first flight of the day.

ATP (Airline Transport Pilot License) An advanced license required to serve as Captain in a large turbine powered airplane.

Base Leg

The second to last course in an airplane's arrival traffic pattern, just before the airplane lines up with the runway.

Bid

Process by which airline pilots determine which airplane they fly and from which seat, where they're based, what kind of schedule they have, and even when they go on vacation. All pilots put in requests, and the one with the most seniority gets their choice.

Braking Action

An indicator for the runway surface friction available for stopping.

CASM (costs per available seat mile)

An airline's measurement of operating costs.

CEO

The only person in the company who gets a couple hundred thousand stock options, a few year's salary, and medical for life when they get fired.

Circling Approach

An instrument approach that doesn't line the airplane up with the runway, requiring the pilot to perform a low-altitude circling maneuver in adverse weather conditions.

CFI

Flight instructor's license.

Chief Pilot — A line pilot's immediate supervisor.

Commercial Pilot License — A basic license that allows a pilot to get paid to fly in entry-level jobs.

Commutable Trip — A scheduled airline trip that starts late enough on the first day to commute to your domicile, and ends early enough on the last day to commute home.

Dead-Stick — An unpowered glide back to Earth with engines shut down, or simulated with the engines remaining at idle.

De-ice — Procedure or equipment that removes structural ice already present on the airplane.

DME (Distance Measuring Equipment) — A navigation radio that displays distance from a station.

DO (Director of Operations) — The Chief Pilot's boss.

DOT — Department of Transportation.

EPR (Engine Pressure Ratio) (eeper) — A measurement of power in a jet engine that measures the difference between the intake and exhaust air pressure.

ETOPS (extended two-engine over-water operations) In a practical sense, it means Engines Turn Or People Swim.

FAA Federal Aviation Administration.

FBO (Fixed Base Operator) A business that handles non-airline aircraft at an airport.

Fed FAA inspector.

Final The last leg of the traffic pattern, when the airplane lines up with the runway prior to landing.

First Officer The second-in-command of a two-pilot airplane, the co-pilot.

Flaps High lift devices on the back of the wings that allow the airplane to fly at slower speeds for takeoff and landing.

Flare Pitching the nose up slightly to shallow the airplane's decent rate during landing.

Flight Director Command bars on the attitude indicator that give the pilot guidance for where to point the airplane.

FMS (Flight Management System) Onboard computer in an automated airplane.

Furlough

Unpaid lay-offs in inverse seniority order when an airline reduces its flight schedule.

Glass

Slang term for a modern airplane that presents the pilot with flight information on television screens instead of analog instruments.

GPS (Global Positioning System)

Satellite navigation system that allows a pilot to accurately navigate directly to any point.

GPWS (Ground Proximity Warning System)

A system that warns the pilot when the airplane is too close to the ground. The enhanced version (EGPWS) incorporates GPS and a terrain database.

Ground-Loop

When a pilot loses control of the airplane on the ground, usually during landing, and it swerves off the runway.

IFR (Instrument Flight Rules)

The regulations pertaining to, as well as the clearance to, fly an airplane without visual references, such as in the clouds.

ILS (Instrument Landing System)

A precision instrument approach that brings a pilot down to a runway in low-visibility or low cloud-ceiling, using navigation radios to line the airplane up with the runway centerline (localizer) and a normal glide path (glide slope).

Instrument Flying

Flying without visual references outside of the airplane's flight instruments.

Instrument Rating

The certification on a pilot's license that indicates a pilot is qualified for instrument flying.

IOE (Initial Operating Experience)

A short period of supervised flying after a pilot is trained for a new position, such as a new-hire, newly upgraded Captain, or a new aircraft type.

Junior Assignment

A crewing process after an airline has exhausted all reserve pilots. Crew scheduling calls the off-duty pilots in inverse seniority order, and if you answer the phone, you must fly, although if you have decent work-rules you'll get some form of overtime pay.

Knot

Measurement of airspeed in nautical miles per hour. This is how a jet's speed is measured in the low-altitude terminal environment.

Mach

Measurement of speed relative to the speed of sound. This is how a jet's speed is measured in the high-altitude cruise environment.

Manifold Pressure

Measurement of power in a piston-engine airplane equipped with constant-speed propellers (controllable pitch propellers).

Missed Approach

The procedure you fly if you do not see the runway upon completion of the instrument approach.

Nautical Mile

Geographically one minute of latitude along a meridian, 6076 feet. This is a unit of measurement with actual geographical significance and is the standard unit of distance measurement in aviation.

NDB (Non-directional Beacon)

Antique navigation radio beacon received by the airplane's Automatic Direction Finder.

Non-Precision Approach

An instrument approach with only course guidance and step-down fixes but no electronic glide path to the runway. This kind of approach will have higher weather minimums than a precision approach (ILS).

OSU

The Ohio State University.

PA

Passenger address.

NTSB

National Transportation Safety Board.

RASM (Revenue per Available Seat Mile)

The revenue generated per available seat-mile, a number that is only rarely ever greater than the airline's CASM.

Raw-Data

Flying the airplane without relying on a flight director's command bars to show the pilot where to point the airplane, a skill that is obviously sharper in pilots with experience in antique, analog airplanes.

Red-eye

A late-night or all-night trip.

Regional Jet (RJ)

A small airline jet, loosely defined. The best description is that if the First Officer isn't making enough money to support a middle-class family, it's a Regional Jet.

RVR (Runway Visual Range)   Equipment that measures the horizontal visibility at the runway during low-visibility conditions.

Slam-Clicker   Crewmember who retreats to their hotel room for the duration of the lay-over.

Slats   High-lift devices on the leading edges of the wings of most large jets, to allow lower speeds for takeoff and landing.

Spin   An aggravated stall.

Spoilers   Panels on the top of the wing that spoil lift to transfer the weight of the airplane from the wings to the wheels during landing, or for higher than normal decent rates in flight.

Stall   The disruption of smooth airflow over the upper surface of the wing; the wing basically quits flying with excessive angle-of-attack (low airspeed or high G-loading).

Stand-up

An overnight trip that doesn't have a legal rest period, so the crew is technically kept on duty for their brief nap at the hotel. Stand-up trips normally only occur at regional airlines and other airlines where the pilots don't have good work rules.

Tail Dragger

Airplane equipped with a tail wheel instead of a nose wheel, as is now conventional in a tricycle gear airplane.

TCAS (Traffic Collision Alert System)

Equipment that commands a resolution maneuver for avoiding an imminent collision.

Throttle

Lever(s) on the center console that control engine power.

Trim Tabs

Tiny airfoils on the back of the airplane's control surfaces that balance stick forces, normally operated through a thumb switch or small wheels on the center console.

Type Rating

In order to fly as Captain on a jet, or any other aircraft larger than 12,500 pounds, the pilot must be certified specifically to fly that airplane type.

V1

Takeoff decision speed, although there is really no decision to make; if you have an engine failure or fire (multi-engine airplane) at or above this speed, it is safer to continue the takeoff than to attempt to stop.

Upset

Loss of controlled flight.

VOR (VHF Omni-directional Range)

Navigation radio station.

Wake Turbulence

Trail of disturbed air in an airplane's wake from wingtip vortices (by-product of the production of lift) and jet-blast. This becomes very dangerous when you are following an airplane twice your airplane's weight.

Notes and Bibliography

(1) *Jonathan Livingston Seagull*, Richard Bach, 1970.

(2) From the famous poem *High Flight*, John Gillespie Magee Jr.

(3) *An Assessment of Thunderstorm Penetrations and Deviations by Commercial Aircraft in the Terminal Area*, D.A. Rhoda and M.L. Pawlak, MIT Lincoln Laboratory, 1999.

(4) *Midnight in the Garden of Good and Evil*, John Berendt, 1994.

(5) Second hand from a relative of his. Possibly paraphrased, so it does not appear with quotes.

(6) Tombstone Economics is a concept thoroughly described in the book *Flying Blind, Flying Safe* by Mary Schiavo, former Inspector General of the United States Department of Transportation, 1998.

(7) *Crabgrass Frontier: The Suburbanization of the United States*, Kenneth T. Jackson, 1985.

(8) Technically the constant speed drive was giving up, which acts like an automatic transmission for the engine driven generator. I was keeping it simple for the book.

(9) This is not an accusation. I was simply bewildered that a neutral party could not interpret contractual language the way it was written.

(10) *Blue Highways*, William Least Heat Moon, 1982.

(11) The fine city of Lynchburg was named after John Lynch, who began a ferry service across the James River at the site. John's brother, Charles Lynch, prosecuted British loyalists in revolutionary Virginia, which left a legacy of vigilante justice, which eventually became associated with hangings.

(12) Wilbur's complete quote is: "All we are is a bunch of rats fighting over the cheese in one great big evolutionary biology clusterfuck."